Kill Talk

OXFORD STUDIES IN THE ANTHROPOLOGY OF LANGUAGE

Series editor: Alessandro Duranti, *University of California at Los Angeles*

This series is devoted to works from a wide array of scholarly traditions that treat linguistic practices as forms of social action.

Editorial Board
Patricia Baquedano-Lopez, *University of California, Berkeley*
Donald Brenneis, *University of California at Santa Cruz*
Paul B. Garrett, *Temple University*
Janet McIntosh, *Brandeis University*
Justin Richland, *The University of Chicago*

Thank You for Dying for Our Country: Commemorative Texts and Performances in Jerusalem
Chaim Noy

Singular and Plural: Ideologies of Linguistic Authority in 21st Century Catalonia
Kathryn A. Woolard

Linguistic Rivalries: Tamil Migrants and Anglo-Franco Conflicts
Sonia Neela Das

The Monologic Imagination
Edited by Matt Tomlinson and Julian Millie

Looking like a Language, Sounding like a Race: Raciolinguistic Ideologies and the Learning of Latinidad
Jonathan Rosa

Talking like Children: Language and the Production of Age in the Marshall Islands
Elise Berman

The Struggle for a Multilingual Future: Youth and Education in Sri Lanka
Christina P. Davis

The Last Language on Earth: Linguistic Utopianism in the Philippines
Piers Kelly

Rethinking Politeness with Henri Bergson
Edited by Alessandro Duranti

Other Indonesians: Nationalism in an Unnative Language
Joseph Errington

Recognizing Indigenous Languages: Double Binds of State Policy and Teaching Kichwa in Ecuador
Nicholas Limerick

Going Tactile: Life at the Limits of Language
Terra Edwards

Kill Talk

Language and Military Necropolitics

Janet McIntosh

OXFORD
UNIVERSITY PRESS

Oxford University Press is a department of the University of Oxford.
It furthers the University's objective of excellence in research, scholarship,
and education by publishing worldwide. Oxford is a registered trade mark of
Oxford University Press in the UK and in certain other countries.

Published in the United States of America by Oxford University Press
198 Madison Avenue, New York, NY 10016, United States of America.

© Oxford University Press 2025

All rights reserved. No part of this publication may be reproduced, stored in a retrieval system, transmitted, used for text and data mining, or used for training artificial intelligence, in any form or by any means, without the prior permission in writing of Oxford University Press, or as expressly permitted by law, by license or under terms agreed with the appropriate reprographics rights organization. Inquiries concerning reproduction outside the scope of the above should be sent to the Rights Department, Oxford University Press, at the address above.

You must not circulate this work in any other form
and you must impose this same condition on any acquirer.

CIP data is on file at the Library of Congress

ISBN 9780197808023
ISBN 9780197808016 (hbk.)
DOI: 10.1093/9780197808054.001.0001

Paperback printed by Integrated Books International, United States of America
Hardback printed by Bridgeport National Bindery, Inc., United States of America

Cover image: Eli Wright, *Saviors* © 2015

The manufacturer's authorised representative in the EU for product safety is Oxford University Press España S.A. of El Parque Empresarial San Fernando de Henares, Avenida de Castilla, 2 – 28830 Madrid (www.oup.es/en or product.safety@oup.com). OUP España S.A. also acts as importer into Spain of products made by the manufacturer.

For those who live through war and try to convey the truth of what it really is.

Contents

List of Figures ix
Acknowledgments xi
Content Warning and Notes on Language xiii

SECTION I. ENTRY POINTS

    Preface   3

  1. **Introduction to Kill Talk**   13

SECTION II. TRAINING

  2. **Yelling**   41

  3. **Insults and Kill Chants**   63

  4. **Broken Rules and Head Games**   81

  5. **"Mothers of America" and "A Woke, Emasculated Military"**   103

SECTION III. COMBAT

  6. **Dehumanization in Combat**   119

  7. **Language as a Shattered Mirror**   143

  8. **Frame Perversion: The Twisted Humor of Combat**   169

SECTION IV. AFTER WAR

  9. **Poetry of Rehumanization**   197

  10. **Combat Paper**   225

    Coda: The Nervous System   253

Notes 255
Work Cited 303
Index 327

List of Figures

Figure 2.1	Script taped to inner door of phone box, Parris Island Marine Corps Training Depot.	60
Figure 8.1	Internet meme: "Nothing says I love my job better…"	171
Figure 8.2	Vietnam War–era Zippo lighter, reading "Yea though I walk…"	179
Figure 8.3	Vietnam War–era Zippo lighter, reading "As I walk…"	180
Figure 8.4	Vietnam War–era Zippo lighter, reading "Let me win your heart and mind…"	181
Figure 8.5	Death Card: "For a job well done…"	183
Figure 8.6	Death Card: "We love you but…"	184
Figure 8.7	Death Card: "Dealers of Death…"	185
Figure 8.8	Internet meme: "Marines be like…"	187
Figure 8.9	Internet meme: "Helping terrorist around the world…"	188
Figure 8.10	Internet meme: "Wartime Miranda Rights."	189
Figure 10.1	Eli Wright at Frontline Studios (photo by author).	229
Figure 10.2	Cutting rag (still from *This Is Not a War Story*, courtesy of writer & director Talia Lugacy and Acoustic Pictures / HBO Max).	232
Figure 10.3	Hollander beater, Frontline Studios (photo by author).	235
Figure 10.4	Walt Nygard pulling sheets (photo by author).	237
Figure 10.5	"U-Turn" © Jim Fallon, 2014.	242
Figure 10.6	"Torture Masks (from left to right: Johnny / Mahmoud / Self Portrait)" © Eli Wright, 2014/2015.	244
Figure 10.7	"Untitled" © Eli Wright, 2018.	245
Figure 10.8	"Family Values" © Eli Wright, 2015.	247
Figure 10.9	James Yee, "Camp X-ray."	248
Figure 10.10	James Yee, "Army. Be All You Can Be?"	249
Figure 10.11	"Standard Operating Procedure" © Christopher Arendt, 2010.	251

Acknowledgments

This project emerged from countless conversations with military veterans I cannot thank by name, since I am keeping their identities confidential. I am so grateful to them for their openness and insight. Beyond those individuals, I thank the following veteran writers, artists, activists, and intellectuals for their talent and enormous hearts. Some of them are not quoted in this volume, but their intelligence and, in some cases, their friendship influenced it profoundly. In alphabetical order, they are Doug Anderson, Chris Arendt, Jan Barry, Camillo Mac Bica, Tyler Boudreau, Michael Casey, Dave Connolly, Sean Davis, Edie Disler, Shawn Dunlap, Bill Ehrhart, Jim Fallon, Preston Hood, Shareda Hosein, Tara Krause, Tom Laaser, Miles Lagoze, Nate Lewis, Marc Levy, Nick Mararac, Rachel McNeill, Caleb Nelson, Walt Nygard, Ben Schrader, Juan Spinnato, Eli Wright, and James Yee. Special thanks as well to Warrior Writers and Frontline Paper (and Combat Paper, by extension) for your truly remarkable work.

For brilliant scholarly inspiration when it comes to interpreting military life and language, I thank Aaron Belkin, Carol Cohn, Jim Dawes, Catherine Lutz, Adam Gilbert, Roberto Gonzalez, Hugh Gusterson, Matthew Gutmann, Kenneth MacLeish, Glenn Petersen, and Alex Pillen. Aaron, an early conversation with you confirmed my conviction that there was something symbolically important about the mixed moral messages I was sensing in military training. Carol, your 1987 article was foundational to this project, and it has been so gratifying to become your colleague and friend.

For their contributions in the form of friendship, feedback, and/or collegial support for this project, I give deep thanks to Asif Agha, Rosa Brooks, Manduhai Buyandelger, Summerson Carr, Jennifer Cole, Sonya Das, Joanna Davidson, Elizabeth Ferry, Kelly Flynn, Susan Gal, Susan Gelman, Kira Hall, Nick Harkness, Rachel Heiman, Larry Hirschfeld, Brian Horton, Emily Ibrahim, Judith Irvine, Deborah Jones, Graham Jones, Elise Kramer, Laura Kunreuther, Smita Lahiri, Sarah Lamb, Ann Marie Leshkowich, Alaina Lemon, Jessica Lowen, Bruce Mannheim, Xochitl Marsilli-Vargas, Norma Mendoza-Denton, Diane Mines, David Parkin, Heather Paxson, Nira Pollock, Carla Power, Christine Rayner, Jennifer Roth-Gordon, Bambi Schieffelin, Antony Seely, Parker Shipton, Merav Shohet, Jack Sidnell, James Slotta, Karen Strassler, David Tavárez, Lynne Tirrell, Chris Walley, and Chip

Zuckerman. This list condenses many complex nodes of conversation and affection, writing retreats and workshops, dinners, drinks, and even a dude ranch, but it will have to do.

Sandro Duranti has been the most supportive series editor I can imagine. I cannot thank him enough for being the champion of this project since I told him about it. My thanks as well to Julia Steer and Jade Dixon of Oxford University Press, for such highly responsive and diligent support.

I am grateful to the National Endowment for the Humanities and the American Council of Learned Societies, both of which granted fellowships and precious time with which to conduct the research and writing of this project. The Brandeis University Norman Funds were also invaluable. And as always, I am beholden to my wonderful Brandeis colleagues, graduate students, undergraduates, and staff for their support and contributions. The students who took my Anthropology of the Military and Policing Class were a particular joy to think with—you know who you are.

Finally: Special thanks to some beloved extended kin who are among my favorite conversationalists: Carey McIntosh, Joan Ferrante, and Seth Lloyd. I am eternally grateful to my wonderful and amazing parents, Ken and Peggy McIntosh, and to my husband, Tom, and children Tobias and Theo, who keep on making me laugh while making me proud.

Content Warning and Notes on Language

The brutal content of this book comes at a historical moment when debates about how to treat disturbing imagery and language are especially acute. Prospective readers should be aware that I frequently refer to acts of cruelty and violence, whether inflicted on military recruits in the United States or on combatants and civilians in the theater of war. Beyond that, these pages are thick with misogynistic, homophobic, racist, and religious insults and slurs, as well as profanity. Such language (along with other kinds of military language) is the object of my scrutiny, and I approach it with bright lights and surgical tools.

I have opted not to alter offensive words with orthographic changes such as asterisks, except in the case of one racial slur that is now conventionally redacted. There are several reasons for my choice to be so direct.

One is that if I were to obscure potentially offensive or upsetting material, some pages might become a blizzard of asterisks. I would also face a slippery slope dilemma; starting this process would beg challenging questions of where to stop. Some of the military insults I discuss, for instance, have dual meanings, such as "haji," which has a positive religious meaning for many speakers worldwide and a deeply insulting, racialized one among some American combatants. I believe it would be confusing to make such words opaque, especially for readers unfamiliar with military slang. Besides, redacting words would make them mysterious, like a box I don't wish to open, when part of my analysis hinges on probing their content.

I consider as well the veterans who may read this book. A number of combat veterans I have spoken to feel a redacted book would fail as an honest account of military world-making, for, to paraphrase the words of one veteran, "the language *is* the experience." As an ethnographer, I believe in the power of trying to climb into peoples' heads with them as best we can to understand their worlds, even if their worlds make us uncomfortable. And while this may surprise some readers, even my peace-loving, politically progressive veteran respondents laughed at the idea of my "bleeping out" offensive words, or using euphemisms to describe what happens in training and in war. To them it sounded silly and prim, as if trying to hold an anaconda with a pair of tweezers. The very bite of the words, in fact, makes up part of the combatant's headspace that I wish to explore.

Some veterans I know were not so much amused as affronted by the very idea of this content warning. One phrased his reaction like this: "Trigger warnings are a function of privilege and an insult to people actually suffering from war. We are educating people for the world they live in, which is not a really nice place."

But other prospective readers will appreciate an alert, in case they want to avoid language that they might encounter as a virtual "punch to the gut," as one civilian reader put it. The accounts in here could disturb people living with past traumas. Beyond that, some young people are socialized to feel that to reproduce hateful language, even if to analyze it rather than "use" it, is to do harm. With this note, I hope to minimize such impressions by letting possible readers decide for themselves whether they are willing to confront the vivid language within these pages. Since some readers might encounter individual chapters in isolation, each chapter title includes a brief note alerting them to troubling content and directing them back to this longer explanation.

A mention of the vexed relationship between language and gender in this book is warranted. Historically, the United States military has operated within a strict and heteronormative gender binary. The past two decades have seen gradual changes: women were permitted to serve in combat starting in 2013, and gay and transgender individuals have been allowed to serve openly since 2011 and 2021, respectively, though as this book goes to press, the Trump administration's military has announced a ban on transgender enlistment. Recruits in the Army and Navy now address their drill leaders using gender-neutral terms, referring to their rank or role followed by their last name, rather than "Sir" or "Ma'am." In 2022, some Marine Corps leaders encouraged recruits to adopt a similar practice, though it remains to be seen how widely this will catch on (and in fact, Trump and his new Secretary of Defense Pete Hegseth may roll back most of the gender-related changes and initiatives I have mentioned). Despite such developments, the Marine Corps (the focus of some of my chapters) remains 90% male, and military parlance tends to use the terms "males" and "females" instead of "men" and "women." While these words may sound clinical, reductive, and restrictive to civilians, they are considered normal and professional within the military, supposedly promoting administrative clarity and consistency. Given the context of this study, I will occasionally use military terminology such as "female Drill Instructor," or "male recruits"; such terms mean that the military has classified them as female or male, respectively. I recognize that such language does not reflect sophisticated understandings of gender complexity, including the way bodies, identities, presentations, affirmations, and attributions may diverge from one another and defy the military's and indeed the wider society's gender classifications.

SECTION I
ENTRY POINTS

Preface

When I was about twelve or thirteen, my teachers assigned two books about war. One was Erich Marie Remarque's *All Quiet on the Western Front*, an account of trench warfare from the vantage point of a young German soldier in World War I. The other was Elie Wiesel's *Night*, a memoir of his childhood survival of Nazi death camps. These books made an undeniable impact on me. As I grappled with the brutal worlds they evoked, my young and sheltered mind couldn't help but question: how could people do such things to one another? I had a vague understanding of vast forces at play, grappling for territory, resources, or some fantasized ethnonational triumph. But I couldn't understand how, within this machinery, a person with a beating heart could be willing to inflict such suffering on others. My encounter with Remarque's and Wiesel's narratives fed my lifelong anthropological fascination with the troubling breadth of human possibility. And nothing has confounded me more than what the poet Robert Burns once described as "man's inhumanity to man."[1]

I remember terrible images and agonizing feelings in those books, but I don't remember taking much away about military language. Some linguistic detail would have been lost anyway, since both volumes had been translated—Remarque's from German into English, Wiesel's from Yiddish into French and then English.[2] But now that my profession has me so focused on the power of speech, I have to wonder: what exactly went on linguistically, in the training of soldiers and in their organic speech communities during wartime, as part of such terrible acts of killing and genocide?

In the face of war's brutality, language might seem like an incidental detail. But US combat veterans who pay attention to it will attest that embodied ways of speaking—from yelling to cursing to joking, and beyond—can be intimately bound up with experiences of kinetic violence. One of my respondents in this project, for instance, is a young Iraq veteran I call Levi, who enlisted shortly after 9/11 to escape what he called his "dead-end, high school drop-out life." By his own account, Levi ended up participating in war crimes in Iraq and felt he would probably spend the rest of his life trying to deal with that fact. He also looks back with chagrin at some of the euphemisms he and his

Kill Talk. Janet McIntosh, Oxford University Press. © Oxford University Press (2025).
DOI: 10.1093/9780197808054.003.0001

buddies used. He makes scare quotes in the air with his fingers as he describes some of the phrases.

> This wasn't an "enhanced interrogation"; this was a fucking *torture*. Right? Or—like—I didn't just "see my buddy take out an insurgent"; I saw him *execute a man*, right? When we sanitize that language it fucks with our heads, because we have this deep-down, inherent aversion to killing—our own kind, especially, right? And so when you can indoctrinate somebody to override that barrier that we have, part of how we get them to do it is dehumanizing and by sanitizing, right? You switch that language and all the rhetoric around to becoming something other than what it actually is. So then we use those other words—those euphemisms—for those things, and detach ourselves from it.[3]

Euphemisms offer a straightforward example of the role of speech in military violence, but some connections between speech and violence are more clandestine, needing to be pulled to the surface for analysis. For instance, one thread I trace through these chapters is an abiding tension between two oppositional linguistic frameworks (you can think of these loosely as "codes" or "registers") that coexist in military talk.[4] One is packed with formal and upstanding locutions—"sir," "ma'am"—and officially sanctioned technical phrases that underplay the sickening edge of violence ("enhanced interrogation" is a good example). The other consists of transgressive language, such as racist and homophobic slurs, profanity, or sadistic jokes. Both frameworks play a role in the military—one upholding a professional and sometimes public face, the other offering an aggressive stance that leans into the prospect of violence. I further argue in these chapters that although profane and other transgressive language has long been officially disallowed in training, some trainers (even if not all) over the last few decades have persisted in using it, a contradiction that indirectly teaches recruits about the norm-violating quality of combat violence. In the chapters that follow, I examine the implications of such linguistic tensions and many other ways that language has helped coax and brace US infantry combatants. I also explore how very different linguistic and symbolic forms in poetry and art can help some veterans manage the torments of memory and demilitarize their own minds.

Readers may have questions about my stance regarding the military. One reason I was shocked by those descriptions of war in my school books was that I had been cosseted by a safe, middle-class upbringing in the United States. Violence was especially anathema in my family, for we had Quaker roots on both sides. Though my paternal grandfather had been a lieutenant with the Army Medical Corps in France in World War I and one of my uncles enlisted in the Navy in the 1950s, my family members were more likely to march against war than to serve. In the Vietnam era, my male kin were pursuing higher education and thus protected from the draft. Recruiters certainly never turned up at my private school to recruit volunteers, and it wouldn't have occurred to me to join the military in the name of class mobility, sacrifice, or patriotism. I was privileged enough to sustain a tender heart and remain blissfully unaware of military affairs.

Now that I'm an anthropologist, it's harder to be quite so oblivious, but it would also be easy to hold the military at arm's length. Many American anthropologists are dismayed that the US military has sometimes paid social scientists to furnish strategic "cultural intelligence," seeing these pursuits as weaponizing cultural understanding while abetting violence and imperialism.[5] Some also consider military culture to be so morally tainted by violence—including the millions of deaths US wars have caused in Vietnam, Cambodia, Iraq, and Afghanistan—that to develop rapport with service members or veterans is to risk being contaminated or corrupted.[6]

But no matter how critical one feels of US military operations, it would be too simple to conflate the strategies of the state with the souls of the infantry doing its dirty work. In fact, such a move would encourage an uncurious and strangely dehumanizing way to practice anthropology. If we ignore the experiences of those whose institutional alignments we don't especially like, it also puts us at a disadvantage when it comes to understanding the dynamics of oppression, for the complex subjectivity of those who wield power is an important element of power itself.[7] And to paraphrase anthropologist Renato Rosaldo, understanding how something works is not the same as agreeing with it.[8]

That said, we should question just how power is experienced among US service members, especially combat infantry. Critics of the military often oversimplify, flattening them as "perpetrators" without considering that many people join the military hoping they will make a positive difference; some join because of a lack of options, and plenty—regardless of why they joined—end up feeling subjugated, even crushed, by the demands of the state. In fact, combatants might be said to have both too much and too little power. In the conflicts of the last sixty-plus years, they have possessed astonishing agency to govern the destiny of entire villages overseas (as no shortage of nineteen-year-old GIs did in Vietnam, for instance), rough prisoners up, and take lives. Yet the disadvantages that direct Americans toward military service are numerous. During the Vietnam era, the draft conscripted about two million American men, about 80% of them working class, and sent them into a futile meat grinder.[9] During the all-volunteer era of the Global War on Terrorism (GWOT) some enlisted in hopes of serving a noble higher cause,[10] but many were also channeled toward the military by limited financial straits. In some cases, childhood trauma—exacerbated by socioeconomic disadvantage—has pushed young people to seek structure, belonging, and father figures in the military. A lack of power, then, is one factor that propels many Americans toward military service.

Once in basic training, furthermore, recruits (and, in an earlier era, conscripts) start to realize how much control they have lost. The language they encounter, though somewhat different across political and cultural eras, will make clear that they are property of the state, potentially expendable, and expected to obey orders they may not agree with. In combat, soldiers may find themselves in situations of impossible moral complexity or compelled to take actions they couldn't have imagined before. Some may also commit violence considered reprehensible even by official military standards, but—in a contradiction I explore in some of my chapters—the structures of speaking and feeling they've absorbed from the military context may have shaken up their moral compass to the point of disorientation. Beyond the matter of their own deeds, some combatants are placed in more extensive danger than they anticipated. A shortage of personnel in Iraq and Afghanistan, for instance, led to involuntary extensions of active duty under the "stop-loss" policies, subjecting soldiers to prolonged physical and psychological risks. The matter of power and agency among combatants can be murky, but facile moral judgments from civilians reflect not our inherent superiority so much as our luck not to have been tested like them.

After the wars in Vietnam, Iraq, and Afghanistan, the conflicts I focus on in this book, some US veterans came home and readjusted, bracketing what happened overseas in the name of patriotic service while enjoying a social boost from their veteran status. For others, re-entry into civilian society revealed a greater sense of powerlessness. Some missed the structure and purpose offered by the military or struggled to find employment. Some suffered physical disabilities incurred during service. But one of the most pernicious war legacies, for soldiers, is the invisible damage done by PTSD and what is now called "moral injury"—that is, the psychological and spiritual distress resulting from having witnessed or taken part in something that transgresses deeply held moral beliefs. Such damage can be confusing to veterans who believe they should be too tough to suffer from anxiety, guilt, or angst yet it is one reason for the fact that the adjusted suicide rate among US veterans has trended up to 66% higher than that of the nonveteran adult population.[11]

Some combat veterans tell me they are tormented not only by what they saw and did, but also by *how they talked about, thought about, and felt about it at the time.* Yet the realms of combatant language and combatant subjectivity seem a black box not only to anthropologists but also to many civilians.[12] Just consider, for instance, the public disturbance in 2022 when Prince Harry described his mindset as he killed twenty-five Taliban while serving as a Forward Air Controller and Apache pilot in Afghanistan. "You can't really harm people if you think of them as people," he explained. "They were chess pieces removed from the board, Bads taken away before they could kill Goods."[13] The international shockwaves from this statement suggested many were stunned to hear his account, which seemed to contravene not only popular fantasies of the genteel royals but also the very liberal humanism Harry and his US allies were supposedly fighting for. But from Harry's point of view, this conceptual framing apparently made the difference between being able to do his job and not.

I describe some of my methods for exploring military language in the Introduction, but here I want to mention some more personal and contextual details: how I initiated some of this work, for instance; what it was like to spend time among veterans coming from lives so different from my own; and the partial nature of this study.

I had a telling false start when first trying to get closer to training in the Marine Corps, the military branch with the most aggressive self-image. I applied to an event called an Educators Workshop at the Parris Island Marine Corps Training Depot in South Carolina. Workshop administrators choose high school and community college instructors to go through a short, toned-down version of basic training, including being yelled at by Drill Instructors (DIs), firing an M16, and being briefly exposed to tear gas. Because boot camp has a way of pulling grit to the surface, some teachers re-emerge saying things like, "I didn't know I had it in me! This could really inspire confidence and purpose in my students." The idea seems to be that the educators will fan back out to towns across the United States and function as informal satellite recruiters for the Corps. But when I filled out the application, I explained I was an anthropologist hoping to learn more about the language of basic training. A Parris Island Public Affairs official told me I had initially been accepted, but a superior officer had then run his eye down my forms and decided the workshop "wasn't a good fit for my aims." More likely, I wasn't a good fit for *their* aims.

So I approached from another angle, working my way through contacts until I was able to connect with the Sergeant Major serving as president of the East Coast Drill Instructors Association, to ask whether I could be a fly on the wall at their several-days-long reunion. Amazingly, he and the authorities on

Parris Island let me tag along. I introduced myself as an anthropologist, which everyone at the reunion found suitably unimpressive. Most of the retired DIs assumed I was a military spouse until I corrected them. They reminisced and talked politics in big groups at the dinner tables, joshed with the young, active-duty guys (there didn't seem to be many female DIs hanging around the reunion), and occasionally went into tongue-in-cheek DI mode while we got food in a mess hall or disgorged from a bus.

Once off Parris Island I conducted some follow-up interviews with former DIs, but I never made formal inquiries of the active-duty DIs who had volunteered to set up the events, mindful that they could not get involved in any systematic research. Still, I socialized with them informally, since they were in the mix of the reunion activities. They were intrigued by my solo appearance, and when I told them I was at the depot to learn about language and considered myself "unshockable," they took this as a challenge, mocking me cheerfully when they finally made me blush. At one point when I handed over a Brandeis University business card, the men started passing it around, exclaiming with a guffaw, "Oh, PROFESSOR! Whoop de do!" and so forth. They were the keepers of masculine power and state-sanctioned authority, and I was swimming like a minnow around the hull.

Beyond those encounters, I conducted interviews with almost fifty veterans of Vietnam and the GWOT, nearly all of them from the Marine Corps and Army. These ranged from one-off conversations to multiple encounters over weeks and months, extending in some cases to meaningful friendships that have lasted for several years. Each individual, of course, had a different response to me. Some were surprised or intrigued that an anthropologist would take an interest in their stories at all, because military and civilian worlds can feel so far apart. One hard-bitten veteran ("Ryan," in later chapters) liked to respond to my naïve line of questioning by puffing on her cigarette and looking at me out of the corner of her eye, saying, "You *amuse* me, anthropologist." Some respondents wanted to talk about their abiding love for the military, like Louis, who was newly immersed in college life but missed the Marine Corps and regretted never having seen combat. (Each time we met, he had worked up another re-enactment of a drill or encounter with a superior officer.)

In some conversations, veterans' memories would spill out as if from behind a dam. I was careful not to ask direct questions about violence, but somehow one person after another would end up going there, sometimes telling me about the worst day of their lives. At least some, though, said they appreciated a rare chance to talk to someone invested in listening, and found it somewhat cathartic. I still worried it would take a toll; their stress was evident in their faces and bodies as they spoke. I followed up with some respondents to suggest outlets for help, from therapy at the VA to veteran's writing groups, and some followed through.

Unsurprisingly, the veterans I got along with the best were those who had grown disenchanted with the US military and its wars. They were reflective and analytical, and many described a dreadful undertow of post-traumatic stress and guilt. Some had figured out ingenious ways of restoring themselves, even if partially, through language and the arts, as I describe in the last two chapters. I spent a lot of time in their company, and with some, friendship grew into collaboration.[14] My affinity for this group, including their cynicism about aspects of military rhetoric, textures my material and should be kept in mind as a qualification about the book in general. You could say that my respondents and I each had our own combination of what Rosaldo calls "insight and blindness," and this book reflects those qualities from all of us.[15]

The focal point of the book is selective, too, in its restricted attention to (primarily) the language surrounding the violence work of infantry on the ground as opposed to, say, the talk of high-ranking military brass, commissioned officers, support personnel, or the drone operators and others who engage in combat from a distance. In focusing mostly on infantry who may end up in close combat, I am working with quite a narrow slice of military experience, for the Army and Marine Corps each has over one hundred Military Occupation Specialties, and most service members never expect to see combat at all, functioning as support personnel, for instance, or setting out on missions defined from the get-go as technical, humanitarian, peacekeeping, and so forth.[16] For readers seeking diverse firsthand accounts of military experience, including some celebratory accounts of the best things military service can do for a person, I recommend the countless memoirs written by veterans themselves.[17] For readers interested in the political underpinnings of US wars, books by historians and political scientists would be far better than this one. My focus is mainly on the language through which infantry combatants across two eras of war curtailed their empathy for "the enemy," entered a zone where ordinary morality is suspended, and came to accept that they would be both instruments and targets of violence.

There are other important caveats to my approach. First, I trace certain linguistic patterns across two eras—the Vietnam War and the GWOT—and various military units, a method with both advantages and disadvantages. By focusing on similarities and continuities, I do not thoroughly account for differences and changes. While I mention the following issues throughout these pages, it would be impractical to provide a deep analysis of the distinctiveness of each branch of the US military, how different historical eras have conditioned and altered the language I discuss, how training policies have evolved over the years, branch by branch and base by base, how the Parris Island

Marine Corps Training Depot differs from the Depot in San Diego, how individual DIs diverge in their personal philosophies on the harshness of training, and how different units establish unique microcultures in the theater of war. My writing is based on specific examples and includes some provisional generalizations, but for the reasons just listed, readers should keep in mind that the utterances I quote should not be taken as universally representative.

Second, a potential shortcoming of my approach is that I have drawn together some of the more extreme aspects of training techniques and combat language, because they are crucial for understanding how soldiers can adopt a mindset of violence. While these intense examples will resonate with many veterans, it is undeniable that some service members will have had a more subdued verbal experience in the military. With its focus on violence, this book does not challenge entrenched images of the aggressive military persona; such an endeavor would require a different ethnographic focus. Still, even if my depiction represents the outer edges of military verbal practice, it reflects a recurring reality in the verbal lives of at least some US combatants over the past few decades, and these verbal patterns bristle with implications.

Third, I should mention a final qualification that raises a relevant tension. In recent decades, the Department of Defense has made extensive efforts to mitigate the racism, sexism, and training abuses that arise in my material.[18] The massive US military bureaucracy, fragmented and flawed though it is, has been lumbering toward changes in its culture, through proclamations and policies far too numerous for me to detail, though I allude to some of them as I go (including in my endnotes). The tension that arises, here, is that although these efforts have made a difference in the top-down messaging and some practices on the ground, there is inherent dissonance in trying to instill sensitivity into what is, effectively, a killing machine. In some cases, cynicism is the stumbling block; I frequently heard younger veterans rolling their eyes or grumbling about "death by PowerPoint" when it came to diversity, inclusion, and sexual harassment trainings. The broader issue is the inherent conflict between liberal values such as mutual respect and bodily integrity and the military's proficiency in wielding violence and death. Moreover, as I explore, some military figures see brutal language as vital to national security because they believe it helps create a hardened killer. (Note that as this book goes to press, Trump's new Secretary of Defense Pete Hegseth has vowed to expunge DEI and sensitivity trainings from the military.) The kind of language I focus on, then, has a persistent lure for those engaged in the state's dirty work.

To check my facts and gather their impressions, I showed excerpts of my material to twelve combat veterans. Though some had less intense experiences than those I describe, most found that the verbal dynamics I capture resonated with them. When I gave the young veteran Levi some draft material to read, he had recently been deeply affected by the twentieth anniversary of the start of the Iraq War. "That war has a dark and fucked-up legacy," he said. After reading, he told me it was "intense" to see the linguistic aspect of his experience analyzed, "especially by someone who isn't part of the military machine but gives a shit enough to translate the process." He suggested a few adjustments but agreed with my assessment that military training places Marine Corps recruits into a structural position akin to "the walking dead." And he concurred that, as he put it, "in training we are crushed by the military system, but then we channel that down to our enemies. Like you say, there's an analogy between the trainer-recruit relationship and the soldier-enemy relationship." Levi went on:

> It really helps and hurts to see this put into a bigger context. It hurts to know my experiences with language and the war were part of this bigger uglier machine. It helps to know my shit is not unique or isolated, and it helps me to come out of my isolation and connect the dots. You put in the work to make sense of our experience, connecting fragments I could not put together because I'm trapped in my afterwar. It's like, we're all locked in a box of our personal experience; I'm aware it's part of a larger whole but we're unable to talk or think about that whole because our experiences were too big and close. You're dumping out all our boxes on the table and recombining them to make more sense of them in a way none of us could do.

Levi was candid that some of the theory was challenging; another veteran, in fact, had characterized a draft of my introductory chapter as "a wall of words," a chastening assessment that sent me back for a rewrite. But Levi also found some of the concepts helpful, akin to "learning a German word for a feeling or dynamic you always wanted to put a finger on; you know it but you don't have the vocabulary to talk about it easily." I was glad that other respondents, too, seemed to find this material illuminating, though admittedly such feedback came from combat veterans who had already developed a critical consciousness about war. Many, in fact, had long been more sophisticated than I was when it came to talking and thinking about "the whole."

In spite of any remaining shortcomings, I hope this book will be engaging to anthropologists and students of language, while being legible to curious veterans and others with military interests. I hope civilians outside the academy will take an interest in this work, too, for soldiers supposedly fight in our name. (As Levi says, gesturing to me, "Blood is on all of our hands."[19]) To make this work more accessible, I have used theory somewhat sparingly, defined theoretical terms as they arise, and placed some theoretical work, extra details, links, and citations in the endnotes for those wishing to go deeper.

I don't dismiss the virtues that military service can inspire—the self-discipline and skills, the extraordinary ability to coordinate group efforts, the bravery and determination, the kin-like bonds of love among soldiers, and the awe-inspiring willingness to make the ultimate sacrifice. When I have glimpses of these qualities, or hear accounts of how they have protected the innocent or saved lives, I am humbled. But my hope is that appreciation of these strengths can abide alongside a deeper understanding of the way the language of combat plumbs human depths as well, sometimes facilitating atrocity and sometimes damaging combatants themselves. Ultimately, I hope these chapters help critics of the military better understand how ordinary people become capable of committing brutal acts, while military enthusiasts might recognize that the noble ideals the military defends in principle are sometimes contradicted by the dynamics I describe. Perhaps those invested in combatants will also take more interest in their health, not merely to return them to "combat readiness," but to restore them to wholeness after battle. Indeed, I hope all readers will be inspired by the final chapters, in which we see veterans brilliantly using new symbolic forms to create a path out of the nihilism of war.

Chapter 1
Introduction to Kill Talk

Randall and I sit together and order Mexican food for lunch.* He is exquisitely polite, as always, wearing a suit that's a little tight around his still-muscular shoulders as he reaches to pour water from a pitcher into my glass. I'm starting to feel that familiar worry: every time we speak about military language, it means speaking about military experience, and Randall sometimes wants to go into the darkest corners of memory, things he's almost never talked about with others. Does he worry the server could overhear? But I remind myself we've done this before, and amid the restaurant's loud chatter, he seems completely focused, insulated in our back and forth. Right now, he's talking about his mixed feelings about the Marine Corps. He's still viscerally proud to belong: "Once a Marine, always a Marine." He imitates the sound of a sharp platoon going by, "so clean and crisp—*clomp clomp* . . . "

Randall survived Vietnam against the odds and managed to lift himself out of a hardscrabble neighborhood, becoming a beloved manager and mentor at his educational supplies company. But he is dismayed by the strange current that still runs through him—the feeling that becoming a Marine and being part of the horror overseas made human life feel tenuous and, sometimes, expendable. One time a few years after he got back from Vietnam, he says, his girlfriend saw a mouse in the bathroom and came running out, screaming. "So I went in there, and I just could not bring myself to kill it. I put it in a bag and took it out to a field and released it. I had no problem taking human lives, and I almost did it even after Vietnam. I can kill a man, but I can't kill a mouse." Randall confesses, with red-rimmed eyes, "I'm the most violent person I know."

What happened? Vietnam's cataclysm of mud, blood, and fighting for your life was obviously a key force; combat trauma puts people to extremes hard to crawl out of. In the 2006 documentary *The Ground Truth*, Marine Corps veteran Sean Huze marvels at his ability to kill and "just not give a shit" because it's "just death." This indifference became the hardest thing to "deal with and

---

* This chapter analyzes words and imagery that may be difficult for some readers to encounter. Please see the "Content Warning and Note on Language" in the front matter for some context and a discussion of the author's reasons for not redacting this material.

reconcile" after the Iraq War. It felt like "the loss of humanity," Huze goes on, which "it's not always easy to tap back into."[1]

But Marine Tyler Boudreau, who also served in Iraq, noticed a related pattern *before* his unit even saw any combat. Noting his own and his buddies' response to another Marine's gunshot wound, self-inflicted at a base in Kuwait to avoid the imminent combat, Boudreau was struck by how they all seemed to have cultivated an "apathy toward death and violence." Casting about for an explanation, Boudreau eliminates several possibilities. "I wasn't coerced. . . . I wasn't trying to conform, or fit in. . . . I genuinely didn't give a rat's ass. . . . For the life of me," he adds, "I can't figure out why. I've heard [other] vets talk about this [too]."[2] Apparently, some begin their acculturation to violence before battle even starts.

Of course, military personnel destined for combat know that they will be expected to kill or potentially be killed for the nation. The philosopher Achille Mbembe developed the term "necropolitics" to describe the way states decide who may live and who must die in service of their agenda.[3] When a government decides to go to war to preserve or advance its interests, it has tremendous power to decide whose lives are valuable and whose are disposable, justifying these decisions in terms of "national security." Within this necropolitical calculus, "enemy combatants" are widely framed as killable and—for the state's purposes, anyway—largely ungrievable.[4] Combat soldiers are somewhat more valued by their own people in this hierarchy of lives; Hollywood certainly loves to showcase their vulnerability, and if they die in war, their funeral will be reverent, perhaps even magisterial. Yet in war, combatants on both sides of a conflict still occupy a position of what anthropologist Kenneth MacLeish calls "necropolitical abjection," being deliberately exposed to death or injury.[5] It is a structural reality: violence and death are anticipated elements of the landscape for some service members.

But how do combatants assimilate violence into their inner lives so they can willingly anticipate the act of killing and swallow the possibility of dying? As I listened to Randall and other American veterans of Vietnam and the Global War on Terrorism (GWOT) in Iraq and Afghanistan describe their military training, and as I observed glimpses of Marine Corps boot camp, it seemed that necropolitical abjection and the willingness to kill were conditioned not just physically, but *semiotically*—that is, by way of meaningful signs, in language and other symbolic forms—before anyone went into battle. And when I track the way US combatants talk during war, some of their speech seems to furnish them with a necropolitical scaffold—an invisible structure that offers shape to their experience of violence[6] and their new relationship with death. In both obvious and subtle ways, language helps combatants imagine themselves as killable killers and manage the moral, emotional, and conceptual implications of this role.

To give a preliminary example of this relationship between language and physical violence, I turn to Randall's account of his training in 1967. He had come up "pretty tough" in a gang-dominated neighborhood of Baltimore, where he was teased for his caramel-colored skin. When the draft for Vietnam started scooping up his peers, he wanted to stay in control. Reasoning his parents would benefit from the government payout if he died, he opted to enlist in "the best" military branch, with those uniforms that look so good. Randall figured he was ready for it, but he was still rocked back when he arrived at the Parris Island Marine Corps Training Depot in South Carolina.

"One or two Drill Instructors [DIs] get on the bus and the first thing you hear is, 'You motherfuckers have fifteen seconds to get off this fucking bus and line up on them goddamned yellow footprints. Now move, move, move, mothafuckas—move, move, move!'" Randall laughed to remember it. "That's how it starts. At first you think this is funny, it's bullshit, and then they run up on you, spit flying: 'What the fuck you smiling about?'"

It was open season, too, on anything that smacked of femininity. During the requisite head shaving, the beginning of boot camp's rite of passage, the barbers would call the guys with long hair "girls." They'd adopt a mocking voice, saying things like, "Oh, that's beautiful, so pretty—where you from, boy? How you want it trimmed?" Randall imitated a loud, lawnmower-like buzz as he mimed an electric razor racing painfully across a scalp. On the first or second day, DIs spelled out the Corps' compulsory heterosexuality. "Is anyone in here gay? Cause we don't want you here. If you realize you've made a mistake, or if you suck another man's dick, if you're shit-packing, then you are not to be admitted in my Marine Corps."

As for other ways of denigrating recruits, Randall says he wasn't targeted by the overt racial slurs some encountered, but one time a DI eyed his skin tone and asked, "What ARE you?"[7] Randall also remembers there was a Jewish guy in his platoon. "I think his real name was Eisenberg. The DIs would say, 'What the fuck is that? You a fucking Jew? Yeah, well, I'm taking that name from you. Your name is now Eichmann. From now on I'm gonna refer to you as Eichmann.'" And all the recruits were subject to generic put-downs. "Your name is 'Private' or 'Scumbag' or whatever they want you to be called. Everybody is 'scumbag,' 'shitbum,' you know. You have no name. You haven't earned the title of Marine yet so you're nobody." If a recruit asked permission to speak, the DI would respond, "Speak, freak!"

Between their yelling and grueling orders, DIs would addle the recruits. "Get over here, pigs!" The guys would rush over in a sweat. "Too fast! Get back and do it again, slower." They'd go back, do it again. "Too slow, ladies! Try again." Shaking his head, Randall called these "weird mind games" that were unwinnable. But there was no ambiguity in how the recruits had to yell as they practiced with their bayonets on dummies or sometimes just running across the fields at Parris Island: "Kill, kill, kill!"

By the end of basic training, Randall says, "You get programmed. It's like housebreaking a dog. You get so eighty-four guys are peeing the same way the same time." He came to accept that he was "a GI, 'Government Issue.' You belong to the USA." While this loss of self-ownership was daunting, he took pride in feeling like a hardened man in accepting it. Sometimes he seemed to channel the DIs while talking to me, repeating their formulations as his own: "If you don't wanna be here, call your mommy. Get your ass outta here."

Randall still thinks there was something "beautiful" about the strength and the pact that emerge from training: the extraordinary ability to work in concert, the physical and mental toughening, and the raw courage of being willing to kill or die for one another, fostered by the kin-like feeling that grows among Marines. He was ready to suffer and to do the worst in Vietnam, and by God, he did. But today, as he rejects the premise of that war, his voice tightens to a rasp. "I killed so many people. For *what*? For nothing." He had become a sacrificial weapon, trapped in the tragic folly of a pointless conflict. And that loosened membrane between life and death continues to flutter within him, an intimacy with violence that haunts him to this day.

The bodily entrainment of Marines and other US soldiers is plain to see, from their skills with weaponry to their taut control over their movements.[8] (In this book, I use the lowercase term "soldiers" to refer to service members in all the armed forces, but I use capitalized terms to specify those in a branch: "Marines," "Soldiers" for those in the Army, "Airmen" for those in the Air Force, etc.) However, the necropolitical role of language in combatants' experience has scarcely been explored by linguistic anthropology or related disciplines.[9] Randall, for one, understood the point of all the drills, fitness exercises, and weapons training, but he also sensed that something hard to articulate was happening to him during all that yelling, verbal abuse, and mind-game playing. The way language was being used seemed to offer a connection to the disposability of bodies and erasure of souls. But how, exactly? How would some of the verbal events Randall describes in basic training, like being cursed at, insulted, and baffled by sadistic games, be connected to kinetic violence in war? Randall could tell there was "a kind of code" that went beyond just new vocabulary into morality itself and that this code was something "you practice every day until it becomes part of who you are."

What kind of personhood did this language set up, and how did its architecture travel from training into combat, taking new forms and having deeper effects?[10]

Randall would continue to learn new code in the Vietnamese jungle and the mud of the Demilitarized Zone at the edge of North Vietnam and South Vietnam. Some of it was obvious, like those racist slurs for the enemy that were easily extended to civilians as part of the crude "body count" the Pentagon used to measure supposed wins and losses in that era. Some of it—which the guys thought of as just "cursing," "shooting the shit," or "military humor"—had less obvious necropolitical implications, yet these still-common tools have an intimate relationship with killing and loss I will explore. And then there were those phrases that rubbished feeling or thinking too much about death, like "It don't mean nothin'," invoked like a talisman at tragic moments.

Randall and the few men from his unit who survived Vietnam would emerge almost mute about their combat experience. Civilians recoiled not only from their morally tainted status but also from the profane, bleak language that issued from their mouths. Hadn't they cared about all the death they witnessed and caused? And—even for those civilians who accepted the notion that communists deserved to die—how did these GIs process their own terror? They were angry and jumpy, but why wouldn't they *talk* about their feelings?

My conversations with Randall reached back to that horror show half a century ago, but there is still a family resemblance between what Randall described and the language many veterans of Iraq and Afghanistan (especially those in the Marine Corps) encountered in training and combat. To be sure, each era of war has its own political climate and argot. Twenty-first-century commanders, for instance, would not risk the reputational danger of the "body count" concept, with its sanctioning of near-indiscriminate killing. It would also be unusual to encounter DIs as overtly bigoted as the ones Randall described, for mainstream linguistic culture in the USA shifted toward greater sensitivity between the Vietnam War and GWOT era, while the military poured resources into diversity and inclusion training. Over the last couple of decades, policies allowed women to officially serve in combat and openly gay and transgender people to enlist, with military brass intermittently trying to implement more humane practices within the ranks. Some younger DIs conspicuously try to avoid the worst abuses of their predecessors. But despite these efforts and changes, the language of combat infantry and their trainers has tended to pull tenaciously toward necropolitical ends, sometimes reverting to patterns that echo those Randall describes. Such training is implicitly committed to the idea that language, used in particular ways, can break down trainees heading for war and remake them into warriors. Once in combat, language can provide a tenuous web to hold soldiers together, sometimes offering a way to shunt or defer the possibility of horror while enabling them to carry out awful deeds.

In fact, the patterns of language use I describe in this book matter partly because they make war more *doable*. Military combat asks too much of a human being. People's minds are not well equipped to assimilate the full implications or the moral depth of killing or being killed; such a reckoning could debilitate one's ability to live, let alone function on behalf of the military machine. As psychiatrist Robert Jay Lifton puts it, "There has to be some level of detachment"—some "psychic numbing"—to apply one's technical skills in war.[11] The language I describe offers a supreme instrument to facilitate this detachment. Such detachment can potentially enhance military force—the volume of fire in a firefight, the relentless pressure applied during a siege, and so forth—while offering a kind of rescue for the combatant. But there is a terrible cost to this facilitation, for if it makes violence more feasible for combatants, it spells more death, mayhem, and misery for the individuals and societies targeted by such violence, and sometimes for the combatants themselves.[12] There is no quantifying the suffering of the victims of such violence, or the guilt or horror incurred by least some of its perpetrators.[13] Military language privileges one state's security (or at least the illusion of it) but not *human* security, in the expansive, human-centered sense of well-being and freedom from fear.[14]

The language of infantry soldiers also matters because of its potential impact on the fabric of our culture. If it can facilitate violence in at least some people, it might also contribute to some combatants returning to society with an altered sense of morality. Combat veterans re-enter the civilian workforce, re-establish domestic relationships, raise children, and navigate the United States' choppy political waters—all while drawing on a subjectivity shaped in part by combat experience and language. I have witnessed how admirably some veterans manage their feelings after war, but others are capable of reproducing war's anomie or enthusiasm for violence. What happens in the military can creep into the wider society, and we ignore it at our peril.

Kill Talk as a Linguistic Infrastructure

The philosopher Hannah Arendt once wrote that violence is "mute"; it "begins where speech ends," after the rational capacity for dialogue fails.[15]

Nevertheless, war's violence is always mediated by language. For one thing, states talk their way into armed conflict, with elaborate rationales that include economic interest, self-defense, ideologies of patriotism, and toxic hostilities.[16] For another, military culture (and I focus here on the United States military) is saturated by what I call "kill talk" among those who serve as instruments of combat. The defining feature of kill talk is its refusal to acknowledge the full relational humanity of and the terrible loss suffered by those on whom potentially deadly violence is inflicted. This book explores how kill talk, in its various forms, encourages combatants to sequester the awfulness of bloodshed and death, "theirs" and "ours."[17]

I think of kill talk as a kind of linguistic infrastructure—a loose collection of disparate verbal strategies that guide soldiers in how to perceive, feel, think, and ultimately act in combat.[18] This infrastructure underpins the experience of having what the philosopher Judith Butler calls a "frame of war," which, in simplest terms, is a structure of meaning that selectively "carves up" experience, fostering indifference to certain deaths.[19] Butler's essays on the subject focus primarily on how visual representations, such as the circulation of Abu Ghraib torture images, help create a frame of war. Those photographs, they argue, framed certain lives as good and "grievable," while depicting "ungrievable" lives as "ontologically, and from the start already lost and destroyed."[20] Such frames shape the wider public's sense of reality and thus their assent to war.

The concept of a "linguistic infrastructure" in kill talk directs attention more precisely to language and to combatants themselves. Imagine this infrastructure as an invisible patterning force that begins with the (re)socialization of those entering the military and continues to evolve in military speech communities during combat.[21] Working in tandem with the political ideologies, military directives, and psychological mechanisms that facilitate inhumane deeds, this linguistic infrastructure offers form to modes of consciousness and shared ways of being-in-the-world. It directs and shunts, but rather than steering water, electricity, or vehicles as a city infrastructure does, its contours and dead ends encourage certain flows and stoppages of perceiving, feeling, thinking, and acting.

Kill talk aspires to block empathy for "the enemy" and to dull the combatant's sense of self-pity; it channels and champions the performance of aggressive military masculinity; it embraces the moral void of war so that combatants might not be grief-stricken and incapacitated by it. This infrastructure helps create conditions of possibility for the deadlier aspects of military experience while shifting combatants' sense of what is thinkable and doable.

I find the metaphor of "infrastructure" helpful because it allows us to think in visual and spatial terms about the directions thinking and feeling can take—extending toward other people, for instance, or skirting around them, or flipping ordinary moral convictions on their head. The word also suggests a patterning force that shows how the intangible entity of "the state" and the vague concept of "military culture" (the deadlier aspect of it, anyway) take hold in the minutiae of talk and experience.[22] It helps to explain how the military nudges the personhood of combatants this way and that, through organizing devices they themselves only partially recognize. For sometimes this linguistic infrastructure offers direct instruction for how to think and feel, but sometimes it merely hints at it. In some of the subtler material I discuss, kill talk seems to offer indirect verbal mirrors or metaphors that resonate with the shattering qualities of combat violence.

Kill talk takes various forms, each adopting a distinctive stance toward kinetic violence and its effects.[23] This book focuses on patterns of kill talk among combat infantry (especially Marines, but sometimes Soldiers) over the last few decades; other variations could be fruitfully explored among, say, commissioned officers or drone operators. Basic training introduces recruits to a structured immersion in kill talk—beyond whatever hints have already breezed around them in the American zeitgeist. Within the first few weeks, many Marine Corps recruits face instructors who yell with such intensity it overwhelms their ability to reason, while the instructor's shredded vocal cords model what it means to push the body beyond pain. The Drill Instructors' (DIs) insults are also pedagogically oriented, stripping recruits of civilian dignity, enforcing military masculinity (an aspiration not confined to male recruits), and indirectly modeling the dehumanization of future enemies in combat. These verbal assaults are further believed to harden recruit sensibilities, as if the language itself were a virtual projectile capable of callousing a person's exterior.

More subtly, DI language has instructive value by virtue of the way it violates not just ordinary norms, but sometimes, military rules themselves. I suggest the military's uncertain control over its violence is indirectly foreshadowed, modeled, and encouraged by the way some trainers use language and other signals. This intricate web of verbal and nonverbal cues creates a morally ambiguous zone while laying the groundwork for how combatants may later confront the enemy.

As kill talk extends into combat, it takes a range of forms. Infantry on ground missions often use bloodless, impersonal jargon when communicating with superiors or when otherwise adopting a "professional" stance. Phrases like "engaging a target," "neutralizing a threat," and "conducting a clearing operation," for instance, can refer to violence while bypassing the fleshy reality of human bodies and their suffering.[24] At the same time, however, a transgressive linguistic register flourishes in the theater of combat. It includes taboo slurs and epithets for "the enemy" and extravagant profanity that signals the speaker's military masculinity while symbolizing, in microcosm, the shocking bodily ruptures of kinetic violence. Such language diverges sharply from the military's sanctioned verbal formalities, leaning almost giddily into the prospect of killing (e.g., "Let's go smoke some haji motherfuckers"). The contrast between official and illicit military language is striking; the loftiness of the official register highlights the grimy, feral stance of the other.

These contrasts sometimes reappear in distinctively patterned jokes that juxtapose prosocial values with the depredations of war. I suggest that when such jokes appear in training, their internal contrasts—like the tensions between norms and their violations, military probity and foul language—offer indirect pedagogy for the future combatant. When combatants themselves generate these jokes, they may offer a sardonic critique of military predicaments but also resonate with, and perhaps even sanction, acts of shocking violence and exuberant sadism.

Other dimensions of kill talk include slogans designed to forestall a combatant's downward emotional spiral, cultivating a stoic attitude toward the possibility of being killed or maimed. After all, in the wars in Vietnam, Afghanistan, and Iraq, service members knew that without a front line, they had to make themselves vulnerable to draw out the enemy. This meant becoming "familiar—comfortable, even—with a certain level of instrumental objectification of their bodies," as MacLeish puts it.[25]

As I delve further into this subject matter, some caveats elaborated in the Preface bear repeating. Not all Marine Corps training experiences mirror the intense scenarios I describe, and not all combatants resort to the most extreme language I recount. The Department of Defense has been striving for decades to mitigate transgressions in training and combat, with real, though contested, effects. In a later chapter, I scrutinize the pushback against such efforts and the accompanying disagreements about how language should be used in the military.

It must be said, too, that there are myriad ways of talking in the US military that do not function in direct service of destruction and harm. The many military branches and units, for instance, cultivate vast and functionally vital technical vocabularies beyond the euphemistic language already mentioned, including acronyms and snappy "brevity codes."[26] Some veterans I talked to emphasized the sheer tedium of military bureaucratese, such as the young Marine Corps veteran I call Louis, who pulled up a MARADMIN (a "Marine Administrative Message") on his laptop and read its dense jargon to me with comic exhaustion.[27] Others regaled me with stories about how military language reinforces hierarchy. To enforce their authority, for instance, officers are prone to speaking with an air of confidence and superior knowledge.[28] Subordinates, in turn, bolster this dynamic by liberally sprinkling their responses with honorifics ("sir," "ma'am," "lieutenant," etc.) and highly obedient verbal stances.[29] And beyond all that, service members have generated an ocean of creative, salty military slang. Some of it helps pass the time during monotonous stretches, while other expressions jab at authority and other irritations, helping soldiers bond while providing an outlet for discontent.[30]

Many aspects of military language, then, get the job done, enforce status differentials, boost morale, and help soldiers find exhilaration on the job. But in this volume, I examine the language that undergirds the necropolitical role of the infantry combatant, the state's killable killer.[31]

Language, Experience, and Context

Why focus on language to understand anything about kinetic violence in war? After all, there are many incentives and forces that can encourage people to kill in war or dull their sensitivity to violence. The menu is extensive: competition over resources and power, imperialism, ethnonationalism, racism and other forms of bigotry, crowd behavior and conformity, deference to authority, abuse during childhood, confused or insecure mindsets among the young people sent into battle. There may be chaotic or incompetent leadership from the highest to the lowest levels. There are the Rules of Engagement that justify and sometimes encourage the lethal use of force against anyone perceived as suspicious (because they are a military-aged male, for instance, or because they look as if they might be carrying a weapon or digging a hole to plant a bomb in). And then there is the psychobiology of combat itself, including fear, exhaustion, vengeance, and the tragic yet adaptive habituation that creeps in as a person gets used to doing something, however awful.[32]

Clearly language is only part of a complex behavioral story, but its role has been under-studied. For language doesn't merely refer to or describe the world; what we say and the way we say it can alter people and their relationships, be they intimate or deadly. I find veteran respondent testimonials persuasive: kill talk insinuates itself into their minds and bodies, helping encourage and shape stances of hostility or indifference.

For a straightforward example, consider Vietnam veteran John Musgrave's memory of the first time he killed a man in battle. It happened at close range, and the man looked him in the eye before Musgrave pulled the trigger. The man died loudly in a pool of blood at his feet, and Musgrave was horrified. He "hadn't yet learned to dehumanize the enemy," he says, and it was too easy to feel for his victim and to think of his grieving kin.[33] After that disturbing first kill, Musgrave recovered his ability to function by telling himself,

> I will never kill another human being as long as I'm in Vietnam. However, I will waste as many gooks as I can. I'll wax as many dinks as I can find . . . but I ain't going to kill anybody. Turn the subject into an object. It's Racism 101. And it turns out to be a very necessary tool when you have children fighting your wars, for them to stay sane doing their work.[34]

Musgrave explains that these turns of phrase had been "modeled by my peers, my instructors, my mentors."[35] His verbal shift had what were, for him, profound implications. With a small pivot in wording, individuals—"subjects," Musgrave calls them—turned into "nobodies," or mere "objects," and the act of "killing" became "wasting" or "waxing," which diminished its severity.[36] Like the optical illusion Wittgenstein made famous, the one that looks like a rabbit or a duck depending on what kind of meaning your eye seeks in it, the object of perception can toggle instantly from a relationally connected human being into a negligible object-like figure.[37] In examples like Musgrave's, we see how words and worlds can merge, and how language can precipitate a shift in consciousness.[38] In fact, in a book of poetry Musgrave wrote after the war, he apologizes to the reader for writing with "obscenities" (by which I think he means both the profanity and the racial slurs that dot his pages) but adds that "the obscenities are not the words I have used to describe [my] experiences[;] *they are the experiences themselves.*"[39] Experience cannot be dissociated from its linguistic medium.

Framing this medium as a "linguistic infrastructure" may bring to mind, for some readers, the literature on the relationship between "language and thought." In anthropology, discussions of this subject often refer to the controversial Sapir-Whorf hypothesis, which suggests that the grammatical structures of entire languages shape distinctive cognitive habits. But rather than making claims about the cognitive effects of obligatory grammatical structures inherent to a language, I join some of my colleagues in anthropology and psychology to focus on optional patterns of language use within the same language, such as adopting certain tones of voice, phrases, styles of joking, and so forth.[40]

I propose that the linguistic infrastructure I refer to as "kill talk" helps foster patterns of thought, feeling, and behavior—"experience," to put it broadly—that make it easier to inflict and accept violence. These chapters do not aim to encompass all possible varieties of kill talk and its accompanying experiences, for many additional ways of speaking within and outside the military encourage indifference to deadly violence. Robin Conley, for instance, documents the subtly distancing language used by prosecutors and jurors in death penalty trials, as they employ phrases like "that criminal," "that guy," or "the defendant" instead of more personal terms, thereby encouraging emotional detachment from the individual whose doom they may seal.[41] Such language offers another framework through which to sequester the human implications of such extreme measures.

Lest I overstate the power of language in war, I make no claim that military kill talk strictly determines thought or experience, because language derives its meanings and effects from embodied, holistic contexts. My more modest assertion is that the language I describe offers certain "affordances"—possibilities or potentialities—that can play a role in organizing combatants' experiences.[42] The stances soldiers adopt with kill talk might help place them into a killing mood or reinforce an already crystallized ability to dehumanize when killing. In some cases, kill talk may serve as a useful defense mechanism, mitigating distress when discussing the violence experienced in combat. Moreover, the impact of kill talk on consciousness may "take" more successfully among individuals already inclined to suppress their empathy.[43] Readers should bear in mind that when I suggest the military's linguistic infrastructure encourages certain thoughts and feelings, I also regard it as leaky, working better for some participants and in some contexts than others. We are, after all, dealing with humans rather than machines, to the state's regret.

Another factor to bear in mind is that kill talk is a collective, interactive achievement, emerging within an affectively charged social atmosphere that pressures people to speak and behave in certain ways and not others. The geopolitics of war create an ambient discourse that frames certain groups as enemies—"communists," "terrorists," and so forth—and this frame is part of the context that gives kill talk its force.[44] At the more immediate level, we must consider the social group in which talk unfolds. The feminist scholar Carol Cohn provides a poignant example, based on her observation that nuclear war strategists in the 1980s simply avoided discussing human suffering. Reflecting on her experience with these groups as they deliberated hypothetical nuclear war scenarios, she notes, "I often experienced the feeling that something terribly important was being left out and must be spoken;

and yet, it felt almost physically impossible to utter the words, almost as though they could not be pushed out into the smooth, cool, opaque air of the room."[45] Nor, indeed, could a Marine trundling along in an M48 Patton tank in Vietnam or a Humvee in Iraq suddenly blurt, "I feel so awful for the poor man I just shot; he must have suffered terribly." Such an outburst would be so hapless, unprofessional, and emasculating that the Marine would find it inconceivable to make such a statement. The social environment encourages some modes of speaking and behaving while deterring others, even as the way military collectives speak creates the context for their action.[46]

In spite of collective pressure, furthermore, service members' ways of speaking and casts of mind are never rigidly fixed. Like all speakers, military personnel are capable of pivoting their stance on the fly. Consider the postcombat account of Eliot Ackerman, a former Marine Corps Special Operations Team Leader, as he tells a journalist about an intense urban battle in Fallujah.[47] Ackerman's commander pulled him aside to say, "My expectation, Eliot, is that your platoon is going to be combat ineffective by the end of the first night." The descriptor "combat ineffective," a fine kill talk euphemism, centers the military mission as the priority, while skimming past the injury or death that would presumably incapacitate the men. Ackerman relates how he dutifully ran up to his platoon guide midbattle to say, "I need to know how many combat effectives you have," foregrounding the countable status of his platoon-mates as mere battle functionaries. He used the term during the battle itself, and again, without a blink, in his postbattle recounting to the journalist, as he places himself back in that headspace.

Later in the same interview, though, Ackerman speaks of the intense "fraternal love" of the men in his unit as they ran into fire to save wounded comrades. He describes the "heartbreak" and "paradox" of being tightly bonded to his buddies while pursuing a mission that would chew up and sacrifice some of them—a reflection that only seems possible outside of that battle's atmosphere. Ackerman thus shifts stance as he moves into and out of kill talk, with one stance distracting from combatants' anguish, pain, and blood by construing them primarily in terms of their "combat efficacy" for the mission, and another intimately describing their inner lives of fear and love as they die for it.[48] The very fact Ackerman and others can pivot in this way suggests that the perspective kill talk encourages is not locked into their psyches forever. This flexibility can hold the seeds of a transformation that can take some veterans into more restorative casts of mind, as we will see.

Irreconcilable Contradictions

I have mentioned an abiding tension between the upstanding face of formal military language and the taboo or unpalatable currents that permeate combatants' speech. Arguably, a similar moral fault line runs through the entire United States military at a vast scale, providing a cultural substrate for the linguistic patterns I discuss. For on the one hand, the military upholds service members as paragons of discipline and national virtue, embodiments of what anthropologist Catherine Lutz calls "super-citizenship."[49] On the other, says Kenneth MacLeish, the violence combatants are expected to undertake sometimes feels "completely contrary to the values of the civilian society they come from and defend."[50] As Marine Corps veteran Tyler Boudreau puts it, some element of "cold amorality" is demanded for the job.[51] And as many have attested, combat sometimes pulls its participants into an ungovernable moral abyss.[52]

The sociologist Werner Binder has observed that there is a long tradition in American popular culture of "'dirty' or law-defying" heroes (some of whom, ironically, work in law enforcement).[53] The oxymoron is familiar, yet we often overlook its inherent strangeness as it fuses two disparate creatures into one like a chimera from mythology.[54] In my conversations with veterans, a sense of unresolved contradictions recurred so often that I came to believe the tension between two sets of imagery, upstanding honor on the one side and moral depredation on the other, is a central predicament in military identity.

Conditions in the Vietnam War made for an especially stark gap between honor and the abyss. Randall, for one, still reels from the moment he lost a more innocent sense of what it meant to be part of that war.

> You know, I come up in this spit and polish Marine environment—you're talking about "Marine Corps pride," and your pants have to be a certain way, your shirt has to be folded a certain way, all this spit shine, and it's serious discipline in the States. Then you get to Vietnam, you see all these dirty guys. Okay, so, they HAVE to be filthy. But it's not just that. These guys are doing things I never even heard about or thought about. Like, I see these dudes sitting in a circle counting stuff and I'm thinking they're playing craps [a card game]. Turns out they're counting fingers and ears and long braids. I say, "Where'd you guys buy the braids?" And they're like, "BUY the braids? What are you talking about?"

The "filth" Randall describes among the combatants in Vietnam was both physical and moral, a stark contrast to the probity and professionalism he evidently expected of the Marine Corps.[55] Later, at the Da Nang Air Base, he would meet "guys who had like plastic bags, like baggies, with EYES. They collected EYES. There were some units that people would scatter, because they'd kill everything that moves. Take no prisoners. Men, women, children, dogs, cats." In such encounters, Randall learned of the macabre GI practice of collecting body parts as trophies, and of GIs emboldened (perhaps by those infamous "free-fire" zones supposedly dominated by the enemy) to "shoot anything that moves."[56]

Randall was certainly not alone in his dismay at the tension between the military's public image of rectitude and its sometimes troubling practices. Military brass has tried to address the matter for decades. Some of their efforts have gone toward polishing the military's public face, through uplifting advertisements and a heightened presence in public rituals.[57] Deeper efforts have gone into adjusting training and command structure. After the stain of the Vietnam War, evolving international law and pressure from activists led the security state to alter war practices on "humane" and "moral" grounds, aiming to minimize civilian casualties.[58] Over the decades, training increasingly incorporated discussions of military law, the Geneva Conventions, and "scenario training" about when the use of force would be justified. Military branches sometimes make a push to shore up their ethical foundations, as in the late 1990s, when the "Marine Corps Values Program" sought to ensure Marines would "epitomize" and "personify" honorable ideals.[59] Within a few years of the start of the war in Afghanistan and the Iraq War, too, the counterinsurgency campaign shifted focus from a "kill-capture" strategy to a "win the population" approach that emphasized an ideal of cultural sensitivity.[60] Policy guidelines during the Obama administration aimed to raise the threshold for the use of force while increasing the use of drones for supposedly more targeted and just killings.[61] And today, the Department of Defense aspires to cultivate "strategic leadership" qualities that include "self-awareness, humility, cultural savvy, and human relations skills."[62]

But critics still argue the violence deemed "just" by hegemonic powers too often involves atrocities rationalized in the name of necessity. Historian Samuel Moyn, for one, asserts that while legal obligations intended to humanize the United States' wars may have reduced dramatic massacres, they sometimes "sugarcoat" war's lethality to "help Americans take the bait."[63] Consider, too, the questionable morality of some actions permitted under the US Rules of Engagement—such as shooting up cars that fail to stop at checkpoints, a practice that led to many civilian deaths during the Global War on Terrorism. Beyond formally recognized war crimes or breaches of the military's own rules (both of which certainly persisted after Vietnam), there is a strong case that much lawful wartime behavior violates the "honorable ideals" the military aspires to. Apparently the rules themselves, and the wide license some have taken when interpreting them, make it easy to transgress normative ideas of morality.[64]

One way to look at this unsettling situation is to suggest that violations of norms, rules, and sometimes laws are unavoidably part of military systems, given that the dominant mode of military power is force and destruction.[65] To capture some of the irresolvable tensions that characterize the US military, MacLeish uses Michael Taussig's metaphor of a "nervous system."[66] For Taussig, a "nervous system" is a system that is supposedly hyperrational and whole, yet still fueled by perpetual unease. As many of the linguistic examples in this book illustrate, a key element of this unease in the military is the impossible tension between officially held ideals and their raw violations on the ground. The microcosmic nervous system evident in the details of language and practice offers a small mirror of military nervous systems at all levels of scale, from the discomfited individual psyche of some combatants to the hypocrisies of the state itself.

I also suggest that some military pedagogy is built on similar contradictions and ambiguities. For instance, despite numerous policies forbidding abuse in training, some trainers in the Marine Corps over the last few decades have believed that they have to break the rules to prepare an infantry edgy enough to handle war's transgressions. Arguably, such moral instability is a feature, not a bug, of military training, because its logic resonates with a combatant's headspace, in which ordinary schemas of meaning and ethics may be thoroughly dislocated.

A related tension arises between Marine Corps training in ethical decision-making and its emphasis on "instantaneous obedience to orders."[67] Ethan, a former Marine turned military lawyer, highlights this contradiction. "It's a huge issue," he tells me from his office. "I mean, you have to have instant obedience to orders. . . . At the same time, you're supposed to follow all lawful orders and know the difference between right and wrong." While some trainers strive to fashion the most ethical soldiers possible, others downplay ethical deliberation, such as Ramon, a retired Drill Instructor who trained recruits in San Diego in the 1980s. When I ask about the role of ethics in combat, he tells me, "When someone is shooting a gun at you, you can't say to yourself, 'Well, I'm just going to take them prisoner.' . . . You tell your recruits, 'You're going to engage and destroy the enemy. That's it.' And destroy the enemy means killing the enemy."[68] All in all, philosopher Jessica Wolfendale argues, modern military training often "undermines the capacity for moral reflection," creating a framework that can perpetuate war crimes such as torture.[69] A certain realism about military pedagogy may have influenced President Donald Trump's reasoning (however flawed) when he exonerated several convicted war criminals in 2019, tweeting in exasperation, "We train our boys to be killing machines, then prosecute them when they kill!"[70]

The irreconcilability of noble ideals and necropolitical practices becomes evident even in something as simple as military buzzwords. Every Marine can recite the famous "core values" of "honor, courage, and commitment"—some carry a wallet-sized card bearing the words—but my respondents reported a vague understanding of how to apply "honor," especially in the heat of violence work. Yes, Marines adhere to impressive principles when it comes to loyalty in combat, such as never leaving a comrade's body on a battlefield. At the same time, quite a few I spoke to defined "honor" in terms of Boy Scout values such as those in the slogan "A Marine never lies, cheats, or steals," rather than in terms of limits on violence.[71] Sam, an Army veteran who worked artillery in Afghanistan, recounts that the Army's emphasis on "integrity" inspired cynical joking in his unit. When Sam made a bad call, he would sardonically repeat the Army officer's phrase, "the backbone of integrity." He added, "Army guys will call each other out for cheating on their wife or having a drug problem once they're home," yet violence during war is nearly always the exception. "The same person slamming your 'integrity' is the one that told you in Afghanistan, 'Just fuck it, shoot all the grenades that way,' and you wound up killing someone you shouldn't have."

This contrast between controlled surfaces and messy underbellies seems baked into and amplified by some of the linguistic practices I detail in this volume.[72] The discrepancy between formal and informal military language can be so prominent that folklorist Elinor Levy has deemed it an instance of "diglossia": a situation in which speakers use a higher status linguistic repertoire in certain situations and a lower status, more colloquial repertoire in others, with the two varieties being clearly functionally separated.[73] However, military ways of speaking do not act like typical diglossia. Officially sanctioned talk and coarse language sometimes co-occur in the same linguistic interaction, sometimes to shift rapidly between markedly upright and unprincipled stances. In Chapter 8, I explore how the verbal duality between honor and the abyss appears in a type of military humor I call "frame perversion"—humor that suspends soldiers between super-citizenship and what are sometimes depraved situations. Again, to paraphrase John Musgrave, the experience and the language cannot be pulled apart from each other.

Empathy and Military Masculinity

My discussions of military language are informed by a backdrop of roiling disagreements in the United States about the importance of "empathy," which I loosely define as trying to compassionately imagine oneself into another person's experience.[74] The concept of empathy was not widely discussed as a core political value in the US until relatively recently. Today, most liberal and progressive Americans would adamantly agree that it is morally good and fitting to care about the suffering of other humans, regardless of who they are. While this principle is terribly hard to fulfill in practice, it has powerful political and cultural implications. Human differences along lines of race, ethnicity, gender, religion, and so forth are not, in this liberal schema, considered legitimate grounds for dehumanization or deprivation.

By now, the notion of empathy has also become a veritable industry, as educators bend their classrooms around it,[75] psychologists deem it a mark of emotional maturity,[76] gun safety advocates tout it as an antidote to violence,[77] career coaches champion it in *Forbes* magazine,[78] "user experience" professionals frame it as a design principle,[79] and Mark Zuckerberg dubiously claims it as a "powerful side effect" of virtual reality.[80] The rise of pro empathy ideology has posed a challenge for the US military, as many centrist and left-of-center Americans reread war's violence not in terms of glories secured but as trauma wrought on vulnerable people.[81] Meanwhile, Americans with right-wing political leanings tend to be more comfortable with the principle that empathy should be reserved primarily for one's in-group.[82]

The human capacity for empathy has probably always been biased—toward those we already identify with, for instance, or the people in our immediate presence—but war tends to cultivate severe empathic sclerosis.[83] The adjustment and suppression of empathic feeling among infantry could be classified, in fact, as a kind of "emotional labor" undertaken at the behest of the state, as part of its necropolitical agenda.[84] For on the one hand, members of the infantry come to identify strongly with those in their unit, but on the other, as kill talk makes clear, the show must go on even if those buddies are wounded or killed. And, crucially, kill talk aspires to block empathic reach toward an often racialized "enemy," erasing their suffering from consideration or making it the subject of mirth or mockery. To be sure, the Pentagon tried to check such hostility during the "counterinsurgency" era that began in 2003, when General David Petraeus emphasized strategic rapport building with populations in the Middle East. This new doctrine aspired to understand populations on the ground—grasping elements of "their culture" and sometimes expressing friendliness and compassion—in order to compete with insurgents and foster political stability. However, scholars have noted that since control was always the objective, the gestures made toward emotional connection in this era tended to be superficial.[85] Not surprisingly, antiempathic verbal patterns among combatants managed to outlive the counterinsurgency doctrine. Such language has a clear necropolitical logic, offering both an incentive and a survival mechanism for those who may ultimately be required to move through the world blasting holes through people.

The hostility to empathy I trace, in fact, suggests that the very definition of military masculinity in the USA could be extended beyond the toughness, aggression, and blatant heterosexual desire characteristic of hegemonic masculinity.[86] The political scientist Aaron Belkin has already added nuance to our understanding, stressing not just toughness but also obedience as part of military masculinity, while further opening the definition to include "a set of beliefs, practices and attributes that can enable individuals—men and women—to claim authority on the basis of affirmative relationships with the military or with military ideas."[87] (Crucially, in this formulation, military masculinity is not just for those with a male gender identity; anyone can aspire to partake of it.) I would add that a key structure of feeling in military masculinity is kin-like affinity for the military unit, coupled with curtailed empathy for outgroups.[88] The functional, "successful" combat infantryman is willing to die for those who share the military mission, while refusing to dwell on the suffering of people targeted or caught in the crossfire.

It is telling that a recent study on Marine Corps organizational culture, commissioned in the wake of a 2017 scandal in which male Marines shared nude photos of female Marines on Facebook, reported that empathy may be a "missing or undervalued core value." The authors themselves had to concede that Marines regarded this claim as "ironic," empathy being "one of the last things people associate with being a good Marine."[89] Miles Lagoze, Marine Corps veteran and director of the documentary *Combat Obscura* (2018) explains the connection this way: "It's hard to imagine what fighting a war would look like if there wasn't toxic masculinity involved ... because you're being trained to kill people, and to not be thoughtful about those things, and to basically be excited to go to war."[90] Meanwhile, as I discuss at length in Chapter 5, many in the military and within the US political right wing associate sensitive language with problematic femininity and national weakness. This language ideology helps legitimate and embolden military kill talk—talk that would be fundamentally unacceptable to many Americans who may not realize that it happens in their name.

Emerging from War

Vietnam veteran Karl Marlantes notes that the feelings associated with taking lives in combat sometimes leak out later in life:

> Ask the twenty-year-old combat veteran at the gas station how he felt about killing someone. His probably angry answer, if he's honest: "Not a fucking thing." Ask him when he's sixty and if he's not too drunk to answer, it might come out very differently.[91]

In fact, there is no one-size-fits-all answer for how veterans feel about killing, then or now; accounts tend to be pretty varied and sometimes internally conflicted. But when combatants do feel numb about what they have done, I suggest, kill talk played some role. That said, whatever effects kill talk has during service do not seem secure. Over time, some combat veterans come to question what they did in war or the legitimacy of the war itself. Some describe their distress in terms of "moral injury," a relatively new concept that points to a spiritual wound caused by the violation of a person's moral compass.[92] Noting how many veterans self-medicate with substance abuse or take their own lives, Marlantes calls on the nation to offer more to help former combatants sort out their grief, sorrow, and guilt.

This book demonstrates that if language can break recruits in basic training and pave the way toward military brutality, language can also offer combatants the possibility of demilitarizing. One recurring theme across several chapters, for instance, is the journey taken by some soldiers and veterans as they come to regret their involvement in war. Sometimes this journey begins with physical proximity to "the enemy," which may break the spell of dehumanization, for the close presence of another person can trigger empathic attunement.[93] In some instances, combatants who regret killing may decide on the spot to renounce slurs and epithets for the enemy, reconceptualizing them as embedded in kinship and community—"somebody's son, somebody's father, somebody's brother," in the words of one individual I spoke to.[94] Shifts in one's perception of the Other tend to be twinned with shifts in language.

The last two chapters of the book, furthermore, honor and analyze the creative work of a subset of American veterans who use language and other semiotic forms to find their way out of their own militarization. One chapter tracks the way veterans, especially those who served in Vietnam, have used poetry to offer commentary on kill talk, grieve for the deaths of fellow combatants and atone for the way they and those around them killed without empathy. My final chapter explores the more recent emergence of "combat paper," a practice that brings veterans together to cut up their uniforms, pulp them into paper, and convert the former social skin of the military self into an open-ended medium on which they print deeply personal and expressive art and writing. These projects offer an antidote to the expressive block so common to former combatants.

Methods and Choices

My fieldwork for this project, conducted intermittently since 2016, took many forms at many sites. All formal research involved military veterans rather than active-duty service members, which means this study offers a recent history of military language rather than a perfectly up-to-date account.

My methods included conducting interviews (most in person and some over Zoom), orchestrating focus groups, engaging in observation and deep hanging out, reviewing documentary footage, reading veteran writings, and monitoring news and social media generated by and about military players. I also attended a multiday reunion of Drill Instructors (DIs) at the Marine Corps Training Depot at Parris Island, South Carolina, where I observed and interacted with retired and active-duty DIs. I later conducted recorded interviews with several retired DIs. (When it came to the active-duty DIs, I socialized and did some informal chatting with them, but beyond the sprinkling of curious questions that followed the drift of our social interactions, I considered them off-limits for recorded interviews or substantial lines of inquiry.)

I also made several visits to a studio in New Jersey called Frontline Paper, where uniforms are transformed into a creative medium. I made numerous visits to veterans' writing workshops in Massachusetts and participated in a summer writing workshop for veterans hosted by the William Joiner Institute for the Study of War and Its Social Consequences at UMass Boston. I attended a workshop for left-leaning military chaplains discussing moral injury, assisted in setting up an exhibition of veterans' art, and attended various military ceremonies and war-related museum events while engaging in conversations with military personnel who were there.

In addition, I conducted open-ended interviews about military language with forty-nine veterans of the American War in Vietnam and the Global War on Terrorism (GWOT). Many were from New England, New York, and New Jersey, with others hailing from the West Coast, central states, and the South. Roughly half of my respondents served in Vietnam, while the remainder served in the GWOT; this division meant about half of these respondents were in their late sixties and older, and the rest were between their early twenties and early fifties. About two-thirds of my interviewees served in the Marine Corps and about a third in the Army, though I also had conversations here and there with veterans of other branches. My respondents were primarily cisgender white male service members, but also included some Black and Latino/a veterans, veterans with Arab-Muslim roots, women, and LGBTQ+ service members. While demographic diversity plays a role in some details of my account, a full exploration of racial, gender, and religious diversity in military language would require a different book. Beyond speaking with veterans, I also spoke with some military-adjacent individuals, such as writing instructors who lead workshops for veterans and a researcher at the Defense Equal Opportunity Management Institute.

I met many respondents through snowball sampling, and some by advertising at two VA hospitals in Massachusetts. Occasionally, respondents would bring buddies along for a casual gathering, like the time I spent three raucous hours at a bar in Tucson with five Afghanistan veterans from the same Army unit. These provided opportune moments to overhear veterans reminiscing, sometimes using the same kind of language they used in active duty. I have changed the names and identifying characteristics of most respondents, and occasionally, to conceal identities further, I have created a composite figure or altered the context in which I was privy to sensitive information. That said, some of my key informants have published writing or exhibited art in the public domain and wish to be identified in my work.

I address two branches of the military in these pages, the Marine Corps and the Army, with a focus on the Marines. Commonalities run through all four military branches, but they also have somewhat different cultures of training, operations, and conduct.[95] The Marine Corps has the highest proportion of men (90%, compared with about 80% in the Army). Its training is famously harsh and cultivates an outstanding sense of belonging—hence their rallying cry, "Semper Fi" (always faithful). Although most Marines go from basic training to the Infantry Training Battalion, those destined to be noninfantry head to the Marine Combat Training Battalion to ensure that, in the Marine Corps' own words, "every Marine is a fighting Marine, regardless of their military occupation specialty (MOS)."[96] In keeping with this spirit, the Corps is notoriously hypermasculine and aggressive; members of other military branches describe it as "hard-ass," "mean," and "intense."[97]

My conversations revealed the playful rivalry between branches, a competition often exaggerated in online memes and tongue-in-cheek remarks. Army veterans, for instance, sometimes enjoy parodying Marines as dumb crayon eaters or empty-headed muscle men. Marines enjoy parodying the other branches in turn.[98] In a mish-mash of truth and myth, some enjoyed telling me that Army recruits get to keep their cell phones in training, that they have so little fear of their Drill Sergeants they'll actually *prank* them, that Army recruits are actually *allowed to smile*. A favorite Marine refrain, though it is a patent exaggeration, is that Army recruits can hold up a "stress card" with a quivering hand if they want a Drill Sergeant to stop bothering them.[99] By contrast with those Army guys, one young Marine Corps veteran tells me, Marines have no "get out of jail free" pass. He thumped the table as he added, "For Marines, it's twenty-four, twenty-five, seven."[100] And yet, everyone knows that Marines and Army alike labored extensively in combat operations in Vietnam, Iraq, and Afghanistan, and members of both branches fought hard and suffered terribly. My respondents who served as Army infantry also confirmed that although some of my material about basic training and kill talk in war has a distinctive Marine Corps flavor, it resonated with them, too. And they had much to add, especially to my discussions of combat language.

I have opted to trace certain linguistic patterns across two conflicts—the American War in Vietnam, which dominated US politics in the late 1960s and 1970s, and the GWOT, which began shortly after 9/11. I am mindful of both similarities and differences between the US military of these eras. The military has been influenced, in recent decades, by a wider social insistence on inclusion and linguistic sensitivity, in ways I discuss in some of my chapters. Of course, the nearly thirty-year lull between wars also saw a major shift in foreign policy anxieties—from "communists" to "terrorists." Each conflict introduced US soldiers to distinctive discomforts and perils: wet jungles versus gritty sand, Agent Orange versus burn pits, grenades versus IEDs, among others. Both wars, however, confronted American troops with the terror of guerrilla warfare and the challenge of distinguishing combatants from civilians.

Many Vietnam veterans, furthermore, experienced a sorrowful sense of déjà vu as they watched the GWOT unfold, fearing that it mirrored the Vietnam War's false premises, difficulty identifying the enemy, and drawn-out, futile bloodshed that traumatized soldiers and devastated the terrain. The Vietnam War cost roughly fifty-eight thousand American lives and three million to four million Vietnamese and Cambodian lives, directly or indirectly. Similarly, the conflicts in Iraq and Afghanistan resulted in millions of casualties, directly or indirectly.[101] Although the number of Americans who died in the GWOT (roughly seven thousand) is lower than the number of those who died in Vietnam, advances in body armor and medical care meant that more survivors would live with debilitating injuries, including traumatic brain injury (TBI).[102]

There were similarities and differences, too, in the composition of these groups of US soldiers. Many who served in Vietnam were conscripted, often from working-class or impoverished backgrounds because it was so easy for others to evade the draft through college deferments, medical exemptions, and other means.[103] Some enlisted out of noble ideals or patriotic duty but others did so because it seemed one of the few available paths to financial security. And the racial inequities were stark: Black men were disproportionately drafted, rarely promoted, and sometimes given the lousiest, most lethal missions.[104] All the US combatants in Vietnam were male, though women could volunteer to serve as nurses or in other supporting roles.

The draft ended in 1973, but low-income backgrounds continued to be a theme for service members in the GWOT. Many recruits after 9/11 came from modest working-class backgrounds, seeing the military as one of the few respectable paths to a reliable paycheck and upward mobility. These days, the military prides itself on its racial and ethnic diversity, with especially high Hispanic representation. Upward mobility has improved for service members of color, even though reports of structural racism remain.[105] Today roughly 18% of active-duty service members are women, who were allowed to serve in combat as of 2013.[106]

While economic and structural dynamics still shape enlistment demographics, ideological and psychological factors also play a significant role. Many volunteers come from military families and view service as part of their family tradition—a pattern the military relies on to meet recruitment numbers, though it exacerbates the military-civilian divide by concentrating service within these lineages. Some young people feel a sense of duty to serve or defend their nation, while others are drawn to the idea of military glory, responding to glossy brochures and TV ads that target them with themes of grit and grandeur. One veteran respondent (who later became a VA counselor) believes that the military's promise of camaraderie, belonging, and strength is particularly appealing to young people from fragmented or abusive homes. And many told me recruiters have a keen ability to sense an individual's longings—whether for financial security, belonging and brotherhood, or a sense of higher purpose—and tailor their pitch accordingly.

If the Vietnam War and the GWOT share a legacy of questionable objectives and failures to win hearts and minds, they also produced a significant number of disenchanted combat veterans. Many, though certainly not all, returned home disillusioned by the gap between their ideals of military service and their actual experience of war. The language I describe may contribute to their consternation, as it encourages dehumanization that some veterans come to regret.

When the War Comes Home

This book argues that language plays an important role in transforming a person into a combatant, helping subsume their purpose into the broader framework of military necropolitics. Part of the military contract—especially for those destined for close combat—involves a process of resocialization that sidelines individuality, desensitizes the self, and alienates the person from thoughts and feelings that once felt authentic.[107] To militarize the self is, in part, to become callous to the feelings of certain others.[108]

At the same time, being militarized can feel empowering to people who want to be part of something bigger and bolder in the face of a perceived threat. My analysis of kill talk may thus bear relevance to the increasing presence of independent, far-right militias. To be sure, the vast majority of service members are not political extremists, and the military sometimes expels those displaying signs of fanaticism or instability. Although a recent Defense Department study indicated a rise in right-wing extremism in the veteran population,[109] a 2023 RAND study argues that support for extremist views among veterans is actually no higher than it is in the general public.[110] Nevertheless, extremists known to have committed or planned a mass casualty attack are disproportionately likely to have a military background.[111] Some militias, furthermore, actively recruit veterans for their weapons training and organizational skills, and militia numbers have tended to surge after a war, possibly fueled by veterans disillusioned by their government and seeking purpose.[112] By some measures, about a quarter of those on militia rosters are military veterans who have, in the historian Kathleen Belew's phrase, "brought the war home."[113]

Rory Fanning, Army Ranger turned war resister, worries that white supremacist militias could be adopting the racist language and dehumanizing tactics he and other veterans learned during their military service.[114] Reflecting on his own experience, Fanning writes, "The people of Afghanistan were never referred to as Afghans. They were only mentioned in the most derogatory terms." He believes this training had "devastating" consequences, including the killing of civilians, and fears this ability to dehumanize others could be easily transferred into today's divisive domestic politics.

A brief look at documentary footage of the Georgia Three Percent Security Force, a faction of the largest militia coalition in the USA known as the Three Percenter movement, reveals an abundance of military language. Engaging in target practice and tactical drills, militia members seem to enjoy commanding militaristic technical terms, snappy acronyms, titles such as "General" and "Corporal," honorifics like "sir," and nicknames such as "Blackout" and "Rambo."[115] They pepper their words with norm-busting profanity as they discuss hypothetical violent scenarios. Their patches and slogans adopt menacing stances: "I am the danger," "Guns up," "Boogieman." Antiempathic encouragements are also in full evidence, as when a self-appointed "General" says, "If it's done by a hostile force, I'm gonna kill as many bastards as I can before they get me and move on without remorse."

Fanning also contends that disenchanted veterans, those "willing to renounce their training," may offer the best antidote to militia extremism.[116] In kind, the veterans I discuss in the final chapters—those who can build bridges between the aggression or indifference of kill talk and the compassion available in other symbolic forms—have been able to show their fellow veterans another pathway.

In the upcoming chapters, I delve into the linguistic infrastructure that supports and facilitates state necropolitics as manifested among US combatants, particularly Marines and Army infantry. Readers interested in the intricacies of Marine Corps basic training—its dynamics of yelling, the removal of first-person pronouns, the use of insults, the imposition of compulsory masculinity, and the sometimes mind-bending intimations of moral nihilism—will find a detailed exploration in Chapters 2 through 4. For those curious about how national political divisions surrounding "PC language," "wokeism," and empathy have influenced discussions about military training and its linguistic norms, Chapter 5 focuses on these debates. Chapters 6 and 7 examine the language of combat itself, including the use of profanity, derogatory terms, and nihilistic expressions that undermine empathy and dehumanize civilian populations affected by conflict. Chapter 8 looks at a type of gallows humor that serves as both a coping mechanism in combat and a subtle encouragement to violence. Finally, Chapters 9 and 10 explore the linguistic and semiotic exit strategies created by veterans who strive to break free of the military's linguistic infrastructure, expanding their empathic connections while grappling with the personal and collective losses inflicted by military experiences.

SECTION II
TRAINING

Chapter 2
Yelling

Night after night, the buses pull up on the tarmac outside the Recruit Processing Center at Parris Island Marine Corps recruit training center in South Carolina.* Usually they are full of young men—still boys, by some measures—with a nervous feeling in the pit of their stomach. They will have sensed the air getting heavy and sticky, and they might have noticed a faint swampy smell. They've seen enough movies to know what comes next, but they still find it startling. A Drill Instructor (DI) storms the bus, shirt tight around his muscles, his belt seeming to float around his flat abdomen, roaring at the neophytes from under his circular hat brim.

"SIT UP STRAIGHT! From this point forward you will only answer me with a YES, sir, NO, sir, AYE-AYE, sir. DO WE UNDERSTAND?"[1]

"YES, SIR!" yell the recruits.

"Now get OFF MY BUS! NOW NOW NOW!"

The young men hustle to plant themselves on a row of yellow footprints painted on the road. The yelling follows them, an acoustic assault, so thick and fast and strangely inflected that each recruit has to listen hard and use herd behavior to know what to do next.

They know they're about to be transformed, but they are unlikely to recognize all the subterranean dynamics of this change and how the acoustic qualities of boot camp will demonstrate how to become a hardened killer. These qualities will also model the disintegration of their personhood and their necropolitical abjection—that is, their killability in the eyes of the state. But more immediate symbolism commands their attention. Those yellow footprints have awaited recruits since the early 1960s, and each assumes the same position, heels clicked neatly together, forcing the body to stand at attention as the DI paces back and forth barking declarations.[2]

DIs have been through their initial speech many times, and it's a performance of intimidation, not semantic clarity. Phrases like "United States Marine Corps" come out about twice as fast as they would in ordinary talk.

---

* This chapter analyzes words and imagery that may be difficult for some readers to encounter. Please see the "Content Warning and Note on Language" in the front matter for some context and a discussion of the author's reasons for not redacting this material.

Kill Talk. Janet McIntosh, Oxford University Press. © Oxford University Press (2025).
DOI: 10.1093/9780197808054.003.0003

DIs slur their syllables, swallow some words, and emphasize others erratically. Addling the listener seems to be part of the point. When I played back a recording (posted to YouTube in 2016 by a noncommissioned officer) three times over, I could discern the following:

> YOU have just taken the first step to becoming a member of America's finest fighting force, the United States Marine Corps. YOU should be standing at a position of attention. That means your heels are touching. Your FEET are at a forty-five-degree angle. Your thumbs are on your trouser seam. Palms rolled inward. Fingers in their natural curl. Head and eyes straight in front. And your mouth is shut. I'll say it again: your mouth is shut. That's the only position for which you should be a Marine [unintelligible] Depot. Do we understand. [The recruits yell "YES SIR!"] And do we understand. ["YES SIR!"][3]

The DI goes on to shout, in a rapid slur, that recruits are now subject to the Uniform Code of Military Justice. He threatens nonjudicial punishment or a court-martial for noncompliance. He shouts about Article 91, on "disrespect" not being tolerated, and Article 92, which states, "You will do what you're told to, when you're told to do it, without question." Each speech segment ends with "Do we understand," but it's a rhetorical question. There's no room to request clarification—only to perform affirmation in the loudest possible voice.

The arrival I've described is fairly typical, but every Marine Corps veteran will describe theirs a little differently. Some DIs bypass the longer speeches at the footprints, instead going up to individual recruits to scream in their ear, "GET ON THOSE YELLOW FOOTPRINTS! EYES FRONT! YOU! QUIT LOOKING AROUND!"[4] Sometimes, two or three DIs stage a "shark attack," swarming individual recruits while screaming at them to assume the "POA"—position of attention—before explaining what the acronym means.[5] One Marine I spoke to described feeling "ripped off" when his bus was greeted by a female DI who was too distracted to give the tongue-lashing he expected; he had hoped for a more bracing, masculine experience.[6] But the classic arrival slams recruits with language that assails and frustrates. There is no sign of anything like "conversation." This is a rite of passage.

From the yellow footprints, recruits are hustled into the Recruit Processing Center, its double metal doors—called "silver hatches"—sporting Marine Corps logos with the eagle, globe, and anchor. Large letters proclaim, "Through these portals pass prospects for America's finest fighting force. United States Marines." A few blocks away at the Parris Island Museum, which is routinely visited by recruits and families at graduation time, a photographic exhibition describes the silver hatches as "the official doorway into a new reality." Their power is preserved through ritualized rules: the recruits pass through them while DIs take a separate entrance.

The events within shock recruits with a whirlwind that continues through the night. DIs act with frantic energy, encircling and approaching the recruits from various angles, purposefully stressing and disorienting them. They describe this as creating "a kind of fog of war," though some of the content seems irrelevant to warfare on the face of it.

A DI yells so thick and fast it's hard to catch what he's saying. "If your shirt is untucked, you gotta tuck it into your pants. If your buttons are unbuttoned, you gotta button your buttons all the way to the top. If your sleeves are rolled up you gotta unroll them and you gotta cuff 'em at the cuff. Scream AYE SIR."[7]

"AYE SIR!"

As recruits fill out paperwork at small desks, a female DI yells confusing instructions at close range, then orders, "Scream AYE MA'AM." If a recruit acts sluggish or confused, a DI might repeatedly palm-slam a desk or locker within inches of their face, scramble the papers as the recruit tries to write, or rock the surface until the papers fall off, sabotaging the very task they've told the recruit to carry out.

In another room, dozens of new recruits stand at attention, still in civilian clothes. A messy pile of their personal effects sits in a heap, and a female DI is rifling through them. She holds up a small notebook and addresses a recruit in a disdainful tone.

"What is this. Is this like an address book? What is this? Is this something PERSONAL?"

"Yes, ma'am," replies the recruit, knowing well enough not to show emotion. The DI tosses it to the ground with obvious disgust. She picks up more items, tossing them to the side as if going through a trash pile. Nothing personal is dear anymore.

The Rite of Passage

In the spring of 2019, I was on Parris Island for several days during a reunion for the East Coast Drill Instructors' Association. The Public Affairs officers on the island had approved my presence, as had the head of the association, telling me to "ask anything you want of the guys," though in the end I listened and observed more than I asked. I was surprised by what I could access at the depot once I flashed my driver's license at the gate each morning and explained my association with the reunion. I could drive freely around the island, observe outdoor training exercises and interactions between Drill Instructors and recruits, and hang out with the dozen or so active-duty DIs, all men, who had volunteered to set up the reunion activities. Off the island, veteran contacts also connected me to former DIs from the Parris Island and San Diego recruit training depots; I spoke to some casually and some in formal interviews.

The active-duty DIs seemed bored when they weren't working on the reunion. I struck up my first conversation with one of them at a fundraiser. I was standing next to an old ventriloquist's dummy, a sort of mascot for the island, auctioned off every year for a retired Marine to borrow. Champing a stiff cigar beneath glowering eyes, the dummy sports a uniform and a DI's "Smokey the Bear" hat.[8] He also bears a red name tag: "Sgt. Marvin Focker, Parris Island." I broke the ice by putting my hand up Sergeant Focker from behind and making his hinged mouth speak: "Hey, maggots!" A couple of DIs laughed.

The dummy invites amusement about the DI's persona, but the DIs couldn't be more serious about the stakes and the efficacy of their performance. From those silver hatches to the Parris Island water tower announcing "WE MAKE MARINES," the USMC (United States Marine Corps) is proud to broadcast they are dismantling mere civilians and reconstructing them into military super-citizens, the ultimate patriotic figures. The notion that basic training produces a superior social being has long been fundamental to US military; in the Vietnam era, new recruits were sometimes told to take a shower to "wash the civilian scum off."[9] At graduation time, clusters of family members wander the island in T-shirts proclaiming themselves "Proud mother / father / uncle / grandmother of [so-and-so]," with the shirt's color indicating the recruit's battalion, and their company insignia emblazoned on the back or front. Civilian kin become lumpen satellites to their Marine, jostling along sidewalks in their ill-fitting shirts while their transformed relative strides, ramrod straight and taut.

When I wandered one day into the Douglas Visitor Center at the heart of the island, a room was set up to await family members. Rows of glossy red metal folding chairs were arrayed before a large photographic display labeled "THE TRANSFORMATION OF YOUR MARINE." Each three-feet-tall picture is titled with a stage of boot camp: "Receiving," "Confidence Course," "Gas chamber / Rappel tower," "Combat fitness test," and so forth. A male or female recruit is captured in a dramatic pose, their silhouette overlain with smaller images of groups of recruits undertaking the same exercise. This sameness is a central goal of basic training: to expunge aspects of the individual and make them a token of a type. The type emerges from physical skill building but also a shift in subjectivity. The way Captain Greg Carroll, former Public Affairs official at Parris Island, put it to me was, "We call it a transformation; there's an intangible character development that goes on."

Learning more about basic training, I was impressed by how DIs almost seemed to be drawing directly on the anthropologist Victor Turner's generalizations about rites of passage, based on fieldwork in sub-Saharan Africa in the mid-twentieth century. Over the course of thirteen weeks, DIs do what ritual elders do to initiates the world over—namely, grind them down "to a uniform condition to be fashioned anew."[10] At the very start, recruits are stripped of their distinctive attributes. Their hair is shaved if male, cropped or lacquered into submission if female; their clothing is replaced with a uniform, and, in keeping with the double meaning of that word, their bodies are reconditioned to behave in unison with the other tokens of the type. DIs subject their initiates to intense physical demands and psychological stress, making them receptive to messages about what they must become. And initiates are repeatedly reminded, through words and actions, that they occupy what Turner called a "liminal" role; they are neither civilians nor Marines but hover in a gray space between clear social identities. To some DIs, anyway, this seems to mean they are to be degraded as virtual nonentities.

Growing up, most of these recruits will have been nurtured by parents who showed some curiosity about their experiences and preferences.[11] American children more than perhaps any others—especially white, middle-class American males—are socialized to believe that while they should be considerate of others, their ideas and their comfort matter. Though many recruits come from less privileged backgrounds, the overarching societal message is that ideally, individuals should have unique personalities with prosocial inclinations, a strong sense of personal agency, and rights of bodily autonomy.

All of these aspects of personhood will be compromised, if not completely erased, during military basic training. In many rites of passage, when the initiates are at their most vulnerable, they are presented with teaching tools of many kinds that instruct them explicitly or implicitly in what their new social role ought to be. Turner calls these tools *sacra* (or *sacrum* in the singular form), from the Latin adjective *sacer*, meaning "sacred." The term doesn't necessarily mean that these tools are religious or holy, but it does underline their importance in teaching initiates bedrock tenets of the society or organization they have signed themselves over to.

Some of the most obvious *sacra* during Marine Corps recruit training include a near-religious profession of devotion to one's rifle ("the rifleman's creed"), instructions about how to use gear and weaponry, physical training that hones the body as a weapon, marching and other motions during close order drills that place recruits in synchrony with their unit, and lectures and lessons about "Marine Corps values." The Corps condemns what they call "selfishness" and aims to reconstruct recruits to set aside their individual preferences—including, potentially, the desire to avoid physical harm—for the sake of the unit's mission and "the guy to the left of you and the guy to the right of you." The full effect inculcates a strong sense of belonging, particularly since the civilian identity that came before it is often symbolically maligned.[12] These *sacra* also play a role in cultivating, albeit to varying degrees, an eagerness for combat and an increased readiness to sacrifice one's life in war.

My purpose in these opening chapters is not to write a comprehensive account of boot camp and its most obvious teachings; others, including veterans, have described it well.[13] Nor is it to focus on the profound sense of loyalty to and affection for one's unit that basic training (and military experience more broadly) tends to instill.[14] This, too, has been widely recognized, often framed in terms of "brotherhood"—a term that highlights a central appeal of military experience for many as well as how marked and marginal female-identified service members sometimes feel.

My focus in this chapter and the two that follow will be on some of the *less* obvious necropolitical teaching tools in basic training in the Marine Corps. If Captain Carroll called the change wrought by boot camp "character development," I frame it instead as a linguistically mediated transformation designed to obscure the service member's vulnerability while curtailing their empathy. For the teachings of boot camp inculcate elements of the new linguistic infrastructure that facilitates the inner life of the military's killable killer.

These chapters compile examples of particularly harsh DI behavior, but as I note in somewhat more detail in Chapters 4 and 5, recent decades have seen efforts to curtail the most extreme training practices across the branches, with mixed success. Readers should also understand that within any given era, DIs have always had a range of personal philosophies about training. While some DIs to this day feel training should be as harsh as possible to build a strong warrior, others feel, in the words of one, that "hazing just isn't effective, except to create a bunch of trauma-bonded recruits." Practices thus vary by individual trainer, as well as by site. One former DI familiar with both Parris Island and San Diego Marine Corps training depots told me that in his opinion, Parris Island, where I conducted some of my fieldwork, is a site of more excesses than San Diego because more of its training happens indoors, making it harder for superior officers to monitor. This simple example highlights how many aspects of military training are subject to variation and contingency.

Nevertheless, yelling, the focal point of this chapter, is a time-honored tradition in the early weeks of Marine Corps training and also a more complex teaching tool than one might assume. I analyze it as embodied language with fleshy qualities as important as the meaning of its words (though I do analyze some of those words in the next two chapters).[15] For one thing, yelling is a force that can cause shock, pain, dizziness, or nausea for some recruits. These forms of stress help grind down the neophyte to make them more susceptible to learning their new role.[16] In this respect, yelling plays a role in that first step Turner described, squashing the recruit's earlier sense of self so they can receive their new identity.

But the yelling doesn't merely brutalize to pave the way to learning, for the yelling itself is a meaningful *sacrum*. Yelling contains *lessons*, in other words. As I explain later in this chapter, its sheer volume destabilizes recruits' sense of their own agency, which contains a durable message about their role as soldiers who must obey others' orders. Yelling also embodies and exemplifies military masculinity—its aggression and its claim on power—in sonic form. DIs additionally seem to construe yelling as a kind of projectile that literally "hardens" recruits, making them more battle ready. At the same time, DIs use yelling to channel corporeal intensity that they hope will translate into kinetic violence down the line. And it demonstrates to recruits one means of forestalling their empathy for others' experiences, an important stance when they encounter enemies in combat. Finally, the actual physical toll of yelling, and the way DIs push through it, mirrors the way soldiers are to persevere through discomfort.

After unpacking the layers of yelling's pedagogic significance, I describe the verbal attenuation of the intimately relational self in boot camp, including the requirement that recruits avoid using the pronoun "I." Boot camp language hammers home the message that individual wishes, sentimental ties to kin outside the military, and personal experiences of weakness and tenderness do not serve the sacrificial military self. All of this linguistic scaffolding offers a provisional shape for military personhood.

Drill Instructors Who Yell

Roughly twenty thousand recruits come to Parris Island each year, and about six hundred Drill Instructors (usually in their twenties or thirties) train them, after passing through eleven weeks of Drill Instructor School. Many DIs volunteer for the job, to move up the career ladder. Occasionally, though, a DI may be assigned to the position by their superiors, pulling them away from a range of military occupational specialties, often as non-commissioned officers. There are class implications for the fact that DIs are gathered from within enlisted ranks, for non-commissioned officers (unlike commissioned officers, who serve as management) needn't have a college degree. The sensibilities of USMC DIs are thus inflected by working-class ideas of masculinity, which (conventionally, anyway) tend to focus on physical fortitude and eschewing signs of weakness.

Almost every dimension of Marine Corps training has, until very recently, been shaped by a masculine default. Only about 9–10% of recruits are female, and in 2019 the USMC became the last branch of the US military to commit to integrating recruit training, in principle.[17] However, reports from observers suggest its efforts in this direction, including mixed-gender exercises such as close order drill, have been halting, and the Corps continues to resist full gender inclusivity.[18] The very inclusion of women in the Marine Corps has bothered traditionalists who fear they may jeopardize and perhaps even taint the Corps' strength. As these chapters attest, military identity in the Marine Corps is based partly on vilifying the weakness associated with femininity, sometimes by symbolically feminizing recruits to spur them to prove their masculinity.

DIs, meanwhile, are expected to furnish the model of an ideal Marine for recruits. Their physical comportment must be as disciplined as a dancer, coiled with potential energy. Some are so strong their upper arms cock outwards slightly before their bent elbows bring their hands back to their sides, like an action figure. (I once saw an Army veteran imitate a Marine Corps DI walking with his arms stiffly held in this position, an exaggeration of inflexible manhood.) DIs push themselves without complaint through illness or injury and never let recruits see them in a state of need or vulnerability, including the simple act of eating. Some bring creative flair to their displays of robotic toughness. Staff Sergeant Thomas Phillips, who served more than seven cycles, described his gimmicks to a journalist. When it was his time to go home, he would "run and dropkick the back hatch [door]. I'd never open it with my hands." Then, he'd set an alarm for one or two in the morning to come into the barracks and yell at the recruits assigned to fire watch (night guard duty): "I was tired the next day, but it proved a point, it was worth it. They were like, 'This guy never sleeps.'"[19] Such physical intensity indirectly teaches recruits that they, too, must override bodily weakness and personal needs. They must subordinate their vulnerabilities to the mission established by the state.

There is, undeniably, a powerful element of performance to the DI persona. This was vividly described by Justin, a former DI now in his forties, now reflective about his own training as a Marine on Parris Island and his later turn as a DI at San Diego.

> Their personal power is intoxicating; it's like crack cocaine. Some of them *are* visually awesome, but they don't all fit the bill. Some are just, you know, *dudes*. But once they put the cover on [the DI's wide-brimmed hat, also known as a "campaign cover"], they feel superhuman, like they're *the most*.

Justin went on to explain that DIs have to protect their mystique. He described an incident in which a fed-up recruit did the unthinkable: he began to storm away from the training space, then wheeled around and punched his DI in the nose. Four other DIs pounced on the recruit and beat him up—but it was too late. The DI who took the punch lost some collective respect, says Justin, because the recruit had "broken the frame," rupturing the illusion that the DI is untouchable. In another instance, a recruit urinated off a balcony in the middle of the night and happened to hit the hat of a DI. The DI should have pretended it never happened, says Justin, because punishing the recruit drew attention to his own humiliation.

Recruits can know that a DI is performing their role, but this doesn't necessarily make them less daunting. As Miles Lagoze describes one of his DIs, "He likes raising [his arms] when he screams, as if he's summoning a demon out of hell. This deeply concerns me, mostly because I know it is a performance, and to perform that well you have to believe it somewhat."[20]

With their varying philosophies and temperaments, Justin adds, DIs may use their power "productively or abusively." DIs may not agree about where to draw the line, or why a line even needs to exist. When Justin was at Parris Island in the early 2000s, his DI would sometimes post him as a "hatch recruit" at the door to keep a watchful eye for "company grade" (commissioned) officers who might not approve of the DI's techniques. One battalion was rumored to develop their own hand signals to warn their DI which kind of officer might be approaching so the DI could modify his treatment of the recruits. The collusion here between recruits and harsh DI tactics is telling; DIs are trying their best to make hardened killers, and many recruits have been willing participants.

The Pedagogy of Yelling

Now, to those Drill Instructors' voices that do so much teaching—not only through what they utter but *how* they utter it. Even outdoors, at Parris Island, the soundscape of recruit training is striking. DIs are expected to project their voices authoritatively, using so-called command voice, which may involve so much rapid yelling that recruits say at times they can't hear themselves think. The yelling is most intense in the earlier weeks of a platoon's training. DIs yell in the squad bay to get recruits organized, they yell during close order drill while recruits move in formation, they yell during daily physical training routines, and they yell during "incentive training", when recruits are singled out for poor performance or entire platoons are punished for the error of one of their members. There's so much yelling that in the initial months of the COVID-19 crisis, there were questions about whether recruits could be properly trained, since it is a time-honored element of the rite of passage to have DIs invade recruits' personal space and yell within inches of their faces, droplets of spit flying.

Recruits, in turn, are expected to yell (or "scream," as we saw DIs ordering new recruits at the chapter's start) at the top of their lungs in response. Often, their first response is not vigorous enough, prompting the DI to demand that they repeat themselves still louder. During recruit training, volume becomes symbolically intertwined with military masculinity. In his portrayal of a DI in Stanley Kubrick's *Full Metal Jacket*, actor R. Lee Ermey drew on his experience as a DI at Parris Island in the 1960s when he improvised lines like "Sound off like ya got a pair!"

On the wooden porch in the back of the Parris Island Brig & Brew bar, beers in hand, several active-duty DIs in their camouflage utility uniforms regaled me with accounts of how they would harangue recruits. "Even if you have fever, chills, diarrhea—you'll keep going and the recruits will never know." They talk over each other, comparing notes on the rigors of the job. Grady, sitting next to me on an Adirondack chair, chortles with amusement as he describes the physical craziness he has endured and the disorientation he's inflicted on recruits. "I can't believe how much yelling is involved," I say. Grady replies, as if it's self-explanatory, "Well, we're creating the finest fighting force." What is the connection, though? How would being yelled at make a person a better fighter?

Aggressive yelling, or some degree of it, anyway, has long-standing precedent in combat training across the Global North. Those who trained for the British Army during World War I, for instance, describe being "shouted at" extensively.[21] But although yelling is a common military training practice, it is not inevitable. A member of the Canadian Forces recently described his training instructors' techniques on an online forum, saying they used motivational phases *without* screaming, such as "You fail because your mind has given up, not your body.... A real soldier is done when his body gives up, not his mind."[22] Upon watching some documentary footage from Parris Island, one Norwegian service member asked in online comments, "Wtf is all the screaming from the officers about? We got yelled at, but nothing like this. Our discipline came from exercise [till] you drop, no sleep, no food and officers that was telling you in a normal way all the thing you did wrong all the time."[23] A recent ethnographic description of basic training in Denmark reports an abundance of laughter, rather than yelling, within and between ranks; humor and jokes are considered vital to creating what the company commander called "a good mood and attitude."[24] An ethnographic study of a military training camp in Finland also makes no mention of yelling; training there seems to focus on enacting physical routines while using low temperatures and inadequate sleep as stressors and techniques of discipline.[25] And one veteran of the Israeli Defense Force claims on Quora that his commanders in boot camp didn't scream in your face as they do in the United States Marines, "because yelling is stupid and accomplishes nothing. Instead, [they would] calmly but firmly tell the errant soldier that what they did is completely unacceptable."[26] Other branches of the US military wrestle more than the Marine Corps with the question of how much yelling is too much, and in recent years Army commanders have made intermittent efforts to keep yelling in check.[27] The very fact that military forces elsewhere achieve their training goals without such extensive yelling suggests there must be some symbolic politics behind the tenacity of yelling in the Marine Corps.

Every social group has its explicit or implicit "ideologies of voice"—that is, cultural ideas about how people ought to use their voices, how this vocal style relates to a sense of self and control, and what personal qualities the style supposedly points to.[28] Listening to Marines justify all the yelling, I noted that many of their explanations were purely practical. DIs need to project their voices to be heard by dozens of recruits on the parade ground or during drills; this, anyway, was the first explanation offered to me by a Parris Island Public Affairs official. The yelling also helps recruits get used to performing under disorienting and stressful conditions, as they must during battle. Marines have pragmatic explanations for *recruit* yelling, too. One theory, related to me several times at Parris Island, is that yelling trains recruits to convey information over the din of combat. "When an individual is yelling in a squad," said the Public Affairs official, "it's so when they do basic warrior training, they can hear each other over the gunfire."

But when I heard these simple explanations, I had more questions. If the point is to be heard by many recruits at once, wouldn't a megaphone do the job? If the point is to accustom recruits to battle sounds, or disorient and stress them with a fog-of-war effect, why not play recordings of explosions and bullets zipping overhead? And what explains all that one-on-one yelling by a DI in what was once a recruit's personal space?

52 Kill Talk

Part of the answer is that the raging authority figure producing the sound, and the hierarchical relationship set up between trainer and recruit, is as important as the sound's amplitude. Recruits report intense anxiety at the prospect of being punished for failing to carry out instructions they may barely understand and anxiety about the barrage of disparagement issuing from the DI's lips—for as I explore in the next chapter, recruits are perpetually reminded that in the eyes of at least some of their authority figures, they are effectively worthless. The yelling also floods the sensorium and drowns out the possibility of resistance while refilling the mind with orders. Some Marines say that while being yelled at in boot camp, they were too agitated to think their own thoughts, let alone come up with a verbal rejoinder. In the face of this chaos and discomfort, personal agency feels attenuated, and it can feel like the only way forward is to follow commands instantly. One 2015 graduate of Parris Island tells me yelling taught him to "follow orders correctly while still being uncomfortable, because that's what most combat is. Bullets flying, whatever. Cramping, whatever. Deal with it, and just do what you're told."

Yelling also contains a lesson about ruthless masculinity, its claim on power, and the pressure to emulate it. In Marine Corps training, yelling is a form of "sonic patriarchy," which the feminist scholar Rebecca Lentjes defines as "the domination of a sound world in gendered ways, as well as . . . the control of gendered bodies via sound."[29] The ideal yell "sounds like ya got a pair," after all—the potential to dominate through ruthless strength and courage, with the proverbial "pair" (balls or testicles) being a metonym for military masculinity. Loud sound also has an omnidirectional quality that territorializes space, a distant echo of the crushing soundscape of US military imperialism overseas.[30] The sound of a DI yelling is the sound of someone who does not care what their interlocutor thinks or has to say in response. As recruits are urged to yell in turn, they are expected to adopt the same mantle of sonic patriarchy. They cannot, of course, exercise power while subordinated in the presence of their DI, but they can rehearse its future promise.

We encounter such ideologies of voice and gender in the following exchange, taken from the documentary *Black Friday Dark Dawn*, filmed at the San Diego training depot in the early 2000s. A recruit (deemed "R," below) has been ordered to hold a piece of paper with information about his newly issued rifle between his fingers, arms stretched straight in front of him, for so long that it hurts. Where this transcript begins, a DI has already been berating him for dropping his arms, for speaking too quietly and with too high a voice, and for saying "Aye, sir" rather than the more formal and effortful "Aye-aye, sir" to signal uptake of the DI's statements. (The italicized, parenthesized profanity below has been bleeped out, but I could lip-read the words. I use repeated letters to show a prolonged vowel, exclamation points to show an especially emphatic tone, and capital letters for especially loud volume.)

DI: Aye-aye, sir. It's three (*fucking*) words! It's three frickin' words! Higher! Hiiigher! Kay what's your rifle and serial number?
R: I can't read it—
DI: [Screaming at the top of his lungs, within inches of Recruit A's ear]—IIIII! IIIII! THIS RECRUUUUUIT!
R: This recruit can't read it sir.
DI: This recruit sounds like he (*SUCKS COCK*)!
R: THIS RECRUIT CAN'T READ IT, SIR![31]

The DI continues to berate the recruit, here, for saying "Aye, sir" instead of "Aye-aye, sir," mocking him almost as if he can't understand simple numbers ("It's three frickin' words"). After reminding him to hold his arms (painfully) higher, he asks him to relate the rifle's serial number, knowing full well the recruit cannot read it while holding the paper at arm's length. Next, he lambastes the recruit for using the first-person pronoun, which recruits are not allowed to do during basic training (as explained later in this chapter), and reminds the recruit what he should call himself: "This recruit." When the DI adds, "This recruit sounds like he (*SUCKS COCK*)," the recruit apparently realizes the homophobic dig is a critique of his voice.[32] The recruit repeats himself louder, as if volume could create the desired display of masculinity.

The idealized form of masculinity Marines associate with yelling creates a dilemma for some female DIs and recruits. In her 2006 dissertation, sociolinguist Catherine Hicks Kennard examined vocal samples from Parris Island and found that while female DIs certainly yell at times, they tend to do so less than male DIs, and on average their yelling is not as loud. Hicks Kennard explains that in order to project the voice, one typically needs to adopt a higher pitch—and female DIs risk losing credibility if they are heard as "screeching."[33] Asked to articulate their ideology of "command voice," then, male DIs emphasize loudness and speed, whereas female DIs focus more on "directness" and confidence. Said one, "We don't feel that we have to... holler and scream at them to get them to produce the same product, you know, the same outcome, the same result."[34] As for learning how to yell themselves, some female recruits say it does not feel right to them—not at first, anyway. On a YouTube video, one young female Marine notes that some women in her platoon of recruits had difficulty yelling as loud as their DIs wanted them to; they seemed too embarrassed or self-conscious to do so.[35]

On the Parris Island parade grounds, I, too, noticed that the female voices didn't seem as loud as the male ones. But it would be a mistake to assume that female DIs are less fierce. I heard anecdotal reports of especially harsh training from some female DIs, possibly driven by a need to prove themselves. A recent study of gender integration at Parris Island (commissioned by the Marine Corps) supports this, revealing that while recruits tend to perceive male DIs as louder in their vocal delivery, more physically demanding, and more knowledgeable about combat skills, male and female recruits alike encountered female DIs they found "scary," "vicious," detail oriented, and intensely demanding.[36] Perhaps some of these female DIs are compensating for their lack of volume, as well as other gender-related traits held against them.

Volume is especially important because of another idea about language, or "language ideology," at Parris Island: DI yelling is intended to harden recruits. The brute materiality of a yell can be an acoustic onslaught as its sound waves resonate through the delicate tissues of the ear and the rest of the body.[37] Ultimately, recruits are expected to become more resilient in response to this, "learning to let stuff roll off them," in DI phrasing, as if they had developed a kind of shell or carapace. This theme recurred so often in my observations that I gave it a name: semiotic callousing. If "semiotics" describes how signs and symbols take effect, with their meanings becoming part of social world-making, then semiotic callousing is the dynamic in which harsh signs (in this case, yelling) supposedly inure people (in this case, future soldiers) to onslaughts of whatever kind. The acoustic blast of yelling may grind down a recruit, but the recruit is also expected to rise up more resistant to assaults. In the next chapter, I discuss another variation on the theme of semiotic callousing, in which the *content* of the words used during basic training is also supposed to harden recruits.

Yelling is expected to thicken the skin, but also to translate into kinetic action. After all, a yell involves raw physicality and strong feeling. It possesses a corporeal intensity that can flow between bodies (which is precisely how some scholars have defined "affect"[38]). The Marine Corps itself recognizes this flow; in popular Marine Corps parlance, the loud voice is supposed to "motivate" recruits, giving them a sense of urgency. Says one DI, "When they hear you coming, they wanna move, because they'll be able to accomplish more by the intensity you put behind it as a DI by yelling and screaming."[39] Recruits, in turn, channel the intensity back as they reply, "YES, SIR!" DIs approve of this expression of visceral voice, because it suggests its potential future conversion into combat force. Through a kind of contagion, then, the forcefully embodied language of the DI is thought to facilitate the future physical violence of the Marine.

I have posited that yelling serves as a practical tool and teaching device along several fronts. It instills anxiety that destabilizes the recruit, preparing them to alter their personhood; it drowns out individual thoughts, which may be replaced by orders; it enforces sonic patriarchy, a kind of domination of space; it ostensibly "hardens" Marines in the making, that they may be more resilient in battle; and it promises to translate into haste and kinetic action, potentially violence. Thinking about these through the metaphor of linguistic infrastructure, the yelling in basic training could be construed as building an invisible groove or track for kinetic violence while obstructing paths for empathy, personal sensitivity, and individual decision-making.

Beyond all of these, I see yet another indirect lesson for recruits in the sheer toll extreme yelling exacts on the body. DIs, recall, are an embodied template of the superhuman physical performance Marines are supposed to deliver. I was struck by how much they talk about the physical challenges of yelling on and off for ten, fifteen, even eighteen hours in a day. DIs develop laryngitis, give themselves hernias, or, in the most extreme case I heard of, pass out from so much yelling. One told me he had blood come up from his vocal cords; another said he yelled so much he "crapped his pants." A DI tells a journalist, "You know, you sleep at night and give your voice time to recover, but that first scream [in the morning] is just so painful. I can't even describe it. It's horrible."[40] Yet DIs will yell through obstacles ranging from pain to sleep itself:

> I'd have a bit to eat at home, but your throat hurts so bad you don't want to eat. I've definitely fallen asleep at the table talking to my wife. I've woken up at night, yelling at my wife like she's a recruit. Screaming at my wife. Jumping out of the bed, yelling at her, IT-ing [incentive training] in my closet and not even knowing it. I woke up in the morning and my wife asks, "Who is Recruit Paige? Because you were yelling at him last night."[41]

DIs learn techniques to prevent vocal cord problems from becoming permanent. Rather like opera singers, they drink tea, hot water with honey and lemon, dilutions of lime juice or salt water, and other funky concoctions. They learn to project from their diaphragms, though this can create its own side effects; Grady told me he had "a half-outie bellybutton from using my diaphragm muscles to yell."

When DIs' vocal cords are damaged, the resulting sound may have its own pedagogical effects. Several DIs told me that as training progresses, they tend to yell through their hoarseness until their voice "cracks," "breaks," or "blows out," after which it may begin to sound different. As part of this, some develop what they call "frog voice": a raspy, gravely vocal fry that emerges through loose vocal cords in quick pops or pulses.[42] Some DIs use such heavy frog voice, you almost can't hear a pitch; the sound is too gravelly. The effect is aggressive, intimidating, and slightly inhuman. Says one Marine, "They don't even sound like normal people when they scream at you. It's more like a distorted croak."[43] Another describes frog voice as "rough and broken, or more accurately, like you would expect a dead man to talk."[44] DIs' voices thus model and point to the breakdown of the body in service of the state, at the very same time that they perform the superhuman transcendence of this breakdown, by continuing to yell.

I can't help but notice all the symbolic work that these yelling voices do. DI's yelling voices don't just intimidate. They represent a sonic microcosm of the social and emotional stances the ideal future Marine is supposed to embody in combat: masculine, aggressive, dominating, self-sacrificing, and—in some cases—hovering mystically in the grey space between human and inhuman, alive and dead.[45] And notice the necropolitics at play, here. These yelling voices instruct on assaulting others *and* sacrificing one's own body. They are the voices of those who may kill and be expected to die.

For some Marines, all of the above may be unpleasant, but it anneals them in a way that they look back on with gratitude. In his 2012 memoir of training, for instance, Marine Corps veteran Patrick Turley admits he may suffer from Stockholm syndrome but remains adamant that the Marine Corps saved him from a wayward life.[46] Louis, the young veteran, told me of his gratitude for the way yelling and being yelled at brought him "out of his comfort zone" and "built his confidence." And plenty of proud Marines look back on the travails of boot camp with amusement; they suffered, the idea seems to be, but now they know how to frame it: it was a rite of passage for their own good, required to toughen them up and bring them into the band of brothers they will forever be loyal to.

Yet other veterans I worked with look back upon their training with dismay. Yelling underscores the lengths to which DIs would go, and their performance of immunity from vulnerability and empathy. Occasionally service members and veterans have even adduced yelling as an explanation for their own malfeasance. While the example may be extreme, consider the infamous My Lai massacre of 1968, in which American GIs mutilated, raped, and murdered hundreds of unarmed Vietnamese civilians on the orders of several officers, including Army Lieutenant William Calley Jr. One participant in the killings, Paul Meadlo, said a decade later, "You have to understand. I was scared of what could happen to me at My Lai and I was scared of what would happen if I didn't obey Calley. That's what they shout at you from the minute you go into the Army."[47]

While there is surely no neat causal line to be drawn between yelling and war crimes, and while in principle service members are encouraged to do some ethical thinking for themselves in the theater of war, Meadlo connects the fear instilled when being yelled at during basic training with the fear of contravening even unethical orders from a military authority. Yelling has a way of foreclosing thought, agency, and rejoinder; it is supposed to translate into aggressive and hardened soldiering, and ultimately, it is a demand to follow deadly orders, laying bodies on the altar of the state.[48]

Erasing the "I" and Curtailing Affiliative Talk

By attenuating thought and agency, yelling can alter recruits' sense of self. Drill Instructors also tinker with recruits' selves by announcing shortly after their arrival that "the words 'I,' 'me,' 'my' are no longer part of your vocabulary." Veteran Will Price describes the ensuing dynamic in his 2008 memoir, recalling a moment when a recruit momentarily lapses and uses the first-person pronoun. His DI rages, "I? I? 'I' is NO LONGER! RECRUIT, GET DOWN AND START PUSHING! . . . DO YOU THINK YOU'RE SPECIAL OR SOMETHING?"[49]

DIs agree this lexical system is designed to foreclose egocentrism and stop recruits from thinking of themselves as individuals. As Sergeant Jennifer Duke explained to *PBS Newshour* in 2016, "We need to break down these individualities they come with, of self and 'me' and 'I.' We need to break them down to basically nothing so we can build them back up . . . as one team, one element, to join our Marine Corps. It's not my Marine Corps, it's not his Marine Corps, it's *our* Marine Corps."[50] Although this tradition has been followed for decades, current DIs tell me it's particularly important in decentering what they see as this young generation's narcissism.

The French linguist Emile Benveniste has argued that using the first-person singular pronoun allows a speaker to "proclaim himself the 'subject.'"[51] When the Marine Corps removes the "I," it forces a workaround. The recruit must use the ungainly formulation of "this recruit" or (for instance) "Recruit Price," referring to themselves as if they are figures in a drama of someone else's making. Put in other terms, the recruit must summon themselves as if they are a cog in the military machine.[52] The inability to say "I" or "me" may also remind the recruit they are liminal nonpersons of a sort—neophytes whose identity now belongs to the hierarchy of the Marine Corps—"recruit" being a lowly title indeed. The first-person pronoun will be returned to them after training, but the hope is that the self will have been realigned, subordinating personal wishes, feelings, and opinions to the unit and the mission.

The Marine Corps also prohibits recruits from using the second-person pronoun "you" when addressing their superiors, lest they sound presumptuous or overly familiar. Recruits must include the honorific "sir" or "ma'am" in all statements to their DI. (Since 2022, Corps leadership has explored mandating gender-neutral salutations, emphasizing rank or position—for instance, "Gunnery Sergeant Smith"—but as of this writing, such changes have not been widely adopted, and the re-inauguration of Donald Trump makes them less likely.) The simplest query or statement must be formally initiated, as in, "Sir, Recruit Russell requests permission to speak to Drill Instructor Sergeant Hendricks." A request to make a trip to the bathroom might be phrased, "Sir, Recruit Russell requests permission to make a head call, sir." Louis tells me his attempts to initiate talk with his military superiors on Parris Island were met harshly. "My DI would be like, 'WHAT?' Not 'Yes, recruit?' It's usually very brutal." He goes on:

> Most of the time they'd kinda cut us off because they knew what the question was. Sometimes you'd start the phrase, "Sir, good morning sir," and they'd be like [in an angry, abrupt tone] "WHAT?" Or, "Is it about gear or is it about drill?" and if it's not either of those they'd be like, "I don't care."

Recruits are not to look directly in their DI's eyes (that's called "eyeballing"), nor smile, for this would not count as proper military bearing.[53] Eyeballing may be met with punishment, including more yelling, as in (from a DI in a particularly bad mood), "Look at me again and I'll set you on fire and put you out with a fork."[54] Gone are the ordinary bodily supplements to conversation like gazing and meeting gaze, moments of human connection that facilitate comprehension and signal "uptake" ("I get you," in other words). One effect of this curtailment is repeated failures of communication. Some of these failures are intentional power plays by DIs. Hicks Kennard found "it is not uncommon for a male DI to go out into the squad bay and 'bark an unintelligible bunch of orders' only to go back into the duty hut and peek through the blinds as the confusion between the recruits unfolds."[55] Meanwhile, the DI's impassive face offers a microcosm of the military's indifference to suffering.[56]

The interactive routines in boot camp thus alter or shut down the affiliative dimensions of communication that anthropologist Bronislaw Malinowski called "phatic communion."[57] The "phatic" aspect of talk doesn't convey important ideas or information; instead, it typically establishes sociability, with "small talk" being a classic example. Malinowski's discussions of phaticity focused mostly on friendly means of establishing contact and opening the channel of communication. But other scholars have expanded the concept of the phatic to include negative ways of skewing the mood between interlocutors. The anthropologist Charles Zuckerman, for instance, explores what he calls "phatic violence" in the way gamblers sometimes "trash talk" their opponents to distract them, "exploit[ing] what we might call the grappling hooks of communication—loud noises, directed gaze, sensorially engaging movements, [and] questions . . . to ensure involvement."[58] To save face, the other players need to keep their cool and resist the temptation to respond.

DIs' stances prickle with phatic negativity as they dominate and denigrate recruits. When they aren't delivering an order that must be instantly assented to and obeyed, they may be issuing a taunt. But if a DI yells "Do you PUKES have what it takes to become Marines?," recruits must not meet their gaze or betray indignation. They must yell back, "YES, SIR!" When a DI rushes up to a recruit and yells three inches from their ear, "YOU FRICKIN' WEAKLING, YOU CAN'T EVEN HOLD UP A PIECE OF ROPE WITHOUT DROPPING IT?," a recruit may be tempted to recoil or lash out in response, but they must not take the bait. They must rapidly calculate whether they can safely answer in the affirmative or negative. Sometimes they cannot do either, since affirming some questions—for example, "Are you as dumb as I think?"—would admit weakness, while negating might seem too contradictory. In some cases, the safest response is to remain quiet. Occasionally, when recruits are unsure of the appropriate response, a DI will feed it to them, like this: "You are a moron. Aye-aye, sir." "AYE-AYE, SIR," replies the recruit.[59]

The DI's phatic grappling hooks sink in deeply but cannot be removed or responded to. This communicative structure suggests that the recruit's personal comfort is worthless. Such dehumanization is framed, like all of basic training, as if it betters the recruits and ultimately serves the nation, for the recruit is to emerge from the ordeal stronger and more self-sacrificing. And—crucially—if the DI's interactions with the recruit offer a general blueprint for the Marine's future engagement with the enemy, then the DI's tactical refusal to establish an empathic intersubjective relationship with recruits[60] offers a scaffold for the Marine's subsequent apathy toward the inner life of the enemy.

Cutting Kin Ties

Basic training in the Marine Corps repeatedly implies that the service member's connections to kin are less important than their new allegiance to the military is. The restriction of earlier emotional attachments is emphasized by recruits' phatically impoverished phone call home shortly after their arrival at the training depot. In the words of one Drill Instructor, this single call is to be placed strictly to "next of kin; that's your mother, father, sister, brother." A row of landline phones awaits, each inside a little white console with a hinged door. A piece of paper with a short script is taped inside each console door (see Figure 2.1). After some simple instructions for dialing, the sheet orders,

Figure 2.1 Script taped to inner door of phone box, Parris Island Marine Corps Training Depot.

"YOU WILL SAY THE FOLLOWING." Recruits are granted about ten seconds to recite the script.

The five-line text—in all capital letters, as if to imply high volume—is clinical and cold. The first words out of the recruit's mouth omit any sign of emotional warmth, instead announcing who they are using military terms of address: "THIS IS RECRUIT (LAST NAME)." Next they offer kin some bare logistic information—they "HAVE ARRIVED SAFELY AT PARRIS ISLAND"—but they abruptly reject any provisions ("FOOD AND BULKY ITEMS") relatives might wish to send them. With precise and impersonal detail, they tell their kin when to expect their next communication ("I WILL CONTACT YOU IN 7 TO 9 DAYS BY LETTER WITH MY NEW ADDRESS"). The last lines of the script avoid terms of endearment, instead reminding relatives of their new role as civilian supporters of a Marine-in-the-making: "THANK YOU FOR YOUR SUPPORT. GOOD BYE FOR NOW."

In documentary footage from 2016 that captures this event, male and female recruits stand in neat lines before the phone bank while male and female DIs yell at those on the phone.[61] The recruits, in turn, yell their lines to be heard above the din. They sound rather like their DIs, in fact, rushing and slurring, without the voice modulation or pauses between sentences that would facilitate comprehension. Some of their voices have a telltale edge of anxiety. "LOUDER," yell the DIs, standing just a couple of feet away. Some DIs instruct recruits not to add anything off script, cautioning, "Don't say 'I love you.'" To kin on the other end of the line, it must sound like the Corps has eaten them alive.

This fleeting phone call home is perhaps the only moment when families have direct sensory contact with the experience of boot camp. I was intrigued to find in 2019 that a website run by and for parents of Marine Corps recruits, recruitparents.com, tried to offer parents some reassurance as they anticipate this call. The site read,

> [There has] recently been a change to the first phone call for recruits. They still have a short, scripted message to say, but at the end parents are given a chance to ask a quick question. Also, the Drill Instructors are not screaming at them while they make their phone call.... Now the recruits can tell their family they love them and give the parents some comfort.[62]

As I read on, however, I saw the "disclaimer." This "change," the website authors added, is "not a written policy but more of an unwritten rule that is left to the discretion of DIs. Some will allow recruits to make their phone call quietly without stressing them out. Others will keep the old school approach and continue to yell in the background." And in fact, in 2022 the official YouTube site of the Parris Island Training Depot posted a video (titled "The First Four Hours") featuring DIs swarming around and yelling at recruits trying to make that phone call. One recruit presses his left hand to his left ear and hunches a shoulder anxiously as he strains to hear the faint voice of his family member.[63] Checking the recruitparents.com website once again in 2023, I found that the passage about a "change to the first phone call" had been deleted.

We have a glimpse, then, of uncertainty when it comes to how abrasive and domineering DIs are expected to be. Should the Marine Corps honor the emotional sensitivities of its recruits? Can it allow any tenderness to be preserved? Or does doing so pose some kind of risk to successful training and, in turn, to national security itself?

Disagreement about such matters roils between and within generations, as well as across differing political ideologies, in the Marine Corps, just as it does in the Army and other branches of the US military. Leaders of various military branches and bases intermittently discourage harsh training and are intermittently met with pushback. Indeed, many military players seem to have an implicit theory about the necropolitics involved: aggressive rites of passage help reconfigure recruits' subjectivity into the role of one who may successfully kill and potentially die for the state. I resume discussion of disputes about how harsh basic training should be in Chapter 5. For now, let us look more deeply at the content of some DIs' yelling, particularly the insults that offer a covert framework for the future combatant's stance toward "the enemy."

Chapter 3
Insults and Kill Chants

Just about everyone at Parris Island has watched Stanley Kubrick's 1987 film *Full Metal Jacket*, with its ear-splitting opening scene featuring a former Vietnam War–era Drill Instructor (DI), playing to type.* R. Lee Ermey was good at recreating his earlier self and didn't need much of a script.[1] If anyone wonders how he came up with his colorful lacerations, they need only understand the Marine Corps as a speech community that passes its verbal art down through the generations. When I attended a luncheon during the 2019 East Coast Drill Instructor's reunion at Parris Island, I was electrified to hear a veteran in his eighties who had served *before* Ermey reenact his own verbal routines.

Wearing a uniform adorned with a black "BUILD THE WALL" pin, the former DI cut a diminutive figure, but his back was ramrod straight as he clenched his fists by his sides. "Are you COMING, BOOT?" He yelled to an imaginary interlocutor. The tendons in his neck strained. "You either DO as I say or I UNSCREW your head, PUKE in your chest cavity, and get you started!"

A through line of verbal brutality in boot camp preceded Ermey and was subsequently boosted by Kubrick's film. Several Marine Corps and Army veterans of the Global War on Terrorism told me their DIs and Drill Sergeants liked to repeat Ermey's lines almost verbatim, suggesting a strange feedback loop between Hollywood's representations of military training and the experience itself. Recruits and DIs alike take some of their cues about authentic training from cinema—probably one of many reasons why some are invested in keeping training harsh.

For an example of such treatment in Marine Corps training from the first decade of the 2000s, consider the incident veteran Patrick Turley describes from his experience at the San Diego Depot.[2] When an overweight recruit balked at a command, the DIs began to snark at him. "Oh, so we want to flinch, huh? . . . We're on our own freaking program, aren't we?" Panicking,

---

* This chapter analyzes words and imagery that may be difficult for some readers to encounter. Please see the "Content Warning and Note on Language" in the front matter for some context and a discussion of the author's reasons for not redacting this material.

Kill Talk. Janet McIntosh, Oxford University Press. © Oxford University Press (2025).
DOI: 10.1093/9780197808054.003.0004

the recruit yelled "No!," forgetting to add the required honorific, "sir." Turley describes the exchange that followed.

> DI Staff Sergeant McFadden's eyes lit up. "'No,' huh? 'No'?! We're drinking buddies now, aren't we, Bequet?"
> "No, sir!"
> "Then what? Are you fucking my sister?"
> "No sir!"
> "You're friggin' nasty, Bequet. Why didn't your mother stop feeding your fat, ugly ass?"
> "This recruit's mother is dead, sir!"
> DI Staff Sergeant McFadden paused and gave him a nod. He turned to leave but then looked back at Bequet. "So that's why she barely moved when I fucked her."

Official Marine Corps and Army documents prohibit trainers from inflicting "verbal abuse,"[3] yet training can involve linguistic interactions many civilians would consider inhumane, from the relentless yelling I describe in the preceding chapter to intense verbal mockery. Drawing on examples from the last few decades, I explore some of the content of what DIs yell. Much of this chapter focuses on insults that position recruits as inferior, feminized, infantilized, and sometimes subhuman—in short, as suitable targets of disgust and aggression. Although the high command of the Marine Corps has tried to curb these extremes and some DIs have accommodated wider cultural changes by avoiding the most inflammatory language, denigrating recruits has been a widespread practice over the decades.

Victor Turner noted that rites of passage often involve a "liminal" period when initiates are treated as lowly because they are in-between social roles. But I interpret military training insults as teaching tools specifically in service of war, even if their pedagogic significance is not always evident to recruits. Like the sheer volume of yelling, for instance, insults are supposed to grind recruits down and ultimately harden them up for combat, another example of what I term "semiotic callousing." Paradoxically, while recruits are meant to become inured to insults, they are also expected to heed the insults' content and learn from it. Name-calling imparts a lesson about cutting kin ties as the recruit realigns their priorities with the military. Sexist and homophobic insults instruct recruits on compulsory military masculinity. They also impart necropolitical lessons by framing recruits as worthless and abject, for despite national rhetoric that exalts soldiers, members of the infantry are expendable, not cherished, in war. When slurs and epithets are directed at recruits, these also serve as a prequel to combat by modeling the dehumanizing language members of the infantry may ultimately use against the enemy.[4] As I will show, this aggressive stance is further encouraged by routine and multifunctional uses of the word "kill" in basic training.

Name Calling

Social theorists have long recognized that the way people are addressed has a way of influencing what they become. The constitutive relationship between words and personhood typically begins in the family. Anthropologist Jack Sidnell, for instance, writes that across many societies, bestowing a name is "associated with the social recognition of some entity's personhood," while linguist Susan Bean contends that in many societies, the names given by family members are considered part of a person's "soul."[5] Over the life course, though, a person may be summoned using quite different terms, sometimes reductive ones, receiving new messages about who they supposedly are. The Marxist theorist Louis Althusser called this creative process "interpellation." When a student hails their instructor as "professor," when a restaurant customer shouts "Waiter!," when an aristocrat calls her adult male servant "boy," the addressees are positioned within some social order and partially constituted by—interpellated by—the roles that have been verbally projected onto them.

In the preceding chapter, I described how Marine Corps recruits are instructed to avoid using the first-person pronoun "I," replacing it with "this recruit." In Althusser's terms, we could say that they must "self-interpellate" as cogs in the military machine. Drill Instructors, too, lodge recruits in the military institution through terms of address. DIs never use recruits' personal names; instead, official regulations permit them to call recruits "Recruit [last name]" or to address them by their billet or job, such as "Scribe" or "Guide."[6] This practice carries a whiff of military necropolitics, whereby each individual serves a role in the military machine and is easily replaced if they become ineffective or killed.

Beyond that, many Marine Corps DIs and Army Drill Sergeants over the last few decades have interpellated recruits in demeaning ways. Some tinker with recruits' given names, implying that their military role requires suspension of their preexisting personal identity, especially as it connects to kin. An Army veteran, for instance, told me his Drill Sergeant changed his name from "Wright" to "Private Wrong." A recent memoir of Marine Corps training describes a DI addressing a recruit with the last name of "Riddle" using the taunt, "Well, well. Riddle me this, Riddle me that."[7] A Marine Corps veteran with a last name beginning with the sound "La-" shared that on the first day of training in 2006, his DI called him "LaFaggot." Some DIs thus treat the names that tether recruits to their families like beach balls to be played with and perhaps tossed out to sea.

Steve, who served in the Army around 2002, tells me his Drill Sergeants liked to pick on the quirks of recruits' bodies or personalities, targeting features that failed to conform to an ideal military type. Steve himself is rangy and angular, and he took flak right away.

> Basically they find anything that's personal about the person, so, you know, if they have a big nose, they say something like that. If they're a little chubby, they will pick on that, you know. They take your insecurities and they totally, you know, they really rip on your insecurities. [If you] see them years later, you know, it's not like they would feel the need to apologize—"Hey, I'm sorry I called you fat when you were a private." You know, like, it's just, everyone knows that they get a free pass just to sort of totally demean you. [My Drill Sergeant] singled me out for being tall and skinny, "like a joint," he said. "You're tall and skinny like a joint. Okay, Joint, I'm going to smoke you." [In military slang, "smoke" means to make a recruit do a bunch of pushups or the like.] After a few weeks, they had nicknames for the people that were always, like, a step behind everyone.

Other nicknames I heard include "Dwarf" (a short recruit), "Butts" (a recruit with prominent buttocks), "Creampuff" (a heavyset, pale recruit), "Wingnut" (a recruit who showed poor judgment), and "Professor" (a recruit who tried to show off knowledge beyond his station). Beyond such tailor-made terms, general taunts directed at individuals or groups of recruits are common (e.g., "Faster, hogs," or "What are you, little girls?").[8] Between conversations with veterans and published accounts, I collected a vocabulary of lacerating put-downs, many in circulation since before the Vietnam War era.[9] These include "crybabies," "snowflakes," "whiners," "weaklings," "wusses," "lazy bastards," "maggots," "hogs," "crayon eaters," "clowns," "retards," "boneheads," "idiots," "turds," "shitbags," "shitbirds," "scumbags," "bag nasties" (military slang for an unappealing lunch), "bags of asses," and a raft of gender-troubled insults, including "ladies," "little girls," "faggots," "pussies," "pansies," "buttercups," "cupcakes," and "sweethearts."

Such terms dance somewhere between playful, absurd metaphor and ostentatious disregard for the humanity and comfort of the recruits. Feminization, infantilization, animalization, objectification, and pollution imagery are common.[10] Sometimes, the insults have specific pedagogic value, particularly in the case of gender-related lacerations that urge recruits to avoid behavior marked as feminine. Meanwhile, epithets like "crybabies," "boneheads," or "lazy bastards" hyperbolically stress a particular attribute and reduce the recruits to that quality or flaw. Name-calling can thus erase the recognition of the person as a whole and worthwhile individual.[11] Notably, some DIs will escalate their insults precisely when recruits show signs of suffering or vulnerability.

Military Masculinity and Feminine Others

Talking to veterans of Vietnam and the Global War on Terrorism (GWOT), I learned that although racial put-downs have become increasingly taboo in military training, gender-based insults remain common. Homophobic and gynophobic language have been tenacious despite many changes and efforts toward gender integration. The Department of Defense is hardly indifferent to this, particularly since female recruits have been increasingly important to making numbers across the branches, and a hostile climate can drive them away. The high command has thus pushed for gender integration and undertaken extensive studies and policy changes in order to curb sexual assault.[12] Nevertheless, many in the Marine Corps have resisted fully gender-integrated training, and the continuing high rates of sexual assault on female service members could be seen as an effort to deter women while enforcing masculine dominance.[13]

If some military players have held tight to a default masculinity, many in the wider society also continue to imagine military strength in hypermasculine terms.[14] Whether one's military ideal is a killer kicking down doors or a strong protector figure, both images are historically entwined with ideas of masculinity. In fact, as Air Force veteran Nick Mararac observes, the image of a strong man facing down danger dominates military ideals even though most service members never see combat, in part because violence has been increasingly delegated to unmanned aerial vehicles such as drones, while national security increasingly relies on technical expertise to combat cyber threats.[15]

Masculinity in the Marine Corps has historically been enforced by framing women as the sexualized and polluting Other. Veterans of the GWOT tell me that until recently, male Marine Corps recruits were supposed to avert their gazes or turn their backs if they came across a female platoon. When someone in Patrick Turley's platoon made the mistake of peeking, a Drill Instructor thumped him in the chest, yelling, "What the fuck were you looking at? ... Were you staring at one of those nasty fucking cunts over there?"[16] One Marine Corps veteran I spoke with, Matthew, said it took him years to get over the "loathing for women" inculcated into him by his training before going to Afghanistan. Women were talked about as "even lower than civilians, just like really unworthy, cheating on men all the time, like homewreckers, or like the source of STDs anywhere in the world; they were going to get you infected."[17]

An extensive 2022 study commissioned by the Corps investigated the dynamics of gender integration and found that in spite of many trainings designed to curtail sexism and sexual misconduct, a hostile version of masculinity continues to be verbally imposed by some Marines.[18] Some male DIs still use gynophobic language, and female Marines share stories about being pigeonholed as "sluts," "dykes," or "bitches"—the last of these being preferable because at least it is authoritative. Male DIs sometimes transmit sexually denigrating expressions in the form of "ditties"—catchy slogans that offer quick verbal shorthand for skilled movements, such as "up the skirt" to reach upward while adjusting the position of one's rifle or "split the clit" or "smack that whore" for other technical sequences. A male Marine who recently graduated reported, "They say that the M-16 is your bitch, and to slap it as hard as you like."[19] Male recruits repeatedly told the researchers they found sexist humor enjoyable, motivating, and a bonding mechanism for male platoons—strengthening the tight in-group important to military masculinity.[20]

Meanwhile, Marine Corps insults link femininity to childish weakness, so when recruits are interpellated as feminine, they are reminded of what they do not want to be. Will Price's 2012 memoir from Parris Island describes how platoons were instructed to put down other male platoons as "bitches," while DIs taunted male recruits: "Hey recruit Price, you just want to hold your weapon with your pinky, like a little girl!"[21] Turley describes one platoon sounding off loudly enough to shake the windows, but their DI still refused to concede to them, saying, "Hooooooooooooly shit. . . . I didn't think it was possible! You all sound even weaker than before. Buncha schoolgirls."[22]

I wondered whether female recruits in the Marine Corps ever internalize the gynophobia seething around them. I had a revealing conversation on the matter with Ryan. Twenty years after her time at Parris Island, Ryan wears rugged boots, hair shorn close to her scalp except for a teal and purple sprout that falls to the left, and a ribbed white undershirt that reveals the sinewy muscles developed from her construction job. She emerged from a ruthless childhood and joined the Marines so "no one could touch her again," going on to become a close combat instructor in the fleet. When deployed to Iraq in 2003, she—like other female Marines, and despite gender regulations in the US military at the time—found herself embroiled in deadly firefights in which she killed without hesitation. Ryan tells me that in her unit, female recruits were demeaned with the same antifeminine slurs conventionally used against men. Military masculinity, after all, is about symbolic prestige rather than merely what gender a body is assigned, and as such, it is not just for guys.[23] And if military violence is about ruthlessly penetrating bodies, there is symbolic logic to heaping scorn on those who tend to be penetrated during sex.

We got into the subject by talking about homophobic language. "Like talking about queers," Ryan was saying. "That's such a huge thing. 'Only queers will do that.' Yeah, stuff like that is really common." I told her I'd heard the classic phrase "Only steers and queers are from Texas" from other Marines.

"Yeah," she said. "'Steers and queers, and which are you?' Yeah, they say that a lot."

"You mentioned they called the guys 'pussies' and 'lady pansies,' and did they call you—"

"'Pansies, Sallies,'" Ryan cut in.

"So the girls were called Sallies, too?"

"Yeah. . . .That's how they insult a girl. So, Sally, I called people, I still call people Sally." Ryan squirmed in her chair to look at her partner, Thea, sitting next to her. Her tone grew amused. "And I still say 'Man up.' I tell myself to man up."

"Yeah, you do, a lot," agreed Thea.

"All the time." Ryan started gesticulating with her cigarette. Her voice rose. "'Fucking man up, bitch! What's wrong with you?'"

"Especially when you're sick," said Thea, and they both started to laugh. Ryan has a serious illness—possibly caused by burn pit exposure—that sees her intermittently bedridden.

"'Man up!' I'll be, like, dying. I'm like, 'FUCK this shit. Get UP, pussy, get up!'"

Ryan's account reveals an unsurprising conflation of gender with sexuality, in which misogynistic taunts are interwoven with homophobic ones. Under the Clinton-era "Don't ask, don't tell" (DADT) policy, which was repealed in 2011–2012, gay service members were not allowed to serve openly on the grounds that their presence would compromise "morale, good order and discipline, and unit cohesion."[24] Homophobia was thus licensed to proceed. Patrick Turley, who enlisted shortly after 9/11, describes how one DI liked to convert recruits' hometowns and states into homophobic place names. Buffalo became "Butt-Fuck O," Oklahoma "Okla-homo," and so forth. Another DI would play sadistically with the rules of DADT: "You know, Guide, they say uncontrollable smiling is a sign of homosexuality. Are you . . . Wait, never mind. I can't ask, so I guess we'll never know." Since recruits were cued to frame homosexuality as both Other and ridiculous, it sometimes became a foil to bond over. When the recruits in Turley's platoon changed into their PT (exercise) clothes on one of their last days, a DI remarked, "Now remember, no matter how cool you, your family, your girlfriend, or whoever thinks you are for going through Marine Corps boot camp, you're still about to look like a fag in those shorts." Turley recounts with apparent nostalgia that it was "the first time we all laughed together."[25]

When I asked Louis about homophobia during his Parris Island training in 2010, he told me in a matter-of-fact voice what his DI asked in the squad bay.

> "Isn't everybody in here gay?" He asked, "Any of you have a big boyfriend at home with a big ball sack?" He also brought that to a point, like, "If one of you is gay, don't try anything with other recruits."

Another of Louis's DIs would confront groups of recruits and ask, "Which one of you nasty hogs likes to suck cock?" Questions about sexuality were against regulation, but these were rhetorical taunts, debasing them all while reminding them that homosexuality would represent a failure of the ubermasculinity Marines are supposed to represent.

Since the repeal of DADT, reports of homophobic language in Marine Corps training have continued to circulate. One anonymous but verified letter from a Parris Island recruit in 2013 reads,

> Don't Ask Don't Tell. Shit may have been repealed, but the USMC sure hasn't adapted. We're called faggots 10–50 times a day. "You think that's yelling? That's sweet, faggot." "Yeah, you would think that's a pushup, faggot." etc. Any time we fuck something up, the DIs tell us "you stupid fucking thing. That's more wrong than two boys fucking." One captain, when giving an ethics class, and talking about how one mistake can change your life/identity told the entire company "you can be a bridge builder your entire life, but you suck one dick and you're a cocksucker till you die."[26]

An Army veteran, Sam, trained at Fort Drum in 2013 and tells me he had a Drill Sergeant who loved to ask recruits, "Are you gay? Are you gay? Have you ever fucked a guy? No? Then how do you know you won't like it?" I ask Sam whether the Drill Sergeants were playing on the idea that after the repeal of DADT they were allowed to "ask." "Oh yeah," says Sam. "That was a big thing. They were like, 'We can ask now, are you gay? We can ask.' But of course, who's gonna say yes to that?" A Marine told me of similar dynamics in his training unit in the same year, saying, "The undertone is still homophobia.

The undertone is like everybody will say, like, 'No, of course not,' but then for the one who's asking, it's kind of like, 'I get to ask these tongue-in-cheek questions now.'" Old homophobic habits die hard, and the traditional imagery of masculine hardness relies on penetrating weak feminine bodies.

These days, there are certainly some openly gay male Marines and DIs, but their acceptance depends on whether they broadcast appropriate masculine hardness. Grady, a DI at Parris Island, mentions over beers he knows two DIs on the island who are gay, but, he adds pointedly, "they're still totally alpha males." Sometimes, acceptance hinges on being able to joke about one's identity. The 2022 report on gender integration in the Corps offers the following account from a veteran:

> Our Drill Instructor, when he told us keep it "tight like pussy; that's how we like it, right?" and most of the platoon said, "Yes, sir," but one [gay] recruit said, "No, sir." Everyone was cracking up.

The same speaker and a friend who trained with him agreed they had grown comfortable with the presence of their gay platoon-mate, and "it's not a big deal anymore." At first they had been concerned the gay recruit might take offense at all the homophobic training language, but "now that we know each other, we know we can make those jokes."[27] This statement concedes that insensitive language has the potential be hurtful, but as I discuss later in this chapter, basic training is precisely a context in which insensitive language and taunts are wielded as a training tool that can supposedly inure people to such harm.

Race, Ethnicity, Religion: Others Within

If gender-troubled insults remain a part of military training to encourage hard military masculinity, racial and ethnic slurs in training have become considerably less prevalent. There is a logic to this trend. For one thing, although military culture prides itself on being distinct from civilian culture, it still has to respond to some winds of change in the wider world. For another, all members of the military are supposed to be "hard" (and hence "masculine"), but the military needs bodies from all ethnic and racial backgrounds. In fact, the military was integrated, by executive order, before the general population was, and although high-ranking military officers have always been disproportionately white, in 1965 almost one-third of American ground combat battalions in Vietnam were African American. People of color have made up at least 40% of US combat infantry ever since,[28] and the Pew Research Center shows a growth of ethnic and racial minorities as a percentage of active-duty forces, from 36% in 2004 to 43% in 2017.[29]

In recent decades, the Department of Defense has invested considerable resources to work against racial and ethnic discrimination, with underlying motives including ethical conviction, social pressure, and pragmatic recognition that recruitment and "operational readiness" will be improved by successful diversity and inclusion.[30] The Defense Equal Opportunity Institute (DEOI), founded in the 1970s in response to the civil rights movement, grew substantially in the Global War on Terrorism (GWOT) era. Over the last fifteen years or so, the military's assessments of equal opportunity have expanded, and the *Defense Organizational Climate Survey* now collects data from over three million people a year in order to assess the "command climate" in matters of discrimination, harassment, and inclusion.[31] Military branches have also seen the growth of DEOI-designed trainings around racial and ethnic sensitivity and diversity. Contemporary Drill Instructors know that racist and ethnic insults pose a particularly high risk to both morale and their own careers.[32]

At the same time, service members have experienced a long-standing tension between ideologies of racial inclusiveness and actual verbal practice. In the Marine Corps, the official line since the Vietnam era has been that the Corps "does not see race," instead perceiving all Marines as "green" by virtue of their uniforms. John Musgrave, who enlisted in 1966, reports all kinds of demeaning feminization, infantilization, and other put-downs in boot camp, but his DI also liked to say there should be no "racial crap" in the Marine Corps, for there are "only two colors[:] . . . forest green, the color of your uniforms, and red, the color of your blood."[33] Yet historically, there have been many reports of service members of color being treated as materially and symbolically "less than," and many who served in Vietnam reported bald discrimination that reflected the broader culture of racism.[34] One of my Vietnam veteran respondents, a Cape Verdean man from New England, says, "It was a racist system, and many of the trainers were white guys from down South. . . . They would use all those ugly words you would expect on us." The historian James Westheider reports that DIs in the Vietnam era sometimes called Black recruits "boys, n*****s, or coons."[35] Stan, a Marine who served in 1968, delivers a more mixed verdict. His DIs at San Diego "would make all kinds of remarks that would now be considered politically insensitive, but they were equal opportunity about it. I don't think I ever heard them call anyone a n***** or a spic." That said, when Stan was trying to make it over a wall with a rope, his DI yelled, "Get up that wall, bean bandit!"

With his dark hair and olive complexion, Stan says, "I realized he assumed I was Mexican American."

I heard relatively fewer reports of racist DI language in the accounts of those who served in Iraq and Afghanistan. Michael, a Marine born in Puerto Rico, couldn't recall any racial or ethnic slurs used by his DIs in 2009, adding, "They made lots of comments just like we're all green, this is the Marine Corps, we don't see color, we're all green." Johnny, a white Bostonian who went to Parris Island in 2005, says, "No way, NO way" would you hear racial epithets used by DIs. Yet bigotry still continues to sneak under the radar. Jason Arment, who served as a USMC machine gunner in the Iraq War, had a DI who liked to tell certain recruits that "their father 'ran back across the border,' or 'got lost, drunk on the reservation,' or 'their momma couldn't pick which one because it was dark.'"[36] Miles Lagoze reports that in 2011, one of his DIs at Parris Island made an Asian American recruit "run laps . . . while screaming 'Me so horny!' over and over again."[37] Louis, of East Asian descent, tells me he did not hear racial epithets when he went to Parris Island in 2010, but a few years earlier he had a friend whose Sergeant "just kept dropping the n-word." At first, his friend "just brushed it off, and he thought it was just like he was just making a joke." Eventually, though, he brought it up to the Gunnery Sergeant, who "sat the [other] sergeant down . . . and said you need to cut that shit out. Because you know, that shit is not tolerated in the Marine Corps. Like, we're all different shades of green but we're all green."[38]

One pattern of ethnoracial insults arose more than others during the GWOT—namely, insults directed at Muslim recruits. After 9/11, Muslims in the US military occupied an uneasy structural position, at risk of being perceived as threats to their nation (because of their Muslim identity) *and* their religious community (for working within the US military as it attacked Muslim nations).[39] A Muslim Army veteran of Turkish descent who served in 2013 tells me his Sergeant called him a "terrorist" once and asked him several times whether he was "working for the other side."[40] Another veteran reports being called a "raghead" and "terrorist" at a Marine Corps Logistics Base in 2015.[41] And the same anonymous letter reporting post-DADT homophobia at Parris Island claimed that an "Indian looking kid" was recurrently told he "looks like a fucking terrorist" by his DIs.

> Anytime he gets mail the DIs don't say his name and instead go "oh, great, more terrorist mail" and drop it on the ground like they don't want to get anthrax, or pretend to listen to it like it's a timebomb. When he answers questions wrong about our classes, they go, "you know why you don't know the answer?" "no sir" "because your brain is full of fucking terrorist information, that's why."[42]

Occasionally, Islamophobic insults have reached a terrible climax. In 2016, a young Marine Corps recruit from Detroit, Raheel Siddiqui, was assigned to a notoriously brutal DI at Parris Island, Gunnery Sergeant Joseph Felix. After three weeks of daily abuse during which Felix called Siddiqui a "terrorist," asked if he "needed his turban," and repeatedly physically assaulted him, Siddiqui took his own life by jumping off a balcony.[43] (Felix was ultimately court-martialed and sentenced to ten years in prison for multiple instances of abuse, including targeting other Muslim recruits.)

Such overt ethnoracial discrimination is hardly ubiquitous in training, but when it occurs, it carries a pointed lesson. Rather than interpellating any random recruit as bungling or problematically feminine, ethnoracial insults scapegoat a minority recruit and interpellate them as the enemy within. This distinctive type of dehumanization singles out racial and ethnic difference—sometimes, difference associated with a geopolitical adversary—as grounds for special derision. And if we accept the loose formulation that DIs are to recruits as Marines are to the enemy, then these insults offer a template for the dehumanizing, essentialist slurs and epithets American service members later wield in the theater of war.

Whatever the insults they are subject to, recruits may also be learning a general lesson about the power of verbal denigration. Perhaps the epithets used against recruits start a cycle in which the verbally abused become verbal abusers, constituting a necropolitical loop that places *both* military participants *and* their targets into the condition of the living dead, offered up to kill or be killed.

Necropolitical Messages That Thicken the Skin

I have suggested that insults imply recruits are lowly and possibly killable, while also suggesting to recruits about how to be ruthless to their own targets in war. A British Army soldier in World War I recognized the first of these roles over one hundred years ago, writing, "To be struck, to be threatened, to be called indecent names[,] . . . all these things take down your pride, make you feel small, and in some ways fit you to accept the role of cannon fodder on the battleground."[44] Others have recognized the second role. One of my respondents connects his experience of being insulted in basic training to his own acts of war. Preston, who served as a Navy SEAL, was trained to hide in wait in the rivers and swamps of Vietnam and sometimes killed his targets by the dozens. He describes himself as having been "numb"; "the feelings," he tells me ruefully, "came later." To be sure, as many combat veterans will attest, killing seems to get easier the more someone does it (though it may later sediment into nightmares, grief, guilt, depression, anxiety, and rage). But Preston also felt that even before landing in Southeast Asia, the verbal component of his training helped steel him for his new role. Sweeping his hand across his white beard, he focused his eyes on a spot on his living room carpet and explained in a raspy voice:

> The insults get you down in that core of BLACKness where you, you can do anything. They want you to be able to say, think you can do anything. And when they train you that way, I think the language is part of it, just to get you to do it.... Even though it was disrespectful, I really feel that they need to have it. You have to [use that kind of] language in order to train them to be killers.

Preston connects his insensitivity to having been insulted during basic training. If you're told you're bad, he seems to imply, you may come to think you can do anything, including killing in the moral void of war.

That said, I never heard Drill Instructors (or former Drill Instructors) acknowledge such stark necropolitical implications of their insults. They would be unlikely to concede, I think, that denigrating recruits could make it easier for future combatants to get into the mindset of being both cannon fodder and killer. Instead, Drill Instructors' stated idea about this language—that is, their explicit "language ideology"—is that tough language simply helps recruits become stronger and harder, part of the "finest fighting force." This logic invokes clearly the concept of semiotic callousing, in which harsh language is supposed to inure future soldiers to onslaughts of whatever kind. Berating is meant to dull recruits' sensitivity to insulting words and, through a kind of transduction of energy, make them generally more resilient in the face of war's physical hardships.

Indeed, military talk often makes a connection between abstract meanings and the physical body, describing insults as if they were small physical projectiles that interact with the surface of the flesh. Recruits are not supposed to allow insults to "get under their skin," veteran DIs repeatedly told me. Instead, the insults are meant to train recruits to "let them roll off." Marines and other service members tend to internalize this language ideology. A young combat veteran, Lexie, tells me the harsh language of military training "hardened us.... It strengthened up the skin, it toughened up the skin." The same metaphor came up in my conversation with the young Marine veteran Johnny, who was telling me that even since the repeal of DADT, "I can guarantee recruits still hear words like 'faggot' if they're around Drill Instructors twenty-four hours a day." I remarked, "If a gay recruit hears homophobic language, I wonder what he feels like." Johnny replied, "Well, I would hope the resiliency started to build. . . . You gotta develop a thick skin." Similarly, on one 2015 Reddit thread started by a gay man considering enlisting in the Marine Corps, two Marine respondents told him he would be fine if he could manage to "have a thick skin."[45] Another gay service member writes that by the end of service, one is supposed to cultivate the ability to "take ridicule—smiling through the most vile and offensive slights with the understanding that they are nothing more than jokes."[46]

In some military discourse, reactions to verbal slights are treated as *diagnostic* of a person's reactions to kinetic violence. Recruits weak enough to crumple at harsh words might be correspondingly vulnerable to whatever menaces the nation (enemies, weapons)—and if a recruit can't handle the words, the feeling is, maybe they should drop out. According to my respondent Liam, who served in the Army in the early years of the Iraq War, language shouldn't make a dent during training. Although he's a peace activist today, I can hear the military stance in his statement that "if you can't handle a couple of insults, then you damn sure can't handle combat." A former Army Sergeant calling into a radio show in 2007 says, "If words hurt your feelings, bullets are going to hurt a lot more."[47] Bruce Yamashita, an officer candidate in the Marines in 1989, relates that when his DIs insulted his Japanese origins, their mentality was, "If you can't take a little ethnic joke, how can you fight an enemy?"[48] Similarly, the authors of the 2022 report about gender integration in the Marine Corps describe what one DI told his recruits at Parris Island: "If this [language] bothers you, what do you think the enemy is going to call you in combat? You shouldn't let little words get to you."[49] The same ideology is evident in one veteran's online response to the 2013 letter reporting homophobia at Parris Island:

> This little faggot should go get his legs and underarms shaved, put on some lipstick and go get a job at a day care telling little kids fairy tale stories. He certainly doesn't belong in the Marine Corps. If a few names bother him that much what is he going to do when the shit really hits the fan in combat? That is what all of the preliminaries are all about. . . . Cussing, name calling is all part of what makes a boy into a Marine.[50]

Again and again, we hear this tantalizing equation: the ability to block off verbal assaults corresponds to the ability to block off the holistic stressors and assaults of combat. As part of the military's linguistic infrastructure, repeated insults are meant to dull the semiotic sensitivities of their target, and sensitivity to the verbal is tantamount to sensitivity to physical projectiles. It is tempting to draw out the implied stereotypes. Does it follow that intellectuals cannot handle pain? That poets cannot manage a fist fight? That a gifted artist will flee when bullets start to fly? And—to reverse the equation—does this mean that good soldiers cannot be sensitive souls, attuned to language, its complex ways of influencing the world, and its relationship with feeling?

I also can't help notice a subtle contradiction in these ideas about semiotic callousing. On the one hand, harsh language such as name-calling is talked about as if it is harmless, as in the old playground maxim "Sticks and stones may break my bones, but words will never hurt me." At the same time, it is abundantly evident that DIs use words as instruments of potential harm in order to train Marines in the making to be tougher. They need this language, they seem to feel, to assail the recruits, perhaps especially in an era when they are more likely to be penalized if they physically injure them.

Kill Chants

Marine Corps training also uses an especially transparent linguistic method to shunt empathy away from the suffering of those targeted in war: frequent repetition of the word "kill." The first time I heard about this, I was speaking to Jay at a veterans' writing workshop. A gifted artist and writer, Jay regrets having joined the Corps and now wears creative outfits like colorful bandannas and leggings with pink on the left side, blue on the right. He tells me that in hindsight, he considers boot camp morally appalling. "You can't believe the things they try to put into you. Like, we greeted each other by yelling 'Kill!' You'd just pass someone on the path and you'd both yell, 'Kill!' and it was, like, just another Tuesday." Jay shook his head as he relayed this, incredulous anyone could toss around such words so casually.

But recruits are routinely interpellated as eager, merciless killers. During Patrick Turley's graduation, a Drill Instructor gave a speech affirming this identity: "In the world of many, there are few. These are the ones they call Marines. Warrior by day, predator by night, killer by choice, Marine by God."[51] Jason Arment relates the USMC Machine Gunners Creed he memorized: "We will cut our enemies down in droves. Our fires will be the substance of their nightmares. We will protect our brothers. The fields of the dead shall serve as evidence of our passing."[52]

Marines who volunteer may be "killers by choice," but their training offers a linguistic infrastructure that deters deliberation about whether to take lives.

As part of this, the word "kill" is often used as an interjection during weapons training and exercise. On one hike, a DI instructed Patrick Turley's platoon that every time the DI yelled "Check him!," they were to reply "Kill!" and strike the pack of the man in front of them.[53] In the 2006 documentary *The Ground Truth*, Marine Sean Huze reports having to yell "Kill babies!" while approaching a target or jogging in formation.[54] Matt Young writes of his training, "We screamed 'kill' for every repetition of cadence during stretching exercises and calisthenics—'1!' 'KILL!' '2!' 'KILL!' '3!' 'KILL!'—to make the thought of killing commonplace."[55] Similar techniques are sometimes used in the Army, too; Kevin tells me of the cadences and chants he learned in his Army bayonet course. "'What makes the green grass grow? Blood, blood, blood. What is the spirit of the bayonet? To kill, kill, kill without mercy.' . . . You had to scream all that stuff out."

As if normalizing the concept while taking it more deeply into their identity, Marine Corps officers and recruits sometimes use the word "kill" in more banal contexts, as in the ritualized greeting described by Jay, above. In Jason Arment's account, recruits were sometimes required to yell "kill" as a greeting (with a head nod) or an affirmative response (e.g., if they wanted to eat at the chow hall). "KILL," he adds, "was the word companies of Marines shouted at their command when they knew they were supposed to say something, but didn't know what."[56] Turley describes his DI directing a squad to "attack the Chow Hall," meaning go to the dining hall to get a meal. As they entered, they were enjoined to sit down and "Kill 37," another platoon in their company. They wound up chanting "Kill kill kill 'em all!" as they marched in past the other platoon to eat. During a military history lesson, Turley's Staff Sergeant would ask a question, and when a recruit stood to answer, his platoon-mates would shout "Kill!" to "motivate" him. If the recruit got the answer right, the congratulations would take the form of (you guessed it) "Kill!"[57] And in her 2015 dissertation, Rachel Lynn Bowman reports that a non-commissioned officer at Parris Island "used 'kill' as a throwaway affirmative in a conversation with my escort lieutenant. . . . The term meant 'great' or 'got it.'"[58] At one point in the documentary *Ears, Open. Eyeballs, Click*, recruits clean the floor while chanting, "Sweep, kill, sweep, kill." Here, "kill" is nested into a rote, repetitive chore, perhaps both being all in a day's work. When a term is used so casually and with so many purposes, it blends into the landscape of cultural expectations.[59]

One former commissioned officer in the Marine Corps, Mike, drew an unnerving connection between kill chants and the possibility of untrammeled violence. Mike now has a white-collar job and spoke to me from behind his desk in a crisp, blue oxford shirt, weighing his words slowly, perhaps reluctant to criticize the Corps he served with for so long. He confirmed that the word "kill" was sometimes used as an affirmation during his officer training. He goes on to describe its use in an academic context:

> It would be very common for someone who is facilitating the instruction [on military history] to say, "Give 'em one!" And then the entire audience would yell "Kill!," right, so that was like a reward or an act like an applause, and this is a Marine Corps applause for them, and so you're rewarding [the speaker] with the word "kill." So I referred to that on my own as "the kill chant," and I had a lot of trouble with it. I participated in it, but it bothered me. . . . Particularly as officers, we were being selected to think and to be discerning, at least that was my understanding of what the expectation was, and when I figured this was a way of brainwashing to just make us, you know, desensitized to the act of violence, to, to build up the, you know, to make killing a GOOD thing. And that's not something that I'm responding positively to. I think that, you know, I should be the one that's—you know, my head is actually above the fray; I'm pulling people back from going too far, or letting them go if necessary—that's like, that's my job as the officer, to control that well. And so I didn't respond to it well.

To Mike, the kill chant has the potential to disinhibit the act of killing, and he worried the desensitization might encourage violence without discernment among the officer class meant to have more rational control over killing than infantry. Presumably the desensitizing effects of kill chants (and the rest of basic training) underpin the unofficial motto Jason Arment reports in his School of Infantry: "Kill absolutely everything you see."[60] Alarmingly, some veterans interviewed for *The Ground Truth* reported that after all the "kill" chanting, they wanted to kill, if only to see what it was like.[61]

The insults and other language I describe in this chapter are components of a linguistic infrastructure that encourages a ruthless necropolitical mindset. The ideal new soldier understands they might be expendable in combat, while also being annealed so they might multiply the state's force. Harsh language encourages penetrative, kinetic violence, while offering a blueprint for denigrating and withholding empathy from killable outgroups. Practices such as the kill chant further bypass empathy and moral deliberation, even reason itself. In the next chapter, I explore some reasons why Marine Corps basic training sometimes violates its own stated principles of respect, reasonableness, and morality and how certain training practices model the topsy-turvy moral universe of combat.

Chapter 4
Broken Rules and Head Games

One summer evening a few years ago, I sat at a sticky bar with Peter and his friend Joe, both former Drill Instructors (DIs) who went through their tours on Parris Island in the first decade of the 2000s.*,1 The men were having a grand time reminiscing about errant recruits, sand fleas, and the quirks of another DI who was so fastidious in the face of his own hunger, he would eat one-quarter of a candy bar and save the rest for later.

The chocolate reminds Peter of a story, and he launches it with a twinkle in his eye. It's about the Guide for one of Peter's old platoons—a recruit selected to carry the guidon (standard flag) in formation and to help ensure the platoon follows the DI's orders when the DI isn't around. One day, Peter's Guide was meant to have located some fitness gear for the platoon. The Series Commander would be coming around for an inspection before long, and the Guide was late. Peter grew more and more animated as he re-enacted the events. (For clarity's sake, I use italics when Peter is imitating the Guide.)

> So Guide is supposed to be getting my gear and I'm going, "Where the hell is Guide. GUIDE?" [He imitates his guide, in a slightly higher voice] *"SIR, GUIDE, SIR!"* "Guide, where is Senior Drill Instructor's PT [exercise] gear?" *"Guide didn't have time, sir!"* So the Series Commander's on my tail, and I was like, "WHAT? I need my gear." *"Sir, Guide needed knowledge."*

"Knowledge" can be militaryspeak for information. Evidently, the Guide hadn't been able to find the gear and needed more information to do so. Peter adopts a tone of enraged disbelief to reenact his own response.

> "Guide needed KNOWLEDGE? I'll give you some knowledge. GET on the quarterdeck!" [The quarterdeck is an area of the floor in a squad bay; the term comes from Navy terminology.]

At this point, Peter glances at me and smiles mischievously to explain.

---

* This chapter analyzes words and imagery that may be difficult for some readers to encounter. Please see the "Content Warning and Note on Language" in the front matter for some context and a discussion of the author's reasons for not redacting this material.

Kill Talk. Janet McIntosh, Oxford University Press. © Oxford University Press (2025).
DOI: 10.1093/9780197808054.003.0005

> When you get 'em on the quarterdeck you wear 'em down—I mean you, ya, ya—[Peter slows down and tilts his head to parody a hyperreasonable voice, as if representing Marine Corps respectability] You instill some—you give 'em IT.

I know what "IT" stands for: "incentive training," which is vigorous exercise ordered as a kind of discipline or punishment. Peter continues.

> I'm, like, instilling knowledge. It's knowledge. [Loud, warrior scream] "AAAHH!" He's doing leg lifts and I'm like, [very rapid, very loud, garbled] "GET THE, GET THE FUCK ON THE—AHHH!"

By this time, Joe had begun to laugh hard, amused by Peter's coy euphemism, "instilling knowledge" and then by Peter's imitation of his own yelling and unintelligible orders.

> So, Guide is yelling back and leg lifting again and again—"*AAAAHHHH!!!*" All of a sudden, Guide lights up like this [Peter gestures to his own face, an agonized rictus]. He's turning red, bloodshot, sweating. I'm like "GUIDE, STOP!" He's still yelling "*AAAHHH!*," and now he's starting to run around. Guide wouldn't stop! So I hit him. [Peter makes a gesture as if slapping someone.]

Joe turns to me, laughing: "NO! He didn't just say that!" Peter continues:

> He wouldn't stop! "*GAAAAHH!!*" I finally, finally took him in the house. "What's wrong, Guide?" [Peter adopts a frantic voice] "*GUIDE NEEDS KNOWLEDGE!*" I'm thinking, what's my general order? What's the general order? He's going crazy on me. So I got some Snickers, some Gatorade [for him]. Then Joe comes by, and recruit is still, like, "*AAAHHHH!*" Joe's like, "Damn, you're gonna get voided [fired]." I had to KICK knowledge to him [makes gestures as if kicking someone on the floor]. I was like "GUIDE, you know your first order is this, second order is this . . ." He finally got calm. "*What happened?*" "I don't know. You went crazy." So, anyway, Guide's gonna go to the wizard [military psychologist]. Talked to him for a while, figured out what's going on, they got him squared away. And today [Peter switches to a tone of pride] he's a Master Gunnery Sergeant in the Marine Corps. [Joe chips in with an "Oorah!"] Attrition was not the mission. I had a command, way back when. Train and make Marines no matter what. I coulda given up on the motivating, and now he's a Master Gunner and I love him for it.

Peter's punishment of his Guide, through yelling, intimidation, and extreme repetitive exercise, pushes the recruit to what sounds like a break with reality. Peter snaps him out of it with a combination of slapping, kicking, sugar, and reminders of his "orders." In hindsight, Peter and Joe find it hilarious, doubtless an easier stance to adopt given the narrative's triumphal ending.

The anecdote speaks to the ideal arc of Corps training. Recruits must be broken, their verbal, physical, and social expectations assailed, and the very act of breaking recruits "motivates" them and gives rise to their excellence as Marines. Today Peter is proud of what he did, and quite possibly the now–Master Gunner loves him back for it. Though some Marines never stop hating their DIs, I also saw no shortage of positive sentiment directed toward past mentors at the Drill Instructors' reunion I attended at Parris Island. Some are grateful the DI's trial by fire toughened them up and granted them entry to an elite brotherhood. Surprisingly, even a glimmer of compassion from a DI can solidify a recruit's loyalty. One Marine's eyes welled with tears as he recounted a poignant moment amid the weeks of berating when his DI finally leaned in and softly inquired, "You okay? You good?" The DI evolution—in recruit experience, anyway—from mere sadist to semisadistic paternal figure is not unusual. That said, a retired Marine told me of a revealing policy. When former recruits get in touch with the East Coast Drill Instructor's Association to request their DI's contact information, he said, "they have to check if the DI wants to be in touch with them. Because some of these guys still want to kill their old DI."

Intense training can evoke intense feelings, including profound hatred and unexpected love. But Peter's and Joe's descriptions point to an additional dynamic. They endorse harsh training as effective, describe it with cheerful amusement, and—like many DIs—reveal mixed or even negative feelings toward top-down efforts to mitigate the intensity of training practices. For although DIs are not supposed to engage in physical or verbal maltreatment, at least some of them seem to find it both tempting and effective.

While attending the Drill Instructors' reunion at Parris Island, in fact, I was recurrently struck to hear former DIs joking about assailing recruits, physically or verbally. The phrase "statute of limitations" was sometimes part of the joke, suggesting some community anxiety about the watchful eye of military law. During a storytelling competition, for instance, one middle-aged former DI who wound up working for NCIS (the Naval Criminal Investigative Service, which serves both the Navy and the Marine Corps) described pranking his former DI decades after they were at Parris Island. He rolled up at the older man's house with his NCIS badge. The former DI didn't recognize him, opening a space for the former recruit to tell him he was "under investigation for abusing recruits" and "there's no statute of limitations." Hearing this, the crowd of former and active-duty DIs roared with laughter; the anecdote clearly struck a nerve. Finally, the man gave the game away by showing the old

DI a photo of them together at Parris Island, offering him heartfelt thanks for turning his life around. But first, his ribbing about the risks the DI had taken would be a way to bond.

Recruits hear official discourse at the outset of their training telling them they will be "respected" and should report infractions up the chain of command. The Department of Defense has been concerned about recruit abuse for decades, issuing numerous directives to curb it and making concerted efforts after high-profile incidents such as the suicide of Recruit Raheel Siddiqui at Parris Island in 2016.[2] Reports of hazing in the Corps dropped by more than 50% between 2018 and 2022.[3] But all the Marine veterans I spoke with trained before the most recent reforms, and the stories I heard from them showed that during the Vietnam and Global War on Terrorism eras, the ideal moral universe described in the official discourse had often been contravened in their training. Such contradictions in the system were echoed by a 2018 internal report on Marine Corps organizational culture, which pointed to a climate of "value conflicts," adding that Marines "described many experiences of mixed messages (perhaps unintentional) from senior leaders."[4] I suggest that historically, an overarching mixed message in Marine Corps training has been that between official principles—particularly the notion that training should exemplify and create honorable, respectful, ethical warriors—and unofficial practices in the hands of at least some trainers.

The disjuncture should give us pause about training priorities. Is it more urgent to create ethically minded soldiers or effective killers? The weight placed on each seems to vary across military players. Many leaders in the Department of Defense, commissioned officers across the branches, and rank-and-file service members fervently believe that the use of force should be carefully and ethically restrained, one way or another. At the same time, some trainers who have worked with young recruits believe that only extreme measures are equal to the gritty job of training future infantry to inflict violence and death. The primary job, for them, has been overcoming restraint, not instilling it. For such trainers, dark methods are the best way to create a killer.

My primary goal in this chapter's descriptions of basic training is not to quantify or report abuse per se (indeed, it isn't clear how to calibrate what counts as abuse in military contexts, as I explain later in this chapter).[5] Nor is it to examine the role of harsh treatment in group allegiance; scholars have already established that hazing can strengthen group loyalty, even though it can also lead to physical and psychological injuries.[6] Instead, I describe the reasons for what I see as a cultural riptide that has historically tended to drag military training, especially in the Marine Corps, toward harsh practices, despite the many efforts to curb these. I consider that the very breaching of military rules, as well as the profusion of incongruous, disorienting signs during training, may carry lessons of necropolitical relevance.

Put another way, I suggest that some of the contradictory messages in Marine Corps training may be a feature rather than a bug. Whether or not this structure of meaning is intentional, and whether it is still as ubiquitous as I suspect, the broken rules, moral transgressions, and breaches of reason that some DIs engage in symbolically resonate with the act of killing. As such, they may be a kind of teaching tool—a *sacrum* in the rite of passage, to use Victor Turner's terminology (see Chapter 2). For if killing is to become more doable, it helps if ordinary thresholds between rationality and irrationality, thinkable and unthinkable have become more crossable. As the military chaplain Zachary Moon has observed, military training needs to alter, or "mutate," what he calls recruits' "moral orienting system" so that they can function in the military as potential killers.[7] To this end, some, even if not all, DIs model transgression by repeatedly enacting the shattering of rules, the distortion of rationality, and sometimes sadism itself. Such acts foreshadow what the psychiatrist Robert Jay Lifton describes as the abolishment of an ordered symbolic universe in war.[8]

I suggest that in training, then, at least some Marine Corps recruits begin to learn about the moral void of combat. The examples in this chapter also highlight the chimerical quality in military identity I have mentioned already—a duality between upstanding, official modes of comportment and taboo or illicit behavior. The contradictions between rules and practices resonate with the linguistic repertoires available in kill talk, in which measured, technocratic, and officially sanctioned phrases contrast with profane and raw language that sometimes adopts a stance of sadistic pleasure. The unresolved tension between "right" and "wrong" also echoes in other linguistic practices I describe, most obviously in the combat humor I discuss in Chapter 8.

Official Rules

So what *are* the standards and values military trainers are supposed to be cleaving to and instilling? I have mentioned a few already. All the branches of the US military can recite creeds that place morality at the core of their stated identity. The seven values most championed by the Army, for instance, are loyalty, duty, respect, selfless service, honor, integrity, and courage. The Marine Corps, for its part, returns again and again to those three words that underpin its code of ethics: honor, courage, commitment. The Corps says repeatedly and in multiple venues that it wishes to create "ethical warriors."

In a substantial 2005 compilation of USMC memos and teaching tools designed for training discussions by Corps leaders, furthermore, we see allusions to "character," "moral compass," "codes of integrity," "respecting human dignity," and a Corps of "the highest moral character in and out of uniform."[9] The "academic" component of Marine Corps basic training, which includes almost forty hours' worth of "core values" discussions, considers topics such as suicide prevention and equal opportunity, the importance of "integrity," and how to make decisions in the face of a moral dilemma. Instructors teach using hypothetical scenarios in which a Marine must make challenging decisions about, for instance, whether to report a leader's ethical violation. Ideal Marine behavior involves reporting infractions up the chain of command and holding oneself and others accountable to the rules. The words "right" and "wrong" make frequent appearances in the teaching documents, with "wrong" being defined as "deviating from moral rectitude as prescribed by law or by conscience; immoral, not just, proper, or equitable according to a standard or code."[10]

Such rectitude is consistent, of course, with the idea of the service member as super-citizen, in popular and military discourse alike. For as the USMC San Diego Recruit Depot website declares,

> [By incorporating the values of] Honor, Courage and Commitment . . . into recruit training, the Marine Corps creates not just basically trained, morally conscience [sic] Marine, but also a better American citizen who will return to society following his or her service to their country.[11]

Moral probity is supposed to be not just an outcome, but also a *means* of training.[12] The Uniform Code of Military Justice forbids abusive physical contact with recruits,[13] and each branch has additionally put forth its own policies about both physical and verbal maltreatment during training. The Army started to ban just about all physical contact for discipline in the mid-1980s, while its Training and Doctrine Command regulations prohibit "vulgar" language and physical or verbal hazing.[14] During the 1990s and the first decade of the 2000s, concern about recruit attrition prompted the Army to undergo systemic changes to further discourage profanity and gratuitous physical punishments.[15] The 2009 US Army Drill Sergeant Handbook adjures Drill Sergeants to "know the difference between being strict/enforcing standards and being abusive/demeaning."[16] "Sometimes you have to get in their faces," one Sergeant tells a *New York Times* journalist in 2005, "but it's not about making them cry. The old philosophy was that you're not ready for combat unless you're made miserable all day."[17]

When it comes to the comportment expected of Marine Corps Drill Instructors (DIs), policy changes began after an infamous scandal on Parris Island in 1956, when a drunken DI forced his heavily laden platoon into the swamps of Ribbon Creek and six recruits drowned. The tragedy initiated major attempts at reform; since then, DIs have been forbidden to physically or verbally abuse recruits and disallowed from touching recruits' bodies except under particular conditions, as when adjusting a uniform or "correcting" a drill movement.

In the first few days of training, today's Marine Corps recruits hear their Senior Drill Instructors give a memorized speech that includes a weighty concession to recruit rights:

> We will treat you as we do our fellow Marines, with firmness, fairness, dignity, and compassion. Physical or verbal abuse by any Marine or recruit will not be tolerated. If anyone should abuse or mistreat you, I expect you to report such incidents immediately to me or one of my Drill Instructors.

The Recruit Training Order (RTO), which is updated every few years, underscores that DIs are supposed to live by this pledge. The 2008 RTO states, for instance, that DIs are to "lead by example" and "forgo fear and intimidation."[18] A reinforcing order signed in 2012 by the deputy commandant for combat development and integration repeats these adjurations.[19] The 2019 and 2024 Recruit Training Orders ban "unprofessional" language, including "all language which is sexually explicit or demeaning to any race, gender, ethnicity, heritage, sexual orientation, or religion."[20] And while the RTO does not explicitly define the word "abuse," it does attempt to unpack "hazing" in its glossary, linking the concept to "initiation" and glossing it as "any conduct whereby one military member . . . causes another military member . . . to suffer or be exposed to an activity which is cruel, abusive, humiliating, or oppressive."[21] At the same time that DIs must avoid such behavior, they must actively respect recruits' dignity.[22]

Despite such orders, a 2015 RAND study found that there is still no consensus among military players about exactly what constitutes "hazing" or "abuse," so the attempted clarifications and prohibitions keep coming.[23] Over the years, the Marine Corps and other branches have seen an outpouring of memos, guidelines, programs, and trainings to reinforce bans on various forms of harsh behavior.[24] In the nation's largest employer, it has sometimes been hard to keep track of the policy churn. New "asks," initiatives, and training protocols can be handed down from on high, but they may wind up in competition with other efforts, their funding source may be unclear, or the details may get lost in the shuffle. But while ordinary bureaucratic dysfunction is one reason why transgressions happen, I suggest there are deeper reasons why some DIs have tended to break the rules.

Crossing the Lines, Codes of Silence, and Pedagogy

Pushing against propriety is part of Marine Corps tradition. We have hints of this in the words of R. Lee Ermey, the former Drill Instructor mentioned in the preceding chapter, who served in the Marines from 1961–1967 and as a DI for the last two of those years (several of his contemporaries were at the Drill Instructors' reunion I attended). Ermey plays the cruel DI named "Gunnery Sergeant Hartmann" in Stanley Kubrick's 1987 film *Full Metal Jacket*. In a 1987 televised interview, a young journalist named Val remarks, "I was afraid to meet you, you were so horrible in that movie.... Was that realistic, I mean is that even possible that anyone could be so sadistic and awful?"[25] Ermey replies, "Yes it was. You have to kind of understand, Val, that we're sending these kids to Vietnam." Val still seems incredulous. "But was there anybody like that? I mean were there people in the Marines who were that—" Ermey interrupts her, saying,

> I'm afraid there was the occasional individual who would take it upon himself to use a little physical force. It was not condoned by the United States Marine Corps, physical nor verbal abuse is not then and it's not now, [but] it's like the speed limit.... When I'm driving 65 miles per hour I've got cars whizzing past me, but it's the individual, it's certainly not the state that allows people to go 80 miles an hour.... So in some cases we have these individuals that seem to think that they can take it upon themselves to do things and get by with it. And Hartmann was one of those people and it certainly did go on.

Ermey's speed limit metaphor is telling. It implies many DIs are tempted to go "over the speed limit"—don't all vigorous young adults do that on the highway? It also clarifies that recruit abuse may be a matter of degree rather than kind, falling along a continuum of ordinary DI behavior. After all, much of what DIs are supposed to do to recruits will stress them out. In fact, much of it *by design* constitutes what many civilians and counseling professionals would already consider verbal, physical, and/or psychological abuse. DIs exert total power over recruits, they deliberately intimidate and frighten them, they force them to undertake unpleasant tasks, they berate and threaten them, and they publicly insult them for poor performance. A widely recognized role of the DI is to be impossible to please, in the early weeks of recruit training, anyway. While this daunting training method has had the most publicity in the Marine Corps, versions of it have existed in other branches, too. As one Army Drill Sergeant said during his 2005 court-martial for his physically and verbally harsh techniques, "It's commonly known that all drill sergeants work in the gray area. If you don't, you aren't doing your job."[26] Since "gray area" work has the nationalist aim of making a hardened super-citizen, there seems to be a tacit agreement among some military players that the ends justify the means, and the means are going to test the speed limit.

Some DIs in the Vietnam War era were particularly draconian, perhaps, as Ermey hints, channeling their anxiety about the grim conditions Marines would face. Historian James Westheider describes DIs at Camp Pendleton bashing recruits between the eyes with a rifle butt and dangling them by their arms over lockers.[27] Vietnam veterans told me plenty of similar anecdotes about being "knocked about" by their superiors, stuffed into lockers, and so forth.

In twenty-first-century training, strenuous messaging from on high has attenuated the physical assaults on recruits. DI Grady tells me that in the final week of training he'll ask recruits in his platoon how many of them "expected to get beat up" during basic training. About one-third raise their hands, he says, and "some of them are disappointed they weren't"—presumably they were hoping the Corps would "make a man" of them by way of violence. His young colleague Adam frames recruit abuse as primarily a generational matter, telling me, "DIs do this stuff at their own peril. But most of the ones doing it are the old guard. We're trying to get them out."

Yet some DIs have continued to break or bend the rules, too, or found ways to create immense physical discomfort without laying a hand on their recruits. In conversation with me, several Global War on Terrorism (GWOT) veterans described being ordered to drink large quantities of milk or water before grueling exercise, to the point that they would vomit.[28] Marines told me of recruits being forced to hold their urine for so long they had to go in their pants. One related being smashed with a bayonet. A Marine who served in the 2010s told me in his third week at Parris Island, a Sergeant (nicknamed "Psycho" by the recruits) broke a recruit's finger and was quietly moved into another unit. When the commissioned officers get wind of incidents like these, they often renew their messaging about the importance of restraint.

The rules about respecting recruits and preserving their dignity are also violated linguistically, of course. The insults I detailed in the preceding chapter are a prominent example. Ramon, who served as a DI at Parris Island in the 1980s, explained that some DIs believe good training requires some verbal transgressions.

> I would hear Drill Instructors call kids faggots, spics, you know. I didn't go all the way there, I don't think that's the way to do it, but I definitely called them things.... The Standard Operating Procedures didn't allow you to do a lot, but—let me explain it this way. Somebody, some desk jockey, who has probably never been a Drill Instructor, wrote a book on how to train, and then he gives it to the Drill Instructor, who looks at it and goes, "This is full of shit. So I'm going to not do anything illegal, but I'm going to train these guys correctly." It's kind of an unwritten code that you're gonna be hard on them and use some offensive language.

Evidently, those rules handed down from on high may be taken with a grain of salt. An additional dimension of "offensive language," Ramon adds, is profanity.[29] I asked Grady while he was setting up picnic tables for a luncheon at Parris Island about the RTO's prohibition on profanity. He clicked his tongue and smiled, saying, "I swear all the time. Motherfucker this, motherfucker that." His colleague next to him winced at the admission, but it wasn't news to me. I had already heard some trainers use so-called minced oaths such as "friggin'" or "daggone" to remain in technical compliance with the rules, but others switch back and forth between these and their profane counterparts.[30]

The tension is evident in a 2004 documentary titled *Ears, Open. Eyeballs, Click*, filmed at the San Diego Training Depot and recommended to me by several Marines. In one segment, the camera follows a platoon on a training hike.[31] It's hot, it's dusty, everyone is heavily laden, and the recruits are clearly on their last legs. Several DIs can be heard trying to "motivate" them. One yells at a recruit who has stopped on the road. "SON OF A BITCH! GET UP! FUCK! ... With this fuckin' shit, get the fuck out of my platoon, sister! ... You're a freakin' puss! That's what you are! Go! Go! Go!"

A couple of minutes later, another DI can be heard chewing out a slow walker. "Freakin' motivate yourself, and get the frig up there.... We shoulda joined the friggin' Army.... 'Cause I'll tell you what, you ain't putting out up to our damn standards." A little later, we see a recruit who has collapsed, complaining his knee has given out. One DI yells, "Get on your feet! Get on your friggin' feet! Your shit ain't broken, son.... I said get the shit, and get on it.... If you ain't dying, you're humping [military slang for walking while carrying a load]. We hump till we die."

Amid word substitutions like "freakin'" and "friggin,'" the profanity rains down—"fuck," "puss," "damn," "shit."[32] To be clear, I don't imagine the main reason profanity appears is simply that it breaks the rules; its use in military training is "overdetermined," meaning that there are countless reasons for DIs to use it. DIs might use profanity because they instinctively grab the most emphatic words at their disposal to transmit their urgent affect to recruits. Maybe profane language also mirrors the harsh realities they want Marines to get used to.[33] Along these lines, the use of profane insults might count as another form of semiotic callousing. Bombarded with harsh language, recruits should learn to inure themselves to feeling "hurt," responding with action rather than nursing their wounds. Swearing is also one way to perform tough American masculinity, and considered unremarkable—even expected—in hypermasculine contexts.[34] Furthermore, since "dirty words" refer to shared and sometimes taboo experiences of the body—sex, genitalia, excretion—they belong perfectly in the military, where privacy is hard to come by and bodies are often filthy or desecrated.[35] Unadorned and profane language also tends to be associated with those with less class privilege, in contrast with the "refined" or "respectable" language people use to self-elevate.[36] DIs are promoted from within enlisted ranks and need not have a college degree, so official prohibitions on profanity may smack of the buttoned-up officer class, or those "desk jockeys" Ramon referred to, out of touch with the enlisted ranks. Looked at this way, profanity may sometimes offer a method of connecting with recruits, especially when it refers to a shared hardship.

But beyond these many reasons why profanity might appear in Marine Corps training, my focus here is on the tension between the prohibition and the practice. The DIs I quote seem pulled between the pressure to constrain their language and the affective intensity and ruthless quality of training. It's as if their emotions are so strong, and the life-and-death stakes in military training so high, the small dam of the RTO cannot hold. Similar dynamics seem to obtain when it comes to other Marine Corps training prohibitions on language, from insults to sexually derogatory and misogynistic remarks.[37]

Like R. Lee Ermey, many DIs will defend their physical and verbal treatment of recruits. Even at their own courts-martial, some DIs have reportedly insisted that "you do not understand[;] that is what you must do to make a Marine."[38] (Nearly 90% of reported hazing incidents in the US military, it should be said, take place in the Marine Corps.[39]) Some justify recruit abuse as a traditional part of the job or suggest that raw aggression is important to DI identity itself. When one military chaplain asked a DI why he treated recruits so harshly, he replied that it is "a rite of passage to hit a Recruit or abuse a Recruit. You are not considered a real DI unless you use some type of abusive means. It's a power trip."[40] Other Marines may concur that harsh treatment is justified. A Marine Corps officer who trained about a decade ago told me he had mixed feelings when reading journalist Janet Reitman's 2017 account of recruit hazing at Parris Island.[41] Though he agreed that some incidents she described were "totally egregious," many practices she described as abuse seemed to him "totally acceptable."

Do recruits push back? New arrivals to the training depots at Parris Island and San Diego hear opening speeches directing them to report abuse if they encounter it. An employee at the Defense Equal Opportunity Management Institute told me that Defense Department officials are greatly concerned about subordinates' ability to report to their superiors without retribution and strive to create structures along these lines, including what are now copious anonymous surveys administered by the military's Office of People Analytics.[42] Such measures may well change the landscape of what future DIs feel they can get away with. But former DIs from both the Vietnam and GWOT eras told me that in their experience, most rule violations went unremarked on by recruits, who accepted them as part of training or were too daunted to rock the boat. Describing his training a few years after 9/11 at San Diego, Will Price notes that his DIs seemed to "know exactly whom they can hit.... They tend to go after recruits like me who they know will never make a complaint against them."[43] Johnny, who trained at Parris Island in 2005, tells me his DI threatened that tattling recruits would be expelled from basic training:

> It's funny, they tell you you can report stuff—they say "You can come forward," and a couple of times during the three-month period, we'd even have these chats one on one with an officer we'd never heard of who would say to us, "How's it going? You can tell us anything." But our DI would give us a heads up in advance, like, "Hey, this is gonna happen and you'd better not say anything or you're gonna get dropped." Saying anything is very discouraged, anything negative. I would wager the person wouldn't say anything, because they want to finish what they started.

To be "dropped" from (kicked out of) recruit training is a source of shame, often interpreted to mean the recruit was too weak to cut it. To report up the chain of command was thus to imperil one's own position. What Johnny describes, in fact, sounds like code of silence akin to the Italian mafia's expectation of omertà, whereby keeping quiet about illicit activities protects the system.

Clearly, some DIs over the decades have found it tempting to bend or break the rules, feeling that harsh treatment is urgently necessary to "train these guys correctly" (in Ramon's words), while recruits have had their reasons for going along with it. I suggest that the very fact of these rule violations, when they occur, carries some underexplored pedagogy. There is powerful symbolism involved when trainers first describe upstanding promises and rules (as in, "We will treat you with firmness, fairness, dignity, and compassion") and then breach them. The contradiction sets up a model for thinking, talking, and behaving in war, as when, for instance, the high emotions during a firefight may override both civilian norms and, sometimes, the military's own prohibitions.[44] Rule violations in training, from physical indignities to taboo language, offer a loose diagram or mirror of the norm-shattering, ungovernable quality of combat violence.[45]

Head Games and the Descent into Moral Absurdity

Sometimes, Drill Instructors go beyond the proverbial "speed limit" by way of unhinged and disorienting demands that may also carry necropolitical symbolism. I had my first hint of such practices while driving past the First Battalion barracks on Parris Island in April 2019. I pulled over to watch a platoon in formation just outside of the building. They had been halted by their DIs, who ran furiously up and down the rows, barking orders. After each command, the recruits yelled "AYE, SIR," in unison. The men ran in place in their olive-green gear, then shifted on command to jumping jacks. A few beats later, they switched to vigorous knee lifts while holding their arms straight in front of them. Then I heard a DI yell something I couldn't make out, and abruptly, in confused fashion, the recruits began pulling their shirts over their heads, holding them extended before them with straight arms. Another order, another "AYE, SIR," and the men placed the shirts on the ground before them, whereupon they were immediately ordered to pick them up again. Then to put them down again. Then to pick them up again. Another order, this time with a rapid countdown ("ten, nine, eight, seven, six, five, four, three . . . "), and the men were tugging their shirts back on. Then off again. Sleeves were inside out, recruits were out of sync, and DIs went from man to man, verbally hammering each for his confusion.

It took me a little time to disentangle what I witnessed, because it merged physical training with orders that seemed designed to flummox the recruits. The first part of what I saw may have been a version of the officially well-regulated but highly unpleasant element of basic training known as incentive training, or IT. Whereas units undergo scheduled physical training, or PT, at least three times a week, with warming up, stretching, calisthenics, strength training, and more, IT is spontaneous and often punitive. A DI may single out a recruit or some segment of a platoon for problematic performance, or sometimes the whole group may be collectively punished for the errors of the few. This shared accountability gives extra incentive to perform well; recruits don't want to incur the wrath of others in their unit. But DIs don't need any grand excuse to IT recruits. They can simply glance at a recruit, notice their gear is a little askew, and, as often as not, send everyone to the quarterdeck or to the sand pit outdoors. Next come orders to do rapid, repetitive exercises—pushups, pull-ups, crunches, running in place with "high knees," "mountain climbers" on the floor, and so forth, which recruits often perform to the point of pain and exhaustion. Some refer to this as getting "slayed" or "smoked."

IT helps physical fitness, but in Marine Corps lingo, it is also described as a means of "instilling discipline and motivation," and "getting through to a stubborn recruit," by ensuring compliance through negative reinforcement.[46] At a banquet table for the Drill Instructors' reunion dinner, a former DI, Jack, tells me the quick repetitions during IT are also designed to improve "MMR," or muscle memory reflex, because "that split second of thinking, or hesitating, gets you killed in combat." Put another way, IT helps to remove the temptation to think when you are given an order. A young DI, Carlos, tells me that during IT, he sometimes gives an order, then adjures his recruits to "be a man." "What does that mean?" I asked. "You do what I tell you to do as fast as you can." While this equation of manhood with compliance may sound paradoxical, the political scientist and gender theorist Aaron Belkin has suggested that military masculinity very often takes this form: both rugged *and* obedient.[47] And as the recruit learns to be obedient, they also learn to self-surveil. Jack tells me IT is often administered for minute details like a boot lace out of place. "You say to them, 'Guess what, Recruit? We know why the Marine Corps is the best: attention to detail. If we go off to war, that's what's going to get you, that attention to detail.'" The USMC Training and Education Command website states, "Incentive training serves as a constant reminder and habit-forming tool for the recruits to police themselves."[48]

In the publicly available discourse of the United States Marine Corps, then, IT is officially named, carefully described, and highly rationalized. DIs also carry "IT cards" in their front pockets that include regulations and reminders about safety limits, such as the maximum duration of certain exercises. By rule, DIs are to check their watches to be sure they aren't going beyond regulations. The card also includes such reminders as how to spot signs of heat exhaustion. The Training and Education Command website states that "under no circumstances is a recruit to be pushed beyond his or her physical limitations."[49]

The unpleasantness of IT may also be justified to recruits on the spot. Staff Sergeant Brian Akers makes the process sound quite reasonable.

> You just don't grab a recruit and say, "Get on the quarterdeck." You explain to the recruit why [they] are up here. Let the recruit know where he is deficient, and you are correcting the problem.... You explain to the recruits as if you would in marksmanship training. If a recruit is not shooting well then let him know what he is doing wrong. IT is no different.[50]

In this rendering, IT is a logical part of the learning process, and recruits understand the reasoning and internalize the idea that these painful exercises aren't gratuitously punitive. In conversation with me, Carlos remarks that "with IT, for myself, I'm gonna be firm, but fair. If you don't do it to my standard I will keep you back and make you do it again, but if you do, I will be fair."

Such presentations of IT give the impression that its protocols have been vetted by physicians and education professionals. The Training and Education Command website is reassuring to prospective Marines and, perhaps, their parents: "Incentive training provides recruits with an instilled urge to do well and stay squared away Marines down the line. Most Marines have fond memories of IT, and it more than likely carries with it a sense of quickly checking oneself over to ensure that one is squared away in mind, body and soul."[51]

But despite the careful rationalizations behind IT as an enforcement of order, its assignation is often unpredictable and notoriously unfair.[52] Not only that, but it is sometimes intermingled with another kind of interactive routine popular in Marine Corps training—a routine I probably saw taking place among those recruits pulling their clothes on and off in confusion. Unlike IT, this genre of routine has no official name, but recruits sometimes refer to it as "being messed with," "games," or, more colorfully, "fuck-fuck games." I call them "head games," to emphasize the way they mess with expectations of human interaction, bearing intimations of a *dis*ordered moral and symbolic universe.

Head games do not happen at a designated time or place, and they can be mixed into IT and many other aspects of recruit life. They are not explained or rationalized, nor do they appear in the public-facing literature by the Marine Corps—instead, they seem to dwell somewhere just below the threshold of "official" recruit life. Different head games share a family resemblance—namely, the demand that recruits do something absurd or pointless, sometimes placing them in an impossible bind. Jack, the former

DI in his sixties, gives me a couple of classic examples: "making someone move sand from one pile to another with a spoon, then back into another pile," or a "'white out,' where after everyone makes their racks [beds] the DIs come through and pull everything apart, pull everything out of the lockers, and make the recruits fix it up again." (I've heard other Marines refer to this gambit as "the tornado.")

Other "games" include making recruits roll around or press their faces into the sand pit in their own sweat and sunscreen until coated with a crunchy layer of sand (called "sugar cookies"), telling recruits to "go mop the rain from the parking lot," making them chase after airplanes taking off on an airbase, making them clean up their own toothpaste and shaving cream after DIs squirt them like silly string, or (an oldie but goodie) making a whole platoon dig a hole to give a burial to a sand flea killed by a swatting recruit (you're not supposed to swat them when DIs are looking).[53] Recruits may have to disentangle their footlocker padlocks out of a giant snarl of intertwined locks or carry their mattresses into the shower room—and yes, the mattresses may be "showered," making for a wet night. Patrick Turley describes the day a DI ordered his platoon to hold their mattresses on the ground while standing at attention and then, impossibly, to lift the mattresses into their arms and rest them on their shoulders to "inspect" their "empty chamber" as if they were rifles. On one hike (or "hump"), two of Turley's DIs sent a recruit back and forth between them to deliver increasingly ridiculous messages, making it clear they were toying with the runner.[54] And some head games include sexually humiliating overtones—crab-walking naked, swapping underwear, and the like. Most of these games go by without remark, but occasionally a DI goes too far and gets caught. One young veteran reports his DI was expelled from the Corps after telling his platoon if they "laughed one more time they'd be playing fuck-fuck games," whereupon he squeezed everyone naked into the shower, "nut to butt," and made them repeatedly squat and stand together.[55]

Ramon, the DI who served at Parris Island in the 1980s, told me of his pleasure in theatricalizing irrationality. Sometimes he folded this into the physicality of his yelling; when a new platoon arrived, he would allow a seemingly level-headed DI to address recruits first, then "charge in, yelling and screaming, and spit's foaming out of [my] mouth. Actually, I used to put an Alka-Seltzer tab in my mouth so that when I was yelling and screaming, the foam would come out." Ramon's evocation of a rabid animal was canny; DIs are terrifying partly because they seem to have lost touch with their humanity and, sometimes, their mind. Recruits are startled as they realize that rationality has gone out the window.

On occasion, Ramon purposefully concocted an absurdly false rationale for punishing recruits, making sure that everyone understood the charade.

> I used to take my recruits to dinner. You'd march them as a platoon to dinner. . . . I would pick up an orange, and they would see me pick up that orange. I'd throw it up like a baseball and walk to the barracks. As soon as they come into the barracks, they would all line up in front of their duty huts, and I'd take the orange and I'd roll it down the middle of the squad bay, and I would go, "I want to know who brought this orange into my house." They're all looking, and nobody's saying anything. You know, start screaming and yelling. It's all just—you're tensing them up. They know it's me [who took the orange]. [Then I'll] go up to one kid saying, "Tell me what you did. You don't want to talk? So get down and give me twenty." So finally, some brave soul will stand up and say, "I did it." I'll go, "You see? Was it that hard?"

Recruits may have to play into a lunatic fiction and sacrifice themselves for the group to bring a head game to a close. Sometimes, however, they're given an order that is truly impossible to carry out, underscoring the absurdity of the exercise. In one video clip on YouTube, a DI calls out a recruit for looking at him, then screams a series of rapid questions and orders:

> "Did I say look at me?"
> "No, sir."
> "Come here. Come here. Did I say look at me?"
> "No, sir."
> "Why are you still looking at me?"
> "No, sir. I dunno sir."
> "Look at the ground. Look up. Look at the ground. Look up. Look at your own face."[56]

Another common mechanism for creating anxiety and frustration during head games is to give orders "by the numbers" by counting backward, often rapidly. The order may be along the lines of, "Go touch that wall in three, two, one—now touch the opposite wall, three, two, one—touch the first wall . . . ." These countdowns may be used on any occasion when an order is given, including those with clear purpose, but they are bound to culminate in punishment when the DI starts from a number too low to be realistic. Here's Ryan describing some details to me:

RYAN: Oh, did anybody tell you about getting dressed by the numbers?
JANET: Yes. They'll count, they'll count down, right?

RYAN: Yes, but it's unrealistic. There is no way. It's not really doable. If they're, if they're doing it by the numbers, it's to fuck with you, because it'd be unattainable. "All right, take that left boot off now. Three, two, one." There are twenty-six laces or whatever on the boot; there's no fucking way. "Oh, good. You want to move slow? Put that left boot back on now. Three, two, one. Oh, good. You want to move slow? Let's go outside."

The recruit rushes their movements, sometimes chaotically. Some report they can "hardly think" during these instances; they merely obey, but they may still be punished in spite of their best efforts.[57]

At the Brig & Brew bar at Parris Island, sitting on wooden chairs on a cool April evening, the matter of head games arose among the DIs as we chatted. Said one, "You take a piece of paper and you roll a pencil into it really tightly. When it comes out, that paper wants to curl. You assign a recruit to use his hands to smooth it until it goes flat. It won't. I've made a grown man cry with this." Another broke in: "I could spend ten minutes, fifteen minutes, and I could have a kid crying just from playing 'two sheets and a blanket.' Easy." (I was too embarrassed to ask what 'two sheets and a blanket' was on the spot. Reddit was to answer the question, later.[58])

Grady explained a countdown technique to me as we sat facing each other on deck chairs. He leaned back, holding the neck of his beer bottle casually between two fingers. An older DI walked by and looked at me inquisitively. "This your wife?" "I wish," said Grady, enjoying the sexual innuendo typical of Marines, and the other two guys we were sitting with laughed knowingly. (Grady had already taken some ribbing from the retired Marines for taking me onto the porch and handing me a beer.) Explaining some head games of his own, Grady said, "We're training people into paying attention." He gestured toward my beer with a finger. "Put your bottle down, five, four, three, two— " I quickly set the bottle on the table. He adopted a harsher tone.

"Did I say put it down with your right hand? Pick it up again. Now put it down with your left hand, fivefourthreetwo— See? You're paying attention now." He gestured at my jeans. "How many inches are your jeans cuffed?"

"Maybe one and a half inches?" I said uncertainly. He fixed his gaze on me.

"One-point-five inches? Are you SURE? How do you know? You didn't measure. Take off your clothes." I laughed nervously. I was reminded of the sexual minefields so many female recruits, and some males, have to navigate. And even within the fleeting frame of this little make-believe demonstration, I was struck by the way Grady seemed to enjoy his power, and the implication, however subtle, that he could cross ordinary boundaries.

Head games grind recruits through states of confusion, frustration, and humiliation. Lieutenant Colonel Michael Becker, commander at Parris Island in the 1990s, explained one rationale of this training strategy to journalist Thomas Ricks. "From the recruit's perspective, it appears to be chaos. War is chaos. And then they see this Drill Instructor—this magnificent creature who brings order to chaos. They learn that if they follow orders, their life will be calmer."[59] In a similar vein, the former DI Jack said to me, "It's all mind games," designed to inculcate "discipline. Discipline," he continues, "is the instant and willing obedience to orders," implying that being barraged by pointless, frustrating head games enhances one's willingness to obey orders without asking for a rational meaning behind them. One Marine wryly tells me the only way to get through head games is to abandon all efforts to understand. "Forget that you have a brain," and just do as you're told.

Following orders without question is clearly an objective of head games, yet notice again the tension with the expectation that recruits should assess whether orders are lawful (a tension observed by Ethan, the military lawyer I describe in the Introduction), and notice the violation of the guidelines requiring respect for recruit dignity. Notice, too, that some DIs also seem to enjoy their cruel and witty innovations, suggesting a sadistic streak. Indeed, other onlookers have reported how much amusement DIs can take in their own head games. One DI tells a journalist how humorous he finds it when recruits stumble and fall or cry because of his nonsensical orders. The journalist asks, "Did you ever get together and say, 'You won't believe what I had these guys do?'" The DI replied, "Absolutely. . . . That's when you know you have a great team. . . . We'd be dying laughing."[60]

As DIs laugh at the spectacle of recruit suffering, they highlight how readily others' pain can be written off. In fact, by actively taking pleasure in that suffering, they signal approval of the wide gap between the DI's and the recruits' experience; one party is empowered, amused, even, while the other party's suffering simply doesn't count. I am struck, too, that some Marines look back on the torment with amusement themselves. A 2021 article in a widely read military publication (*Task & Purpose*) solicited readers' accounts of the "funniest military punishments" they knew of.[61] One account reads,

> We had a guy who was not too bright. He screwed something up when we were at the range, so my drill instructor made him face the mirror. The drill instructor then told him to yell things at the mirror and point, "You're stupid!" "I'm not stupid. You're stupid" "NO! I'M NOT STUPID, YOU'RE STUPID!" Each time, it escalated. I still believe that the kid at some point really was arguing with himself.

Another account from the Army concerns a recruit considered "DUMB" who "drooled and his nose was always running." When he showed up to formation with his boots on the wrong feet, the Drill Sergeant made him repeat, "I'm a pimp, I walk with a limp, I wear my shoes on the wrong feet." The raconteur adds, "The way he stuttered, snorted and drooled his way through that sentence made it hilarious for the entire 9 weeks we were there."

The atmosphere created by DI treatment of recruits seems infectious in the sense that head games appear to prepare recruits to violate moral norms. When DIs display exuberance in irrational behavior, it suggests that within a militarized mindset, logic and conventional morality can be upended. DIs' overt enjoyment in causing humiliation also provides recruits with a model for ignoring or even taking pleasure in the enemy's suffering during combat. Reflecting on such dynamics, Miles Lagoze reflects after his tour in Afghanistan that "our DIs had given us the gift of laughter[,] the ability to find the suffering of other people absolutely tickling."[62]

My interpretation of head games resonated with some Marines I showed it to. One, who served in Afghanistan, wrote to me after reading some of my draft material.

> I kept getting hit with flashbacks and old memories from my own experience, while learning about the underlying mechanisms behind the stuff that happened, and the function of the DIs behavior. While it may not be totally calculated on the part of the DIs (they'll say it's just about tradition, discipline, whatever), the institution keeps perpetuating the same behavior for a reason. I was struck by how well you dissect the "fuck fuck games" and ITing, and it made me realize there is a kind of sexual-humor-death balance going on in the unwritten rules vs. the written ones that I think directly relates to war crimes and other "misbehaviors" that happen overseas. The gruesome, unsettling stuff we laugh about in country would not be funny without having gone through bootcamp first, and witnessed the absurd behavior of the DIs, which facilitates this accustomization to the horrific, in a way.

All in all, the semiotic techniques of rule violations and "head games" are multifunctional. They break down recruits' comfort through humiliation and anxiety while demonstrating the contingency of rules and old moral bedrock. Their senselessness, non sequiturs, and sadism may also have a kind of productivity, offering a template for the cruel and sometimes pointless absurdities of combat. Yet they cannot announce themselves as pedagogy, because the lessons are so contrary to what we conventionally imagine learning is supposed to be about—and contrary to public advertisements of military training as a value-laden framework.

Recruits do not always register the contradictions inculcated by their training. Some also believe that hazing is an ultimate good, because it teaches

Marines to put their discomfort in perspective while furnishing a positive bonding mechanism.[63] And consider Patrick Turley's summation of his time at boot camp. His DIs routinely struck recruits, made them drink water until they vomited, and played such extreme head games that, Turley writes, "every day [at Parris Island was] the equivalent of being mentally raped." His lowest point was when he was notified on the firing range that his father had died unexpectedly and he would have to go home on emergency leave. Before he could go, some DIs on the range "found me.... They tied my hands behind my back with duct tape and began pushing me around, yelling that I was 'nasty' and that 'the Marine Corps didn't want me, anyway' and spitting in my face." Turley was stunned but returned after a week to complete his training. A few pages later in his account, he proudly states, "Since I've gotten here, I've learned being a Marine isn't about action, being in shape, and looking good in a uniform. I've learned it's about honor and integrity and standing for what is right."[64] Turley leaves the tension unspoken: "honor and integrity" were preached by the same men who inflicted "mental rape."

Chapter 5
"Mothers of America" and "A Woke, Emasculated Military"

Marine Corps veteran Will Price, in his memoir of basic training, remarks Drill Instructors (DIs) have "had a lot of their power taken away from them in recent years.* They still abuse us for sure—that's their job—but it's not like it used to be, when they could do just about anything and get away with it."[1] Price himself wishes the discipline were harsher, "because some of these nasty recruits need a lot more punishment than they're getting." In a similar vein, several veterans I spoke to defended recruit abuse as a useful lesson about the hard knocks to come. Some worried about cultural changes that have influenced young people to demand institutions pay more attention to their feelings and sensitivities. A retired DI, Fred, griped about the winds of change while we ate scrambled eggs and toast at a Parris Island mess hall early one morning in 2019. "What are they going to give these Marines at graduation," Fred asked with a rhetorical flourish. "A dress? But then," he went on, "it's a whole generation of entitled liberal snowflakes."

I was curious to know what Ryan would think about all this. She had served in the Marine Corps for several years before and after 9/11 and was involved in heavy combat and killing that still torments her. I told her about one of my conversations at Parris Island.

"Some of the active-duty Drill Instructors were talking about how 'Oh, we can't stand it now. It's this young generation. They're so savvy and manipulative. They know that when the recruits start talking about, thinking about self-harm, we have to send them straight to the "wizard" [the DIs' sardonic term for a military psychologist]. We have to take it seriously. But, in the good old days—'"

"—in the good old days," Ryan echoed, knowingly.

I continued to narrate the DIs' position. "'We didn't have to take it seriously. We could just keep pulverizing them.' So now, they're [like], 'What do we do?'

---

* This chapter analyzes words and imagery that may be difficult for some readers to encounter. Please see the "Content Warning and Note on Language" in the front matter for some context and a discussion of the author's reasons for not redacting this material.

Kill Talk. Janet McIntosh, Oxford University Press. © Oxford University Press (2025).
DOI: 10.1093/9780197808054.003.0006

The wider culture is saying, 'Hey, it's not okay for you to be tormenting people to the point of them wanting to take their own lives during basic training.' But some of the DIs are like, 'But we have to.' What do you think of all this stuff?"

Ryan had strong opinions. "I think that it's—okay, let's be real. If you can't handle it, I don't want you standing next to me with a gun when the shit hits the fan. I want you to go home and cry to mommy. Like, go now, from boot camp. Bye."

"So there is something to it."

"Yeah, we're not, we're not talking about the kid you want to work at Macy's next to, you know? If you can't fucking handle it, how do I know you're going to haul my freaking bloody ass corpse out of a bad situation alive? I don't. You're a fucking puss. Bounce."

Fred's and Ryan's invocations of dresses and pusses and crying to mommy frame antiabuse efforts as problematically feminine and antithetical to a strong military. Fred also links it to the bleeding-heart political left wing. Their stances speak to a broader issue concerning gender and the military—not just service members' strong or weak bodies, but gendered relations within the nation. In the 1980s, feminist scholar Jean Bethke Elshtain argued that American women's given role in war was to sacrifice their sons, even as men learn to sacrifice themselves while taking other lives. This framework made for a sentimental view of mothers weeping in their bedrooms but almost sacred because of it—"beautiful souls" virtuously looking after hearth and home.[2] By contrast, a dominant framework I found in the Marine Corps derides the image of mothers at home weeping for their recruit children, because their emotional and linguistic sensitivity could imperil the very nation. This framework articulates with a broader conservative structure of feeling that has old roots but new strength since the rise of President Donald Trump and far-right Republicans in the US.[3]

In this chapter, I trace a thread between the military discourse about problematic maternal figures and the conservative hostility in the United States toward what they snidely refer to as "PC" (politically correct) or "woke" language and political attitudes. I show that these hostile stances, circulating through both military and civilian life, endorse ruthless language and ruthless deeds—and correspondingly strict limits on empathy—as crucial underpinnings of hard masculine realism important to national security.

As I hope I have made clear, the United States military is internally politically diverse and divided about matters such as harsh training. Many military officials are intent on fostering diversity and inclusion and addressing sexism and abuse, while initiatives from the Military Equal Opportunity office aim to transform the culture from within. Some current and former DIs, like Tyler Boudreau, feel that harsh training is a mistake because it risks "alienating" recruits from the institution. After all, he tells me, the military needs to respond to the cultural moment and accommodate the shifting tolerance levels of the young generation they need to work with.

But veterans, politicians, and civilians who lean conservative tend to align with the idea that when the military prioritizes comfort, it imperils the nation. Hard realities mean that some must suffer—service members on the one hand, enemies on the other—for the good of the USA. Those who are vulnerable or marginalized, furthermore, deserve no special sensitivity or concessions. Understanding this structure of feeling helps us refine our understanding of American military masculinity, while explaining why the linguistic infrastructure of kill talk has been so resilient in the face of objections from both within and without the military.

Mothers of America

The image of the worried mother seems a common preoccupation for several of the former Drill Instructors I spoke to. Sitting at a banquet table during the Drill Instructors reunion, for instance, one DI remarked to his peers,

> You know, San Diego is next to the airport. You got the guys at the airport control tower looking over your parade grounds! Mark here could see his own house from the depot. It means there's more surveillance, so it's harder to be a hat [a DI]. You got mothers looking on saying, "You're abusing my baby!"

Some Marines, anxious about softening training practices, have invoked a bugbear they call "Mothers of America." The phrase can be found in an old marching cadence that sets up a sardonic tension between weak mothers and hardened Marines: "Mothers of America, meek and mild / Send to me your sweet young child / We'll make him drill and we'll make him run / We'll make some changes in your young son."

It turns out there is no such organized group as "Mothers of America," but many Global War on Terrorism Marines and other veterans I spoke to believed that the phrase designates a real organization—some kind of regulatory agency, perhaps, or at minimum a vocal collective that meddles with basic training by advocating for recruit rights or safety. Ryan, for instance, told me for a long time she had believed that "Mothers of America didn't like seeing their kids in such bad shape at graduation, so they objected, and now the end of the Crucible [the grueling three-day final test in boot camp] is a few days before graduation so their kids can clean up." Johnny said when he went through Parris Island in 2005, "One thing they'd constantly say was, 'Because of those Mothers of America we can't do anything! You guys have it so easy.... We can't go as hard as we had it.'" Louis, who trained a few years after Johnny, similarly described Mothers of America as an organization that had pressured the Corps to lighten the stresses of basic training.

> I guess in the past when recruits went to basic [training] there had to be someone who advocated for the rights of recruits.... So even though our rights were limited, they had to, you know, keep something there.... Like, we always had to have at least three meals a day. Obviously water. I'm not really too sure what else Mothers of America regulate. I know they at least have some influence in all branches of service.

Marine Corps veteran Michael, who went through Parris Island in the 2010s, also had the sense that Mothers of America were an influential organization—and that they were imperiling Marines overseas.

MICHAEL: The DIs made a note of telling us constantly that, it's the Mothers of America that don't let us hit you.
JANET: I've heard this, yes.
MICHAEL: So, you're being made to be like less—you're being made weaker because of the Mothers of America and if you die in war it's because, it's going to become their fault that you die in war.
JANET: Were they saying, like, "Mothers of America" as in capital letters, as an organization?
MICHAEL: Yeah, that's the sense that I got, but I never looked into it after, but it was like they had organized and that they were behind all the changes that took place.

These mythic "mothers" represent forces of sympathy and feminine weakness that threaten to get in the way of the suffering many Marines feel is crucial to basic training. Maternal tenderness thus may imperil the safety of soldiers in combat. No wonder recruits' mothers are recurrently insulted by DIs in basic training, as DIs work overtime, they believe, to cut the apron strings.

One Facebook page that had almost forty-four thousand followers before it was removed around 2022 was titled "MARINES AGAINST MOTHERS OF AMERICA," in all caps.[4] The page itself had little content, but it linked to another (now defunct) page on "causes.com" where Marines and USMC veterans complained that "mothers" were trying to make basic training too easy.[5]

Consider these contributions from 2013, when commenting was fairly active. (All errors are original to the postings. I have redacted the posters' names for privacy, except to clarify that one of the below posters has a feminine name. All the other names are masculine.)

- C—— B——: Put a stop to the downward slope of my generation, starting with the country's elite warriors. Cut your goddamn umbilical cords, pussies. Stop whining and be a MAN (or woman).
- A—— R——: I have a saying that fits the mothers of america, pussification of a nation . . . carry on!
- M—— S——: As being a Marine and no longer being in I think Mothers of America need to leave the things that the Marine Corps did back when I was in 6 years ago alone not step in. Its the Marine Corps its suppose to be hard!

Or this exchange between two participants in 2015:

- K—— B——: Mothers of America makes boot camp for females easy and doesn't prepare them for the real Marine Corps.
- C—— D——: I agree I served from 07–12 and they were trying to make boot camp easier for boys becoming men while I was in. I don't agree with that and when they are in combat will mothers of america come and save them from those towel head fuck by saying oh its to hard on him you can't do that you have to stop.

On the Facebook page, someone wrote, "The tree hugging mothers should no [know] nothing that happens at boot camp." Basic training should be, in other words, a black box to civilians, especially maternal "tree huggers," the latter term being a classic disparagement for empathic leftists. A poster under the name Sylvia W. countered, "But we do [know what happens in boot camp], so now what? Would you like it if your family turned their back on you?" J—— S——, Marine veteran, responded,

> It's about letting the marine corps and the DIs do their jobs. . . . When I see a kid cry every night cause its too much or he got hit to be corrected and he writes home to mommy and she contacts their congressmen to do something about it and now u have kids getting passed along and graduate. Then god forbid they have to see combat they cant [sic] handle it.

One D—— M—— conceded that "Marine Corps training is hard, difficult, probably inhumane and sometimes unethical," but the Corps needs to "weed out those who aren't fit to do it" and oppose anyone who "meddles" with the training. Others called Mothers of America "smothering" and "overprotective" and asserted that they are "crippling the Marines," saying, "Coddling is not an option." Added B—— C——, "When I was in, when we got promoted we got pinned, where they smacked the chevrons in." In other words, the new insignia supposed to be pinned to clothing was literally pounded into the flesh of the chest. He goes on: "Mothers found out, protested and now if its done its quiet.... It was a long tradition and u were happy to have it done."

Only one contributor to this "Marines Against Mothers of America" group, M—— C——, noted that he searched the internet and could find no trace of an actual group named "Mothers of America." He concludes the notion of the group is "mostly a rumor and an urban legend," which got started because of references to "moms back in the real world who wine about little Johnny being yelled at." When I asked Ramon, the DI who served in the '80s, whether Mothers of America was real, he said,

> No, it's not. But if I had a son, and he wrote [a letter of complaint from boot camp] and I read it, I'd tell him, "Take a teaspoon of cement and harden up." If my wife read it, [she'd say], "Oh my God, what are they doing to my baby? I need something done." Because, to be quite honest, women are just very sensitive, and that's the way it should be. [But] the mothers of America could make the job hard.

"Mothers of America," then, has been a convenient effigy, a mythical construct to assail. The concept emerges from a felt crisis of military masculinity that has been extended to anxiety about national security. It is a metonym for empathic or nurturing principles—loosely mapped onto women, young generations, and the political left wing—that might compromise military necropolitics—that is, the state's need to make infantry into potential killers who might also die. Although men and women alike, including many within the Department of Defense, have objected to military hazing and abuse, the phrase "Mothers of America" essentializes such criticism as primarily a matter of feminine handwringing and harping.

Empathy Politics

"Mothers" aren't the only weak link in the nation. Fred's anxiety that Marine Corps strength is imperiled by a "generation of liberal snowflakes" emerges from a nationally widespread conservative idea that liberals (especially younger ones) are excessively fragile.[6] Liberals themselves would probably retort that they are not fragile so much as attuned to their own emotional states, as well as empathic with the vulnerable—an imperative that drives certain left-wing political priorities. For although empathy is a ubiquitous human capacity, its cultivation (or not) is a social achievement, ideologically played up or down depending on contingencies of the historical moment and social group. Among many left-leaning Americans these days, empathy has become a leitmotif—an ideal that informs everything from parenting and teaching to professional life and the deeds of the state.

When it comes to politics, American liberals and progressives have increasingly valorized what could be called "empathy without borders" as a humanistic moral virtue.[7] The political ramifications are widespread, and one implication is that the state should recognize and be considerate to those who have experienced marginalization, particularly along lines of gender, sexual orientation, and race. This heightened sensitivity plays out in legislation while fostering widespread attention to "trauma," based on the notion that harsh life events can damage the psyche. Leftist discourses of empathy without borders capture a utopian ideal, however unevenly followed in practice, and this ideal aligns with a reluctance to send troops to war and the notion that abuse should be disallowed in military training.[8]

To many Americans whose politics lean right, however, the left's emphasis on empathy is excessive. They argue that the concept of trauma is too often used as an excuse for inaction or incompetence. Liberals' heightened valorization of feelings, they claim, fosters a "victim mentality" that weakens both individual character and American society as a whole. Furthermore, a prevalent right-wing discourse suggests that the left's focus on emotions stems from an infantile dependence on parental figures such as nurturing mothers, concerned teachers, coddling institutions, and the welfare state. George Lakoff highlights this contrast, noting that conservative views of the state often follow a "strict father" model, while liberal views align with a "nurturant parent" model.[9]

Another aspect of right-wing skepticism concerns the seemingly infinite generosity of empathy without borders, which could spread resources dangerously thin. They argue it is better to protect and strengthen the in-group, though the definition of this in-group varies among conservatives. (Is it "Americans," plain and simple? Or those Americans deemed better "patriots," often implicitly defined as fellow conservatives? Or is the in-group overtly defined by cultural or phenotypic whiteness?) In such frameworks, policymakers cannot afford to dwell on the suffering of, say, the millions languishing in prison, would-be immigrants broken by the Sonora Desert or by harsh treatment in ICE detention, or Muslims feeling disenfranchised by a refusal to support their new mosque. The first Trump administration epitomized this antiempathic stance toward immigrants, minorities, and other marginalized groups, with supporters donning T-shirts proclaiming "Fuck your feelings." Such dynamics led journalist Adam Serwer to claim that "the cruelty is the point" of the Trump era.[10] In contrast, when President Biden made his first remarks to the nation as president-elect in November 2020, he presented the ideological counterpoint, stating, "The people have chosen empathy."[11] Trump will be inaugurated for his second presidency as this book goes to press in 2025, and to the extent the he controls the tide, it will once again shift direction.

"Win Wars or Be Politically Correct?"

The state's interaction with potentially vulnerable service members has been a matter of intense concern within the military, as noted in Chapter 3. The need to recruit and sustain an all-volunteer force since the repeal of the draft has meant that in recent decades, the services have initiated various reforms to appeal to broader racial, ethnic, and gender demographics. The Defense Equal Opportunity Institute has been strenuously working to curtail racism and gender-related discrimination, while making an impassioned argument that "Total Force readiness" hinges on inclusion.[12] Pentagon officials have also been mindful of the toll of veteran suicide rates and have pushed for more mental health related resources. The 1991 Tailhook scandal brought sexual politics into the spotlight, bolstering efforts to make the military sensitive to women, while activists have pushed the military toward greater inclusion for LGBTQ+ individuals, sometimes including education about gender-neutral pronouns. Today, military policies help gay service members move to states where they can be legally married and (since the repeal of Roe vs. Wade) fund service members to travel out of state to obtain an abortion.[13] And some members of the high command promote mentorship rather than mere domination among drill masters—partly as a concession to younger generations who expect more care.[14] At Parris Island, some Drill Instructors restrain themselves accordingly, aware that not all recruits will respond well to harsh treatment. A DI named Miguel told me, "If someone's been yelled at at home their whole life, it may not have a good effect." They might respond better if you hold them up as an example: "'Everyone notice how recruit Johnson just did that? Do it like he does.' And recruit Johnson will respond to that."

But such initiatives and gestures toward sensitivity have met with variable support from different presidential administrations and have precipitated a tug of war among military players concerning military identity. After all, the multibranched and sprawling United States Armed Forces are hardly a political monolith. Some young people join the military before they have formulated clear political opinions; once enlisted, they may see their role as following orders, no matter who the Commander in Chief is. Those willing to express a political allegiance are divided. On the one hand, a numeric majority of active-duty service members and veterans identify as Republican when polled,[15] and recruiting efforts probably exacerbate this trend by focusing on the southern states because conservative values of aggressive masculinity and respect for authority are more prevalent there.[16] And yet, about a third of troops tend to prefer Democrat candidates, while some military leaders have been vocal in their critiques of Donald Trump.[17]

Not surprisingly, conservatives inside and outside of the military have argued for decades that changes in the direction of inclusion and sensitivity are downright dangerous to national security. Journalist Stephanie Gutmann, author of the 2001 book *A Kinder, Gentler Military: How Political Correctness Affects Our Ability to Win Wars*, argues that training standards and America's war readiness began to decay in the 1990s. Between the need to recruit and the rise of peacekeeping and humanitarian missions (or "playing social worker to the world"), the physical strength and aggression key to military success started to take a back seat to feminization and psychological comfort.[18] This shift coincided with heightened linguistic sensitivities, described by one Staff Sergeant in 1998 as overweening concern about "what you say, how you say it, and to whom do you say it."[19] But serious fighting, says Gutmann, involves "triage" that requires setting aside not only luxuries but also simple human decency, for the "values" of the battlefield have little to do with liberal society.[20]

Gutmann's book was rapturously received by conservatives, and online comments reflect the nerves she struck. The remarks of Guttmann's supporters recurrently associate femininity, empathy, and "PC" liberalism with the prospect of losing wars. A military wife writes in an Amazon review, "The military is now beginning to learn that the practices utilized in order to make the military seem more palatable to the masses have been mistakes.... You will have servicemembers bending over backwards to be PC, rather than to look after their jobs and duty to their countrymen." A former Marine Corps officer conflates women's bodies with military weakness when he writes, "The nation can't have a kinder, gentler, pregnant, military and defeat the barbarian hoards [sic] that we face." And an Army veteran who fought in Vietnam titles his review, simply, "Win Wars or be Politically Correct?"[21]

Not long after Gutmann's book sparked national conversation, other veterans defended the importance of harsh language in basic training. In the online comments following a 2004 article wondering whether the Marine Corps training had "gone too soft," dozens complained about the Corps cosseting recruits. "All this PC shit about 'harsh language,'" writes one in disgust.[22] Responding to a recruit who complained about his treatment, one veteran likened harsh military language directly to the importance of strict parenting:

> As a parent when raising kids I used a few words to my kids that perhaps were not politically correct and smacked them when the need was there and their little egos did not get damaged and they have gone on to become responsible adults. This little crybaby should be sent home to his Mama so she can cut his meat for him.[23]

On a 2007 NPR show about efforts to make basic training less "mean," a chief Army Drill Sergeant at Fort Leonard Wood Drill Sergeant School explains that he encourages other Drill Sergeants to follow the acronym AURA: "acceptance, understanding, recognition, and appreciation of our soldiers that show up today." One woman caller, "Allison," approved of the change, saying she had backed out of the training process back in the day because she objected to being so insulted. It was so harsh, it made her feel "worthless.... If I'm made to feel like nothing, why do I want to do this for you?" But an Army Sergeant who self-identified as "Ernesto" called in to say that between 1986 and 2007, he noticed this "big difference":

> [Drill Sergeants] are much more delicate in their language because when I train soldiers ... I give it to them loud and extremely filthy. And when I talk, I have a few people say they're insulted by my language. I say, Well, we're not going to go to nursery school, we're going into combat, and if words hurt your feelings, bullets are going to hurt a lot more. And it seems that the soldiers we're getting now [are] much more sensitive and much more delicate.... If you yell at a guy and use profanity that insults his mother, then he's going to say, Well, hell, I don't want to do this anymore, I'll just get myself kicked out.... But I've always felt that the way to keep them in is to give them an *esprit de corps* and a sense of accomplishment, not stroking his hair and kissing his neck and making him feel warm and fuzzy.[24]

Ernesto neatly echoes the concept of semiotic callousing when he explains that emotional sensitivity to words equates with sensitivity to kinetic violence ("bullets"). He sneaks in a whiff of homophobia with his derisive allusion to "stroking [the recruit's] hair and kissing his neck," implying that affectionate impulses could lower military resolve. For Ernesto, to "yell at a guy and use profanity and insult his mother" is the best recipe to create a successfully hardened combatant.

As conservative discourse about the US military continues to thrive, the anxieties and tropes of each successive era join the narrative stream. Over the last ten years, complaints about military training reforms have merged with complaints about liberal college students, sometimes sardonically deemed "social justice warriors" with a "woke" agenda. When the Muslim recruit Raheel Siddiqui took his own life on Parris Island after being harassed by an Islamophobic DI in 2016, online defenders of harsh training adopted the same "snowflake generation" discourse as the former DI Fred, earlier in the chapter. One added, "Hazing? Are you kidding me? What do you want, 'time-outs' and 'safe spaces'?"[25] Meanwhile, an opinion piece in the conservative *Washington Times* complained that President Obama's "politically correct" military would spell doom: "Militaries are used to kill people and break things . . . having a military comprised of social justice warriors won't cut it in the next war."[26]

When Donald Trump appointed the Marine Corps General James Mattis as his first secretary of defense in 2017, Mattis seemed initially to reinforce Trump's politics by issuing a call to review all "unnecessary trainings" so as to focus energy on "warfighting readiness."[27] Regardless of Mattis's intentions, some of my veteran respondents interpreted his words as code: the military was making too many concessions to cultural sensitivity, to nontraditional service members (including gays, who had only just been allowed to serve openly), and to coddling beside the point of the military mission. At the Parris Island parade grounds, a retired Marine named Marty gave me an enthusiastic earful about Mattis. "His nickname was Mad Dog," says Marty admiringly. "He says a lot of things that aren't considered politically correct; you couldn't get away with that now." (Mattis would later distinguish himself by resigning from his position as Donald Trump's Secretary of Defense and accusing Trump of trying to divide the nation. "Politically incorrect," yes, but he clearly had his own moral red line.) During the Trump administration, right-wing watchdog groups also came down hard on the military's diversity and inclusion initiatives.[28]

But the pendulum would swing toward more inclusion efforts under the Biden administration, as the armed forces devoted renewed attention to their "culture and tone." A primary goal, in the words of Sergeant Major Julie A. M. Guerra, would be for "America's sons and daughters [to] come inside of our formations . . . and know that they are safe."[29] The Army held "listening sessions" about racial tensions in light of the Black Lives Matter movement and produced recruitment advertisements such as a 2021 ad featuring an Army corporal with two mothers. Predictably, the alt-right Senator Ted Cruz tweeted in response that the Army had become "woke" and "emasculated."[30]

The term "woke," in African American English, originally meant being attentive to racial and social injustice, but in the mouths of critics it has taken on the same acid tone as "PC" and used to denote hypersensitive and unreasonable political liberalism. Cruz would use the triggering term again in 2022 when he tweeted a response to a 2022 Russian recruiting video featuring a virile-looking young man jumping out of an airplane and firing a rifle at a terrorist. "Holy crap. Perhaps a woke, emasculated military is not the best idea."[31]

Around the same time, right-wing commentator Matt Walsh sardonically titled one of his shows, "Don't Worry. Our Army of Feminists and Gay Activists Will Protect Us."[32] The talk show host Jesse Kelly appeared on *Tucker Carlson Tonight* to rail that "woman-friendly" and "gay-friendly" sensitivities in the military could result in "thousands, maybe tens of thousands, maybe hundreds of thousands of Americans" dying. Instead, he argued, the military should strive to attract and train soldiers who are "flat-out hostile," stocked with "Type A men who want to sit on a throne of Chinese skulls."[33] Carlson himself suggested that Ibrahim Kendi's book on antiracism, assigned to some Navy personnel, was further weakening the military.[34] Other conservative complaints would directly target sensitive and inclusive language. Former Secretary of Defense Mike Pompeo, for instance, wrote an opinion piece for *Fox News* in September 2022 lamenting that Air Force Academy cadets were being told to replace terms such as "you guys" and "terrorists" with terms that have been deemed "less offensive." "We have put pronouns over potency in our fighting forces," he wrote. "This smut is nothing more than repackaged Marxist dogma. . . . A woke military is a weak military."[35] In summer 2023, House Republicans took action by adding an "antiwoke" amendment to a budget bill in order to prevent the Department of Veterans Affairs from reimbursing abortions, subsidizing transgender health care, and flying Pride flags.[36] The members indicated their aim was to "end the Left's cancerous woke policies in the Pentagon undermining our military's core warfighting mission."[37] And Army Veteran Pete Hegseth, Donald Trump's presumptive nominee for Secretary of Defense as of January 2025, complains bitterly in his most recent book about elites in the military who have rendered it "woke and weak."[38] He believes war, though, will quickly re-establish priorities: "Sometime soon, a real conflict will break out, and red-blooded American men will have to save [military officials'] elite candy-asses."[39]

By 2023, representatives of the conservative Heritage Foundation and Republican Senator Tommy Tuberville were repeatedly fretting that "wokeness," with its anxiety about "toxic masculinity," was hampering rather than improving the military's ability to meet its recruiting goals.[40] A June 2023 article by a Navy veteran in the conservative *Washington Examiner* frets about retention, contending that by drawing attention to racial and gender differences, "the core of the woke movement has created aggressive division and intolerance throughout the armed forces, which weakens our fighting spirit." The author goes on:

> The fact that the world's greatest fighting force is now embracing an ideology counter to the warrior mindset is going to turn a lot of people away. The young men and women who want to serve this country do not want to join a culture that shuns warrior tenets and so-called "toxic masculinity" while praising people for being victims.[41]

While some prospective recruits may worry they won't get the bracing initiation they hope for, the Army's own marketing research has debunked the notion that concern about "wokeness" has seriously compromised their numbers. A 2022 survey indicated the main reason young people tend to shy away from military service is the possibility of being injured, killed, or sexually assaulted or incurring PTSD—in other words, being casualties of military violence rather than aggravated by military tenderness.[42]

All in all, conservative discourse conflates disparate liberal efforts—antiracism initiatives, accommodating women in the military, LGBTQ+ inclusivity, suicide prevention, a culture of "listening," and verbal sensitivity—and treats them as intertwined menaces to national security. The wide extension of empathy in "wokeness," furthermore, is repeatedly associated with inadequate military masculinity.[43] A clear casualty in this discourse is empathy for service members who deviate from the prototype of a cisgender male warrior. But the structure of feeling some conservatives recommend for the military is one of aggression without empathy—with the implication that harsh treatment during training can help service members harden their hearts for the enemy when they face outward, fulfilling the necropolitical demands of the state. It does not seem to matter to them that most service members affected by liberal military initiatives will never go to battle, since most service members never deploy into a combat zone.

Over twenty years ago, Stephanie Gutmann worried that the military was falling prey to a "general cultural drift in the United States that brought us, by the century's end, to a government that hovers, wrings its hands, and worries whether everybody's having a good time."[44] Her image of the liberal state, here, is of a neurotic maternal figure whose well-meaning concern will be its own downfall. Between the "Mothers of America" historically hated by Marine Corps DIs and the weak, "feminine" liberalism so hated by conservatives, empathy is repeatedly branded as antithetical to masculinity and thus military success. And with its many impressionistic mappings, conservative discourse treats psychological comfort and well-being among military personnel as outright threats to national security. At the same time, the right-wing discourse in favor of brutality within the military presents a question: how do proponents of military personnel eager to "sit on a throne of Chinese skulls" reconcile such a structure of feeling with the glowing slogans that celebrate "honor" and "integrity" among military super-citizens? Is indifference to suffering the best virtue our nation can offer?

If the nation is spending hundreds of billions of dollars a year on national defense, it behooves Americans—whatever their political stripe—to understand not only our military's international impact, but also its reverberations in the souls of those charged with doing its dirtiest work. Such changes begin in training and continue in the theater of war, when members of the infantry are placed in impossible situations and rely on the linguistic infrastructure of kill talk to help them do their jobs and deny, compartmentalize, and repress the human implications. In the next chapter, I begin to examine some components of this linguistic infrastructure in combat.

SECTION III
COMBAT

Chapter 6
Dehumanization in Combat

In preceding chapters, I described Ryan, the Marine deployed to Iraq in the early aughts, still all sinew, prickling with traumatic memories.* When she enlisted as a teen, Ryan was determined to prove herself worthy after a miserable childhood of abuse. She became a close combat instructor at a training base, teaching the strikes, chokes, and knife techniques that allow Marines to kill hand to hand. She warned me not to touch her inadvertently. "If you come at me from any angle," she told me, "I'm going to annihilate you." When she was "in country" with a light armored infantry, Ryan was involved in dozens of firefights and other deadly encounters as she traveled in vulnerable convoys. The formal prohibition on women in combat proved meaningless. "I have seventeen confirmed kills," she told me more than once, as if still coming to grips with it.

Ryan seemed to enjoy relating the merciless training she received at Parris Island in 1999, just as she enjoyed telling me how she excelled there. "You're not a Marine in boot camp; you're a piece of shit." For Ryan, as for so many others, the verbal callousing seemed necessary to weed out or harden the weak before combat. "If you can't handle it, I don't want you standing next to me with a gun when the shit hits the fan. I want you to go home and cry to mommy. When you're in Afghanistan, no one's going to go, 'Oh, you're too stressed, hold on. Let me put my gun away.'"

Yet Ryan looks back with dismay at her own deeds in Iraq. Being called a scumbag or a Sally was motivating for her in training; her indifference made her feel tough. But the words that dehumanized the enemy, she now thinks, were more pernicious. "From the minute I got to boot camp," she says, her higher-ups were "pumping terms into me," including "towelheads, sand n*****s, and all that." She arrived in Iraq, she says, primed to hate, and assumed she was killing primitive people who liked to murder Americans without cause.

---

*This chapter analyzes words and imagery that may be difficult for some readers to encounter. Please see the "Content Warning and Note on Language" in the front matter for some context and a discussion of the author's reasons for not redacting this material.

The children in Iraq were the pivot point, for her. We sat outside a bar early one October afternoon, elbows on an aluminum table, Ryan drinking vodka and coke while gesticulating angrily with a cigarette. She was telling me the Marine Corps had tried to convince her to treat Iraqi kids as potential enemy combatants.

> They told us, "You can't trust them. They strap them with bombs." The reality is, I didn't see any kids strapped that way. All I ever heard was them telling me that they would strap or shit. And I can't tell you how many kids we fucking shot. How many kids we shot because they told us that shit. And none, no fucking child that I ever fucked up ever had anything on them. So when there was this little boy shot in the leg, I picked him up. You know, I'm a fucking American. You want to kill kids? Do it without me.

Ryan threw the wounded boy over her shoulder to run him behind the line of fire for medical aid. He was holding a sharp piece of metal, "like a shank," and in his fear, he managed to stab Ryan a few times in the back, bloodying her as she carried him. There was something about the incident that made Ryan think. The boy shouldn't have been shot to begin with, and was so terrified, he lashed out at the person trying to bring him aid. He probably thought Ryan was a monster. Maybe some of the Iraqis Ryan had thought were monsters had been all right, too. And maybe the military lines about "towelheads" and kids trying to kill Americans couldn't be trusted after all. The military was steamrolling over Ryan's sense of right and wrong—a moral compass she glosses as being "American."

Ryan goes on, telling me how disenchanted she became about the entire conflict in Iraq. She became convinced that 9/11 was an inside job, because the US had such a strong military presence in the Middle East before 2001. She realized she had heard Islamophobic slurs at Parris Island back in '99. Maybe the US had been cooking up an excuse for a fight. The US military, she concluded, "was already training us to hate the thought of them, before it ever happened. . . . So we just went over there and killed a bunch of families, just because you told us they came over here and did all this shit, but they didn't."

Rethinking her years of service, Ryan leaned back in her chair, propping her knee on the table's edge and running her fingers through a shock of purple hair.

> I lost a shit ton of friends over there. I killed people for [the US government's] lies. And I was so brainwashed into "it's us or them." . . . Once you realize that you killed a bunch of people—they're out *there*. They didn't come over here and

blow up shit. [The US military] fucking brainwashes you so bad, it's like, "You're defending your family, and you're defending your home." You're not. You're just killing people because they were born someplace else. And it's still a lie. And everybody likes to act like, "I did it because I'm a fucking man." In the grand scheme of things, at the end of it all, do you think it matters why you took a life? Don't say. It was still a life. It was still somebody's dad, and somebody's son, and somebody's uncle, and somebody's brother.

Ryan doubts the war made a difference to national security. She doubts the idea that killing in combat is noble because it's supposedly "manly." And she has adopted a completely different stance toward those she killed. The shift from calling someone "towelhead" to calling them "somebody's dad" marks a journey of conscience. Where Ryan once saw ungrievable and nefarious beings, she now imagines socially embedded, loved, and loving fathers, sons, brothers. "A life," in other words. A full human life.

In the last chapters of this book, I explore more of these conceptual journeys among regretful US veterans who have turned to art and writing as they finally imagine the humanity of their putative enemies. In this chapter and the next, I examine the language US combatants in Vietnam and the Middle East used to construe the enemy as deplorable and killable. Taking a human life violates most ordinary ethics and religious precepts, so killing in war is easier if the combatant can reconceptualize the deed as acceptable, perhaps even obligatory, or—at the very least—meaningless. Kill talk offers a conceptual infrastructure that encourages this end.

This chapter focuses on labels that create a linguistic distance from the enemy while positioning them as less than fully human. As I will discuss, racist labels were widely used by Americans in Vietnam, often without question. Times have changed, and some American soldiers fighting in Iraq and Afghanistan opted mainly for technical descriptors such as "the enemy," "insurgents," "hostiles," "enemy combatants," "threats," "targets," or "OPFOR" (used when service members would pretend to be "opposing forces" in training exercises). Some preferred general moralizing terms such as "bad guys" or the playfully profane "shitheads." Others still circulated racial, ethnic, or religious slurs and epithets. Such language is increasingly taboo in mainstream US society, but it remains part of the military's linguistic underbelly.

Although such dehumanizing language does not guarantee dehumanizing thought, nor is it a requirement for killing, soldiers attest that the terms I discuss, when used in the context of combat, are often accompanied by distinctive states of mind.[1] Slurs and epithets constitute the enemy as homogeneous rather than individual, as racially inferior, as lower on the animacy hierarchy (a scale or gradient of how alive, animated, and thus relatable an entity is considered to be), as less vividly thinking and feeling, as less relationally embedded, or as generally less grievable.[2] The potential effect of these terms is not only conceptual (the entity to be killed is not quite a person), but also relational and physical, curtailing the invisible tendrils of empathy while disinhibiting aggression. The linguistic infrastructure offered by slurs and epithets thus aspires to block the extension of empathy outward and encourage the extension of kinetic violence.

Certain terms for the enemy, furthermore, have potential consequences that extend beyond enemy soldiers, for they semantically encompass entire racial, ethnic, or religious communities. Inspired by colonial and Orientalist ideas about racial hierarchies, they conceptually bundle civilians with enemy combatants. Later in the chapter, I also show how US military racism reveals itself in less obvious linguistic moves, particularly the use of "mock language"—the often-mangled terms and phrases borrowed from the language of "the enemy." By distorting Vietnamese and Arabic and using them primarily for derogatory or hostile talk, mock language indirectly derogates the social groups that speak those languages.

Of course, the broad political and kinetic conditions of war establish the framework that anchors and facilitates the potential of these ways of talking. Stateside rhetoric about evil communism or terrorism, for instance, encourages combatants to view the enemy as morally wrong, a threat to the nation, and often as racially inferior. The conditions of battle in Vietnam, Iraq, and Afghanistan—at times chaotic, terrifying, and enraging—further intensified this mindset.[3] Testimonies from veterans, such as those in the documentary *The Ground Truth*, reveal that US soldiers sometimes experienced "peer pressure group killing," whereby those who refrained from killing risked being teased or shamed.[4] The willingness to kill civilians, when it happens, can also be stoked by many factors, including poorly defined rules of engagement, commanders who condone or ignore misconduct, and the psychological extremes of combat.[5]

But the linguistic infrastructure I describe both emerges from and contributes to a broader climate of violence. One soldier in the same documentary notes that in the tight culture of his military unit, without easily available alternatives of talking and thinking, he felt "trapped in the bubble" of dehumanizing the other. In a similar vein, a Vietnam veteran named Dave tells me he felt his thoughts and ultimately actions in Vietnam were constrained and channeled by a closed linguistic system.[6] "In all my training," he adds, "I heard the word 'Vietnam' fifteen times, but I never heard the word 'Vietnamese'. It was 'slope', 'dink', 'gook'. And we were going to 'zap them', 'terminate them', 'grease them'. It was like any genocide."

At the end of the chapter, I present evidence that shifting away from racist and dehumanizing language often coincides with experiential shifts in how a combatant perceives the enemy. The causality here can be hard to discern: does the realization of the enemy's humanity precede a verbal shift or follow it, or do they occur simultaneously? Regardless, some service members eventually adopt new terminology that frames their targets as more human. Many report that wordless encounters—looking into the enemy's eyes or sensing their vulnerability—helped them realize they could not sustain the gap between their dismissive terminology and the actual human being.[7] Still, such feelings of guilt, grief, or mercy hardly affect every soldier. A recent study of Dutch veterans found that many successfully used strategies that included "compartmentalization" to avoid the experience of moral injury.[8] Other soldiers may remain entrenched in anger, fear, or indifference, committed to a militarized worldview that erases the suffering of the enemy. Such individuals may have been especially good at internalizing the infrastructure of meaning offered to the combatant so they can sleep at night.

Dehumanized Dehumanizers

In Chapter 3, I described how Drill Sergeants and Drill Instructors insult recruits to semiotically callous them, hardening them in body and soul. As their superiors address them in these ways, recruits come to sense their own expendability in war. This process may also make them more willing to kill, as they begin to conceptualize themselves as other-than-human. Former Staff Sergeant Camilo Mejia offered his eyewitness account during the 2008 Winter Soldier hearings, an event inspired by the Winter Soldier Investigation of 1971 that heard Vietnam veterans' testimonials about war crimes. Mejia described brutalizing Iraqis at checkpoints and remarked, "You cannot act as a human being and do all of these things."[9] More subtly, when trainers dehumanize recruits, they provide a semiotic example—a tutorial, if you will—of how soldiers might dehumanize the enemy in the field of combat.

This formula isn't consciously recognized by all, but some of my more cynical interlocutors seemed to catch a glimpse of it. In a conversation shimmering with resentment about her service, Tina, a young Army veteran, wrinkled her brow emphatically as she explained it to me, "You have to TAKE OUT a piece of your humanity and then you have to take the humanity out of the enemy side in order to FUNCTION in the military."[10] The relevant aspects of humanity may differ in both cases—the combatant's deficit is in compassionate feeling, while they perceive their enemy as devoid of important suffering or soul—but both are ultimately hollowed out.

A short personal essay by Paul Crenshaw makes the connection between these paired dehumanizations.[11] Crenshaw was in the Army National Guard in 1990 at the start of Operation Desert Storm. He describes the obscene sexual references and occasional identity-based insults his Drill Sergeants used against recruits. Crenshaw himself became "Crankshaft or Cumshot or Cocksucker, depending on who was doing the calling." Others were called "Crotch-face," "Rape Kit," or "Ballsack." A Vietnamese American recruit, starkly enough, became "Gook." Crenshaw believed the Drill Sergeants so named them "to break us down so we could pull closer together," and recruits mimicked this verbal practice, perhaps, he speculates, out of sublimated fear. He writes,

> Our Drill Sergeants were constantly calling us cocks and cunts, threatening us with physical violence. We were scared all the time—of our Drill Sergeants, of the base where we had been sent to train, of the future—and to keep the fear from flying out we flung bravado at one another in our choice of words.

In the final paragraphs of Crenshaw's reminiscence, we see how derogatory epithets for recruits furnish a model for dehumanizing the enemy.

> In our final days of training, as we wound down toward release and finally began to relax a little, Saddam Hussein invaded Kuwait and we were all called together so the Drill Sergeants could tell us we were going to war. We stood there in stunned silence until someone—Talleywhacker, maybe, or Hot Ding-a-ling, said we'd fuck that fucking towel-headed sand [n*****] right in the fucking asshole is what we would do, and we all cheered with our hoarse voices standing there in our young boots.

Reductive Slurs in Vietnam and the Global War on Terrorism

The derogation of the enemy through slurs and epithets, excluding them from ordinary moral rights and obligations, has deep and wide precedents the world over. Before and during the Holocaust, the Third Reich framed non-Aryan people as *Untermenschen*, subhuman, and specifically deemed Jews "rats": animalistic, insidious, and pestilent.[12] During the 1990s genocide in Rwanda, state radio encouraged Hutu people to refer to Tutsi as *inyenzi* (cockroaches) and *inzoka* (snakes), laying the conceptual groundwork for their extermination.[13] Basic training in Europe has historically tended to reduce the enemy to "mad dogs," "vermin," and other such categories.[14]

In the US military, the catch-all term "the enemy" has been widely used in all conflicts. However, in backstage military talk not intended for public ears—at least not these days—racial, religious, and other slurs and epithets have often been employed. In the 1960s and '70s, service members sometimes used terms like "Charlie" to refer to their Vietnamese enemies, but frequently used racist slurs carried over from the Pacific theater in World War II, some of which originated during the invasion of the Philippines (1898–1902).[15] US military personnel also have a history of using the phrase "Indian Country" to refer to unpacified war zones.[16] The phrase invokes "savagery" in the enemy while conflating white conquest and supremacy across eras and battlefields, including Vietnam, Iraq, and Afghanistan.[17] Emboldened by such metaphors and long histories of prejudice, some military personnel during the Global War on Terrorism (GWOT) were prone to use racist and Islamophobic epithets, though authorities in the Department of Defense strove to curtail these, especially once the counterinsurgency campaign was underway, placing an emphasis on "winning hearts and minds."

News footage recorded in Vietnam occasionally reveals how American combatants used such slurs in that era, freely doing so on camera. When Army Lieutenant Conrad Braun gave a televised interview shortly after a battle with the North Vietnamese Army (NVA) in Vietnam's central highlands in February 1967, he dispassionately and repeatedly used the epithet "dinks," underscoring the enemy's faceless killability.[18] Describing how his unit was overrun, Braun says,

> They just tried this sneaky stuff. . . . One time, one dink crawled up on the platoon perimeter and uh, Owen Mapes shot him, shot him in the leg and just uh, left him out there. Dink's two buddies came up to help him out and Mapes just emptied a magazine [of] automatic fire and killed all three of 'em.

In the above excerpt, Braun drops the article to use "dink" as if it's a proper name, highlighting the interchangeability of one enemy to another. Later in the interview, Braun describes how he planned to destroy the personal effects of his fallen comrades and kill himself as his unit was outnumbered. "I was about to just blow it all up with me rather than let dink get it. He definitely wasn't going to get us." In such statements, "dink" becomes a mass noun, a singular "he," as if all "dinks" have merged into one entity, embodying a not-quite-human enemy principle.

At the same time, when "dinks" are differentiated, it is often merely to count their inert bodies. The US administration infamously relied on "body count"—a phrase that erases the subjectivity and social entanglements of the living who die in war—as a spurious means of gauging US success in Vietnam. Accordingly, Braun offered his dispassionate tabulations: "There were dinks in threes and fours piled up outside that platoon perimeter." Near the interview's end as he sums up the carnage, Braun says, "[My buddy killed] about ten, eleven, twelve dinks I think, out there. I think I personally can account for three." He continues, "[The] body count now, I think, is eighty-three." Quantifying the deaths, Braun disregards the suffering; after all, statistics don't bleed.[19] Meanwhile, Braun names, individuates, and humanizes his own buddies—"Owen Mapes," "Spec-4 Jones," "Sergeant Brown"—and describes their acts of valor in the face of grave injuries.

Immediately after the interview, in which Braun uses the term "dink" eleven times, the camera cuts to NBC studio anchor Bill Ryan, who endorses Braun's "professionalism":

> These men . . . have raised American military tradition to the highest level in our history, and they have done it by becoming thoroughly professional soldiers. They could not do less than that and have a reasonable chance to survive in a strange land and a type of war strange to American military experience.

In the 1960s, then, an NBC anchorman, a figure of cultural authority and respect at the time, seemed to accept that epithets for the enemy were the argot of military expertise, seemingly necessary to warfare and to making do in a "strange land."

One would be hard pressed to find mainstream media apologists for such epithets today, particularly considering the shifts in the American zeitgeist that have put a critical spotlight on racist language. Documentary evidence from the twenty-first century suggests it is rare to hear US combatants from the GWOT using racial slurs in front of a camera if they are self-conscious. If popular terms for the enemy in Vietnam were "gook" and "dink," recent combatants are more likely to default to phrases like "the enemy," "this dude," "their guys," or "shitheads." One popular military meme, in fact, makes a nod to this trend, adding a bloodthirsty twist: "It's not about race. It's not about religion. I just like to shoot assholes."

Yet the GWOT still inspired some service members to reach for racist and Islamophobic language, including mocking terms like "towelheads" and "ragheads," "camel jockeys" or "sand jockeys," the overtly racializing "sand n*****s" and "sand gooks," and "hajis," from the Arabic term for a person who has made a pilgrimage to Mecca. Reports from the earliest years of the

GWOT suggest some superior officers flung epithets with vigor. One account describes a senior officer telling journalists, "The only thing these sand n*****s understand is force and I'm about to introduce them to it."[20]

Consider, too, the account of Mike Prysner, who went through basic Army training in 2001 and deployed to Iraq in 2003 with the 173rd Airborne Brigade. Testifying at the 2008 Winter Soldier hearings, he said,

> When I first joined the Army, we were told that racism no longer existed in the military.... We would sit through mandatory classes and every unit had this EO [Equal Opportunity] representative to ensure that no elements of racism could resurface.... And then, September 11th happened and I began to hear new words, like "towelhead" and "camel jockey" and, the most disturbing, "sand n*****." And these words did not initially come from my fellow soldiers but from my platoon leader, my Sergeant, my company first Sergeant, Battalion Commander. All the way up the chain of command... these terms were suddenly acceptable. I noticed the most overt racism came from veterans of the first Gulf War. Those were the words they used when they were incinerating civilian convoys... [and] bombing water supplies knowing that it would kill hundreds of thousands of children.[21]

For at least the first decade of the GWOT, then, some military trainers linked dehumanizing epithets to embodied acts of killing. This happened in spite of the efforts of military EO offices to curtail racist language, suggesting again a gap between officially sanctioned scripts and informal, taboo language in the military. One Army reservist relates that he encountered chants and songs with lyrics such as "kill ragheads, kill Osama bin Laden."[22] At the firing range, he says, commanding officers would refer to the pop-up targets as "Talibans," "bin Ladens," "hajis," or "ragheads." Matt Young reports that during his Marine Corps training in 2005, the Drill Instructors made a similar connection: "Hajiis, they said. Muj, they said. Targets, they said. Do it again, they said. You hesitated, now you're dead. Do it again. And again. And again. Now do it right."[23]

Like Prysner, Geoff Millard—the Washington DC chapter president of Iraq Veterans Against the War—insists the use of the term "haji" was rife at every level of the chain of command in the early years of the Iraq War, up to the highest ranking Army officer during his deployment, General George Casey.[24] Millard also recalls an incident from 2005, a traffic control point shooting, in which a mother, father, and two young children were killed. (Such shootings were a recurrent tragedy at checkpoints. Jittery about suicide bombers, US service members were apt to fire on vehicles at the slightest sign of potential threat, such as a flash of metal inside the vehicle, or the failure to slow.) Millard was present when the incident was briefed to Colonel William

Rochelle of the 42nd Infantry Division. Rochelle turned to his division level staff and said, in what Millard describes as a "very calm manner," "If these fucking hajis learned to drive, this shit wouldn't happen." Millard looked around incredulously and saw not a blink of dissent.[25]

The Racialized Enemy: Polluting, Animalistic, Inhuman

Most of these terms, of course, reflect and perpetuate broader racist histories in the West, emerging from an essentialist notion of a great chain of being that places whites at the top.[26] In the United States' geographic imagination, Vietnam, Iraq, and Afghanistan have been seen as primitive places where the US is entitled to impose its political and extractive will. Racist terminology evokes attitudes not just of superiority, but also of revulsion. As the late anthropologist Mary Douglas famously observed, human beings tend to naturalize their social order by treating those outside it as essentially polluting.[27] Psychological studies confirm that when a single slur targets a person, others tend to distance themselves from that target, consciously or not.[28]

In theaters of war, American combatants sometimes bought into the notion that the enemy carried a polluting essence. One Vietnam veteran told me his platoon called the infections they got from elephant grass "gook sores." Army veteran Marc Levy was so committed to the idea of the Vietnamese as a pestilent species that he recalls one day with particular chagrin. His squad had mowed down nearly everyone in a group of Viet Cong. A young woman fighter survived the hail of bullets, and as Marc walked past her, she clawed at his thermos for water. Marc describes his inner state to me: He could not imagine her as human. He didn't care whether she lived or died, and if she touched his thermos, he told me, he wouldn't drink from its "contaminated" opening again.

The contaminating horror of the enemy other could be invoked by a word but was felt in the body. Marc tells me what it was like to encounter the term "VC" in 1970—an abbreviation for Viet Cong[29] suffused with prejudice when it issued from American mouths. As we sat in his living room, Marc shifted into a hushed voice (written in italics below) as he recalled the way the word itself was both tantalizing and alienating:

> That one drill sergeant . . . talked about *the VC*. . . . It was like something out of the movies. The VC, you know, *they weren't real* [to us recruits]. . . . The way he said it, they were just something taboo. . . . *There's something mythic about them*. They had some kind of aura around them.

Marc added another term: "When you hear that [other word], 'gooks,' it's dread." He clutched his upper arms and shuddered, as if shaking off a chill. The term itself seemed to embody the suspicion and fear that gripped the entire US. As the philosopher Achille Mbembe puts it, the logic of modern war tends to involve the "perception of the existence of the Other as an attempt on my life, as a mortal threat or absolute danger whose biophysical elimination would strengthen my potential to life and security."[30] For Marc and others, terms of reference were enough to invoke this "logic," which was affectively and intracorporeally felt by young American troops.

Beyond their hierarchizing and affective charge, many labels for the enemy promote a conceptually impoverished model of the other.[31] Slurs like "slants," "hajis," and "towelheads" selectively highlight a supposed trait of the group, reducing it to that negative description. As linguist Anna Wierzbicka notes, while most labels group people according to a cluster of properties, hyperbolic epithets that categorize based on a single property indicate that for the speaker, this property "looms so large that it determines his way of seeing the referent, to the exclusion of other properties."[32] This labeling method obscures the enemy's positive or at least complex thoughts and feelings,[33] helping create the psychological distance that can facilitate the act of killing.[34]

American combatants heading to Vietnam, Iraq, or Afghanistan often encountered dehumanizing generalizations about the enemy long before facing them in the flesh. In the Vietnam War era, claims included "They don't grieve for their dead the way we do," "They're not human," "Gooks don't bleed, gooks don't feel pain, gooks don't have any sense of loyalty or love," "The only good gook is a dead gook," and "Dead gooks have a special stink."[35] Vietnam veteran Rion Casey summarized one slur, stating, "Gooks are close to being animals."[36] These myths, posing as citable folk wisdom, construed the enemy as an altogether different species.

Similarly, military personnel propagated hostile generalizations about insurgents in Iraq and Afghanistan during the Global War on Terrorism. Sean Davis recounted that during his Army National Guard training at Fort Hood, a captain instructed him that "the ragheads don't have the common courtesy to give the American soldier a fair fight.'"[37] Other respondents heard claims such as "Towelheads are eager to blow themselves up to make a point" or "You can't trust a haji." These hallucinations were presented as timeless, essential truths, dehumanizing millions of people in one sweep.[38]

The fantasies embedded in wartime slurs become even more evident in the fact that US soldiers of color have sometimes used racist terms for the enemy. The dynamic bewildered Vietnam Veteran and poet Dave Connolly, who once described to me being startled to hear a young Black veteran refer to Iraqis as "sand n*****s." But oral histories of Black veterans who served in Vietnam reveal their use of racial slurs against the Vietnamese.[39] While some, like the renowned poet and veteran Yusuf Komunyakaa, consciously avoided such derogatory language because of its similarities with racism in the United States, this was not universally the case.[40] The experience of being subjected to racism does not necessarily prevent individuals from perpetuating their nation's bigotry.

In fact, when a nation identifies an "enemy abroad," it often triggers a pattern of projection, whereby citizens extend the nation's internal hierarchies to a global level of scale. Anthropologists Susan Gal and Judith Irvine would describe this semiotic pattern as "fractal."[41] The term "fractal" originates from geometry and refers to structures such as ice crystals, tree branches, and fern leaves, in which a pattern at the microlevel recurs at progressively larger scales. Societies sometimes create fractal symbolism that replicates their ideas about local social structure at a broader, international level.

Consider the symbolic oppositions powerful Americans have established to support the idea of their own superiority—male versus female, straight versus gay, white (supposedly racially superior) versus Black (supposedly racially inferior). All of these conceptual oppositions have been deployed in domestic (even household) politics, and in times of war, the US may subtly and not-so-subtly project the stigmatized half of each binary onto the enemy. The military, in other words, could be said to construe itself as symbolically white, masculine, and straight relative to its Others, as these qualities are commonly associated with superiority and strength. Recall, for instance, how Ryan, in Chapter 3, used gynophobic words like "pussy" to derogate civilian-style weakness. According to Jasbir Puar and Amit Rai, for a brief while after 9/11, domestic homophobia in the US was temporarily overshadowed by homophobic discourses about sexuality in the Arab world, even as gays in the US were, in some regards, considered morally recuperated.[42] A similar projection occurs when a Black service member deems an Iraqi a "sand n*****," asserting the Iraqi's inferiority. These fractal dynamics reveal how centrally ideas of "race" are about symbolic domination.

To be sure, as the philosopher David Livingstone Smith reminds us, one "cannot just 'read off' dehumanizing attitudes from the words people use," for language does not always neatly correspond to mental states.[43] Outside of combat, for instance, a speaker might use an epithet with an ironic stance, or as part of an affectionate joking relationship, or—as I am doing now—in an analytical frame, critical of the dehumanization it suggests. Furthermore, since the limits of thought are not strictly determined by the limits of one's terminology in any given utterance, it is entirely possible for one's inner attitude to transcend a reductive term and see an enemy as something more than what the term connotes.

Nevertheless, veterans' testimonials about how words encourage states of consciousness in war are telling. In the introductory chapter, we met John Musgrave, who attests he could not have gone on killing in Vietnam if he had not reframed his targets from "human beings" to mere "gooks." Another Vietnam veteran, my respondent Doug Anderson, affirms this in his poem "Kill Him with a Name": "We were taught to call them gook, / slope, slant, and worse, / because it's easier to kill / that way, easier to sleep at night / if you've merely crushed a roach / under your boot heel."[44] Ivan, who served in the Army in the central highlands of Vietnam in 1969–1970, told me of the role language played in his own willingness to kill.

> You heard gooks, chinks, and stuff of that nature. So it just falls on your ears and you just absorb it.... I was naïve; it didn't register as being racist or anything at the time.... That's how they basically get you to think of the enemy, so you don't have any problem killing them or wanting to.

In summary, many combatants attest that slurs and epithets helped them sidestep the humanity of the enemy, making acts of killing more manageable. The philosopher Giorgio Agamben, who wrote extensively about how political systems determine the conditions for life and death, would recognize these epithets as fostering what he called a "state of exception," in which ordinary laws, political protections, and norms are suspended for certain kinds of people.[45] For combatants, then, such terms distill a justification for suspending the rights of others, whether or not this justification aligns with official governmental rhetoric.

Civilian Casualties

Those who formulate idealized plans for war, of course, hope that violence and dehumanization can be trammeled and aligned with the constraints of the Geneva Conventions and Rules of Engagement. In a passage from a book on military ethics, for instance, two philosophy professors argue as follows:

> Our troops cannot and should not avoid dehumanizing their enemies to some degree. Just as it is their responsibility to only kill certain people in certain ways at certain times, it is the responsibility of leadership to help them accomplish this by training them to only dehumanize certain people in certain ways at certain times.[46]

I couldn't resist sharing this with Marc Levy, since I knew how absurd such moral agility would sound to his ears. Marc went through basic Army training in 1970 and was a willing killer within a month of his arrival in country. He replied, "I read these lines and laughed. Was this written as a joke? The thinking is so out of touch with reality, it's frightening." Some of the "reality" Marc alludes to, I suggest, emerges from the conceptual world of military epithets.

Because the slurs and epithets used by service members have tended to fixate on racial, ethnic, and religious properties, they have been easily generalized across entire populations, devaluing both combatants and civilians. There is no question that many additional factors contributed to high civilian death rates in Vietnam and the Global War on Terrorism. Both conflicts, for instance, were predominantly guerrilla wars without front lines and involved ambiguity about who was fighting for which side, occasional fire from within populated zones, and the perpetual fear of ambushes or IEDs. US military leaders in Vietnam emphasized "body count" as a mark of success, which encouraged reckless killing. But meanwhile, the derogatory terms used by combatants often extended beyond enemy fighters to anyone loosely associated with their derogated group, making civilians more readily killable.

Vietnam veterans have attested that their military epithets were flung like a wide net across the people of the region. According to Army veteran Haywood Kirkland, "As soon as I hit boot camp in Fort Jackson, South Carolina, they tried to change your total personality. Transform you out of that civilian mentality to a military mind. Right away they told us not to call them Vietnamese. Call *everybody* gooks, dinks."[47] Reporters Michael Sallah and Mitch Weiss, in their Pulitzer Prize–winning account of the war crimes of one US unit in Vietnam, describe the wide extension of epithets by Army men: "These Vietnamese were no better than the Vietcong, they said. They were all gooks, and none of them could be trusted."[48] Some military personnel talked about the "mere gook rule": killing a Vietnamese civilian "did not count" in the minds of many American combatants, because the dehumanizing term so readily extended to encompass them.[49]

Dave Connolly describes how on his first day in Vietnam, he encountered a shocking display of genocidal prejudice. He recalls "a Black Sergeant First Class and two Black Specialists were all handing out ammo. They said, 'You're here to kill gooks. Kill any gooks you see.' It was open season." Dave was shocked by the naked prejudice and later lost patience with it and with the superior officers who sent infantry into combat for personal glory. After his disillusionment reached breaking point, he and several others would be court-martialed for dragging a Lieutenant by his feet and dipping his head in a urinal. "At the court-martial, they said, 'You're going to jail for assaulting an officer in uniform, blah, blah, blah.' I said, 'But it's okay to kill every fucking gook I see?'"

In Afghanistan and Iraq, too, slurs and epithets extended to civilian populations. Army veteran Anna tells me of the rules of thumb as she learned them a decade ago. "[We heard] the word 'haji' in the sense of, like, an Iraqi is potentially a haji, [and] a haji in that context is not a good person.... You should be wary of them, because you never know." In the 2008 Winter Soldier hearings, veteran Mike Prysner said, "When I got to Iraq in 2003, I learned a new word and that word was 'haji.' Haji was the enemy. Haji was every Iraqi—he was not a person, a father, a teacher, or a worker."[50] Sean Davis describes a US Colonel in Iraq talking cynically about his interpreter: "I can't trust the fucker. He's a raghead too."[51] Matt Young explains that during his Marine Corps training in 2005, "The infantry taught us to use language like 'haji' and 'raghead' and 'target' and 'towelhead' to dehumanize not just enemy combatants, but every Iraqi or Arab person we encountered."[52] Perhaps the dehumanization in the military's linguistic infrastructure contributed to a disturbing 2006 finding by the Marine Corps Mental Health Advisory Team survey: only 38% of Marines believed "all non-combatants should be treated with dignity and respect."[53]

Mock Language

When US combatants appropriated and distorted the term "haji" for their own purposes, they engaged in a long-standing linguistic practice aimed at debasing speech communities. Anthropologist Jane Hill pioneered the study of what she termed "mock" versions of languages, particularly focusing on Anglo-American usage of "mock Spanish."[54] Mock Spanish often involves grammatical and other errors, reflecting a lack of respect for the language and its native speakers. It also uses Spanish terms to convey negative or taboo concepts—for instance, *loco* instead of "crazy," *caca del toro* for "bullshit," or Donald Trump's infamous allusion to people crossing the southern US border as "bad hombres." Notably, in mock Spanish even neutral Spanish phrases like "hasta la vista" or "adios" may be adopted in an aggressive or derogatory manner, as seen in the *Terminator* movies. Hill argues that such uses of Spanish not only arise from but also reinforce negative stereotypes and attitudes toward Spanish speakers.

While American GIs in Vietnam used a few neutral Vietnamese terms for basic communication with locals, many of their Vietnamese-inspired slang terms had negative connotations. The dynamic is especially striking given that South Vietnamese fighters were allies in the war. GIs used mock versions of Vietnamese both in conversation among themselves and in hostile exchanges with Vietnamese people. "Dinky dow" was a widespread GI phrase used to mean "go crazy" or to be crazy, from *điên cái đầu* (crazy in the head).[55] The Vietnamese *đi đi mau*, meaning "let's go" or "go quickly," was sometimes shortened to "di di" and typically used to tell children to "scram." GIs sometimes paired the phrase with a threat, as in "di di mau or die." "Doo-mommie," used to curse at someone, was an US English approximation of the Vietnamese phrase *dụ má mày*, which roughly translates to "mother fucker."[56] A popular phrase was "xin loi" (from the Vietnamese *xin lỗi*), meaning "I'm sorry," which American GIs sardonically printed on helmets and flak jackets, or muttered to Vietnamese enemies in the spirit of the dismissive English phrase "tough shit."[57] Occasionally, says veteran Doug Anderson, Marines would ironically use "xin loi" in place of "it don't mean a thing," that well-worn phrase used "for shutting down the heart in order to get through another day after a buddy had been killed" (see Chapter 9). One veteran told me his buddies would say "croc-a-dao" to mean "dead" or "kill," usually as a threat to a Vietnamese individual: "I croc-a-dao you." This may have been a mangled version of relevant Vietnamese terms.[58] GIs using these pejorative phrases were not interested in pronouncing them carefully. They were flung around in hostility, carrying implications that Vietnamese speakers are off their heads, dislikeable, and killable.[59]

American combatants in Iraq and Afghanistan also showed casual disregard for the meanings of terms they encountered there, sometimes changing them in a pejorative direction. In Iraq, for instance, the word "mujahideen" in its most general sense means a person who fights on behalf of the Muslim community. US service members shortened it to "mooj" (or "muj") and used it as hostile slang for Iraqi insurgents. The name "Ali Baba," from the folk tale "Ali Baba and the Forty Thieves," became a term for any enemy or criminal. "Yalla," a versatile Arabic term that denotes a wish for something to get started or move forward, has been simplified and somewhat semantically inflated to mean "hurry up" or "run." "Marsalama," a corruption of the Arabic *ma'a salama*, or "go in peace" (literally "with peace"), was stripped of its religious connotation and came to mean "see you later."

Americans adopted the term "haji," which originally referred to a religious pilgrim, not only to label "the enemy" but also as a pejorative adjective to describe what they perceived as the dubious nature of local customs, places, and objects. A "haji shop" referred to an Iraqi-operated store on military bases, sometimes selling pirated DVDs Americans called "haji discs."

"Haji armor" referred to the scrap metal welded to the sides of a Humvee by an Iraqi mechanic to give it extra protection. "Haji patrol" meant an Iraqi escort detail. Hart Viges, who served in the Army in 2003, describes the stance of denigration associated with the term.

> And then we went to Baghdad and pretty much ran that town into the ground. You know, there was no real structure there, no police, no authority except for us. And we took full advantage of that in the treatment of the people and in just overall viewpoints. I mean, myself, I never really consider myself a racist person, but everything was "haji this," "haji that," "haji smokes," "haji burger, "haji house," "haji clothes," "haji rag." "Haji" is the same as "honky." It's the same thing. I had to catch myself.[60]

Like the epithets "towelhead" and "raghead," which debase cultural practices, mock versions of local terms desecrate familiar and sometimes sacred signs. Terms like these wouldn't catch on if US service members did not have a loosely shared reference point of disdain for the people on the ground.

Gentler Dehumanization

Notwithstanding these examples, the broader shifts in US language ideology since the Vietnam War era have meant intermittent signals from superior officers to curtail racist talk about the enemy. A recent "organizational culture" report commissioned by the Marine Corps describes tensions within and between ranks about the importance of senior officers setting an upstanding example for their subordinates. Some apparently persist in using derogatory racist language (whether about the enemy or other service members) under the pretense of "joking" or by merely asserting, "That's just how Marines talk."[61] But the cleanup message sometimes gets through.

Operations Officers began instructing their ranks to refrain from using the term "haji," for instance, as early as 2005, coinciding with General David Petraeus's efforts to rebrand US military operations in Iraq and Afghanistan. A respondent who went through Marine Corps Officer Candidate School in 2006 told me racial slurs did not make an appearance during his training, except the use of the phrase "haji squat" to describe a type of exercise (inspired by the ability of some Middle Eastern men to squat-sit). Army veteran Tom says his friends in basic training around 2015 told him, "Okay, you can't say 'haji' now. We can't call them 'raghead' anymore." Lennie, who entered Parris Island in 2015, tells me, "I heard a lot of terms like 'towelheads' before entering the Marine Corps, from movies and from other people talking, but when I definitely went into boot camp, there was, like, less emphasis on race [from the Drill Instructors] and more just emphasis on 'the enemy.'" While this verbal shift has played out unevenly across military branches and units, verbal sensitivity has generally been on the rise. Overtly racist and Islamophobic epithets for the enemy are now expected to live a more clandestine existence.

What labels for the enemy remain publicly acceptable, then? One hides its troubling politics in plain sight: "terrorist." The term does not overtly attach to a particular racial, ethnic, or religious group, yet it has been disproportionately applied to Muslim religious extremists (far more than to white Christian extremists at home) and creates a reductive caricature of the motives and morality of those the US fought against in the Global War on Terrorism. In kind, some veterans tell me the phrase "primitive terrorist" was common when they served in Iraq or Afghanistan. "Terrorists" are framed as barbaric, hate filled, and vicious enough to target civilians, in contrast to putatively civilized and just "soldiers" in war—yet as anthropologist Talal Asad has argued, the contrast is untenable, given that legal-moral guidelines are often breached in war, and wartime strategy often necessarily kills civilians.[62] Also morally simplifying is the now-common phrase "bad guys," which even appears in official military literature. A handout for the Marine Corps Basic Officer training course concerning prisoners of war states, "If we catch a bad guy, we obviously want to keep him locked up."[63] And then there are profane options such as "shitheads," echoing what Drill Instructors sometimes call recruits.[64]

When it comes to professionally sanctioned language in recent years, terms such as "insurgents," "targets," and "enemies" are preferred. On the face of it, these are racially, ethnically, religiously, and geographically neutral. They do not lump people together based on any quasi-biological or otherwise essential attribute, and they seem less likely to be extended to entire demographic categories (e.g., all Vietnamese, all Muslims or Arabs). However, the words are hardly free from reductive implications. "Enemy," for instance, carries with it a frisson of dread about an evil Other. "Target" treats a human being like an object. Many of the professionally accepted terms still drain their referent of full humanity, dodging the moral depth of killing.

It should be said as well that among those who don't serve as infantry but instead practice the military's heightened capacity to kill from a distance using drones and bombs, we sometimes see striking referential absences. In Mathias Delori's study of French fighter jet pilots who participated in the war in

Libya in 2011, he found no epithets, no vicious and hateful language, and no particular interest in tabulating bodies, which could not be seen anyway. Just "coarse" and celebratory discussion of the pilots' bombs and their "successful mission." "The dead enemy," writes Delori, "simply does not count."[65]

Relationality and Abandoning Epithets

Tyler Boudreau, who served in the Marine Corps until 2005, attests that once soldiers build up their defenses, "they can neither see, nor hear, nor feel the humanity of the people whom they've shut out."[66] Yet sometimes that humanity rises up to confront the American combatant, and some kind of empathy subtly permeates their consciousness. Close encounters with the adversary, including direct eye contact, keen observation of their unique features, or hearing their apprehensive voice, can trigger a profound recognition of their shared humanity, fragility, and intricate connections within society.[67] The moral philosopher Jonathan Glover deems this shift a "breakthrough of the human responses," including a richer in-filling of the other person's reality.[68] Linguistic shifts may correspond with such subjective shifts, and these changes sometimes happen rapidly. For as I explained in the Introduction, speakers can shift stance in the span of a single breath, allowing their consciousness to step toward or away from the military's necropolitical priorities, toward or away from a recognition of the other.[69]

Consider Lieutenant Braun's subtle footing shift (which is not really an empathic one, but telling nonetheless) in the same interview discussed earlier in the chapter, when Braun moves momentarily away from enemy epithets while foregrounding Vietnamese prowess in battle. The interview had been in process for several minutes, and Braun had indicated he considered "dink" a synonym for "NVA" (the North Vietnamese Army) and indeed for any Vietnamese.[70] But near the end of the interview, Braun shifts stance to enunciate a certain respect for the enemy. "What do you think of this war?" asks Howard Tuckner. Braun replies,

> War stinks, I think. I'd like to go home, but I'll stay it out. We'll win, no sweat. I'm just—just hanging on over here. We got—they say we fought crack NVA troops. Well, we lost some crack troops ourselves, but there's no doubt in my mind about winning. We'll never be whipped over here. But, just a, just a funny thing. I have the greatest respect in the world for the NVA. They've got their fine soldiers. They're good shots, they come charging at anything.

Braun first shifts into using "NVA," instead of his preferred and racializing "dink," when engaging in reported speech ("they say we fought crack NVA troops"). But after changing footing with the phrase "But just a funny thing," he begins to discuss his "respect ... for the NVA," mentioning their competence and bravery. The term "NVA" here highlights their status as members of a trained military force, rather than as pestilent racial others, and Braun's stance shifts from disparaging to admiring. The interview clarifies the way an epithet congeals "as-if" abstractions that a speaker can move away from if they choose a different term. In a more extreme example, Sallah and Weiss describe the shifting stances of a GI who had come home from Vietnam deeply disturbed. He would sometimes rant about how "the gooks were all the same and how he should have killed more" but sometimes express regret about opening fire on "unarmed men, women, and children."[71] Evidently, here was a man wrestling with his own antithetical attitudes toward Vietnamese, one evoked by a dehumanizing epithet and the other with a humanizing description.

Combatants often mention meeting another person's gaze in combat as a moment of stance shift. Shared gaze can trigger an intimate, intercorporeal sense of mutual awareness and human sameness. Hart Viges, in his Winter Soldier testimony, recounts such a moment and shows the connection between labels and experience. Viges had his sights on a man in a doorway with an RPG on his back,

> but when I looked at his face, he wasn't a bogeyman, he wasn't the enemy; he was scared and confused, probably the same expression I had on my face during the same time. He was probably fed the same BS I was fed to put myself in that situation. But seeing his face took me [a]back, and I didn't pull the trigger. He got away.[72]

Consider as well the torment of Marine Corporal Jeffrey Lucey, who took his own life at the age of twenty-three after telling his family members about the moment he realized the humanity of his supposed enemies in Iraq. His father spoke to the camera as part of the documentary *The Ground Truth*.

> He was told to "pull the fucking trigger, Lucey." And then he shot that man. And then he shot the other man. He looked at the man and he could see the fear, the terror in the man's eyes. And Jeff said, you know, all of a sudden, he just wondered was [the man he shot] there because he had to be there like Jeff was? And then he just thought about him being—

Lucey's mother breaks in, saying, "His family. He said he could see this boy's family; that he must have had a mother, father, or maybe a wife, children, whatever.... And he told his sister that his gun was shaking as he was aiming at him." Lucey's sister adds, "He told me he was a murderer. He said, 'Don't you understand? Your brother's a murderer.'"[73] Jeff shifted his categorization of himself to this label that, in his telling, bears the full moral weight of taking a life. The word "murderer" shocks the listener, being so out of place in the military's necropolitical lexicon that suspends such moral judgment about killing in war.

Along similar lines, Sean Davis recounts how close contact with Iraqis led him to question his dehumanizing stance. A Humvee in his convoy was ambushed and Davis and his squad rushed into a nearby grove trying to find the triggermen. They found "an old man in a white dishdasha talking to a boy in dirty hand-me-down clothes," and his squad buddy whispered, "Let's get these motherfuckers." It wasn't clear whether they were the culprits, says Davis, but at some level he "wanted to kill them." He realized, though, that there was beauty in the way "the sun cut through those orange trees and fell on the old man's white robes," and Davis approached the man and boy to speak. "After talking to them," he writes, "I didn't see them as enemies—just a grandfather taking his grandson for a walk."[74] From "motherfuckers" to "a grandfather and his grandson," the descriptive language shifts to a tender frame. And in speculating that the boy may have worn "hand-me-down clothes," Davis reveals himself beginning to contemplate the networks of care and relationship that surround this young Iraqi.

Several weeks later, Davis was moving door to door on a search for insurgents when he encountered an Iraqi man in his forties who spoke excellent English. The man said he studied at University of Illinois Urbana-Champaign but moved back to Iraq to bring his father to the hospital for kidney dialysis. He told Davis that Iraq hadn't been as bad under Saddam, who "left most people alone."[75] Later, says Davis, "I couldn't stop thinking about what the English-speaking man out on the road had said.... Were these 'terrorists' just fatherless sons wanting revenge?"[76] Again, the shift in terminology shifts the concept from an evil Other to a person enmeshed in affectively poignant and powerful kinship ties.

Not long after, Davis was assigned to an air assault Quick Reaction Force team, flying over villages in a helicopter. He could not switch off his new awareness of the loving relationships among Iraqis that had him rethinking their humanity. "Looking down at the houses I realized that each one held a family, each one was a home, each home had children, mothers, fathers, grandparents. That wasn't something I thought about in training and now it was something I couldn't avoid thinking about."[77] Not long after, when Davis was instructed to shoot a group of men in a sector he had been assigned to, he found himself "staring" at the men around a campfire. "I lost my breath and the bottom of my stomach dropped out. We were really going to have to kill these men."[78] His reluctance to shoot is evident in his noun choice; they were not hajis, shitheads, motherfuckers, or even "guys," but dignified "men." Davis opted to engage them verbally before shooting and learned they were merely security for the Baghdad Zoo. Nobody died there that day.

Sam, who worked on a base with Afghans, says that unlike the other American men in his unit, he sometimes went to the Afghan section and hung out with them. He came to view them "as people, because I would talk about my sons and they would talk about their sons. And they wanted them to have a good education, I wanted—you know.... They'd bring me their fresh watermelons; we'd share cigarettes, and [I'd] just be like, 'You guys are just human, different but human.'" All of this made Sam question the euphemisms of war. He had told me his artillery unit would use phrases like "wipe out a grid" when firing on a portion of a village, adding, "We use words that are like 'casualty,' but you're killing a human soul." He wondered whether kill talk might constitute a grave misrepresentation, adding, "I questioned if I've actually done what I'm supposedly doing." Sam seems to grasp that the language of war has the power to distort perception by framing the act of taking a life as something devoid of emotional consequence.

A final example captures the moment Doug Anderson, a medic in the Marine Corps, realized he could no longer use the slurs he had learned in basic training. In a poem, Anderson describes how his men had set a Vietnamese village on fire "to kill its vermin."[79] But when they dragged a man out of a hole where he was hiding, his vulnerability became visible in pathetic detail.

> And he blinked
> in the glare, all five feet of him
> covered in mud so that even his
> black pajamas were gray with it
> he didn't look like anything
> you'd want to kill...
> He just stood there, maybe hoping
> for a quick death, just a shot
> to the back of the head,
> no interrogator to slip a hat pin under his nail.
> I knew then I couldn't say *gook* again.

Those who find themselves broken by remorse after service are sometimes not merely guilty about what they (and the entire military apparatus) did, but also how they labeled and conceptualized others. Wartime epithets seem to have collateral damage—civilian lives, yes, but also, more subtly, some of the service members who did this cruel labeling. When they look back in hindsight, some are appalled by their deeds and also their past mindset. Recovery thus requires new language, new stances, what social theorist Alfred Schutz called a "Thou-orientation" that grasps the human existence of the people once so vilified.[80]

Chapter 7
Language as a Shattered Mirror

> On its way to confront the crowd of onlookers the person-thing [the US Marine] steps into a fleshy pile and stoops to investigate.* It is the suicide bomber's face, blown completely from his skull. It is amusing to the person-thing. The person-thing thinks it is wonderful and hilarious and physically amazing. It holds the bomber's face in front of its own and screams at the crowd through plump, blood-flecked lips, watching the crowd's reactions through empty eyeholes.
> —Matt Young, Marine Corps infantry, based on his three deployments in Iraq[1]

If you listen to American combat veterans for long enough, you may hear them talk about violence that exceeds your imagination. For my part, I was surprised by how often tame questions about military language led to respondents relating devastating accounts of combat behavior that I had not solicited. Sometimes I had the sense that as they got to know me, they wanted to externalize burning memories in front of someone who would listen without judgment. A couple of veterans told me combat was on their mind because of their years-long incredulity at the gap between civilian spaces—an aromatic café, or their living room sofa with its wool throw blanket—and the surreal violence of the war etched into their mind and body. Even to talk about war meant to reckon again with their knowledge that organized, polite people, including themselves, carry within them terrible potential. As one veteran friend, Steve, put it to me while we looked at an exhibition of the terrible aftermath of the My Lai massacre, "They make too much of My Lai, as if it was this *exception*. But there were a thousand smaller My Lais. This is just what war does; it puts you into the abyss."[2] Plenty of soldiers have come home and managed to compartmentalize who they were in war, but for others, the abyss lingers. Steve, a bear of a man, sweet and gentle in my presence, confessed that

---

*This chapter analyzes words and imagery that may be difficult for some readers to encounter. Please see the "Content Warning and Note on Language" in the front matter for some context and a discussion of the author's reasons for not redacting this material.

he had "huge emotional walls, huge investment in staying emotionally cold. I'm not afraid that I'll cry. I'm afraid that I'll kill."

The flip side of becoming a killer in combat is the grim reality that a soldier can be eviscerated at any moment. This uncanny knowledge remains with many, evident in classic PTSD behaviors such as needing to sit facing the door, and sometimes it appears in ruminations about the impossibly thin line between life and death. One day, I sat over drinks with three Vietnam veterans after they made a public appearance to speak about their antiwar activism. They didn't find themselves together often, and when they were, they had a rare chance to talk about the past with those who would understand. One man was marveling at how his body remembered combat details, like knowing how far away a round was from his ear, depending on if it made a sound like "ZZZK" or "TISZZzzz." Ari, a gangly man with salt-and-pepper curls who was drafted in the late '60s, wanted to talk about surviving the war by the skin of his teeth—including an incident when he was wounded by the bones of the man sitting next to him. He took to wearing two flak jackets at a time, sleeping with one wrapped around his head. "Nobody wanted to be near me after a while, because anyone near me died."[3]

Again and again, I heard about how the experience of combat makes people into killers while haunting them with the prospect of their own demise. Terrifying weaponry is not the only force that makes death more thinkable. I have described the pedagogical elements of military training (especially in the Marine Corps) that narrow the gap between life and death, reason and unreason, human and inhuman. Through the rigors of basic training, its deindividuation and semiotic callousing, some may find themselves heading toward the "person-thing" Matt Young characterizes in the epigraph to this chapter, with less feeling for suffering and perhaps even for the prospect of their own body's dismantlement. Once members of the infantry are in combat, the slurs, epithets, and mock language discussed in the preceding chapter may render some deeds more doable than before. And language is one of the few resources available to help humans to cope, however provisionally, with the impossible situations posed by combat. Linguistic frameworks can situate violence, suggesting how combatants should conceptualize and experience it, while offering techniques to manage the shattering of their world.

In this chapter, I examine the evasive language, ubiquitous profanity, and nihilistic slogans that are part of kill talk. The modes of speech I discuss here are quite disparate in some respects, including the fact that some are considered "professional" and some are not, but all of my examples have something in common. They encourage a militaristic stance toward killing or being killed by minimizing suffering, whether by distorting or denying its significance or leaning into the violent rupture of bodies and expectations.[4] All the tactics I describe in this chapter and the next are components of the linguistic infrastructure that supports state necropolitics and, thus, complicit in the state's denials of life by way of a representational repertoire that, looked at one way, is profoundly broken. At the same time, the same tactics can additionally be interpreted as "coping mechanisms" in the sense that they appear to help combatants function in the face of the necropolitical challenges of war. These verbal gambits aspire to deny suffering or to represent suffering as positive or fun, thus shunting empathy away from those killed or injured in war—for it is impossible to function as a successful combatant when overwhelmed by such empathy. They reinforce aggression and sometimes offer a poetic reinforcement of war's nihilism, approvingly echoing war's violence or embracing the idea that meaning and morality don't matter. As coping mechanisms, however, they are not always wholly successful, nor do they always stand the test of time. Sometimes the very extremes of the language I describe—its obvious workarounds, the way it tries to blot out pain or deny moral assessment—catch up with combatants who come to realize the language conceals profoundly disturbing realities.

Doublespeak and "Fun" Misery: Erasing Suffering

In 1987, the feminist scholar Carol Cohn published a groundbreaking article on the language of nuclear defense strategists, based on several weeks of training with them. Their slick acronyms and technical terms made war maneuvers "racy, sexy, snappy" to talk about. Their euphemisms for bombs and bombing sanitized the effects of weapons of mass destruction, describing supposedly tidy "clean bombs," "surgically clean strikes," and "counterforce exchanges." And then there were the sexual metaphors, which emerged in garish glory as the men (they were all men) pondered hypothetical nuclear strikes: "thrust to weight ratios," "deep penetration," losing one's nuclear "virginity," even "releasing our megatonnage in one orgasmic whump." Such language, Cohn argued, helped "make it possible" for them to "do their macabre work" by flattering their masculinity while disregarding the lethality of nuclear scenarios.[5]

Cohn was struck by the fact that although these terms and phrases denote massively violent maneuvers, their connotations are bloodless. The available lexicon doesn't just downplay the flesh and blood consequences of war; it erases them from the field of consideration and awareness. After several months of learning defense intellectuals' professional discourse, Cohn herself felt locked into this mode of thought when in their speech community. To speak about hypothetical nuclear engagements with this group of men meant avoiding talk about suffering or sentient human bodies, for talk of human pain was stigmatized as feminine and weak. The language that remained available, Cohn argues, precipitated a cognitive shift.

> I could not use the language to express my concerns because it is physically impossible. The language does not allow certain questions to be asked or certain values to be expressed.... [And] if I was unable to speak my concerns in this language, more disturbing still was that *I found it hard even to keep them in my own head*.[6]

Cohn's experiences offered intimate confirmation of what psychologists have long claimed—namely, that euphemisms can serve as mechanisms for what they call "moral disengagement."[7] In a similar vein, former Army captain Lana, who oversaw a nuclear missile storage site during the Cold War, tells me her unit's language repeatedly skirted the reality of suffering. A "nuclear release order," which she now calls an "omnicidal folly," was nicknamed "popping the cookies," cheerful slang that sounds like opening a package of dessert or perhaps that phallocentric slang for a woman losing her virginity, "popping her cherry." Lana is equally horrified, in retrospect, by the phrase "lower yield" to describe nuclear weapons that still had deadly force much bigger than Hiroshima or Nagasaki. "It was an OBSCENE misnomer," she says.

The evasions of military wording influence the thinking of both the general public and military personnel themselves, often sidestepping moral hypocrisies or potential dilemmas. Sometimes this takes place through linguistic absences. Marine veteran Eliot Ackerman, for instance, describes how the US military engaged in the targeted killing of Taliban commanders and al-Qaeda operatives along the Afghanistan–Pakistan border but refused to call these "assassinations" because Executive Order 1233 banned assassination, deeming it anathema to US ideals.[8] Sometimes, the evasions concern how words are defined. Consider the way civilian victims of US drone strikes in regions such as Pakistan, Syria, and Yemen have been classified as killable "militants" if they are simply moving through space in the company of a known terrorist.[9] Examples like this resonate with Benjamin Lee Whorf's insight about the way language can shape our sense of reality, with potential life-and-death stakes. As a fire inspector, Whorf had spoken to workers at the site of a blaze and realized they had been smoking around gasoline barrels they habitually referred to as "empty." The phrase implied the drums were inert or safe, making it hard for the workers to conceptualize the drums as potentially dangerous because of lingering fumes.[10]

The linguist William D. Lutz agrees that military verbal distortions can reshape our sense of the world, famously stating that "in war, the first casualty is language."[11] Within the sprawling US military, various communities of practice use Orwellian euphemisms that reflect their specializations. These are not merely delicate means of protecting listeners' feelings, like the phrase "passed away" instead of "died," but potentially misleading or deceptive terms. Lutz defines them as "doublespeak": "language that avoids or shifts responsibility, language that is at variance with its real or purported meaning [and] that conceals or prevents thought."[12] By way of example, Lutz invokes the word swaps the president and Pentagon offered the American public during the first Gulf War: "efforts" or "visits" for bombing attacks; "soft targets" for human beings; and "degrading," "sanitizing," "impacting," or "taking out" targets to mean dropping bombs on people and buildings.[13] Probably the most famous example of military doublespeak is "collateral damage" for civilian casualties, now sometimes replaced by the snappy "civ-cas."[14] While this terminology can seem wildly incongruous when placed next to its real-world referent, most military doublespeak feels like "professional" language to those who use it and probably to many outside of the military. Such language allows the institution to maintain control, for its bloodless and bureaucratic confidence has an unobjectionable tone on the face of it, while placing an obscuring gauze over the real-world effects of violence.

Military personnel engaging in face-to-face acts of violence, including cruelty and torture, can be enabled by doublespeak, too. At the US military prison in Guantanamo Bay, Cuba—"Gitmo," in military parlance—officials encoded doublespeak into their documents even as Army personnel on the ground generated more casual euphemisms. I heard directly about this dynamic from one of my respondents: the now-public figure James Yee, who was assigned to be one of the first Muslim military chaplains at the prison.[15] James is a proud 1990 West Point graduate who served in Saudi Arabia as an Army Lieutenant and Patriot Missile officer. Having converted from Lutheran Christianity to Islam in 1991 and studied religion in Syria, James was posted to Guantanamo Bay in 2002 and assigned to counsel Muslim detainees.

It quickly became apparent that the more than six hundred detainees were not, as far as he could tell, hardened terrorists (at the time, the CIA had detainees of "higher value" at its various secret "black sites"). James soon found himself disturbed by the human rights abuses they related to him, from the desecration of the Quran to outright torture. When he began to make reports to his superior officers, he was arrested, nicknamed "the Chinese Taliban," and accused of conspiring with the enemy. After seventy-six days in solitary confinement, suffering untold damage to his psyche, family, and reputation, James was released without charge.

I met with James several times in New Jersey, where he now lives alone and frequents the studios of Frontline Paper to create drawings and prints on paper made of military uniforms (see Chapter 10). Polite but reserved, he carries an air of sadness and disquiet. He still loves the ideals and the way of life he mastered at West Point. But he knows the US military to be capable of profound abuse, including its refusal to honor the humanity of its putative enemies. In James's opinion, cruelty at "Gitmo" was facilitated by what he calls the military's "play on words."

In fact, although I thought our conversation might focus on his artwork, James knew I was interested in language and wanted to tell me at length about the disturbing language games he encountered. Some of the now-notorious euphemisms at Guantanamo Bay provided legal cover, such as calling prisoners "detainees" so they could not be protected by the international law that applies to prisoners of war. Torture was renamed "enhanced interrogation." And although officials publicly claimed that the detainment camp had no solitary confinement, James told me that in the so-called disciplinary cell block,

> they had cells . . . which weren't made from the steel mesh of the other cells; they were made from steel walls or steel panels, so [the prisoners] couldn't see in or out. They mostly were kept in the dark. And those were referred to as Maximum Security Units or they were known as "MSU," but essentially it was solitary confinement.

Anything prisoners were allowed to have in their cells, from religiously important items such as prayer caps to essentials like a bedroll and a Styrofoam cup, were deemed "comfort items," implying the prisoners were being cared for or even cosseted, which they decidedly were not. And, James adds, "prisoners never went to 'interrogation.' They always went to what we called a 'reservation.' It was a 'reservation' with their interrogators, basically." James ventriloquized the way a guard might say it, making it sound almost like a dinner date: "Like, 'Detainee 005 has a reservation at five o'clock.'"

These terms can all be found in the Guantanamo Bay Standard Operating Procedures from the era, suggesting that—as the public now knows—they were institutionally endorsed as a means of concealing severe prisoner treatment.[16] Less formally, prison officials and guards generated their own creative phrases that bring me to an additional type of military speech—namely, language that occludes suffering while inflecting it with a sardonic air of enthusiasm or amusement, as if misery were fun. James describes how the guards talked about the sleep deprivation they used to "soften up" detainees (another euphemism, so engrained that James used it without remark), making them more susceptible to other forms of torture.

> The sleep deprivation policy that they had, I remember it being called "Frequent Flier," where they would wake up the prisoner every, you know, every hour, and then move them to another cell. It's what they called their "Frequent Flier Program."

This phrase likens the prisoner's deeply uncomfortable forced motion to an airline passenger's accumulation of points or privileges with their flight mileage. The wording is both playful—as if inflicting this suffering were a game—and dismissive of the prisoners' agony. As Cohn puts it, "Speaking about [a disturbing concept] with that edge of derision is exactly what allows it to be spoken about.... It is the very ability to make fun of a concept that makes it possible to work with it."[17]

The prisoners mustered small forms of resistance, of course, using whatever options were available. These gestures were an indication of grave misery, but US military personnel downplayed them, verbally reframing their rebellion as silly and impotent. Sometimes, James relates, after a prisoner was tortured,

> they would tell fellow prisoners and then they'd stage a disturbance. So sometimes the prisoners threw water. Actually it's a mix of water and human excrement—feces and urine. So the guards referred to those, the water throwing, as prisoners throwing "cocktails."

At times, he adds, detainees would stop eating in protest, but camp staff referred to this not as hunger striking, but as "voluntary nonreligious fasting," an official euphemism used to fend off scrutiny from human rights watchdogs.[18] In a related vein, James believes that many prisoners wished to take their own lives, but in public reports officials downgraded all but the most severe suicide attempts as "self-harm" or scorned it as "manipulative self-injurious behavior."[19]

In his singular position as a confidant, James heard story after story about prisoners' emotional and physical pain. But his higher-ups were implacable and assumed his empathy was a sign of deeper political allegiances. Perhaps the charges against James testify indirectly to the power of euphemism at Guantanamo Bay, which established expectations for necropolitically "appropriate" subjectivity among US service members. If you were in the US military system, you were not meant to feel for the enemy, so James's fellow military personnel seemed in disbelief that one of their own could empathize with the detainees. When James treated prisoner suffering as real, he came to seem less relatable, even dangerous, to his peers in the US military and was ultimately recategorized as Other.[20]

According to reporter Margot Williams, writing some seventeen years after James Yee left the island, the military commissions prosecuting the remaining post-9/11 detainees were still engaging in abundant doublespeak. "Euphemism is a foundation of the torture structure," she writes. She lists enabling phrases such as "intelligence requirements," "countermeasures to resistance," "negative reinforcement," and "conditioning strategy." Williams was taken aback to encounter even a "euphemism for [a] euphemism" when a military psychologist said, "You want to watch the use of euphemism for what you're doing. Don't be fooled by 'enhanced interrogation,' you are doing coercive physical techniques."[21] While this phrase at least concedes that force and bodies are at play, it remains detached from detainees' suffering. US military players refuse to paint the picture of detainees' cold sweat of fear, glances of pain, or frenzied movements of panic. To hear of these things can put one in the mind of them, and a primary purpose of necropolitically appropriate language is to shunt empathic thoughts of suffering out of mind.

From some of James Yee's examples from Guantanamo Bay, we can infer the guards generated their own off-the-record "creative" phrases. Across the military, alongside officially sanctioned doublespeak, service members have come up with slang and other creative descriptions that frame a grim situation as fun, as if to playfully divert the speaker or hearer from discomfort, risk, and violence. As discussed in earlier chapters, a general spirit of laughing at others' discomfort is handed down by some Drill Instructors (DIs) and Drill Sergeants. In Chapter 4, for instance, I described the DI Peter's winking allusion to "instilling knowledge" into a recruit by wearing him down with painful leg lifts so intense he nearly lost his mind. A 2020 tweet from the official Marine Corps Recruit Depot at Parris Island account has a similar alchemy; the image depicts recruits being yelled at while undertaking painful training exercises, but the caption reads, "This is where the fun begins."[22] Framing pain as playful or pleasurable is one mark of military masculinity, indicating toughness and willing—even enthusiastic—obedience to painful orders. But if, as I have suggested, the recruit in training has a somewhat analogous role to the enemy in combat, then what applies to the suffering of recruits sometimes applies to the suffering of enemy combatants.

Hence, the theater of war brings countless snappy phrasings that seemingly enjoy their own rhymes, alliteration, and playful allusions, while contrasting ironically with the misery on the ground. In Vietnam, weapons and equipment received ludic nicknames, some of which evoked the innocence of childhood: "Puff the Magic Dragon" (an aircraft that could strafe with automatic weapons fire), "Snoopy" (a C-130 flareship), "Jolly Green Giant" (a crane helicopter involved in combat rescue operations). "Toe Poppers" and "Bouncing Betties" were two kinds of mines that terrorized American GIs. Switching a weapon like an M-16 to fully automatic fire was called "rocking 'n' rolling." The act of dropping napalm followed by ordinary bombs was called "nape and rape."

More recently, journalist Evan Wright describes Marine Corps officers who prepared a reconnaissance battalion in Iraq by warning them about nerve gases that "make you dance the funky chicken until you die" and blistering agents that make the skin "burst up like Jiffy Pop."[23] Iraq itself was nicknamed "the sandbox" by many US combatants: the site of child's play. "Shake and bake," revived from the Vietnam era, refers to attacks that combine cluster bombs, conventional bombs, and sometimes napalm.[24] Bodies burned to death—in Vietnam, Iraq, or Afghanistan, and whether friend or foe—are "crispy critters."[25] "Full battle rattle" means wearing about fifty pounds' worth of gear. Shooting someone is "lighting them up"; shooting into an area to draw fire from the enemy so that they'll disclose their location is "recon by fire." A "death blossom" ensues when a startled member of the Iraqi security forces sprays fire around indiscriminately. Such uses of language mirror the topsy-turvy moral universe of military necropolitics, to which participants acclimate themselves by characterizing gruesome reality with a light touch.

Combatants also possess abundant terms for their own acts of killing, many of which can be loosely sorted into the two categories I have noted: institutionally sanctioned doublespeak, which often sounds bureaucratic and emotionless, and colloquial slang that sometimes conveys a sense of grim "fun." Many of the latter terms could be considered "dysphemisms": word substitutions with a derogatory or taboo valence, which contrast with euphemism's mild or softening quality. Like slang generally, such terminology helps create camaraderie, in this case through a shared sense of dark humor or knowing mastery. But whether the terms for killing are euphemistic or dysphemistic, they all steer consciousness away from recognizing the suffering and loss involved.

Sophie, who served as a combat helicopter pilot during the Global War on Terrorism (GWOT), tells me her unit "never directly said we 'killed.'"

152 Kill Talk

When planning a mission, their euphemisms included "moving ammunition," "hitting the target," and "neutralizing the enemy." These, she says are "nice ways of saying, 'We're killing this Iraqi,'" adding, "we incrementally adapted to the point where we didn't even understand how bad it was." Other officially encouraged terms include "neutralize," "take out," "engage," "destroy," or "disable" the enemy. Accounts of a deadly skirmish might talk of "securing a landing zone," "clearing a field," or "covering one's pursuit objective." Another phrase, "firing a stopping shot to the cranial cavity," offers a strikingly clinical way of describing a headshot—one that dehumanizes by omitting any acknowledgment of the mind within.

As for slang verbs for killing, many options since (at least) the Vietnam War era lean into violence while broadcasting a cool and casual stance toward it. The same words may also be used to refer to the killing of one's own, enabling the speaker to adopt a cavalier stance toward terrible loss. The repertoire includes "grease," "hose," "waste," "smoke," "fuck up," "light [someone] up," or "blow [someone] to hell." Words like "whack" and a GWOT-era variant, "schwack," have an onomatopoetic quality that echoes the sound of a projectile slamming into flesh, potentially implying some satisfaction in replicating it. The interjection "get some," popularized by a scene in *Full Metal Jacket* when a helicopter machine gunner repeatedly yells it while shooting civilians, was adopted by some combatants in the GWOT, probably with awareness that it evokes the sadistic aggression represented in that film.

Recent examples of dehumanizing language around killing include phrases like "slaying bodies," as seen in an internet comment on why people enlist: "Let's be honest, everyone joins to slay bodies." Similarly, the term "stacking bodies" appears in memes like "When you joined up to stack bodies but all you do is listen to PowerPoints" and on t-shirts bearing slogans such as "USMC: Stacking Bodies since 1775." Modern terminology for killing also reflects internet culture, with phrases like "deleting some terrorists" and "unaliving some assholes." Online, "unalive" often avoids triggering content filters that flag posts about sensitive subjects like death and suicide, though in some cases, the word constitutes a deliberate effort to speak gently about something difficult. In military contexts, using a term like "unalive" may nod ironically in the direction of this sensitivity.

Sam, recounting his time working artillery in Afghanistan, told me his unit had coy, jokey ways to avoid talking directly about killing people.

> There was one mission where the Taliban leader that was always shooting at us....
> He would come up over the mountains with a donkey with all of these RPGs [rocket propelled grenades] and mortars on the back and then sit down and then shoot

at us. There were three guys with this donkey, and this donkey was super important because it was the only way they could get their ammunition up and over this mountain.... So their guys were trying to escape... and we started shooting them. I mean we killed them [all], but the way we said it was, "We got one donkey." You know, it's a playful way for us to be like, "I got the donkey, yeah." You make a lot of jokes.

Perhaps it is not too far-fetched to see such language games as similar to the macabre behavior Matt Young describes in the excerpt at the start of this chapter, in which a US Marine holds up the skinned face of a suicide bomber with bemusement, using it as a mask to horrify a gawking crowd. Why not, if death has been framed as fun by military language all along? Verbal play along these lines appears to bond military speech communities, offering them a creative palette that speaks with twisted pride to their ability to endure.

It is important to note that the repertoire I have been describing, which ostentatiously denies or dodges the vulnerability and suffering of those in war, is not the only way service members talk about violence. Despite the abundance of euphemisms, dysphemisms, and other kinds of word substitutions for killing, plenty of combatants have used more plain or frank language: "I killed/shot/blew him up," "We crushed him with the tank," "She opened fire and hit two enemy combatants." In Chapter 3, I described how "kill chants" routinize the word "kill" in Marine Corps training. Such direct terminology does not directly speak of suffering, but at least it does not hide behind euphemism or jokey slang. Sometimes service members will combine plain-spoken, matter-of-fact language with additions from the kill talk repertoire, such as jargony euphemisms, denigrating words for the enemy, or profanity underscoring aggression—as in "Let's kill those motherfuckers." Such combinations highlight the diverse verbal stances available to them in framing their actions.

An example from Miles Lagoze's memoir exemplifies how plain language about killing can intermingle with official and unofficial word substitutions. As a cameraman for the Marine Corps, Lagoze was invited by a platoon to "tag along and film them schwack somebody."[26] We can assume, here, that Lagoze is ventriloquizing the slang of the platoon. In the end, Lagoze filmed a sniper named Warren firing on a presumed Taliban. After the deed, Lagoze turned on his camera again to interview Warren so that he could get a good sound bite for the Marine Corps. Both men knew, says Lagoze, that "as long as [Warren] sounded professional and didn't curse or talk about 'killing hajis,'" the video had a good chance of being released to the public. Here we see an example of mixing plain verbs ("killing") with kill talk slang ("hajis"), as well as the Marines' consciousness of dual registers, one official and the other off the record.

Lagoze goes on to explain that when he first tried to get a sound bite, Warren went overboard with the official jargon, "talking like a robot, reciting Marine Corps textbook definitions about the mission of surveillance target acquisition teams." Finally, though, they got their take. There's no talk of "hajis," just plain reference to "two men" and to "spotting both the individuals." Warren adds that after surveilling the suspicious man, "that's when I engaged him. He went down on the first shot. Statistics show that about every Taliban a sniper takes down saves about three Marines' lives. . . . It's something I take very seriously."[27] Warren thus represents his deed—which he describes euphemistically as "engaging" and "taking down," not "schwacking"—as both moral and honorable.

Levi, who was a medic with the Army in Iraq, is keenly aware in hindsight of the way word substitutions for killing worked on the psyche, mentioning both dysphemisms and euphemisms at play in his military specialty.

> In my job, having to do a lot with, like, dealing with the dead, handling the dead, we don't refer to them by those most direct, simple terms. Yeah, they say, "Somebody got whacked." Or "wasted." Or, you know, "He's gone," or whatever. But never do we actually say like, "I killed a person" or, like, you know, "So-and-so is dead." You know, it's just like—I think there is an avoidance of that, which is part of the whole indoctrination or dehumanization process, that we separate ourselves from death. . . . It's a coping mechanism to detach yourself or distance yourself a little bit from what it actually is that we're dealing with.

That said, the language never strictly determined his thoughts or feelings, and Levi admits that the available slang never completely "took." "Something I always struggled with a little bit was not being able to detach myself from it and see [the death and suffering] as anything other than, like, what it actually was." Today, he connects this struggle to his sense of moral injury; he saw and did things that caused harm to others, but when his language downplayed the violence, he says, he "couldn't reconcile it."

Two decades after the United States withdrew from Vietnam, veteran James Soular would still be ruminating about military euphemisms and baffling language such as "We had to destroy the village in order to save it." "The Vietnam War," he adds with frustration, "clawed insistently at one's sense of reality with its oxymora." Soular was especially vexed by jargon that seemed to contradict itself, such as "aggressive defense" or "peace offensive."[28] When military language avoids confessing the harm military deeds cause, it may play a role in numbing affect or otherwise helping some combatants cope with the otherwise unthinkable, but, as Levi and Soular imply, it may also be competing with an underlying sense of the hard realities of suffering. For some, in fact, the language's very denials may ultimately draw their awareness to what is being denied.

"Fuck"

In the opening paragraphs of his 2021 memoir, Iraq veteran Kacy Tellesson describes what it was like for him to shift into a Marine identity. Language features prominently in his description. First, he says, the Marine Corps "whittles away your personal vocabulary," replacing it with "fast technical terms" and "quick syllable bursts," a striking characterization that evokes the sound of an automatic weapon firing. Second, says Tellesson, beyond the acronyms and specialist's language, the word "fuck" becomes so prevalent that it "might be the only intelligible thing [a civilian] could pick out from our conversations on the range."[29] Indeed, when I told veterans that I was doing a project on military language, a number responded with something like, "So I guess you're writing about the f-word?"

In Chapter 4, I briefly discussed the use of profanity in training, highlighting why Drill Instructors sometimes use it despite its prohibition under the Recruit Training Order. In the heat of combat, however, no such prohibitions exist, and profanity becomes ubiquitous, serving various neurological, emotional, semantic, and social functions that suit the extremity of warfare and play a role in the military's linguistic infrastructure.

Combat videos from Iraq and Afghanistan illustrate how profanity is embedded in the language of soldiers. It often serves as an intensifier in moments of urgency, as in commands like "stay the fuck low," or expressions of shock, such as "holy shit," exclaimed when a soldier's helmet is struck while he stands on a tank in northeast Afghanistan.[30] At other times, the profanity conveys frustration and anger, as when a soldier, after his unit suffers casualties, bitterly observes that civilians on the road are "fuckin' smiling at us."[31] In some cases, profanity is part of a combatant's offensive stance. A 2017 video captures US Special Forces ambushed by ISIS on a mountain pass in Afghanistan. The footage is punctuated by the sounds of automatic rifle fire and RPGs, occasional shouted directives, and profanity-laden commands like "Start shooting that shit" and "Smoke that fuckin' [unintelligible]," as a helmeted soldier points into a gully, urging his platoon to aim their weapons there.[32] In these moments, profanity serves as a predicate ("fuckin'") or a noun ("shit"), implying that the target of violence is degraded or dehumanized.[33]

While rewatching Miles Lagoze's 2017 documentary *Combat Obscura*, composed of footage he collected in Afghanistan, I noticed the abundant profanity when his unit is caught in a firefight. In concert with the sound of automatic gunfire and bangs of artillery, we hear Marines cursing: "Jesus fuck" and "holy shit." A Marine is hit: "Oh FUCK." "Oh SHIT." Another Marine is hit: "Hey, I'm fucking bleeding!" "All right, this motherfucker's bleeding."

Soon after, several men wait for a medevac chopper in a small, mudpacked room while a medic cleans Lagoze's small shrapnel wound. About seven guys chatter in overlapping discussions that I cannot pull apart, but in almost every audible sentence the word "fuck" appears, multifunctional and following its own grammatical rules—special qualities of profanity noted by linguists.[34]

- "One of us just go out there and fucking tell Charles to shoot the cars down, so I thought 'fuck it' . . . "
- "Fucking death, man"
- "Well the blood is fucking—it's stopped flowing already"
- "It's fucking stupid, dude"
- "Yeah it is. I don't know what the fuck is going on."
- "What the fuck is there"
- "Who the fuck is anything"
- "He asked—said Fazaj, fucking . . . "

A few minutes later, while they carry a wounded man on a makeshift stretcher toward the chopper, one of them says, "Advance to the fucking bird."

According to cognitive scientists, profanity is processed differently from most language, being more directly connected to the emotional centers of the brain.[35] Neurological damage to the limbic system, a deep brain region that helps modulate aggression and anger, can lead to inadvertent swearing.[36] Swearing can also increase pain tolerance, probably because it can trigger a fight-or-flight adrenaline rush in the speaker.[37] Even hearing another person's profanity can lead to increased heart rate and shallow breathing,[38] so an urgent swear word in the middle of a firefight—"Hey, I'm fucking bleeding!"—can mobilize those nearby to act.[39] Swearing may additionally have cathartic effects, providing relief from emotional turbulence.[40] These close connections between words and embodied feeling suit profanity to the shock and rage of combat, as well as the need for urgent or violent action.

The intermingling of adrenaline and strong feeling helps explain the language in one firefight in Vietnam (representative of many) that Marc Levy described to me. The GI who was walking point for Marc's squad was a few meters into the jungle when he came running back into a clearing, screaming, "Dinks! Dinks!" As the unit's medic, Marc took cover and listened as his buddies switched from a racist to a profane epithet to fire their weapons: "They would raise up and scream and curse, 'You motherfuckers!' *Ba-ba-ba-bom*, and down. 'You motherfuckers!' and down." The profanity, he told me, seemed like a way of "gearing themselves up"; it was bound up with the visceral, hostile energy they needed to muster for their deadly act. Profanity may be functionally similar here to the way US soldiers in the Middle East used heavy metal and rap music with driving beats and profane lyrics to get "wound up," "amped up on an adrenaline rush," or "crunked" before heading out of a base to fight.[41]

Here we see one role of profanity in the combatant's linguistic infrastructure: it can channel feeling into kinetic violence, sometimes affecting and mobilizing others in the vicinity to do the same. But there's more to profanity than an adrenaline rush or an affective surge, for it involves more complex, social meanings. For one thing, as noted in Chapter 4, swearing is conventionally associated with masculine toughness rather than feminine delicacy.[42] Connected to this, when military trainers break rules to use profanity against recruits, they are tapping into the logic of semiotic callousing, in which hard language is supposed to produce hard fighters. When combatants use profanity, it thus marks them as hardened members of a masculine in-group. Sam, who served in an Army artillery regiment in the mountains of Afghanistan, explains that profanity can signify a military identity. In his unit, he tells me, "the f-word was almost glorified; we swore like sailors. The more you use it, the more 'military' you are."

More subtly, one veteran shared that he favors profanity because he experiences its sound and "how it feels in my mouth," as "strong and determined." Grunts are attuned to brutal kinetic realities, and the very form of profanity seems to affirm this mindset. In English, profane words ("fuck," "shit," "cock," etc.) are typically monosyllabic and end with hard, "plosive" consonants.[43] The intense form of this language draws attention to itself, with the sensuous qualities of the sounds mirroring a sense of urgency, rage, action—and maybe violence itself.[44]

To some combatants, profanity's terse, forceful quality carries authenticity and candor. Sam, for instance, tells me profanity is part of speaking "directly" about raw truths, which he considers important if one is not to obfuscate war's violence. When the Taliban "bombed the crap" out of their base and his unit returned fire into villages in the nearby mountains, his men found themselves confronting violence so raw, they lost patience with jargon and doublespeak that felt too distant from their experience.

> The guys get so sick of all the Rules of Engagement details and euphemisms—words like "insurgent," "kill radius." . . . We like directness; we respond to things that are immediate and make sense. [Things that are] immediate, bare-bones, live-or-die make sense. . . . Swearing is a quick way to be direct.

Ironically, in the same conversation Sam told me that his unit would refer to enemy dead as "casualties" rather than "human beings," admitting that such depersonalizing euphemisms were common currency. His was also the unit that alluded to "getting a donkey" as a tongue-in-cheek euphemism for killing several Taliban. But here, he voices the ideology that "swearing" is better at capturing the reality of violence "directly" than formal military registers, which tiptoe around brute experience while attempting to micromanage combatants' discourse and actions via the Rules of Engagement.

What Sam tells me next adds another layer to the significance of profanity in the military: it transgresses civilian norms. "One reason we swear so much in the military," he says, "is we CAN and we WILL; the rest of the world might have conventions, but we don't have to do what the rest of the world does." In discussion with me, Vietnam veteran Doug Anderson also flagged this dynamic.

> Cursing is subversive; it's a way to speak obscenely against authority. The words your mama and the schoolmarms told you not to say all explode through the repression in existential situations. Your mama and the schoolmarms are not in the existential situation with you, so, fuck it.

In other words, profanity is part of that rebellious underbelly of military life that violates norms of propriety.[45] Doug's formulation suggests that profanity may even have spectral overhearers: the word police of the civilian world, feminized as "your mama and the schoolmarms."[46] His phrasing implies disdain for verbal constraint in the war zone's "existential situation" of life or death. Notably, just as profanity disregards the conventions of "the rest of the world," so does combat, which shatters rules and casts participants into a moral void. Profanity again mirrors the broader ways in which combat contravenes ordinary life.

When I asked a young veteran, Dirk, why Marines swear so much, his reply also pointed to a sense of combatant exceptionalism.

It's part of Marine Corps dark humor, and it keeps us sane, helps us deal, because we're nonstop pushing ourselves. This life is not natural, or not normal. It's constant stress and sleep deprivation, constantly pushing ourselves beyond where our mind thinks we can go. And when you're in combat, do you think we're holding back?

Dirk may be referring partly to the neuropsychological assistance profanity provides, as discussed earlier in this chapter. But he also implies profanity has a mirroring quality, reflecting the shattered world of war. Profane language is at home in contexts that are "not normal"; both profanity and violence are extreme, breaching normal expectations. During the existential upheaval of combat, Doug Anderson adds, "there is the deep notion that everything is going to shit." Everything disintegrates in war, as the boundaries and protections that support normal life and bodies themselves fall apart. Using profanity models and mirrors such disintegration.

Indeed, just as speaking with profanity shatters norms, its semantic meaning denotes bodily rupture. Common profane words used in combat—"fuck," "shit"—describe the breaching of bodily integrity, as things go into or come out of bodily orifices. Queer theorist Leo Bersani has suggested that the anatomical realities of sex, involving a sometimes-aggressive rupture of bodily boundaries, may shatter the conceit of an intact self and signify the "breakdown of the human."[47] Profanity may be suited to combat because it meditates, however fleetingly, on the puncturing of bodies.

In a related vein, US English slang makes explicit connections between profanity and the shattering of the world; "getting fucked" or "screwed" are common ways to allude to being badly or violently treated and left in an abject state. This verbal culture may piggyback on a psychodynamic sex-and-death connection[48] that is enhanced by military culture, as evidenced by the words of the young Marine who told me, "I'm a Marine, so to me, fucking is killing is fucking is killing."[49] Beyond this conceptual mapping, further semiotic mirroring is at work. The act of penetration—whether by a phallus or a weapon—breaches a bodily boundary. When chanted or screamed in a fit of rage, the phrase "fuck you" can feel like a virtual projectile. The rhyming of sex and violence in military language also taps into a conservative cultural idea of "fucking" as masculine aggression that violates and injures the feminine. Examples like these illustrate how military masculinity connects the violent, symbolically potent act of rape with the experience of war.

A further resonance between combat and profanity may stem from their shared invocation of bodily taboos. Semantically, profanity brings offstage animalistic bodily functions in front of the curtain, violating norms of polite sociality. In combat, Marines and soldiers are tasked with violating other taboos and boundaries, turning bodies inside out with their weapons. War is rife with polluting "matter out of place"; blood, brains, intestines, and excreta are spilled and scattered.[50] Soldiers' bodies may be reduced to abject bodily functions, exhausted and contaminated through penetration by projectiles or evacuation by fear. As Doug Anderson puts it in conversation with me, "Something about being scared shitless makes us think about shit."

The entire phenomenon of combat, in fact, is morally polluted; ordinarily, people are not meant to kill other people. The deeds of war are thus a desecration, spoken of in desecrated language. An Iraq veteran I spoke with encapsulated this when he said, "Some of the guys I went in with after 9/11 just wanted to kill things. Just fuckin' bloodlust." Ryan, the Marine with seventeen confirmed kills and a guilty conscience (see Chapters 3 and 6), tells me, "I feel like I could spend the rest of my life trying to make up for that shit. . . . I just want to be a good human, and no amount of 'good human' is going to make up for that shit." Profane language, therefore, captures and reflects profound bodily, moral, and existential violations.

A striking encounter between US Army men and Afghan civilians, captured on tape by journalists from *The Guardian* in 2008, shows how combatants sometimes twin profanity with a ruthless necropolitical stance and lack of empathic understanding for civilians. In the video, US troops head for a frontier village, frustrated because their base is being targeted daily by rockets from Taliban positions in the nearby hills. Their goal is to persuade the few remaining villagers to provide information about the Taliban or to encourage them to defend themselves with the AK-47s each household is permitted to own. A corporal attempts to communicate with a couple of Pashtun elders through an interpreter, but the process is hampered by inadequate translation, cultural misunderstandings, and conflicting agendas.

One Pashtun elder tries in vain to explain the village's dilemma through an allegory, which the subtitles spell out: "In our country, we grow wheat, and we have ants. There is no way we can stop the little ants from stealing the wheat. There are so many little ants it is almost impossible to stop them." The elder's analogy suggests that the sheer number and persistence of the Taliban make it futile for the villagers to attempt to stop them. The translator fails to convey any of this to the US soldiers, though he does translate the elder's additional point that the Taliban have been beating up their young men. Upon hearing this, the corporal addresses the translator. "Ask him if he's got any guns here. I don't wanna take 'em, I just wanna know— " At this point, the corporal pauses, then bends at the hips to speak into the translator's face with a menacing tone, continuing, " —why he didn't shoot him in the fuckin' face." He turns to walk away, adding, "I fuckin' hate this town." The following day, the US base takes more rockets from the same village, leading the corporal to fantasize about "cleaning the town out," presumably with violence.[51] His use of profanity during the interaction with the elder seems intertwined with frustration, aggression, and a lack of empathic curiosity about the struggles and perspectives of anyone in the village.

A meme posted by a (now-defunct) veteran-owned company that sold militaristic clothing and gear ("Valhalla Wear") further exemplifies how profanity can enact the suspension of empathy. The meme features an image of heavily armed US combatants aiming assault rifles at some unspecified target in the desert. The text reads, "Deployment thoughts: It's weird. I still feel guilty about killing that rabbit with a pellet gun when I was a kid, but I couldn't give two shits about the Taliban dude I killed the other day." The language in the first portion of this statement is reflective and empathic: "I still feel guilty." The final statement, "I couldn't give two shits about the Taliban dude I killed the other day," marks an aggressive stance not only in what it says but how it says it, using a notable shift of footing keyed by profanity ("shits") and slang ("dude").

These many features and functions of profanity add up: it marks the speaker as tough and norm busting, it mirrors the rupture of bodies in combat, it seems to channel libidinous energy into aggression, it is associated with lack of empathy, and it appears to help direct strong feeling into violence. Some veterans attest that in their experience, in the context of war, anyway, profanity facilitated the act of killing. This is not to claim that profanity on its own creates aggression—in fact, psychological studies furnish no clear evidence for such an argument.[52] Rather, when a person is already in combat, using profanity seems to enhance the military's necropolitical priorities. Two Vietnam veterans, Preston and Ivan, confirmed this in conversation. We spent one long afternoon together in Preston's living room, with Ivan's enormous white Great Pyrenees draped over my lap. After a couple of hours of conversation, Ivan spontaneously opened up about some of his worst experiences of combat. He described a horrifying event in which his unit members killed two Vietnamese children. I asked him whether he remembered anything about "the language the people would use to be in that mindset." Ivan replied by mock-ventriloquizing the way he remembers speaking in combat.

> Hey, in Vietnam every fucking thing you ever fucking said, every fucking moment you fucking said something. You know, 'Motherfucker you just fucking do that.' It created a sense of security in that you were capable of doing horrendous acts if you had to, without feeling any compassion. And you would be able to do things that are downright illegal if you had to. . . . There was no boundaries.

Preston agreed about the link between profanity and boundary violations.

> The language gets you into that taboo area which, you know, it's not only do you think it, but it gets you, yeah, 'FUCK, I can do that.' You know. It's everything into that taboo area, where, you know, they'll mentally get you into that taboo area, as well as the verbal, and I think the verbal gets the mental.

Both men imply that the taboo of profanity echoes and facilitates moral boundary violations. Preston adds that "the verbal gets the mental," suggesting the stance carved out through language encourages a mental stance—and this, in turn, helps condition acts of killing. We see vividly in their words that profanity can play a key role in the military's necropolitical linguistic infrastructure.

"It Don't Mean Nothing"

Some veterans look back at kill talk as tragic for the way it stifled thinking and feeling about loss. I would receive a rich education on this matter from Dave Connolly, who arrived in Vietnam as part of the 11th Army Cavalry Regiment, right after the Tet Offensive in 1968. Dave has a round face, boyish despite the white hair that lies flat against his head. Circular glasses frame his kind eyes, and he speaks in a tenor voice with a South Boston accent that I hear every time I picture him in my mind's eye. Through conversations over the course of several years, I would learn about his family members who helped smuggle arms to the IRA, about the time he accidentally saved Steven "The Rifleman" Flemmi in a bar fight and spent years deflecting Whitey Bulger's invitations to join the Winter Hill Gang, about his disgust with the wars prosecuted by the United States. Military service was supposed to be part of his proud community's identity. "All our dads were in World War II," he says, "and all their younger brothers were in Korea. That's how we were raised. We were supposed to march-step into the next war, be Southie boys, and do what you're expected to do." But, he adds, his grandfather was "in my other ear. 'They're gonna make you into cannon fodder,' he said."

On this occasion, Dave and I sat in his living room under a quilted American flag, hung in a frame with a peace sign soldered to the top edge. Dave was telling me about the first time he knew he'd killed a North Vietnamese Army soldier.

> Right away when I saw what I did, I threw up. And then I went off by myself and cried and got called a pussy. And it was—the other guys just said, "That don't mean nothin'. It's just a gook. Just a gook."

While his platoon-mates devalued Vietnamese deaths, Dave was disturbed enough to consult the 11th Armored Cavalry Chaplain, who happened to be from South Boston.

> I went to him, and I said, "You're Irish. If you don't understand what's going on, how about 'Thou shalt not kill?'" And he said, "Except for gooks. You are here to do your job; do it."

Dave couldn't square it. His mind kept drawing connections between that slur and the way the English discriminated against the Irish. "I was like, okay. But Irish kids are 'nits' that'll become lice." He invoked another contemptuous term for people of Irish descent. "You know, I'm a 'Mick'!" Dave knew from experience that the slur didn't erase the human being. He was right about his own psyche, anyway. He would be haunted for decades by the image of that first man he killed—his shining hair, his cheekbones, his black-and-white scarf.

> They wanted me to think, "Don't mean nothin'." That's not how it feels. That's not how it feels today. If I didn't take nine milligrams of Prazosin every night, I would never sleep again.[53] I would see his face. You know?

The butchery on all sides would get so much worse. Out of eighty-odd men in his unit, fifty-nine were killed in action and everyone else was hit: "It was a fucking slaughter, to no end." By the end of the war, Dave would be shot in the arm, knee, and gut, and left with nerve damage from a partially broken neck. He would become a vociferous antiwar activist, writing poetry to process his memories and political convictions. One of his poems reflects on the common saying GIs in Vietnam used to cope with the horrors: "It don't mean nothing"—the same phrase the guys in his unit directed at him after his first kill.[54] The poem describes Dave in his first days in country, observing the nineteen-year-old soldier who commanded his squad.

> On his second day there,
> they went down into Bien Hoa city
> with their brand new guns,
> just hours after the VC had left,
> and strolled along a wide,
> European style boulevard
> lined with blossoming trees
> and the bloating bodies
> of Americans, dead for days.

> He puzzled at their leader,
> the nineteen year old veteran
> with the pale, yellow skin,
> bleached, rotting fatigues,
> and crazy, crazy eyes,
> who hawked brown phlegm
> on each dead American saying,
> "That don't mean nothin;
> y'hear me, meat?"
>
> And everywhere he went,
> there were more,
> down all the days and nights,
> all kinds of bodies,
> ours, theirs, his,
> until nothin meant nothin.[55]

The young sergeant refers to the living GIs as "meat"—inert flesh—while dismissing the death before their eyes: "That don't mean nothin." Yet even his purulent spit is significant. The projectile functions like an emphatic index, physically connecting with the bodies as if to point to them, while desecrating them with a disgusting bodily fluid, perhaps implying they mean even *less* than nothing.[56] Dave was baffled by this behavior at first, but such words and deeds reflect the politics of death in war. The sergeant was living out his combat trauma while also, in effect, training the new members of the unit how to negate their own humanity. The phrase "don't mean nothin" applied to "all kinds of bodies," on both sides of the war—for in military necropolitics, all are potentially expendable.

American GIs used the phrase "It don't mean nothing" both descriptively and prescriptively during the Vietnam War, like a suggestion for thought. The phrase fights against the obvious. A violent death is intensely meaningful, spilling over with significance and emotional implications for the living.[57] Furthermore, in the model of semiotics developed by Charles Sanders Peirce one hundred years ago, such meaning unfolds over time in a kind of chain; one idea or feeling leads to another, becoming its own signifier that begs for interpretation, so that the chain builds its links, unfolding with deeper cogitation. An intensely meaningful event continues to unfold, leading to perseveration and—sometimes, if the meanings are terrible—debilitating the thinker.

The phrase "it don't mean nothing," then, is a metasemiotic injunction, or a sign about signs, instructing people how to interpret the signifier that is violent death. In war, the suggestion is, it's best not to interpret violent death and to treat it as meaningless and unimportant so as to block the unfolding chain of thought and feeling. "It don't mean nothing," in fact, seems a fine example of a bromide that psychologist Robert Jay Lifton would deem a "thought-terminating cliché" for the way it poses as folk wisdom but shuts down discussion, debate, and thinking.[58] In the final words of Dave's poem, "nothin meant nothin," we hear the narrator resigned to the nihilism of this stance. The first "nothin" here makes sense only if it's glossed as "everything," but the poet is so bereft of meaningfulness that he cannot even bring himself to say that word.

As part of the linguistic infrastructure of kill talk, the phrase "it don't mean nothing" appears to have been an effective technology to help block feeling for some American combatants. You can hear it in documentary footage from a jungle somewhere in Vietnam, in which an off-camera journalist interviews a US squad leader, Lyman "Gene" Dunnuck.[59] Wearing Army green fatigues and a neatly trimmed brown mustache, Dunnuck tells the journalist that "I got five people I got to worry about beside myself, so I make sure all them get back, get myself back; [then] I'll be satisfied." In a hushed voice, presumably trying not to draw fire, the journalist asks Dunnuck how he got his "nickname."

"Killer?" replies Dunnuck, with a smile. "Killed a coupla gooks in a bomb crater one time," he says with a little laugh, scratching his neck. The two were taking a bath, he explains, when Dunnuck threw a couple of Claymore mines into the crater and detonated them, then riddled the men's bodies with several bursts of M60 machine gun fire. Dunnuck gives another quiet laugh, saying, "Just proves don't take no baths while you're in the field."

The journalist follows up. "What's your feelings about killin'?"

> Don't have any. Doesn't *mean* nothing. Guess you could say it was a job to do, that's all. Either you get killed or you kill him.... You don't [got to] have no feelings about it, you know. You see a dead gook, it don't mean anything, you know.

For Dunnuck, the self-protective verbal strategy may have contributed to his success in battle. According to the voice-over on the documentary, he was "among the most respected" soldiers in Charlie Company. He was invested in the welfare of his unit, but any empathy for the Vietnamese people had been terminated by the conditions, and evidently the language, of combat. For him, the verbal renunciation of meaning seemed to facilitate an affective vacuum.[60]

The Global War on Terrorism (GWOT) had its own versions of "It don't mean nothing." Miles Lagoze, for instance, describes one of his Drill

Instructors telling his platoon about killing an entire family at a checkpoint in Iraq when they failed to stop their car after warning shots were fired. The Staff Sergeant indicated he "did what he had to do," adding, "That's the way it fuckin' goes, rah?" "Oorah," the platoon responded, reinforcing his boldly proclaimed indifference.[61]

In a conversation about military humor, Sam told me about "tactical patches" sold in places like Army and Navy stores. They're supposed to look like they're officially issued, but private vendors sell a range of images and slogans, from "Freedom isn't free" to the phrase in circulation since the Vietnam era, "Kill 'em all and let God sort 'em out." Sam's unit liked the patches that attached with Velcro. The guys would "play" with them, putting them under their collars or the flap of their sleeve pocket and flipping the fabric up to flash the message. Sam had one that read "Fuck it," suggesting indifference to the matter at hand—another mechanism of foreclosing feeling.

> I'd flash that when people said, "You good with that, Sergeant?" "Fuck it" is like, "whatever." There was one tactical patch with something like "My give-a-shit meter is at zero." Or sometimes people would make a joke, like, "What's that?" "Oh, that's the last fuck I gave. I give zero fucks now."

I talk to Sam about the phrase from the Vietnam era "It don't mean nothing." He says, "Yeah, when we had a buddy die or kill himself, our phrase is, 'It is what it is.'" The maxim reminds me of casual American appropriations of Buddhism that aspire to confront conditions in the world without analysis or denial—without, in other words, further elaboration of meaning. Some GWOT veterans describe the fatalistic phrase as therapeutic for the way it leans into acceptance, but for Sam, it suggests a tough confrontation with the brutality of what has transpired, for "there's no comfort." Other variations on this theme include "Embrace the suck" and "Suck it up," both of them adjurations to accept hardship rather than objecting to it. In Kurt Vonnegut's surreal and satirical take on World War II, *Slaughterhouse Five* (1969), characters confronted with death used a phrase that sounds like a verbal shrug: "So it goes." It brings to mind the way one soldier in the Iraq war would listen to a Lil John song called "I Don't Give a Fuck," chanting its refrain over and over to steel himself for battle.[62]

Phrases like these may help some combatants handle existentially charged situations, but they cannot forestall thought and feeling every time. After all, nobody would need to use phrases like "It don't mean nothing" if it weren't possible to be in doubt about it. In a crowdsourced online repository of military slang, one veteran defines the statement as "a phrase you said when you were really disappointed, and ... something really meant something to you. It was a thing to say to keep you from going crazy."[63] One day when I accompanied Dave Connolly to Salem State University, he informed a group of students that "It don't mean nothing" was "a self-hypnosis phrase. But," he continued, "our fuckin' problem is that it *all* meant something. And we got home and it chewed its way out—drinking, drugging, beating people in bars, being a real pain in the ass to cops." The only reason judges didn't lock him up and throw away the key, in fact, was that he has three purple hearts, a matter that kept coming up during sentencing.

It Means Something

The way language is used in the US military—its technical lexicons, coy or witty euphemisms, profanity, and foreclosures of meaning—almost never confronts the experience of violence or the costs of it head on. Kill talk offers terrible workarounds, denials of the suffering that Americans inflict on others, and denials of the suffering of service members themselves. And in profanity and euphemism, there may be encouragements to violence through boundary rupture, ludic reframing, and dehumanization. Some combatants embrace all these linguistic devices as markers of masculinity, toughness, and the willingness to suffer on behalf of a greater cause. Others, though, may use kill talk to crutch their way through combat, while sensing they may yet be haunted by the suffering they try to block from their minds.

Dave Connolly, of course, is among the haunted. In military kill talk, he sees not only a device to facilitate the role of the killable killer, but also a calamitous cover-up of the state's misdeeds. Recovering the meaning of war requires pulling back to connect the combatants' terror and misery to the structures of power that shelter the privileged.

In October 2022, Dave sent me another poem, with a dedication: "For Janet McIntosh, who gets it." I think Dave knew we agree about the cost of those bromides like "It don't mean nothing" and the personal suffering and political catastrophes they try to sweep away.

> "It Don't Mean Nothin' Redux"
>
> It was a thing, always was,
> but we didn't know because
> we were rightmotherfuckingthere
> in the shit thisclose and then
> came out the other side,

upright, some mostly unhurt
and had to hold onto somefuckingthing
or cry.
You getting this? Eighteen, nineteen,
boys on both sides, some of whom
had never been with a woman,
had never lived yet,
yet taking lives
or losing theirs,
some listening to Officers
on the other end of both side's radios
who don't have the balls
to come out here with us kids.
It did and will always mean what?
Come on, Amerika, answer me.

Chapter 8
Frame Perversion

The Twisted Humor of Combat

> You're standing here today in your crisp, new uniforms. Your shoes, your brass—they gleam just like mirrors. You look sharp! But always remember . . . until the day that you die, deep inside each and every one of you there has been born and bred an individual who will always be that dirty, sweaty, filth-encrusted, ripped-trousered, camouflage-painted, magnificent little son of a gun whose brethren have kept the wolf away from the door of this nation for over 200 years. Go forth as Marines!
>
> —Commander's speech on the parade deck at Parris Island[1]

Military life offers a welter of conflicting messages.* Contradictory stances are baked into Marine Corps training, as crisp and tidy uniforms contrast with sweat and muck, while Drill Instructors (DIs) solemnly announce they will treat recruits with respect before humiliating and debasing them. The head games DIs play with recruits (described in Chapter 4) sometimes appear to dramatize the lack of reason and care in war, while the enactment of contradictions in training may illustrate how easily the military's official claims and the rules of ordinary social life can be subverted. In the Commander's address in the epigraph to this chapter, we see the way military symbolism evokes a layered persona: publicly pleasing and neatly lined up on the surface, but filthy and feral deep down.

Military linguistic styles can embody these striking contradictions, too. Logistic military speech, for example, is full of dry acronyms and technical jargon, but another register bursts with salty, playful slang. The language of military decorum—including politeness, honorific terms of address, and "values talk" about honor and integrity—contrasts with profanity and insults that sometimes feature prominently, even when against military rules.[2] In a fine

---

* This chapter analyzes words and imagery that may be difficult for some readers to encounter. Please see the "Content Warning and Note on Language" in the front matter for some context and a discussion of the author's reasons for not redacting this material.

Kill Talk. Janet McIntosh, Oxford University Press. © Oxford University Press (2025).
DOI: 10.1093/9780197808054.003.0009

example of the tension, the Army Colonel and trained linguist Terrence Potter has observed that at West Point, conventions of official, formal language contrast with the denigrating nicknames cadets sling back and forth while out of earshot of their superiors.[3]

All military speech repertoires have their role. The formalities and politesse are important for the chain of command and sustain the burnished public face of military honor. The snappy technical words make high-stakes deliberation efficient while projecting mastery and know-how. Slang establishes camaraderie while providing a safety valve for discontent—as when referring to Marine Corps or Army cooks as "death from within," or payday as "the day the Eagle [the US government] shits."[4] As I note in the introductory chapter, one folklorist has suggested the contrast between formal and informal military language equates to "diglossia," a situation in which a community uses two distinct language varieties in different situations, a prestigious one for formal occasions and a more colloquial one for informal.

The concept of diglossia captures some aspects of military linguistic dexterity, but it suggests a neat contextual gap between polish and profanity that doesn't capture the way military symbolism can deliberately merge these modes of being. Consider, for instance, the spirit of contradictions in the famous apothegms by Marine Corps General James Mattis. Mattis has been esteemed by military players for being simultaneously "deeply thoughtful and extremely aggressive," as one profile puts it.[5] He also specializes in paradoxical statements. His advice to Marines about how to succeed in Iraq was, "Be polite, be professional, but always have a plan to kill everyone you meet."[6] When he met with local leaders in that country, the story goes, he told them, "I come in peace. I didn't bring artillery. But I'm pleading with you, with tears in my eyes: if you fuck with me, I will kill you all."[7] Rather than separating composure from ruthlessness, Mattis's most famous utterances place these disparate stances together. And Marines love to quote him, seeming to find his statements amusing, satisfying, affirming.

This chapter focuses on a type of military humor characterized by similar contrasts. The meme in Figure 8.1, circulated online by Marines, offers an illustration. Its visual format resembles a corporate inspirational poster, and it starts in an upbeat tone: "Nothing says I love my job better . . . ." But the language and image twist into a startling resolution: "than tossing a grenade in a room with a smile." In this sardonic statement, the Marine or Soldier takes pleasure in violence.

Frame Perversion 171

Figure 8.1 Internet meme: "Nothing says I love my job better..."

Soldiers know their humor can be grisly to civilians. One blustering text I found on social media, for instance, reads,

> We kill people for a living. It follows that we aren't politically correct.... We willingly charge in to the most dangerous, miserable conditions, and we emerge on the other side with blood on our hands and smiles on our faces. We achieve this with the use of the most profane, dark sense of humor imaginable.... Semper fucking fi.[8]

Yet again, we see imagery of a "smiling" combatant twinned with violent imagery, while the dignified Latin slogan of the Marine Corps, "semper fi" (always faithful), is punctured by profanity. A familiar oxymoron surfaces here: Marines are simultaneously the most honorable and the most norm-defying people you will ever meet. The recirculation of this text suggests that such chimerical stance taking is important to some Marines' sense of identity.

When I asked one Marine to explain the "tossing a grenade with a smile" meme, he replied with a grin, "It shows how badass we are." Yes, but as I came to recognize it as an example of a common pattern, I suspected there's more to say about what it means to push oppositional material together like this. I call the dynamic "frame perversion," defining it, more specifically, as the layering or commingling of frames in ways that juxtapose the prosocial or positive with the antisocial or hostile.

In his work on language and behavior, sociologist Erving Goffman defined a "frame" as an understanding or definition of the social speech situation.[9] A frame offers the sense of what is happening, the relationships and attitudes being established, and the expectations at play. Taken very broadly, as I do here, the concept could be used to loosely encompass several terms in language studies, including "register" (a repertoire used by a particular persona or in a particular social situation), "stance" (the attitude a speaker adopts), "voice" (the speaker's tone), and "genre" (a specific type of text). As we will see, any of these specific elements may be involved in the contradictions struck by frame perversion.

I use the term "perversion" because in the examples of military humor I analyze, a prosocial frame is contradicted, even violated, by the introduction of hostile material. Military frame perversion often begins with a prosocial template—a respectable frame established by, for instance, an inspirational poster, a prayer, a nursery rhyme, or a jocular tone—but it shifts almost immediately into a dark, threatening, irreverent one that viciously negates the positivity. Sometimes these discrepancies appear nearly simultaneously, but in many examples, they have a poetic structure that uses the prosocial frame as a matrix into which an antithetical toxin is inserted. This U-turn veers away from norms and ethical considerations, and the term "perversion" captures this journey into the nonnormative, even the inhumane. Readers will surely recognize the resonance between this military comedy and the contradictory frames I have discussed in training, including its head games, transgressions, and irrationalities. Variations on the theme of frame perversion are so ubiquitous in military semiotics that they clearly do something for participants. What could that be?

I suggest that in military humor, frame perversion encapsulates and encourages military necropolitics. As part of the military's linguistic infrastructure, these memes and jokes offer combatants another means of attenuating sensitivity to suffering, whether their own or that of others. They set a tone during training that casts doubt on prosocial norms and makes the unthinkable and illicit thinkable and doable; after combat, they lean into one's involvement in violence. Frame perversion can also mirror what is sometimes a dual identity among members of combat infantry, who sometimes uphold an orderly, professional side for the public while adopting a dissolute one behind the scenes.[10]

To be sure, frame perversion has multiple affordances, offering varied potentials for meaning making. In some cases I discuss, it may provide service members with a means of processing the dreadful moral situations they find themselves in or even of critiquing the military as an institution. But most of the examples below display a jarring inversion of positive expectations, suggesting deliberate and wanton opposition to (the perversion of) everything a moral person is ordinarily supposed to be.

Situating Frame Perversion in Theory

It can be hard for civilians to relate to the twisted humor of the combatant.[11] Those who have seen their moral bedrock blown to pieces and lived through the disjointed, hallucinatory qualities of war sometimes meet violence and discomfort with levity.[12] Marc Levy, the Vietnam veteran I mention in previous chapters, collected numerous examples of what he calls "tasteless, obscene, unforgivable, lawless jokes whose wit and irony strip combat of its mythic bones, look death full in the face, and somehow make it comical."[13] Some of these jokes follow a frame perversion pattern, like the spoof of "The Night before Christmas," retitled "When the Third Platoon Gunned down Santa Claus." In the new lyrics, the platoon mistakes Santa for Viet Cong and calls in artillery salvos that blow his legs off. A Colonel orders them to cover up the error, down to "burying his goddamn bag."[14] Elsewhere, veteran Larry Rottmann relates a horrendous joke about a so-called gook stretcher that juxtaposes the concept of a "stretcher"—a piece of humanitarian equipment one uses to transport the injured to care—with the image of torturing a Vietnamese captive.[15]

Sometimes, says Levy, grunts themselves wonder "why we found [these] funny."[16] Yet many people use playful language to mitigate extreme situations and lighten the darkness. This is evident in the ironic wisecracks sometimes heard among first responders, or emergency room physicians and nurses. Decades ago, sociologist Antonin Obrdlik suggested that gallows humor among civilians during World War II was vital to morale, providing a psychological escape. Similarly, the geographer Jennifer Fluri describes how twenty-first-century Afghan civilians used humor to cope with the misery of living in a war zone.[17] Humor and irony are not unusual in grim circumstances, and frame perversion is obviously a variation on this theme.

There are clear psychological and collective dynamics involved in laughing in the face of hardship. Laughter bonds communities, establishing out-groups while enhancing camaraderie within the in-group.[18] Laughing about violence may also be a way of rejecting the prospect of shame among its perpetrators.[19] Humor distracts from grief, too; as one veteran notes, sometimes "if you don't laugh, you'll cry."[20] Psychological studies clearly establish that humor can offer emotional release, diffuse tension, and reframe a crisis, with possible physiological and mental health benefits.[21]

Other scholars have seen subtler virtues in humor or sarcasm in times of hardship. Anthropologist Michael Lambek, for instance, describes irony in the face of illness as a kind of wisdom or savvy—an almost therapeutic "inner recognition about the contingency of truth[,] ... a stance that gives ambiguity, perspective, plurality, contradiction, and uncertainty their due."[22] In this reading, irony has an interpretive, quasi-analytical function. When it comes to the service members I talked to, many find it appealing to ironize and mock the way the military's upright self-presentation conceals the gritty realities of military life. In this fashion, humor can also thrive as informal critique.

All these coping mechanisms are certainly part of humor in war. At the same time, the material I focus on in this chapter also suggests a symbolic return, again and again, to the theme of how the world can be upended. For some scholars, such patterns will remind them of the theoretical vein in humor studies that asks what makes something funny to begin with. Incongruity plays an important role in these theories. The linguist Victor Raskin's "semantic theory" of humor, for instance, suggested that many jokes involve two contrasting "scripts," or interpretive frameworks, and that the "text" of a joke is at least partially compatible with both scripts.[23] Many jokes start by encouraging the listener to interpret the text using one script and, at the punchline, shift frame to an opposing script, as in this joke: "Why the long pause?" asked the bartender. "I dunno, I was just born with them," replied the kangaroo.[24] Others have elaborated incongruity theory with the suggestion that humor results from benign threats to a person's sense of how the world should be.[25]

In the cases of frame perversion I discuss, there's no question that opposing or unsuitable items placed side by side beget amusement. But the violations of "how the world should be" in the examples I discuss are hard to construe as "benign." Rather, military frame perversions often depict violent acts that have real immanence for the combatant.

Furthermore, the cases I discuss in this chapter involve a specific *kind* of incongruity or shift, from a prosocial or professional frame to a deadly one. They detonate a bomb amid conventional morality and sociality, almost reveling in destruction as they elicit the service member's wry laughter. This, I suggest, has effects distinct from those typically described in the humor literature. If a common argument is that preexisting psychological distance from tragedy makes jokes like these funnier,[26] I suggest that rendering the tragic funny through frame perversion helps *create* psychic distance from it. In other words, my interest is less in what makes these violent jokes funny and more in what the humor might do to a person's understanding of violence. For instance, a common psychological reaction to one's own violence is what psychologists call "perpetrator disgust," which some players overcome by learning "to accept or even enjoy the violence."[27] The humor in frame perversion is part of the military's necropolitical linguistic infrastructure that may both enable violence and help combatants cope with it when it happens, whether by their hand or to their body. Frame perversion jokes, especially told and received in a military context, refuse to be appalled by violence.[28]

Notice, too, that there is a structural resemblance between frame perversion and profanity in combat. In the preceding chapter, I discussed how profanity violates norms and symbolizes in microcosm the rending of the flesh; in these respects, it offers a symbolic anticipation and echo of the violence of combat. Frame perversion may be similar, offering a distinctive shape for thinking and feeling within the military's necropolitical linguistic infrastructure. US combat humor, with its simultaneity of opposites, might be not merely a coping mechanism but also a symbolic mirror of spiritual turmoil and anomie and an encouragement to unmoor the self from conventional morality.

To go deeper into this idea, I turn to the work of anthropologist Alex Pillen, who analyzes the strange relationship between atrocity and what she calls "non-sense," or signs and symbols that don't make sense in any ordinary way. Based on her fieldwork in post–civil war Sri Lanka, Pillen notes that "wartime subjectivities" are often engulfed in "the simultaneous presence of contradictory moral frameworks ... [particularly] the coexistence of a prewar morality with a violent new reality in people's hearts and minds."[29] Not only that, but, she adds, this "inhumanity and cosmological turmoil are reflected in linguistic and performative expressions."[30] Her examples focus on how the simultaneity of opposites—such as ritual symbolism that enacts both caretaking and murder toward the same figure—reflects what she calls "'cosmological damage' in the aftermath of the extreme violence of twentieth century civil war."[31]

If Lambek underscores dark irony as a kind of wisdom, and Pillen suggests the "simultaneity of opposites" reflects subjectivities roiled by war, my analysis of frame perversion in the US military adds an additional possibility. I suggest that there is something both pedagogical and enabling in the military material I discuss and that it connects to the combatant's necropolitical subjectivity. Perhaps inasmuch as these jokes encourage a moral void, they can assist the combatant to do the necessary. As the psychotherapist Edward Tick, who has worked with veterans for decades, explains the sequence: "In order to kill, one must invert one's sense of good and evil."[32] In Chapter 4, I suggested that during the "head games" of basic training, military higher-ups sometimes ironically layer cheerful stances with aggressive acts to presage deadly behaviors and to encourage not more encompassing vision (as in Lambek's model), but occluded vision when it comes to human suffering. Military semiotics are designed not only to cope with hardship, but also to channel affect and curtail empathy, rendering certain lives less grievable while encouraging an illiberal necropolitics. A chronic tension in military life—hard for military personnel to state directly but expressed nonetheless in the symbolic output I describe—is that noble military ideals aren't easily reconciled with the realities of war. In combat, killing gets messy, moral purity seems unsustainable, and normal schemas of meaning, ethics, even humanity may be thoroughly dislocated. Frame perversion mirrors and even celebrates this dynamic, as can be seen in the following examples.

Cadences

The pedagogical aspects of frame perversion begin in basic training. Classic examples can be found in "cadences." Sung or chanted in rhythm while marching, while running in formation, and during drills, their lyrics are passed down through generations of military participants. Though cadences are often modified or semi-improvised, their patterns are part of military folklore. Their call and response segments and entertaining lyrics fend off boredom or exhaustion while enhancing camaraderie. They also have a mandatory ritualistic element, in the sense that singing along is not only patterned, repetitive symbolic behavior but also more or less required. If a Drill Instructor initiates a cadence, recruits will find militaristic ideas issuing from their lips. As with other aspects of military training, the Department of Defense has tried in the last couple of decades to discourage racist, sexist, and overtly brutal expressions in cadence calling, but the message has not altogether done away with these.

Traditionally, cadence subject matter includes the unfaithful spouse or girlfriend (those are known as "Jody cadences"), the polluting or hateful qualities of the enemy, the prospect of one's own death or injury, and the epic dimensions of one's own aggression. And some cadences engage in frame perversion in their representations of violence, like this example I collected from a Marine who served in Iraq:

> Little yellow birdie with a little yellow bill
> Landed on my windowsill

> Lured him in with a piece of bread
> Then I smashed his little fucking head.

This cadence employs the singsong quality typical of a child's nursery rhyme, creating an initial frame of tenderness akin to a caregiver's recitation to an innocent child. The text orients affectionately to a yellow bird, focusing on its aesthetic details and using the diminutive term "little." The speaker entices the bird to come closer, whereupon the scenario takes a jarring turn, culminating in profanity and deadly violence. The final use of the word "little" is particularly striking, as the diminutive occurs in a frame of apparent rage or sadism.

The next example also starts with the poetic structure of a benign children's song or nursery rhyme, then describes killing everyone in sight.

> I went to the market
> Where all the families shop
> I pulled out my K-bar [a sharp knife]
> And started to chop
> To the left right left right left right kill
> Left right left right you know I will
>
> I went to the church
> Where all the families pray
> I pulled out my machine gun
> And started to spray
> To the left right left right left right kill
> Left right left right you know I will[33]

The rhythm of the lines, "left right left right left right," invokes both the playful repetition one might hear in a children's song and the barked instructions of a DI ordering a march. The final phrase of each stanza, "you know I will," has an air of particular menace.

When such nightmarish texts appear during that susceptible liminal period of boot camp, their frame perversion has a pedagogical edge. In training contexts, in fact, one can most clearly see the contrast with Alex Pillen's examples of the simultaneity of opposites. Her material comes from a population tending to its wounds in the aftermath of civil war. Cadences in the US military, though, are presented to individuals undergoing reconditioning to become weapons themselves. Their function is transparent to Levi and his friend Russ, both of whom trained in the Army in the early aughts.

LEVI: There's a lot of really sadistic cadences that we sing and revel in and make jokes of and all that kind of stuff.

[The two reminisce about a variation on the theme of the "little yellow birdie" cadence.]

RUSS: I take it as they're trying to break down what's acceptable human behavior and what they expect out of you. So it's part in jest and part very real when they say—you know, one of the cadences is, there's multiple versions of it, maybe, but it's, you know, it's like, "I went to the schoolhouse where all the kiddies play. I pulled out my M-16, and I began to spray. Kill, kill, kill, kill"—and then it's like, "I went to the market"—you know, so they have different versions of it, but essentially it's all things that are all basically war crimes you're not supposed to— [Russ laughs uneasily] I mean, they tell you to kill the enemy, too; they sing about that. But you also sing about killing unarmed civilians, and I think that's a very—I think the purpose of that is they want to break down in your head what you think is acceptable human behavior.... I mean, they're, essentially, they're getting you ready to do that, in a lot of ways, I think.

Beyond cadences, DIs in the Marine Corps use other forms of frame perversion as they underscore that conventional norms do not hold in the military. In a recent YouTube short, one DI describes how he responded when his recruits wished him "Merry Christmas" on Christmas morning. (Christmas and Santa Claus, with their evocations of childhood innocence and good cheer, are popular themes in military frame perversion.) "I was like, OH! It's Merry Christmas, is it? Well ho-fucking-ho." He describes how he then tormented the recruits, making them dump out their footlockers, kicking their belongings everywhere, and so forth. "I was like a fricking orchestra conductor there, just, you know, of pain and suffering. I got kids over here crying and freakin' out, kids over here getting slayed...." He laughs to remember it.[34]

Zippo Lighters

Once "in country," the creativity of combat infantry tends to both celebrate and comment wryly upon military necropolitics. A prominent medium for US soldiers' creativity in the Vietnam War era was the Zippo brand metal lighter, carried by nearly every GI. Initially used to light cigarettes, these lighters were eventually weaponized in "search and destroy" missions, during which they were used to set fire to thatched dwellings and entire villages. Many GIs brought their Zippos to engraving stalls in South Vietnam cities or on large bases, personalizing them with words and images of their choice. Some selected the particulars of their unit, a map of their stationed area, or the name of a loved one. The engraved lighters looked cool and, in the words of one veteran, "felt tough." For many GIs, Zippos may have been that simple, but some requested popular slogans that turned their Zippos into a venue for predigital memes of sorts. Many such slogans would start in one register or tone, only to take a dark twist.

A common engraving on lighters, for instance, would open with Psalm 23:4, then abruptly shift into profanity and intimations of hostility.[35] The example in Figure 8.2 reads, "Yea though I walk through the valley of the shadow of death I will fear no evil for I am the evilest son of a bitch in the valley." The biblical voice is evident in the words from the famous psalm, including the archaic term "yea." Then the tone darkens, claiming profane evil rather than piety for the psalm-quoting self. The familiar reverence of biblical language makes the profanity feel particularly jarring. The frame shifts so thoroughly that the second use of the term "valley" seems to refer not to a figurative space of Christian perils, but to a literal valley, perhaps in the Vietnamese highlands, where the "evil" combatant stalks his enemies.

Figure 8.2 Vietnam War–era Zippo lighter, reading "Yea though I walk..."
Photo credit: Lightergallery.com.

The example in Figure 8.3 slightly modifies this popular text while retaining the archaic register of biblical language with the term "shall" before veering into an aggressive contemporary voice: "As I walk through the valley shadow of death [sic] I shall fear no evil for I'm the evilest son of a bitch." (Another common ending was "for I'm the meanest motherfucker here."[36]) Again, the piety in the first half of the text is subverted by the profane and "evil" sentiments in the second half.

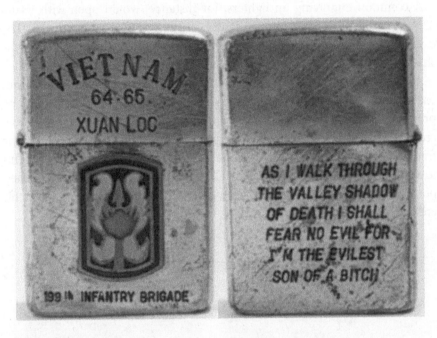

Figure 8.3 Vietnam War–era Zippo lighter, reading "As I walk…"
Photo credit: Lightergallery.com.

On other Zippo lighters, the golden rule was perverted into a deadly intimation: "Do unto others as they would do unto you, only do it first."[37] Another Zippo slogan transforms the gentle, aphoristic phrase about the wisdom of nature—"[X] is nature's way of telling you [Y]"—into a snarky observation about war violence: "A sucking chest wound is nature's way of telling you that you've been ambushed." In Figure 8.4, we see an especially popular Zippo phrase: "Let me win your heart and mind or I'll burn your god damn hut down."

Another variation on the same theme is, "Give me your hearts and minds or I will wreck your fucking huts."[38] The American use of the phrase "winning hearts and minds" can probably be traced to President John Adams, who liked to claim that the American Revolution had been driven by a change in the minds and hearts of the colonists. During the 1960s, President Lyndon Johnson frequently alluded to a persuasive "hearts and minds" campaign in

Figure 8.4 Vietnam War–era Zippo lighter, reading "Let me win your heart and mind..."
Photo credit: Shutterstock.

Vietnam, hoping to turn the North Vietnamese people against Communism. However, American GIs learned to be cynical about this phrase once they saw that the brutality of their war was hardly converting anyone. A deeply disenchanted 1974 documentary about the Vietnam War was titled, simply, *Hearts and Minds*.[39]

This instance of frame perversion—"Give me your hearts and minds or I will wreck your fucking huts"—may have served multiple purposes. For those who had lost faith in the war, it could amount to political critique, an expression of frustration toward the lofty rhetoric of politicians out of touch with the grim realities of war. But for others, or perhaps even for the same individual, the phrase could evoke exuberant sadism. Both meanings might be available—a performance of counterpolitics, or yielding to the darkness. In ostentatiously performing the combatant's moral abominations, Zippo slogans hover ambivalently between cynicism about military violence and license to commit it.

The phrase "hearts and minds" continued to circulate during the Global War on Terrorism and remained subject to jaded reworking, in the vein of frame perversion. In his memoir about the war in Afghanistan, for instance, Miles Lagoze describes the pattern of paying off families and forcing them to leave their homes so that US soldiers could move in, then writes, sardonically, "hearts and minds," followed by a thumbs-up emoji.[40]

Death Cards

The use of ace of spades cards, sometimes called "death cards" in the context of the Vietnam War, furnished an additional medium for the pattern of frame perversion. The United States Playing Card company and other companies such as Bicycle Cards sent over crates of specially printed packs of ace of spades cards (sometimes marked "BICYCLE SECRET WEAPON").[41] Unit leaders or individuals could special order decks printed with their identification (e.g., their Company, Battalion, or Regiment) or sardonic text of the sort I describe in this section. Americans would leave these cards on the body or in the mouth of deceased enemy fighters or scatter them across villages and trails to intimidate the enemy. The Army veteran Dave Connolly tells me his superior officers handed out packs of ace of spades cards printed with his unit's information. I wondered whether anyone worried about reprisals, but he says the men weren't really thinking about that. "It was another level of PSYOPs [psychological operations]," he explains. "Masculine chutzpah, kind of like gang warfare. We were meant to throw them into a hooch [a dwelling] or leave them on bodies."

American GIs entertained a myth that the suit of spades symbolized "death" to Vietnamese. This belief may have emerged when the French occupied Indochina, bringing fortunetellers who used spades to predict death and suffering. However, it doesn't seem the cards represented anything in particular to many Vietnamese peasants until US soldiers repeatedly left such cards on the bodies of their victims, effectively reassigning the symbol to mean violent death at American hands.[42]

The very use of cards in the context of killing involves an element of frame perversion. The ace of spades originated, of course, as one card in a deck typically used for games, not deadly deeds. The act of leaving a single card behind as a trace also evokes the tradition of "calling cards" (or "visiting cards") in eighteenth-century and nineteenth-century Europe, where aristocrats making social calls would leave decorative printed cards on a small tray to indicate their visit. Calling cards are precursors to modern-day business cards. Playing an ordinary card game, visiting a friend's home, or handing over a business card obviously involve social interactions fundamentally different from conducting violence. And while calling cards or business cards imply the prospect of an ongoing, cordial relationship, leaving the death card sends a terrifying message. The combatant not only marks their presence but also takes credit for the death, mocks the body (by, for instance, leaving the card in the deceased's mouth), and hints that they may return to inflict further damage.

Sometimes the content printed on individual death cards engaged in frame perversion as well.[43] The card portrayed in Figure 8.5, for instance, juxtaposes contradictory tones and stances. The ordinary spade icon is overlaid with a

Figure 8.5 Death Card: "For a job well done..."
Photo credit: Sergeant Herb Friedman.

skull and crossbones. The text opens in the register of a tradesman advertising his skills with a calling card or advertisement, featuring a seemingly endearing and harmless nickname: "For a job well done, 'Squeaky,' call . . . " This is followed by a shift into a profane and menacing voice: "Deadly / The ass kicken mother fucker / I deal in death." The pun involving the word "deal" refers both to dealing cards in a game and dispensing something—in this case, death.

The card in Figure 8.6 reads: "NVA/VC [North Vietnamese Army / Viet Cong]: We love you but we've come to kill you." It adds a sardonic suggestion of how to get in touch with the US unit's medic, who, of course, has no

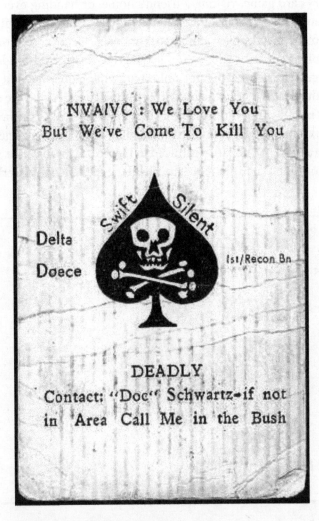

Figure 8.6 Death Card: "We love you but . . ."
Photo credit: Sergeant Herb Friedman.

intention of helping the enemy. The card thus invokes simultaneous opposites: love and medical assistance, set alongside a promise of murderous violence.

Similarly, the card in Figure 8.7, headed "Dealers of Death," blends the format of a service advertisement with its death threat: "We Specialize in V.C. Extermination / 24 hour Service / Special Mercinary [sic] Rates." Using the professional language of an extermination service invokes the classic image of the supposedly polluting and subhuman Other who deserves to die. The card

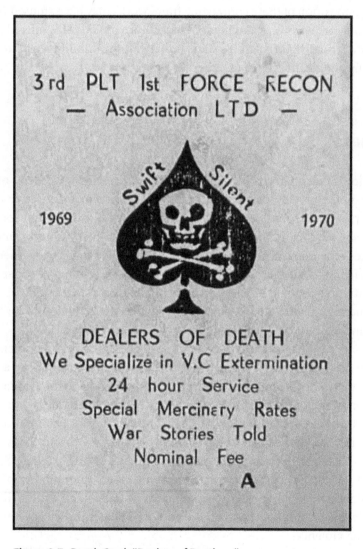

Figure 8.7 Death Card: "Dealers of Death..."
Photo credit: Sergeant Herb Friedman.

also promises the card dealer will tell "war stories," sardonically integrating the social framework of storytelling into the context of violence.

Regardless of how much these details were understood by Vietnamese (likely very little), leaving such cards among the dead was purportedly "good for morale" for US troops. But the frame perversions depicted on the cards also reflect and amplify a distinct positioning within the moral universe. Conventional, prosocial frames, whether professional or friendly, are overlaid with grisly intimations, akin to a horror movie in which a child's party or sunny Sunday afternoon abruptly turns bloody, upending the moral order. The juxtaposition of these contrasting frameworks may have amused GIs, but it also mirrors war's abandonment of social norms. The cards offered a semiotic infrastructure for affective stances that endorsed indifference to others' suffering and death.

Memes

The Global War on Terrorism has spawned its own innovative forms of frame perversion. Over the past two decades, US service members have created thousands of memes that have zipped around online communities. To be sure, these have their limitations as windows into "military culture," since they partake of the irony, hyperbole, and nihilism common in the wider meme culture zeitgeist. That said, certain military memes pull frame perversion into a twenty-first-century mode of expression, as they mingle positive themes with menace. Figure 8.8, for instance, contrasts an invitation to an "Easter egg hunt" with the image of a soldier throwing a grenade at ISIS.[44]

Beyond the obvious frame perversion set up by the contrast between activities (an Easter egg hunt versus grenade throwing), this meme carries a subtler disjuncture. The formulation "[X] be like" is a common opening for a meme, appropriating Black English syntax ("be" rather the standard "is") to set up a dramatization of something a type of person says or does. The condition dramatized by the "[X] be like" setup is usually amusing or positive, not violent. With a quick internet search, for instance, I found a meme reading, "Students be like / I don't need to write it, I will remember," and another picturing an enthusiastic looking elderly white man: "Men be like / I'm finally ready to settle down." But the example in Figure 8.8 violates those expectations by invoking violence.

The meme in Figure 8.9 features an image of a Marine roughly grasping a barefoot man—presumably an enemy combatant—by the back of the neck

Figure 8.8 Internet meme: "Marines be like . . ."

and frogmarching him through what looks like a combat zone. The text, written in a stencil font reminiscent of military printing, reads, "Helping Terrorist [sic] Around the World / USMC Assistance Program." This tongue-in-cheek slogan of a fictitious organization mimics the tone of a charitable NGO, starkly contrasting with the harsh physical treatment depicted in the image.

The example in Figure 8.10, a meme credited to the veteran-owned clothing company Valhalla Wear, begins by invoking "Miranda Rights," which are typically read to a person upon arrest in the USA. The meme adopts the list format of these rights, starting with "You have the right to . . ., " establishing a formal and legalistic frame. However, this expectation is quickly subverted by profanity and aggression: "You have the right to get fucked" (in the sense of being the target of bad or violent deeds). The remaining "rights" continue in this vein, threatening violent retribution for backtalk and sardonically suggesting that the person apprehended in war has a right to talk to a lawyer—if they "can find one in the next 30 [seconds]," which, of course, they cannot. When they fail, they revert to the first "right" again ("the right to get fucked"). The ultimate message is that in a time of war, the enemy's rights, civil or universal, are irrelevant.

Figure 8.9 Internet meme: "Helping terrorist around the world..."

Frame Perversion 189

Figure 8.10 Internet meme: "Wartime Miranda Rights."

Again, we can read more than one affordance (i.e., more than one potential function or meaning) into this meme. For some, it may encourage human rights violations, while for others, it may serve as a critique or a reflection of cynicism toward official wartime formalities and ideals. This last theme emerged during a conversation I had with Sam, the Army veteran introduced in Chapter 6 who served in an artillery unit in Afghanistan. We were sitting together, looking through a Pinterest page of military humor I had archived, when he paused at a picture of a tactical patch that read, "My idea of help from above is a sniper on a rooftop." Sam drew my laptop closer and started to laugh. He explained one reason Army guys would find that funny is their frustration with the constraints of official language. Commanding officers often used public-facing formalities that left him longing for more direct expression of what actually happens in combat. He elaborated further.

> Big Army is in charge of our language, you know? Because I am [Sam made scare quotes with his fingers] "first and foremost a representative of the United States of America." I have to say things like "winning hearts and minds." And then, like, the grunt on the ground is really, "Call it what it is and tell me I'm going to kill somebody, and I kill somebody," right? . . . You know we just—we don't have time for those formalities. It's almost like—I guess it's like you write an academic paper in college,

you know? That's not how I speak, but I have to present that image. . . . But it doesn't get the job done when I'm talking to somebody, you know?

In another conversation, Sam was full of snark about the contradictions he noticed between lofty Army slogans and the gritty realities of service, especially when he was promoted to Sergeant.

> You know wearing the uniform, you represent America, America is professional, America looks good—you know? . . . Like, we have to present a narrative of being these educated, smart, tactically proficient, very physically fit, confident people who have their heart in the right place and are also willing to shoot a gun. It's not like reality but . . . we're meant to recite our shared virtues, like "loyalty, duty, respect, selfless service, honor, integrity, and personal courage." . . . There's the creed of the non-commissioned officer that went, "No one is more professional than I"—so it's like, when you're doing something really unprofessional, you would just joke and be like, "No one is more professional than I."

For Sam, then, military humor offers cynical commentary on the gap between public-facing euphemisms and idealistic expressions—"no one is more professional than I," "help from above," "hearts and minds," and so forth—and the messy or brutal reality of what happens on the ground, which is better expressed in raw and unabashed terms.

The internet teems with further examples of military frame perversions. Illustrations can be found in the memes that read, for instance, "Dear Diary / I like totally smoked a terrorist today," "I enlisted to make a difference / And I can make 30 differences per magazine," "Hearts and Minds campaign / Giving two to the heart and one to the mind," and "My parents told me I could be anything / So I became a weapon." A final example is a meme featuring a close-up of a bright-red drop of blood on a blade of grass. The caption starts with a popular marching cadence—"What makes the grass grow? Blood blood blood. What do Marines do? Kill kill kill"—then invokes good environmental citizenship: "Marines: Environmentally friendly since 1775." Again we see a frame of life-giving care intermingled with deathly language. Even the visuals in this meme involve semiotic perversion, as the fresh green blade of grass representing life and hope is besmirched in a twisted world where the blood Marines spill, rather than water, somehow makes the grass grow.

Talking to the Dead

Evidence of frame perversion in combat is hard to come by for an outsider, but an incident captured in the 2018 documentary *Combat Obscura* includes a stance shift that resonates with the verbal maneuvers we have seen. The footage was shot by Miles Lagoze, who at the time was serving as a Marine Corps cameraman assigned to gather video material in Afghanistan for USMC Public Affairs. Lagoze retained the outtakes and, to the Marine Corps' dismay, edited them into a powerful film billed as "the footage the USMC doesn't want you to see."[45] In one incident, the men in Lagoze's unit shoot and kill someone they believed to be an armed enemy combatant but later realized was an Afghan civilian.[46] The footage begins as the Marines enter an area just outside a dwelling made of packed mud. One Marine has leaned his rifle against the wall, and another can be heard off camera saying, "No, wrong building." The dead man's body lies against the dirt wall in a splatter of blood, face down, his left knee and arm bent, and his feet bare. A Marine leans in to grab the man's shirt and roll him over, while saying in a jocular, satisfied tone, "Jus' like a deer."

A couple of the men talk about the logistics of breaching a door while this is happening. Right around this moment, the group appears to realize that the dead man was unarmed. "Oh shhhhit," says one voice with irritation. A couple of voices can be heard: "He didn't have a gun on him, did he?" "Goddammit. No, he didn't." The camera cuts briefly, then a Marine approaches and steps over the man's legs while addressing his bloody corpse in a friendly tone that almost sounds like that of a sympathetic doctor: "All right, buddy, how you doing today?" As the Marine begins to lift up his arm to inspect his wounds, we suddenly hear a palpable and cruel sneer in his intonation: "Looks like you just got ffffuuuucked. Oooo, hand!" He examines the man's bloodied hand with evident curiosity. "Right in the fucking hand." Inspecting the man's entrance and exit wounds, the Marine says enthusiastically, "Oooo! Through and through!" He concludes in a tone of mild interest that "he lived for a little while."

I read all of the men's words aloud to two Vietnam veterans, Preston and Ivan (see Chapters 3 and 7), to hear their reaction to the abrupt shift in tone between feigning a cheerful greeting, then sneering at the man's bloody demise. To them, this instance of frame perversion served as a coping mechanism. Preston said, "Yeah. They're playin' over it. It's like they play over it 'cause they don't want to admit it's real. It's a form of denial." Ivan jumped in: "Keeps you somewhat sane in an insane situation."

Wave Tactics

In each case of frame perversion I have discussed, one voice, sometimes the first in a sequence, invokes a conventionally valued frame. Then, abruptly, a dark, hostile, boundary-crossing, or existentially threatening message lands. As cadences, slogans, memes, and combatants' talk switch from cheerful, child-friendly, holiday-friendly, family-friendly, sacred, professional, or legalistic frameworks into exuberant endorsements of violence, they flip an executioner's switch from life to violent death. Their extreme toggling from chipper or prosocial to bloodthirsty, the gross mismatch of registers and themes, highlights the incongruity, throwing into relief the monstrous quality of the deadly frame. Not one of the messages returns to innocence; they transition instead from life to death, and the undertow is clear. Nihilism wins in military humor.

I have suggested that when presented in training, frame perversion throws conventional moral order into question and is part of the linguistic infrastructure that subtly works on the future combatant's inner world. The frame perversions generated by combatants themselves resonate with and apparently reflect combatant subjectivity. They reflect war-weary cynicism about formal, official, prosocial attestations, sometimes critiquing the military's own façade, and they mirror the devastation of moral expectations. They also seem a microcosm of some of the bizarre paradoxes combatants may be ordered to enact. Marine Corps veteran Tyler Boudreau describes wrestling with the "disparity" between the notion that the US military was in Iraq to "demonstrate our humanity" and the subjective experience of "embracing the violence," even killing with "elation," as a necessary condition for pulling the trigger.[47] In fact, one of his narratives about combat experience highlights the way that frame perversion in military humor resonates so well with the terrible semiotics of combat. Boudreau describes how, in 2004, General Mattis ordered Marines to smile and wave every time they passed an Iraqi to display their goodwill, as part of the counterinsurgency campaign. Yet this encouragement to be diplomats and potential killers at the same time did not sit easily in the minds of wary Marines, who found themselves pointing rifles with one hand and waving with the other. Boudreau reflects on the contradictory poetry of the situation:

> It was a struggle because one does not generally wave and smile without some notion of humanity, [but] I don't think one can point a loaded weapon at a person without attaching feelings of hostility. . . . [The] paradox confounded me both emotionally and psychologically.[48]

Mattis's "wave tactic" policy inadvertently created the very semiotic dynamic—frame perversion—of so much dark military humor. It became, says Boudreau, a "tension in the consciousness," because "these two mentalities don't go together. I'm trying to connect with you or I'm trying to steel myself because I might have to kill you."[49] Indeed, whether or not its confusion stems from counterinsurgency tactics, war tends to present combatants with moral murk again and again. The journalist Kevin Sites, who interviewed combat veterans about their worst experiences, summarizes it like this: "Killing turns everything on its head.... [It] is a lifelong sentence to contemplate the nature of one's own character, endlessly asking, 'Am I good, or am I evil?' and slowly growing mad at the equivocation of this trick question whose answer is definitively yes."[50]

Reading a draft of this chapter, Doug Anderson, formerly a corpsman with the Marines in Vietnam, remarked that this material's dislocations and internal contradictions reminded him of the dynamics of "moral injury." "You cross your own boundaries all the time in combat. The public thinks we are behaving like Eagle Scouts and thinks when we return we'll be the same old well-behaved people we were when we left." But there is no such moral purity, he says. Combatants are left to dwell in "their own internal contradictions about war." In the next chapter, I explore how some veterans, Doug included, have used a very different linguistic strategy—namely, poetry—to exemplify, to probe, and to mourn the moral injuries of war.

SECTION IV
AFTER WAR

Chapter 9
Poetry of Rehumanization

"Portrait of a Boy at Dawn"

The green metal bird shimmies
North along the muddy banks,
Sweeps south, flying high, low,
A risky business feeling them out,
The tall slender reeds bowing
Beneath us.

We bank hard right, dip again
Blowing the green curtain down,
The boy equally stunned,
His mud-laden AK no match

In the forever time,
His astonished face, his forever *No!*
When *brrrraaapp* flips him backward
His starry cartwheel a bloody splash
Dissolved in mud.

In the cool morning air we nose up,
Thankfully pull away, his immense
Frightened eyes follow me,
Forever wake me at home.

—Marc Levy[1]

In the previous chapters, I have explored the brutality of US military "kill talk" among infantry: its suppression of individuality and vulnerability during basic training, its evasion of grief and empathy during combat, its occasional indulgence in sadism, and its promotion of the killable killer mindset.* Some combat veterans normalize this verbal repertoire; they don't necessarily bring

---

* This chapter analyzes words and imagery that may be difficult for some readers to encounter. Please see the "Content Warning and Note on Language" in the front matter for some context and a discussion of the author's reasons for not redacting this material.

Kill Talk. Janet McIntosh, Oxford University Press. © Oxford University Press (2025).
DOI: 10.1093/9780197808054.003.0010

it into civilian life, but they consider it to have been a matter-of-fact aspect of their military experience. Others look back on it with moral distress, seeing it as entangled with psychic challenges they experienced on returning home, and sometimes with their mounting critiques of the warmongering state. Increasingly, such veterans have turned to the language arts for a very different verbal medium through which to process what happened in war.

Consider what Marc Levy's poem above achieves that military language never could. The title indicates this is a "portrait of a boy"—already a pivot from combatspeak, with the term "boy" evoking vulnerability and potential that military epithets for Vietnamese people certainly did not. And, in fact, the "portrait" captures a *relational* moment between US combatants and the boy that—again, unlike military kill talk—allows us a flickering window into the awareness of both sides.[2] As the narrating voice in the helicopter describes the American GI's sensations of gliding, banking, and "feeling out" enemies as if on the hunt, it also makes the boy's experience legible—his astonishment and horrified objection. There is a tenderness in describing his lacerated body as a "starry cartwheel"; for a split second, the image almost mirrors a carefree childhood, as well as a flashing celestial body. In the final stanza, the reader feels the protective luxury of superior technology—the helicopter lifts the GIs away in the "cool morning air"—in tension with the doomed boy's accusing eyes, indelible on the conscience. Marc's poem (I will use the first names of the poets I know personally, for continuity with the other chapters) spells out a terrible crack in military necropolitics. Combatants are supposed to mete out death without a second thought, but this poem consecrates the boy's suffering, and the moral authority of his objection, "forever."

If kill talk strives to curtail emotions that might threaten the state's agenda, poetry "invites you to feel," in the words of poet and critic Muriel Rukeyser.[3] Veteran poetry explores old feelings and invites new, expansive, subversive ones. It helps the writers themselves hold up inchoate memories to give them new clarity of meaning, thinking, and feeling far beyond the discouraging linguistic infrastructure offered by the military. And their poetry can give unlikely veneration to godawful experiences. Extracting these terrible happenings from the recesses of the mind-body, veteran poets closely observe their details, probe them for profound implications and, in this way, honor them.

Veteran poetry varies in proficiency, from the novice's crude catharsis to the mature art of the seasoned, but all the veteran writers I have spoken to attest they benefit from the genre. Its form and expectations open possibilities not available in either kill talk or ordinary narrative. To begin with, the very notion that one will write "a poem" invokes solemn creation, prompting the writer to draw breath, stand at a distance from the events portrayed, and adopt a new angle of approach.[4] Poems can speak in many voices, and some writers find this lifts their inhibitions. One instructor who works with veterans, for instance, told me they felt "much freer to be critical of the military in verse." For some, poetry's condensed language and attention to imagery allows them to capture truths that eluded them in the fog of war.

A poem, too, allows a writer to work within a fragment of time, without having to produce a fully emplotted narrative.[5] Take, for instance, Dave Connolly's short poem titled "Food for Thought, 3:00 a.m." He writes,

> They moved in unison like dancers in a ballet,
> the spider 20 inches from my rifle,
> the Vietcong 20 feet farther out, in-line,
> each slowly sliding a leg forward.
> I let the man take one more step,
> so as not to kill the bug.

Dave tells me he wanted to make this poem powerful by "getting it down to the second," placing the reader inside his mind, "like you're looking down the rifle with me." This poem aspires to share a fragment of wartime subjectivity to help the reader grasp, in Dave's words, "just how unholy it got."

Poetry's invitation to metaphor can step in when language cannot "say a thing straight" (the phrase comes from Vietnam War veteran and poet Bruce Weigl[6]). We see this dynamic in Doug Anderson's poem "Xin Loi," the title of which means "I am sorry" in Vietnamese.[7]

> The man and woman, Vietnamese,
> come up the hill,
> carry something slung between them on a bamboo mat,
> unroll it at my feet:
> the child, iron gray, long dead,
> flies have made him home.
> His wounds are from artillery shrapnel.
> The man and the woman look as if they are cast
> from the same iron as their dead son,
> so rooted are they in the mud.
> There is nothing to say,
> nothing in my medical bag, nothing in my mind.
> A monsoon cloud hangs above,
> its belly torn open on a mountain.

War's aphasia left Doug with "nothing to say" to the parents' pathetic gesture, but in his poem, nature grieves the tragedy; the monsoon cloud's belly has been rent open like the child himself, and the rain of sorrow is imminent.

In this chapter, I examine a selection of poetry from veterans of the conflicts in Vietnam and the Global War on Terrorism, focusing on how they process war's haunting aftermath. Over the last two decades in the USA, "poetry therapy" (sometimes referred to as "poetry of recovery") has become a means of helping people express and unburden themselves.[8] Having watched veteran poets read their work out loud, too, I am struck by their whole-body involvement as they reevoke their past. The writers may shake, rock, or sweat, sometimes needing a few hours to "come down" after a reading. Vietnam veteran Lamont Steptoe wept as he read aloud his memories of fear at one reading I attended. "Do you know what it's like to come under mortar fire? To pray in the pauses. To think this may be your last day? Or hour? Or second? Do you know what it's like?" The crowd was there, and some of us tried, however imperfectly, to imagine ourselves into his skin. Such events offer the possibility of what Jonathan Shay calls a "communalization of grief" in which listeners can "listen, believe, and remember."[9] The realities of war may thus be recognized and elevated, rather than being "stuffed" as kill talk would have it.

But this communalization is hardly a mere matter of feeling, for there is a decidedly political dimension to much veteran poetry. As the poet Carolyn Forché describes the genre, "poetry of witness" exhorts against forgetting by attesting to what has happened at the hands of the state.[10] The author's account is candid and heavy with truths—a form of unfiltered and frank speech scholars have termed *parrhesia*.[11] Their writing may be "therapeutic," but it does much more than clear the mind; it serves the public good as well.

The Rise of the War Poets

The act of writing poetry stepped into what was a terrible silence and lack for some veterans. In an unpublished memoir about his Global War on Terrorism (GWOT) service as a Marine, Maurice Emerson Decaul writes that Parris Island excelled at making recruits into "efficient, rational killers" but left a gap he describes as "lack of instruction on how one is supposed to manage oneself after crossing the killing boundary."[12] After all, training and combat encouraged "the demonstration of mental toughness by not seeming to be too affected by death,"[13] but this display—enhanced by the linguistic infrastructure I have described—did not neatly establish the limits of experience. Grief and guilt still managed to seep through.[14]

While the US military now offers more postdeployment assistance than it did in the Vietnam era—PTSD screenings, tips for "adjusting to a normal routine," logistics for locating benefits and health care—some returning combatants still experience crushing emotional and moral disorientation.[15] At Parris Island, amid a conversation about combat in the Middle East, a couple of young veterans discussed how Marines adjust to civilian life after experiencing combat. Dirk said he still hasn't fully returned because he "loves war" and is considering rejoining to go back into a war zone. Noah shrugged and said, "You just have to deal." Javier said, "It's a matter of maturity.... Some of these guys are more mature than others."

If the US military hopes that service members can rely on personal qualities to handle the juxtaposition between their warrior and civilian selves, other societies have more systematic methods. Atavip of New Guinea, for instance, undergo prewar rituals to place fighters into a state of dissociation during combat. As a result, they consider themselves relieved from personal responsibility for killing.[16] Historically, some Indigenous American societies would stage purification rituals for the entire community, cleansing combatants of their deeds while enlisting non-combatants in their welfare.[17] Systems like these offer a framework of meaning through which fighters can achieve some distance from what they did.[18] But as Tyler Boudreau, former Marine and Drill Instructor, suggested to me, it is hard to communalize the return from war in societies like our own, in which the very decision to go to war is not collective to begin with. In such cases, restoration at the level of the whole society seems a fantasy; reintegration can only happen at the microlevel.

If the US military offers no holistic structure for returning soldiers, the nation as a whole seems to have endorsed the option of talk therapy. One might imagine a pressing need to narrate war experience.[19] But for US veterans, talking about combat experience is notoriously challenging. The generation that fought in World War II, for one, was famous for its masculine stoicism. Many simply did not discuss their battles, nor were they expected to. A generation later, Vietnam veterans came home to an America that glared at them accusingly. There was little room for them to talk about where the dreadful stereotypes—"baby killers" and the like—were wrong and no sympathy if veterans wanted to process the ways in which they were right.[20] The diagnosis of PTSD, which now invites sympathy and therapeutic treatment, was not even formally identified until 1980. And some veterans simply did not wish to narrate their grim memories. Many preferred not to relive them and had been trained by the military to squelch their feelings anyway.

By the time of the first Gulf War, Americans were determined not to repeat the miserable homecomings of the Vietnam era or to worsen the newly acknowledged PTSD resulting from combat. This resolve, however, has led to three decades of civilians greeting veterans with the platitude "Thank you for your service," without comprehending why this phrase might receive a mixed reception or why it falls so short of the act of listening with an open mind.[21] Even when their interlocutors are well meaning, many veterans find simple conversation inadequate for expressing anything significant about their inner lives after war. Kevin Basl, who served as an Army mobile radar operator in Iraq, found himself struggling to communicate about the war after matriculating into college. "How was I supposed to sum up two deployments in a few sentences? How could I explain what it was like to load metal boxes containing the remains of soldiers onto a plane at night in the desert? I stopped telling people I had been in the military."[22] War's violence tends to defy ordinary language. In Army veteran Eli Wright's poem "Game Over," he writes, "We came home incomplete, / with no words to describe / how our hearts are now beating us black and blue / for some of the things we had to see and do."[23]

Indeed, the communicative divide between combat veterans and civilians involves at least three gaps. One is between the experience of war and the capacity to put it into words. I have already noted (as in Chapter 4) that military training sometimes hints at war's irrationality and internal contradictions. Many scholars have additionally noted that trauma tends to silence the tongue and that ordinary language is maladapted to describe violence anyway.[24] As the anthropologist E. Valentine Daniel puts it, "Violence is an event in which there is a certain excess: an excess of passion, an excess of evil. The very attempt to label this excess ... is condemned to fail."[25] Combatants tend to remember war nonverbally; as Kevin McSorley puts it, their bodies "carry war in ways that are at once intensely felt and intractable, and yet seemingly unstable and unknowable."[26] And while conventional psychoanalytic approaches suggest trauma can be addressed if incorporated into a meaningful story, perfect coherence often eludes those with post-traumatic stress. According to trauma theorist Cathy Caruth, traumatic experiences are never wholly assimilated; they defy understanding, and as a result, "knowing and not knowing are entangled in the language of trauma and in the stories associated with it."[27] When ethnographer Zoe Wool spoke with US veterans injured in the GWOT, she found their reminiscences fragmented; for them, "the war remains in tiny pieces."[28] Doug Anderson tells me that like many Vietnam veterans, he spent years after the war losing himself in drink and the cultural exuberance of the late

'60s and early '70s. "I was just numb," he says. Only "a long unwinding" could start to bring his inchoate feelings and thoughts about war to the surface.

The second gap is the acute experiential divide between combatant and civilian. The civilian's ignorance can be maddening, and the chasm may feel impossible to traverse. This dynamic can be seen in Ken Burns and Lynn Novick's documentary about the Vietnam War, when Ron Ferrizi offers an anecdote from his days as a LOACH (light observation helicopter) crew chief in 1967. Ferrizi says when he returned from a combat mission to the firebase one day, an American journalist approached him. "Wow," she said, "can I ask you a couple of questions? What was it like out there?"

> How does it feel that a .50 caliber just opened up, shooting a half-inch piece of lead at you? [*Ron pulls hard at his mustache, wincing as if frustrated.*] It's hard to describe. It's shitty. [*He laughs briefly, bitterly.*] I mean, isn't it, isn't it apparent what it's like? Wanna know what it's like? Go look at it! Go out there, go see the bodies. I was ready to whack her. Yeah, I wanted to blast her. I was ready. [*He points an index finger skyward, shaking his head.*] Whoa. [*His voice rises and his face reddens in seeming fury.*] You wanna know what it's like? BOOM, there it is! I'll give it to you, right now! You wanna feel it? You wanna see it? I'll give it to ya! That's what you want? Is that what you want? [*After a brief editorial cut, the camera returns to Ron speaking in a more composed way, though still with a furrowed brow.*] I don't wanna tell you what it's like 'cause I don't wanna remember it! But that's the insanity that it brings out.[29]

Ferrizi seems to bristle for several reasons. Why should he relive the horror just to entertain or titillate this naïve journalist? Even if he did, he says, "it's hard to describe"—in fact, maybe the only way to convey the visceral dread of the situation would be to show her the bodies or menace her with actual violence. If words can't translate the lived experience, the gap between combatant and civilian can never be closed—a gap that can result in mass denial of war's realities and veterans' needs.

The third gap is between civilian and military language. Combatant language doesn't work in civilian life. The jargon is impenetrable, the euphemisms evade, the profanity offends sensibilities, the nihilistic, fatalistic statements feel irreverent, the humor is twisted. I met one veteran at the Joiner Center writing workshop who said he had tried to put military language out of his mind; it "disturbs" him now, and the way he talked when he returned alienated his family and friends. Looking pained, he said, "It's been very hard for me to adapt, linguistically."

Vietnam veteran D. F. Brown suppresses the macabre combat humor I discuss in Chapter 8, even if—as he explains in a poem—he still finds it funny: "I can tell true stories / from the jungle. I never mention / the fun, our sense of humor / embarrasses me. Something / warped it out of place / and bent I drag it along."[30] Embarrassment about combat language is surely one reason why veteran John Musgrave included a preface to his poems, explaining they reflect "the language of teenage warriors"—yet he also explains why he can't write in other terms. The words are not merely "descriptive"; rather, "the obscenities *are* the experiences themselves. In these poems, I have used the language of my war."[31] Some veterans prefer to stick with the word substitutions I describe in Chapter 7—the ones that sound bizarre and stiff to civilian ears. "Even now," Decaul confesses, "writing the word Kill makes me nervous. I'd much rather use euphemisms such as 'eliminate a threat' or 'process a target.'"[32]

Even when veterans speak candidly and intelligibly, some civilians may struggle to handle what they hear. Marc Levy once read several of his war and postwar vignettes aloud on video,[33] then came across a librarian's review of it. Deeming his accounts unsuitable for high school students, she complained that Marc spoke "through gritted teeth" and sounded "so angry." Marc was incensed by her reaction. He tells me,

> [I felt like] this woman has no idea. She's so disconnected. She's so out of it when it comes to combat and war. But in hindsight it makes sense. I can understand fully now that civilians, especially American civilians, compared to others, have a more romanticized, sentimentalized, mainstream-generated perception of war.

After Vietnam, some veterans didn't necessarily recognize how the war had affected them. Many tried to pick up the pieces and block out their war experiences, even if signs of trauma would emerge years later. Some told me it felt like a sign of weakness to seek therapy. A couple of them remarked they worried they would offend a therapist if they were honest. Glenn Petersen writes of his enduring inner conflicts about talking about the war; acknowledging his pain goes against his self-image as a stoic, he worries he will be seen as "seeking sympathy or trying to draw attention to myself."[34] It was a turning point for some when the veteran-led "rap groups" ("rap" in the sense of casual talk) emerged in the 1970s, offering a rare space for veterans to speak candidly with mutual understanding and without self-censorship.

Writing their experiences down, even without an audience in mind, was a watershed moment for some veterans. It happened spontaneously for Marc Levy. Once home from war, he slept for years with a canteen of water from the jungle by his bed and a weapon next to him—first a loaded .25 automatic pistol under his pillow, later a machete under the mattress, then a meat cleaver. For reasons even he doesn't fully understand, he also began to keep a notebook at hand so he could write down his nightmares upon waking. He wound up publishing two volumes of his war dreams. Over the years, Marc transitioned into publishing poetry and prose.[35]

Other Vietnam veterans, too, salvaged themselves through writing—sometimes taking inspiration from antiheroic World War I poets such as Wilfred Owen and Siegfried Sassoon. Together they would go on to create an extraordinary network of soldier-poets. Larry Rottmann, Jan Barry, and Basil T. Paquet, for instance, formed 1st Casualty Press (as in the saying "The first casualty of war is truth"), which published the first anthology of Vietnam veterans' poetry in 1972, titled *Winning Hearts & Minds: War Poems by Vietnam Veterans*. William (Bill) Ehrhart, also an inspirational leader in the movement, explains in a retrospective essay that "most of the soldier-poets [in this volume] were not really poets at all but rather soldiers so hurt and bitter that they could not maintain their silence any longer."[36] Ehrhart subsequently edited down some five thousand submissions for a second volume of Vietnam War poems, titled *Carrying the Darkness*. Some of the poets who emerged over the years would be widely anthologized and recognized, including Bruce Weigl, Yusef Komunyakaa, Michael Casey, Doug Anderson, and David Connolly.

Several of these men helped found the William Joiner Center for the Study of War and Social Consequences at University of Massachusetts Boston. Its summer veteran's writing workshops, one of which I attended, were run for many years by veteran poet Kevin Bowen; these were sites of great colloquy and creativity. Some GWOT veterans came to writing after Lovella Calica founded the nonprofit Warrior Writers in 2007 to counteract veterans' social isolation. Chapters rapidly emerged in several cities, and Warrior Writers fostered public readings and anthologies as well as a manual for leading veteran writing workshops. The workshops offer an accepting space and writing prompts that sometimes focus on experiential detail—the act of putting on one's first uniform, the smell of cordite, what it feels like to click a safety on or off, and so forth—to help writers connect with the minutiae of memory rather than feeling pressured to write "poetically" or in sweeping terms. Warrior Writers has also worked with Combat Paper and its offshoots, described in the next chapter. Further writing initiatives, such as the National Endowment for the Arts' Operation Homecoming, have brought writing workshops to VA medical centers, as an accompaniment to conventional therapy.

The early efforts of veteran poets aren't always artful, but why would they be? Without training in the craft, most people don't have a strong sense of how to make words across the poem hum or collide in meaningful ways; how to exploit formal elements such as meter, musicality, or line breaks; how to pace a poem's evocation of images and voices. But many veteran poets describe their lyrical poetry of inspection and revelation as "cathartic" and, in some instances, life-saving. In what follows, I interpret several poems and, sometimes, analyze what their writers say about the process in order to understand how veterans use poetry to speak back to kill talk.

Metacommentaries on Military Language

While setting up an exhibit of veterans' art and poetry at the Fifteenth Street Quaker Meeting House in Manhattan, I came across a poem Jan Barry had printed in letterpress at Frontline Paper in New Jersey.[37] It read, in part,

> Modern sons and daughters
> Are carefully educated
> In how to dispatch, eliminate—
> But not call it murder;
> Torment, but not call it torture

Veteran poems about the military's verbal infrastructure are not unusual. Distance makes it easier to look back in dismay at the way they used words to discredit the suffering of the enemy or to dodge the emotional brunt of killing. Some veterans reflect on how kill talk rendered the enemy opaque. Marc Levy's spare poem "Peacetime," for instance, opens by recalling the words the GIs would use to talk about heading into combat.[38]

> We gave it names
> Like contact,
> Movement or
> Bringing scunnion.[39]
> We psyched ourselves up
> Scowling, "Time to kick ass
> And take names."
> But never talked about
> The human beings

Such word choices move between bloodless euphemism ("contact") and visceral profanity ("kick ass"), but none of the available options humanized the enemy. The poem proceeds to describe the mounting tension before an explosion of violence, after which the cycle would "start all over again." Marc returns at the poem's end to reflect on the GI's experience, trapped in the ghastly rhythms of tense anticipation and explosive combat, sometimes without a word or thought to the people on the other end of these encounters. The poem ends,

> That's how it was.
> That's how we lived . . .
> And never mind the human beings.
>
> Never mind.

Note that the poem highlights the relationship between language—they never *talked* about the human beings—and consciousness—they didn't *mind*, in the sense of casting their attention to, the human beings on whom they inflicted violence. Marc's double line break throws his final phrase into relief, as if to impress on us the horrifying implications of the neglect he once shared in. Similarly, in Doug Anderson's poem "Kill Him with a Name" (see Chapter 6), we see that those broken by regret after service are often remorseful about not merely what they and the entire military apparatus did to others, but also how they *labeled and conceptualized* those others. ("We were taught to call them gook, / slope, slant, and worse, / because it's easier to kill / that way, easier to sleep at night / if you've merely crushed a roach / under your boot heel.")

Other veteran poetry, too, tackles the erasures in military doublespeak and the ruthless military profanity that captures certain hard truths. At a 2008 reading, Vietnam veteran Thomas Brinson recounted his disgust at a certain military euphemism. "A C-130," he read, "carrying a full load of flag-draped coffins," coffins that Air Force personnel referred to as "fallen angels." "Fallen angels?" Brinson seethed. "I've seen K.I.A.'s. There's nothing angelic about them."[40] Bryan Alex Floyd's poem recreates the language of a Lance Corporal lecturing the new guys in Vietnam: "To be scared is okay . . . but don't expect sympathy. / Sympathy is a sad word found in the dictionary / somewhere between scab and syphilis . . . Know this about this fucked-up war / that will never unfuck itself— / Life in Vietnam is a sea of shit."[41] Again, such metalinguistic writing highlights the erasure of compassion in the lexicon of the Vietnam War—in this case, compassion for US soldiers themselves.

And Floyd's final lines underscore the way profanity mirrors the debasements of a war zone.

In 1997, Vietnam veteran David Bianchini sent a friend an extraordinary prose poem of a letter from the Fairton Correctional Facility, indulging what he calls "all my wordy psychotic abandon."[42] Titled "To Shane," this stream-of-consciousness piece consists partly of words and phrases uttered by Vietnam War combatants, separated by ellipses. By isolating them from context, Bianchini confronts the reader with their moral perversions (see Chapter 8), flanking horrifying images of weapons, destruction, and death with flippant and sardonic intimations of fun and joy.

> Flaming frolic... jungle rot and joviality... magical mayhem... medal monkeys... bouncing Betty's... compresses for crispy critters... give him a cap to the noodle... Yippee for genocide... the goody-goody soup of human bone... butterfly bombs... human cotton candy... Cinderella with a scythe.

Assembling these barren responses to suffering, Bianchini puts them on freakish display. One phrase, capitalized and bracketed by quotation marks, repeats a grim ostinato: "'IT DON'T MEAN NOTHIN... DON'T MEAN A THING.'" That saying, as I explain in Chapter 7, was used after a terrible death to encourage combatants not to think or feel. Bianchini seems to emphasize that it made urgent demands on consciousness—and its recurrence in his prose poem sounds deranged. Bianchini deems himself "psychotic," but might the war's necropolitical language be equally troubled?

Marine Corps veteran Jeremy Stainthorp Berggen, assigned to mortuary duty in Iraq, composed a poem titled "PTSD" that attacks the platitudes other service members offered him to handle his distress.

> He said, c'mon suck it up
> They said, it's time you just moved on
> She said, wherever you go, there you are
> And all I heard was
> Nagging voices
> Barking orders
> Missile raids [43]

The phrases Berggen critiques, here, are examples of thought-terminating clichés—along the lines of "It don't mean nothin'" or "It is what it is"—that aid and abet military necropolitics. But even if the military had offered a contemplative vocabulary, Berggen implies, the soundscape of war drowned out the potential for clarity. The poem goes on to rethink the term "PTSD" itself, experimenting with new possibilities to capture Berggen's experiences: "Post Terror Soul Disorder," "Pathetically Trying Slowly Dying," "Potentially Terminal Spiritual Disease," and, finally, "Please Try Something Different." Rather than accepting PTSD as the glitch of stressed-out neurons, Berggen recasts the old acronym to reflect his "soul" and "spiritual" ailments. By the poem's end, he connects his distress to broader maladies of the nation-state: "I mean, just give me . . . / A war that hasn't started / A country without greed."

These poems document a damning litany of verbal failures. The anodyne euphemisms—"fallen angels"—that deny the ghastly effects of violence. The frame perversions in oxymora like "butterfly bombs" that suggest a moral void. The refusal to mention the humanity of those on the other side and the ugly racial slurs that treat them like abominations. The adjurations to stop seeking meaning—"It don't mean nothing," "Suck it up," "Move on"—that dismiss the need to feel and think after loss. Poems like these imply that at least some of the moral injuries of war stem not only from a military-industrial complex hungry for war, and not only from the brutal effects of war's violence, but also from military kill talk.

Poet and critic Martin Espada writes that if "phrases such as 'weapons of mass destruction' bleed language of its meaning, then war poets must restore the blood to words."[44] By way of example, Espada cites Wilfred Owen's famous poem "Dulce et Decorum Est," with its images of World War I combatants fumbling for gas masks and a dying soldier with "white eyes writhing in his face." Owen's poem concludes with a rebuke to the popular martial rhetoric of a century ago. He condemns the Latin phrase from Horace, often inscribed on memorials, *Dulce et decorum est pro patria mori* (It is sweet and fitting to die for one's country), as "the old Lie." Espada writes, in response to Owen's poetic example, "the most powerful poems of communal grief, for me, insist upon intimate, concrete, particular details, images, and narratives. Grief must have a human face; consolation must have a human voice."[45] Veteran poetry forces a reckoning with the human horrors and sorrows that kill talk attempted to skirt.

Reawakening Feeling, Metabolizing Grief

In Vietnam, Preston Hood was a SEAL, a Navy elite special operator trained for highly specific, often grueling, missions. He once embraced the tough image, he says, to the point of literally eating glass in a bar to show off. Kill talk helped him be "emotionally detached"; the war's racial slurs and profanity helped get him into a mindset of what he calls moral "blackness," or a "taboo area" where anything is doable. Once he was in that headspace, Preston says, "Killing was easy. I never thought about it; it didn't matter. It was like tying your shoes. It wasn't traumatizing at all."

A turning point came, though, after a firefight in which Preston shot a young teenager who had been part of a group of Viet Cong. The boy was moaning in pain on the floor of a dwelling, and looked into his face. Preston found himself reaching into his pocket and giving him a shot of morphine before running outside. Though the choice happened without thought, his best explanation is this: "I wanted his death not to be awful." In this moment of nascent compassion, he tells me, he began to "turn back into a human being." He would think about this a lot in the years to come.

Still, Preston emerged from the war in fits and starts. For a long time, he says, "I lived my life on the edge, almost like on a suicidal edge," not caring much whether he lived or died. "I didn't talk to anybody for years and years and years; we were expected to stuff it." In a short film about veterans' struggles, Preston expresses total disenchantment with what he had been required to do. "There's no apple pie, there's no God, and what you did was bad, you know. At the time, I guess it was what we needed to do, 'cause you're trained to kill and you think you're doing good for your country, and yet again you know it's not the right thing to do. When you think about it now."[46]

Preston also started to rethink the language of war. Of the phrase "it don't mean nothin'," he tells me,

> It really *does* mean *something* the way I interpret it, and this was just our way to play *over* it—*not* deal with it when we're supposed to be dealing with it. You know, and it was just a way to try and forget someone died. It was like another conditioning thing, and that to me was one of the most conditioning phrases *ever* that we went through. It's the worst thing we probably could have done, is stuffing it.

When he couldn't stuff it any longer, in the 1980s, Preston finally sought therapy from the VA, but he didn't like the therapist, who "mostly wanted to toss medication at you and be done with you." But he had an intuition that writing might be helpful. He used to write as a young person, and he had begun to meet veterans from Vietnam interested in meeting American veterans through the William Joiner Center. Having grown up in a society that valued poetry, many of the Vietnamese veterans had memorized poems about grief and trauma. To Preston, they also seemed not to bear anger toward their

American counterparts. Maybe, he reasoned, poetry could be a medium in which to "metabolize" all the killing, to grieve, and mourn, and become fully human again.

In fact, Preston had started writing a poem during his months in country, but couldn't finish it. "I couldn't get blood to ink," he laments.[47] "My mind would withhold and couldn't write the trauma of Vietnam." In the end, this poem would take him twenty-five to thirty years to complete. Titled "Rung Sat," it is named after a large mangrove swamp area in South Vietnam where the North Vietnamese Army and Viet Cong had infiltrated and Preston would lie in wait to kill. (For the complete poem, see notes.[48])

The first lines came to him earliest. They capture the visceral terror of living on the edge of death, as in, "I wade ahead / fall through myself like a stone, / enemy voices passing only meters away." Over time, Preston added devastating images from memory:

> Blood trails along the river
> . . .
> shallow graves dug quickly,
> brown-uniformed & black pajamaed bodies,
> rice bowls & fish heads—
> children half-buried in dirt.

Preston tells me it took nearly three decades to write the final lines of the poem, which read,

> I am a man half in the water, half out;
> my legs suck into mud.
> My hands hold my head outstretched—
> hasten to deliver me among the dead.

In that final image, Preston is mired, perhaps sucked into the miasma of killing and fear. He begs for deliverance, seeming to offer up his own head as a plea. He tells me, "at the end of that poem I felt, I felt like John the Baptist. I was trying to recover my humanity, and I didn't really know it at the time as much as I do now. . . . My writing was my salvation after war." John the Baptist had emerged from the water, proclaiming the baptism of repentance for the forgiveness of sin. He would go on to scold King Herod for his sins, but Herod would behead him in vengeance. The complex figure in Preston's poem seems to represent a tumult of stances: the offering of his own life (head) in hope of forgiveness, but also a quasi-suicidal gesture, as if his own death might be the best mercy and perhaps atonement.

Preston tells me writing can feel "shamanistic." Poems will "sometimes just flow through you," against what he calls the military's "code of silence." "When I was writing it made me feel good; I didn't know why." His theory is that just as snakes bring forth their new selves by shedding their skin, the poet releases an outgrown skin with each poem, for a small rebirth.

Doug Anderson, who served as a corpsman (medic) in a Marine rifle company in Vietnam, also tells me writing poetry was the medicine that reawakened him from the emotional numbness of combat. In "North of Tam Ky, 1967," Doug describes what that blockage felt like as he crawled through a clearing to a buddy who had just been shot.[49]

> I had inside me in those days a circuit-breaker between head
> and heart that shut out everything but the clarity of fear.
> I felt nothing for you then, rolling you over, looking for the exit
> wound . . .
>
> I knew only the muzzle flashes too close in front, the sniper
> cracking on my left and I flipped the switch and went cold.

Twenty-three years later, the poem adds, Doug is still "tinkering" with those same wires, "a filament flickering in the heart and then the blaze of light." There is hope for feeling after all these years, perhaps especially through words.

Rehumanizing the Soldier

If kill talk aspires to dull the sensitivities of US combatants so that they are not destroyed by grief when battle buddies die, the rejoinder of much soldier poetry is to linger on horror or pity to rehumanize their dead. While conventional narratives and storytelling have been important to many veterans as they articulate and share their stories,[50] poetic form has the ability to suspend a moment in time. The critic John Berger notes that "the poet approaches language as if it were a place, an assembly point, where time has no finality, where time itself is encompassed and contained."[51] This lack of finality, says Berger, gives the poem and its observations a kind of "immortality." War poems can thus consecrate the magnitude of combat tragedy, as if to speak back to the military apparatus: You cannot erase people so easily.

Dave Connolly, the Army rifleman who served in 1968–1969, became a force to be reckoned with among the antiwar activists and Vietnam poets. Some of his poetry perseverates on the moment he lost two buddies in combat, a loss that would feel like a black hole in his life. Jerome had arrived on the same flight to Vietnam as Dave, and Billy would join them three weeks later. The three of them, all about nineteen years old, survived the terrifying operations in and around the Michelin rubber plantation, where dozens of US soldiers died. On a fateful evening some weeks later, the trio was assigned to an observation post on a perimeter with little cover. They lay toe to toe as the night gathered. Dave remembers the frogs singing near the tree line, then falling silent. Someone out there was moving.

Dave remembers that Jerome smiled and winked, getting into a crouch and moving his head up to get a bead on the enemy. He was shot instantly in the eye, the bullet spinning him around. "I can smell his blood as I'm talking to you," says Dave. Dave and Billy put their rifles on a berm, emptying their magazines and throwing grenades. An RPG ripped through the berm, the force and shrapnel blowing Billy into Dave. Dave clambered out from underneath Billy's body and grabbed his M-16. He remembers screaming for a medic, weeping, shooting toward the VC again and again long after their weapons fell silent.

In a prose piece titled "Incident near Ap Bac Ba Ria," Dave describes how the military's indifferent language helped him conceal his grief in front of the other grunts.[52] He still remembers the dead men by their combat nicknames ("Ratshit" and "Weasel," on which more later in this section), and these recur in the writing that perpetually takes him back into the moment.

> In the morning, I was hard as one of those pieces of teak down below, full of Fuck Its and It Don't Mean Nothings in front of those other brothers; they understood. Some of them cried as Ratshit and the Weasel were bagged, but not me, not in front of them.

While the phrases kept his tears at bay, he could never forget the moment those boys were vaporized. Something like kinship went with them. "Ratshit still winks and smiles at me sometimes, just before being shot in the eye. And Weasel still rushes at me, and embraces me, all bloodied and blown open. And I wake, and cry. I wish I had then." His performance of indifference in 1968 hurts to remember.

In a diner in South Boston, on an unseasonably warm mid-December day, we are eating turkey sandwiches with burned fries. "Ratshit and Weasel, their deaths," Dave tells me, "I'm still writing about it, because I CANNOT let go of it." I say something like, yeah, I see you approaching it again and again. I know you've dreamed about them a million times. "Yep," said Dave. "You need to keep circling it." He shows me a poem that enlists the reader midstory:[53]

"Why I Can't"

Ratshit and the Weasel and I
are behind this dike, see,
and Victor Charlie,
he's giving us what for.
And Ratshit, he lifts his head,
just a little, but just enough
for the round
to go in one brown eye,
and I swear to Christ,
out the other.
And he starts thrashing,
and bleeding, and screaming,
and trying to get
the top of his head
to stay on,
but we have to keep shooting.
A B-40 tunnels into the dike
and blows the Weasel against me.
He doesn't get the chance
to decide whether or not
he should give up and die.
Now I'm crying
and I'm screaming, "Medic,"
but I have to keep shooting.
At this point, I always wake,
and big, black Jerome
and little, white William,
my brothers,
are not dying beside me
even though
I can still smell their blood,
even though
I can still see them lying there.
You see, these two,

> they've been taking turns
> dying on me,
> again and again and again
> for all these long years,
> and still people tell me,
> "Forget Nam."

This poem suspends those agonizing seconds, refusing to bury the dead. But poems like this are not mere effusions of one man's compulsive memory. They are a political rejoinder to silence. To paraphrase the author Annie Ernaux, sometimes autobiographical writing does not merely translate the past, but transmits it, ensuring that its subject matter *exists*.[54] And John Berger suggests that poems are a privileged site for this insistence. In fact, he uses a war metaphor to make his point:

> Poems, regardless of any outcome, cross the battlefields, tending the wounded, listening to the wild monologues of the triumphant or the fearful. They bring a kind of peace. Not by anesthesia or easy reassurance, but by recognition and the promise that what has been experienced cannot disappear as if it has never been.[55]

As speech acts, Dave's elegiac poems sanctify the men's deaths, refusing to allow the state to delete them with impunity. In making the deaths indelible, he highlights how precious their lives *should* have been. Again, John Berger on a poem's "promise": "language has acknowledged, has given shelter, to the experience which demanded, which cried out."[56]

And what about the language politics surrounding those nicknames? I've described how Drill Instructors gave recruits insulting nicknames to detach them from their roots and reframe them as disposable (Chapter 3). In a war zone, combatants may also give each other "tags"—catchy mnemonics that, in Vietnam's "meat grinder," had a pragmatic angle. "Brothers came and went," Dave told me. "They were wounded or killed so fast you couldn't keep names straight." The tags implied the interchangeability of recruits, one dying and another quickly taking his place. They also reflect the ribbing often found in homosocial groups—affectionate, but just barbed enough to perform heterosexuality. "The Weasel looked like a Weasel—his nose stuck out farther than mine," says Dave. "A guy we called Smoke was the color of a smoke fire. That's how you kept things straight in your mind. . . . I was Mad Dog or Deadly because I wasn't afraid. . . . Ratshit," meanwhile, was "a big, Black kid from Baltimore. We couldn't come up with a nickname for him as we already had a medic who had the same looks and the nickname Buddha. Ratshit's nickname came the first time he sneezed: no 'achoo.' It sounded like he said 'ratshit,' so that was his nickname, which he hated." (Though his tag may have been inspired by the sound of his sneeze, it's easy to see why Jerome didn't like it. In fact, as I hear it with today's ears, it sounds racist, though no such idea seems to have been on Dave's mind.) The dubbing of battle buddies with these casual, sometimes unwanted tags was an index of war's indifference to people's prewar sense of identity and full humanity. But here is an example of terminology failing to fully steer thought and feeling: Dave has spoken and written to me many times about his wholehearted love for both men.

Still, in some of his poems, Dave pushes against the tags' dismissive implications. In "Why I Can't" (quoted earlier in this section), for instance, he switches midpoem from their tags to their given names, Jerome and William. Dave also shows me a rhyming poem in a packet of unpublished material that makes a similar shift. Titled "For the Weasel, KIA 02/08/69," it addresses one of his dead friends directly, beginning,

> I had this dream the other night
> and in it you weren't dead
> and we went fishing on your pond.
> Remember? Like you always said?

The poem describes Dave's experience of waking up crying, then continues:

> Weasel, you were dead before you hit the ground,
> hit through and through and through,
> I tried; I really tried to save you,
> but there wasn't shit that I could do . . .
> I think of you so often, Billy;
> it's like you're still right here by me.

Again, the figure in the poem shifts from his war incarnation, "Weasel," to a present moment when he has his birth name back ("Billy," the diminutive of William). In an email, Dave tells me he had promised both Jerome and William's mothers he would never reveal their last names, since "their mothers were so horrified at how they died."

> Why did I tell you their [first] names? They were young men who would have been of worth to America if they were not wasted. Both of them were hard as nails when the shit came and like loving uncles to the little kids in the villages. . . . I had to humanize them with a real name despite my promise about their last names and will keep that promise even though all of our mothers are long gone.

"Weasel" and "Ratshit" capture Dave's voice of that time, and the ruthless play of language in the military, but, Dave concedes, they aren't as "humanizing" as their given names. Meanwhile, just as Billy and Jerome perpetually haunt Dave, they populate and repopulate his poems, giving the lie to that phrase "It don't mean nothin.'"

Rehumanizing the Enemy

Kill talk aims to stifle the spread of empathy, yet at the Joiner Center's veteran's writing workshop, empathy emerged as a recurring theme. Veterans spoke of the empathy evoked by poetry in their writing classes, wrote about their empathy for the people they once fought against, and lamented what they saw as a decline of empathy in the American public. One Global War on Terrorism veteran said he was pursuing a master's degree in "empathy and transnational communication." The collective ethic focused on expanding the will to humanize others.

Many veteran poems look back in sadness at the bleak, constricted reality of their consciousness in war. Take, for instance, Bill Ehrhart's "Time on Target."[57]

> We used to get intelligence reports
> from the Vietnamese district offices.
> Every night, I'd make a list
> of targets for artillery to hit.
>
> It used to give me quite a kick
> to know that I, a corporal,
> could command an entire battery
> to fire anywhere I said.
>
> One day, while on patrol,
> we passed the ruins of a house;
> beside it sat a woman
> with her left hand torn away;
> beside her lay a child, dead.
>
> When I got back to base,
> I told the fellows in the COC;
> it gave us all a lift to know
> all those shells we fired every night
> were hitting something.

This deceptively simple poem reveals the shifts in Ehrhart's consciousness over time, suggesting radically different perspectives on the same scene. The final stanza reaches back to Ehrhart's wartime mindset, as he recounts cheerfully telling his comrades what he'd seen, giving them an emotional boost, "a little lift"—notice the affectionate language—to know they were doing their job and "hitting something." What did they hit? Back then, "telling the fellows" might have involved the common military slurs for Vietnamese people. Writing in hindsight, though, Ehrhart uses tender words—"woman" and "child"—as he sets the scene of destruction, letting each term linger with a line break. The mind's eye can picture his unit trundling by while she sits grievously wounded, immobilized in shock next to the little body, her life, like her house, in ruins. When Ehrhart shifts into the combatant's stance of satisfaction in the next stanza, we are suitably jarred. The ironies in this poem highlight the empathically barren subjectivity of the combatant.

Like the failure of empathy Ehrhart depicts, the act of killing, treated by the state as a mechanical necessity to winning a war, is crucial subject matter for many veteran poets, who retrieve it from silence and linger on its afterlife. Bruce Weigl's "Song of Napalm" includes an image he cannot shake:

> the girl runs only as far
> as the napalm allows
> until her burning tendons and crackling
> muscles draw her up
> into that final position
> burning bodies so perfectly assume. Nothing
> can change that, she is burned behind my eyes
> and not your good love and not the rain-swept air
> and not the jungle-green
> pasture unfolding before us can deny it.[58]

Weigl is an agonized witness. His very eyes are scarred by her death, shaping his vision forever. The reality of the girl's death cannot be undone by present-day goodness—a lover, the loveliness of the natural world. Note that the poem impresses her image on the reader's mind, too, by putting the details of her suffering in our sightline as well as his. Poetry of witness confronts an ontological challenge of war: it is so hard for those who are not there to believe in the suffering it causes.[59]

Doug Anderson's "Infantry Assault," another lament about the deeds of war, opens midmemory: "The way he made that corpse dance by emptying / one magazine after another into it." The poem continues in this vein, unspooling twenty-one lines of imagery in a single sentence as the men in his unit descend into bloodlust. (In fact, an M-16 clip contains twenty-one rounds, so the numerical structure of the poem mirrors a single 1.5-second burst of the rifle fired on full automatic, even as the poem's arc brings us to the consequences of such an act.[60]) The final lines of the poem read,

> the way when all the Cong were dead, lined up in rows,
> thirty-nine in all, our boys went to work on all the pigs
> and chickens in the village until
> there was no place that was not red, and
>
> finally, how the thatch was lit, the village burned
> and how afterwards we were quiet riding back
> on the tracks, watching the ancestral serpent rise
> over the village in black coils, and
>
> how our bones knew what we'd done.

Doug's decision to omit the implied "I remember" before each image propels the poem with a stream-of-consciousness intensity, leading to a dreadful stopping place: "our bones," where silent knowledge festers.[61] With this poem, Doug releases war's secrets onto the page, restoring blood to words, to invoke Espada's phrase,[62] and also reviving the public memory of war. The poem does not absolve but ruminates on a crescendo of unthinking brutality—a pattern repeated by US troops over the years (consider the title of Nick Turse's 2013 Vietnam War history, *Kill Anything That Moves*). "Our bones" should stand for the bones of our nation, while the smoky "ancestral serpent" rising over the devastated village evokes the reptilian evil wrought by American combatants when the state puts them into situations that defy moral reasoning.[63] The poem's intimations of guilt challenge the myth that the US military is a force for good.

Some veteran poets zero in on those experiential shifts whereby the combatant recognizes the humanity of the enemy, often through eye contact or proximity. Here, for instance, is Doug Anderson's "My Enemy":

> We imagined him as wily, reptilian,
> squatting in a hole alive with snakes,
> or underwater breathing through a reed,
> his gelding knife glimmering in the green,
> leering with the cruelty he'd inflict on us
> if he overran our lines. But now,

> see this prisoner two-thirds our height,
> grey-faced, legs caked with mud,
> ribs showing, his rotten teeth
> outsize in his shrunk skull. How he
> stands there in the rain, dazed, perhaps
> looking past the torture to his death
> and maybe there, he'll find some sense to this.[64]

The pitiful sight of this tiny, starving man is the ultimate rebuttal to the military's portrayal of a demonic, cruel enemy. In the final lines, Doug bridges the empathy gap, speculating on what the man might be feeling and thinking. The poem thus captures a pivotal moment when his consciousness shifts from what philosopher Martin Buber would call an "I–it" relationship to an "I–thou" relationship, in which the other is no longer a "thing."[65] In an unpublished version of this poem, Doug sees this encounter as the moment that deterred him from using the military's lexicon of racial slurs: "I knew then I couldn't say *gook* again." Indeed, for many veterans I have spoken to, the act of moral recuperation is intrinsically linked to rehumanizing people through the language used to characterize them.

A related poem by Michael Casey, one of the first Vietnam veteran poets, is dedicated to the frail, elderly Vietnamese man his unit brought in for interrogation: "For the Old Man."[66] The poem describes removing a sandbag from the man's head to reveal a huge bump, indicating he's already been beaten. He begins to bow repeatedly to each GI in turn. In Vietnam's syncretic Buddhist-Confucianist-Taoist religious ethos, bowing with clasped hands would likely have been a gesture of humility and respect, but the American men (mis)interpret it as "prayer":

> To Booboo, Delbert, and me
> He kept it up too
> He wouldn't stop
> His whole body shaking
> Shivering with fright
> And somehow
> With his hands
> Clasped before him
> It seemed as if
> He was praying to us
> It made all of us
> Americans
> Feel strange.

Casey tells me that the man's abject bowing and clasped hands were "clearly a 'please don't hurt me' supplication," but his poem highlights how "strange" the GIs felt, perhaps sensing their unsuitability for being positioned as merciful gods. (In an earlier draft of the poem, Casey had written "Christians" instead of "Americans.") At the time, the American combatants may not have been able to pinpoint why the event made them "feel strange," but by now the writer understands that the event not only signified cultural misunderstanding, but also stood as a moral indictment. The poem's title, which dedicates the work to the old man, feels like an apology or penance.

For some veteran poets, their perception of civilian Others remains distant yet imbued with curiosity, longing, and, at times, tenderness. Hugh Martin is one such writer. In the final lines of his prose poem "Responding to an Explosion in Qarah Tappeh," he observes two small Iraqi girls "in flowing, flowery dresses, the hems swaying against their feet," who "cry softly, moderately, like sorrow was something they were trying for the first time."[67] Another poem describes three Iraqi policemen dancing slowly with their Kalashnikovs held against their bodies as they listen to a Kurdish lute and the haunting sound of a man's singing voice.[68] A third depicts the body of a suicide bomber, "gone at the torso," that "twisted toward me, flailing out / his thin, dead arm, like he wanted / to hold my hand."[69] That horrifying moment becomes almost beautiful, as the poem evokes the human connection lost in war.

Some veteran poets have honored their former enemies by attending to their voices. As US veterans like Bill Ehrhart and Bruce Weigl came to understand Vietnam's extensive poetic history, they brought other veteran poets with them to Vietnam to meet their Vietnamese counterparts in 1985 and again in 1990. The William Joiner Center sponsored several conferences that would involve veteran poets from both the US and Vietnam.[70] Weigl, Kevin Bowen, and others also began to translate Vietnamese veterans' poetry themselves. Americans in Vietnam had occasionally found documents on those they had killed that turned out to be lyrical poetry, featuring images of moonlight, mothers, wedding boats, grief, and heaven. *Captured Documents*, published in 1994 by Thanh T. Nguyen and Bruce Weigl, for instance, features a heart-wrenching group of poems removed from the bodies of North Vietnamese Army and Viet Cong. Phillip Mahoney published a 1998 anthology titled *From Both Sides Now*, interleaving American and Vietnamese accounts of their war experiences.

Larry Rottmann's 1993 book, *Voices from the Ho Chi Minh Trail*, illustrated with photographs by North Vietnamese veteran Nguyen Trong Thanh, includes poems written in the voices of Vietnamese veterans Rottmann interviewed. In one poem, Rottmann animates the compassion of an old farmer who watched a US fighter jet crash into his field. "Since the American had no one to say prayers over him / I built a small altar on the wreckage. / Each week, I still burn some joss for that young man / who died all alone so far from his ancestors. / Many times the local cadres have ordered me to stop doing that, / but they are all too young to know about important things."[71]

On one of his return journeys to Vietnam, Bill Ehrhart distributed copies of a poem titled "Making the Children Behave."[72] In the poem, Ehrhart casts himself back to the time when villages in Vietnam were "strange" to him and "nothing ever seemed quite human" but himself and his unit. Now that his empathic imagination is alive, he can begin to imagine what those village denizens think of him. To them, he was and is the bogeyman:

> Do they think of me now
> in those strange Asian villages
> where nothing ever seemed
> quite human
> but myself
> and my few grim friends
> moving through them
> hunched
> in lines?
>
> When they tell stories to their children
> of the evil
> that awaits misbehavior,
> is it me they conjure?

As these war poets expanded their hearts, their critical perceptions of war broadened as well. While most war poetry could be read as "political" in the sense that it recuperates lives the state disregarded, some works overtly criticize the implacable structures of the state, or the relationship between the citizenry and the wars prosecuted in their name. In Doug Anderson's poem "Same Old," he describes his "immediate choking fear" as he ran into crossfire to treat the wounded, then coming "home to a country that watched / the war on TV at dinner. No one put down / their forks: it was all in a box."[73] American civilians can't grasp the ontological reality of war overseas, and in the absence of widespread public outrage, the military-industrial complex continues to fatten.

Doug concludes the same poem with the small sound of human loss. Much like the profiteering often ignored in war, the grief of its victims frequently goes unacknowledged. Yet this suffering, for him, is the last word.

> Always a war somewhere and underneath
> the crack of rifles, the sound of money
> sliding down the chute, and a
> whimpering of mothers over here, over there.

Chapter 10
Combat Paper

After Drew Cameron returned from eight months as a field artillery soldier in Iraq, he moved to Burlington, Vermont.* He was restless and disillusioned, so he joined Iraq Veterans Against the War. He was also casting about for a creative outlet and signed up to take a papermaking class with a civilian friend, Drew Matott.

One night in 2007, Cameron took his desert fatigues out of his closet and put them on for the first time since coming home. In Iraq, the uniform had been his social skin, signifying his absorption into the military. It had likely been manufactured by prisoners—wards of the state, like soldiers. Military uniforms vary in style and color—green for the jungles in Vietnam, beige for Iraq's sands, dress blues for formal occasions, and various camouflage patterns that go in and out of style depending on the branch—but at their core, they are all the same. They project the wearer's super-citizenship, offering a veneer of probity behind which lies the murk of battle behavior and the soldier's marginalized status in the realm of necropolitics. After all, bodies in uniform are interchangeable, easily replaced in the event of death or injury. Each one of them, in a sense, is reducible to the "unknown soldier."

Cameron and Matott had an idea. Cameron would be photographed cutting off his uniform piece by piece, releasing this envelope of bad memories, toxic masculinity, and false promises. He tackled the left arm first, and though it felt subversive, he was also flooded by what he calls "this overwhelming feeling of empowerment and emotional expression." He started cutting and ripping harder until the uniform was piled before him in shreds, in an act he has described as both "liberation" and "reclamation."[1]

The two Drews began to experiment. A cotton uniform can be macerated in a pulping machine, then pressed and dried to become paper, flecked with threads. Cameron began to pulp uniforms, first his own and then others' castoffs, cutting out the badges and zippers, reducing the fabric to small squares so they could be transformed. Cameron used his new uniform paper

---

* This chapter analyzes words and imagery that may be difficult for some readers to encounter. Please see the "Content Warning and Note on Language" in the front matter for some context and a discussion of the author's reasons for not redacting this material.

Kill Talk. Janet McIntosh, Oxford University Press. © Oxford University Press (2025).
DOI: 10.1093/9780197808054.003.0011

to print an Army logo, then riddled it with bullet holes, printing below, "There's wrong... and there's Army wrong." Both Drews created a piece called "Breaking Ranks," which featured repeating images of Cameron standing in uniform, with a single standout image of him ripping the fabric off himself. They had opened a new expressive medium, an expanse for painful feeling and singular insight.

Cameron and Matott would bring the craft to other veterans, several already working with the Vermont-based initiative Warrior Writers (mentioned in the preceding chapter) and some, members of Iraq Veterans Against the War. The Combat Paper Project, as it was eventually called, took on possibility as small groups of volunteers would load materials into a van and host papermaking workshops for far-flung veterans who had served in Vietnam, Bosnia, Somalia, the Gulf War, the Global War on Terrorism (GWOT), and beyond. The project and its offshoots, such as the Frontline Paper Project in Branchburg, New Jersey, and Matott's international Peace Paper Project, would be widely recognized for the transformational genius of the core concept. (I will use the lowercase phrase "combat paper" to refer to paper made from military uniforms in all these venues; Combat Paper, capitalized, is an organization run by Cameron, and the term is trademarked.) The veterans who run workshops don't usually use the word "therapy"—it's off-putting for many, sounding touchy-feely, patronizing, or deterministic—but they sometimes talk about mutual healing and often about transformation.

Participants come to the table with a range of experiences and political stances that can hardly be reduced to "antimilitary" versus "promilitary." Just about all of them feel something new when making combat paper, but exactly what they feel is highly individual. That said, for veterans wishing to move away from their own militarization, combat paper has been powerful. What its inventors seem to have discovered, in anthropologists' terms, is one of the few available rites of passage out of the United States military. The combatant's linguistic infrastructure, their kill talk, aspires to contain personal vulnerability, attenuate empathy, and distort the moral compass. Kill talk offers a repertoire of doublespeak and euphemisms, it-don't-mean-nothings and twisted jokes, slurs and f-bombs, to shunt away unwanted shock, guilt, horror, or hesitation over violence. Some veterans follow this script successfully, but as we have seen, some find themselves in acute distress down the line.

The writers in the preceding chapter attest to the capacity of poetry to work on this suffering. Yet for some who have experienced war, says anthropologist Alex Pillen, "extreme experiences require a vocabulary outside the realm of ordinary language."[2] Making combat paper lifts away the dulled, deindividuating military skin, freeing what lies beneath while offering a new medium for reckonings that can be verbal but can also involve a tactile and visual end run around words. The papermaking process pulls memories to the surface, allowing the service member to externalize, rethink, articulate, and sometimes expunge otherwise inchoate and trapped pain. The rite thus offers a new format for eloquence outside of the military's pitiless, mission-driven repertoire.

The personal agency in the combat papermaking process is surely part of the alchemy. After a year or two in the military machine, some veterans lose sight of where the military ends and their person begins. The uniform offers a starting point for this question, being a kind of transitional object, somewhere between the military and the self. The combat paper process manipulates the material until it is far less military and far more self. By undoing the state's configuration of the uniform—its standardized pattern, its encompassment of the body, its zippers and official credentials—the papermaker seizes power over the terms of the state and wrests from it a medium for personal expression and, sometimes, disobedience.

Many combat paper creations have a melancholic vibe, but they don't merely sit in loss.[3] For some participants, combat paper fosters new community and growing political attunement to the way service members are subject to the state's crude vision. It also offers creative ways of articulating this dilemma. The queer theorist Ronak Kapadia has described how artists in Afghanistan, Iraq, and other nations targeted during the GWOT have found sensuous and tactile ways of articulating the "disqualified knowledges, histories, geographies, and memories preserved by the 'lower' senses of empire's gendered, racialized Others."[4] Although US combatants played a central role in marginalizing and Othering those nations, they, too, have sometimes been damaged by their own state's warmongering, and their damage has also been sidelined. Returning veterans are expected to recite familiar bromides: they are "proud" to have "served their country" and "fought for our freedom." Such language, the homecoming part of the military's linguistic infrastructure, offers no path for critique or dissent. For those veterans who feel themselves morally injured by their participation in war, combat paper opens the possibility of a dissident aesthetics.[5]

Inverting Military Initiation

Eli Wright says combat paper saved his life. He enlisted in the Army shortly after 9/11 and served as a medic in Ramadi, Iraq, where he had expected to give medical aid to US troops. Instead, he was assigned to stabilize the vital signs of Iraqis who were being "interrogated," which amounted to keeping them alive for the next round of torture. After Iraq, Eli was stationed at Fort Drum in New York, where he helped build the first active-duty chapter of Iraq Veterans Against the War. He got a black tattoo of a paper clip on his right hand to signify "People Against People Ever Re-enlisting—Civilian Life Is Precious" (PAPER CLIP) concealing it from his superior officers with a Band Aid.[6] Around the same time, Eli joined the Combat Paper Project. After leaving the service in 2008, Eli was among the early instructors who would bring combat paper far and wide to art studios, universities, military bases, and other venues where veterans could be found.

I first met Eli (pictured in Figure 10.1) in 2018 at the Frontline Arts studio in Branchburg, New Jersey, where he sat at his laptop amid paper-drying racks, a huge, old letterpress in the back corner, and rollers and brushes lining the walls. He is slight, with sandy-blond hair, a trim beard, and sleeve tattoos. He can be guarded, and when I first walked in, he looked up and fixed his gaze on me for a beat or two. But I smiled first, and he broke into a grin.

At Frontline, Eli works with Studio Manager Walt Nygard, a former Marine and Vietnam veteran turned artist. Walt cuts an imposing figure, with straight, black-to-gray hair, a short, white beard, and eyes so intense that it took me a moment to perceive the kindness behind them. Over time, I would come to learn how differently Eli and Walt think about the military. Whereas Eli sees the military as abusive to recruits from day one of boot camp, Walt, whose father and son also served, believes service to be a respectable path for kids who don't thrive in school and a way to "stand up and be counted." Eli is candid that his nerve endings are frayed, while Walt says he's "not into the touchy-feely stuff." What they agree on: combat brings trauma, and over the last sixty years the United States has prosecuted abhorrent, unethical wars.

Talking to Eli and Walt, I was struck by how well their papermaking workshops accommodate a range of stances toward the military. After all, for some veterans, anguish comes not from military participation, but from leaving the institution that gave their life shape and meaning.[7] My contacts tell me there is a lot to miss: the adrenaline, the sense of purpose, the frisson of power, the intense camaraderie, the military identity. One former Marine relates that she missed having "the structure that tells you what to wear and when to wear it"; even if the uniform reduces individuality, it can also function as a supportive exoskeleton. And the war journalist Sebastian Junger has written poignantly about the anomie many US veterans experience when they lose the communal bonds of their unit, as thick as kinship.[8] That said, some veterans both

Figure 10.1 Eli Wright at Frontline Studios (photo by author).

loved and hated their experiences at war, in an ambivalent tangle, and some who come to make paper are not so much nostalgic as empty, numb, or deeply troubled. The moral inversions of combat and the various military efforts to deflect vulnerability, empathy, grief, and regret leave some feeling they lost their humanity.

Whatever their experiences, veterans have been offered no clear way to process them. My discussions of basic training in this book just scratch the surface of the prolonged and potent rites of passage endured by those entering military service. Military institutions pummel, harden, train, indoctrinate, and celebrate the new inductees. Soldiers' tools, including kill talk, may or may not be enough to help their psyches through combat and offer little to help them make meaning of it all. So why is there no rite of passage to transition service members back to civilian identity? "At the end of it all," says Eli, "you're just handed your DD214," a certificate of discharge from active duty. Some societies, including some Indigenous ones, put returning combatants through rituals that bracket their acts of violence, purify them of wrongdoing, and reintegrate them into ordinary society where otherwise there would be a gulf.[9] In a moment of curiosity, I asked one Drill Instructor (DI) at Parris Island what kind of ritual he could imagine to "undo" things and reintegrate Marines into civilian society. He paused to think. Given what a shock boot camp is, he couldn't picture anything that would counter it except another violent shock to the system. "It would have to be so extreme," he said, trailing off. He seemed to be imagining a ritual that looked like a film of a DI smoking a recruit, played backward.

The early combat paper folks didn't think of their process as a demilitarizing rite of passage, but they intuited ways of inverting symbols and structures given to veterans by the military. Part of the magic has to do with the meanings that surround the uniform, and the meanings evoked by its dismantling. Many healing rituals find a way to materialize inchoate problems—illness, emotional discomfort, the sour taste of a relationship gone bad—in the form of symbols so that they can be manipulated, with corresponding effects on the psyche or body.

In a classic account of a healing ritual among Cuna Indians, for instance, the anthropologist Claude Lévi-Strauss explains how a shaman aided a pregnant woman experiencing a stalled labor.[10] The shaman gave her mysterious pains meaning, through wooden figures that represented a violent conflict in the woman's body in which good spirits battled dangerous ones. In this way, the shaman mapped the woman's struggle onto materialized signs and then, through incantations, narrated a positive outcome to encourage her labor progress. In a related vein, Victor Turner describes rituals among central African Ndembu people that strive to remove afflicting spirits causing pain or illness by concretizing them in the form of a small sac or some other perceptible form that a shaman appears to extract from the body.[11] Apparently, subjective experience can be reorganized when an external symbolic language reorganizes its terms. Along similar lines, Eli explains that the process of remaking his uniform into paper and art feels like releasing something—like taking his war experience and "letting it outside of me, [so] I can carry it around in this physical form, but it's not trapped inside anymore."[12]

Cutting Rag

"We don't throw scissors in their hands immediately," says Eli of veterans who join a workshop for the first time. Cutting their uniform to pieces is probably going to feel like a shock, so it's important for veterans to sit together first and find some common ground. Sometimes the conversation flows organically, just unstructured talk. Sometimes the leaders offer writing prompts from Warrior Writers to loosen thoughts and feelings up. Eli might give them a prompt about the uniform itself. What was it like the first time you put on a uniform? Or the last time? The garment may look inert, but it's haunted by memories and feelings. Writing may draw these out.

Now veterans begin to "cut rag," a phrase dating to the early days of paper mills when paper was made from old rags rather than trees. After the Battle of Gettysburg, Eli tells me, rag pickers on the battlefields found a windfall of cotton and linen uniforms and bandages. Sometimes he tells the veterans in the studio that newspapers documenting the battle were themselves printed on the uniforms of the dead. A uniform can march a person to their death, but it can also be repurposed to speak of it.

Still, the idea of cutting one's uniform is a brazen act, for uniforms represent military identity while humming with the authority of the state. When I described the combat paper process to some service members, they were shocked. One Marine looked to the side before saying, "You don't DO that kind of thing to a uniform." Another guessed that "you wouldn't find many Marines" willing to participate in Combat Paper, since "Marines take their uniforms seriously. . . . I bet you'd find mostly Army guys doing that paper thing." When folks are invited to a papermaking session, some deliberate for weeks before deciding they'd be willing to cut.

The pulping machine can only take postage-stamp-sized squares of fabric, and you must remove anything it can't pulp. Buttons, Velcro, seams, unit patches—Eli tells the veterans these are "unserviceable," using a technical military term to meet them where they're at. "There's a lesson in there. You need to let go of what's not serving you anymore, let go of the detritus."[13] There are a lot of ways to cut: scissors, handheld rotary cutters, bare hands—or two people yanking on either end of a shirt that doesn't want to give way.

Figure 10.2 shows a veteran using scissors to slice the fabric of his uniform into strips. "We're deconstructing the order of the military," Eli tells me, "turning it into chaos and out of that chaos recreating something new."

Figure 10.2 Cutting rag (still from *This Is Not a War Story*, courtesy of writer & director Talia Lugacy and Acoustic Pictures / HBO Max).

All kinds of items may spill out of pockets and seams, like little flashbacks. Cigarette butts. Pictures of a spouse. Sand. Pebbles from some far-flung location, sewn into a seam for private reasons. The larger items have to go, but workshop organizers don't believe in washing the uniforms. They may smell of sweat or carry grime from faraway locations; they may even be stained with blood. Those will be blended into the paper, given new purpose.

Hearing and feeling the ripping of their uniforms, "breaking that weave," in Eli's terms, offers veterans a new sensorial experience. By all accounts, this collective act around a table changes the atmosphere in the room. Emotions run high, extending to laughter and sometimes tears. Sometimes there is only the sound of cutting and shredding. Sometimes participants joke about uniforms that were always too tight or too loose or ask whether they could also pulp their boots, their beret, their rifle. Sometimes the mood turns dark with a grim war story, and people may talk about losing their faith. Eli tells me he sometimes hears phrases like "Where the fuck was god?" He thinks more veterans lose their faith than find it in the nihilistic experience of war.

Walt's uniform still reminds him of the grit and tenacity of service and of how proud he was when his son enlisted. Cutting is "sacred" for him, and if he drops a piece on the floor, he'll pick it up reverently rather than sweeping or throwing it away. Jenny Pacanowski, a former Army medic, says,

> It all seemed very dumb to me at first, in all honesty. Then when I started doing it, it was a totally different thing [and I] started thinking about all kinds of shit. I was in my own zone, like I didn't even realize anybody was there anymore; it was just me and my uniform and I was just tearing that shit up and tearing down all the walls that I had put up over the years, and I wasn't drunk, and I was clear headed, and I loved it![14]

For Eli, the uniform had come to feel like chaos, destruction, and death, and ripping into it was a release of pressure. Cutting felt like, "You don't own me anymore. I'M going to own this and own my story now." One woman who had been subject to military sexual trauma told me of cutting up donated uniforms with a couple of the men at Frontline when she had a sudden realization: "We're cutting all these CROTCHES out." The guys paused for a second, then seemed to realize what she was alluding to. If clothing can stand in for people, maybe dismantling it can address their worst deeds.

Marine Corps veteran Leonard Shelton turned to combat paper years after his final tour in the Middle East. In his most traumatic moment, which he described to journalist Kevin Sites, he had to cover up the charred body of a buddy killed by friendly fire. His grief and rage were overwhelming, and he remembers looking at his Gunnery Sergeant "to help me with my feelings. Nothing." A few years later, he began to cut his own stomach, arms, and legs, saying later, "I had to put my pain somewhere."[15] In one documentary about combat paper, Shelton zips a rolling cutter back and forth across one of his badges, saying, "I feel pissed off. I feel like I got fucked over quite a bit. I feel that I've been used and I don't want to represent what has used me anymore."[16] On another occasion, Shelton put scraps from twenty years' worth of dress blues into a single pulp slurry, saying, "That's twenty years in my hands, right here. I gave up a lot of years, and I've seen a lot and I've done a lot. But when I cut up that uniform, I'm searching for a new name so I can find out who I am."[17]

For a few years, Eli headed to the Washington, DC, area every couple of months, holding papermaking workshops at alternating locations, between the Walter Reed National Military Medical Center and Fort Belvoir, often working with active-duty service members who aren't allowed to participate in partisan political activities. Sometimes those workshops feel politically benign; active-duty folks or veterans want to do something like pulp the uniform of a friend killed in action to make a memorial image or poem. No matter what, Eli gauges his audience carefully and tends to avoid openly critiquing the military during a workshop. I say to him, "It's so wily! It's so subversive!" He says yes, "it all comes out of an antiwar position, but we have ways of doing it softly." Sometimes, he likes to say or do things that "resonate" with military thinking even as he plants a few hints of critique—"puts the bait there"—and participants can take it up if they want to.

Occasionally Eli offers this anonymous quotation as food for thought: "Rags make paper. Paper makes money. Money makes banks. Banks make loans. Loans make beggars. Beggars make rags." While this short verse targets the harmful causal chains of capitalism, it might inspire some to contemplate other structures as well. "Rags" (cloth) make uniforms, which make soldiers, which make the military, which makes wars, which make not "beggars" but those who feel lacerated by the military machine. And these beggars may end up finding combat paper and making their uniform into rags, then paper, and then something the military never anticipated.

Pulping the Uniform, Pulling Sheets

Eli takes me to the basement of Frontline Paper so I can see the Hollander beater, based on a design from seventeenth-century Holland, that pulps the uniforms (see Figure 10.3).[18] It has an oval "raceway," a loop about four feet long. Water and little fabric squares zip around this track until they reach a grinder wheel that churns fast and loud. When introducing the machine to veterans, Eli likes to give a brief history lesson about papermaking to establish that the participants are part of a long, proud tradition. "After all," he tells me with a tinge of amusement, "everything about the military is about tradition, and we're forced to respect and regurgitate it on command, whether we like it or not." He describes how each participant is directed to take a handful of uniform scraps and toss it into the beater. I say it reminds me of bereaved people casting a handful of dirt into a grave, but Eli has another image in mind. While veterans move scraps into the beater, he incants, "All hands feed the machine." "They can interpret this however they like," he says, "but what I'm thinking is 'We all feed the war machine.' I want them to think about their role in militarism."

Over the course of a few hours, the beater breaks the fabric into pulp while keeping its long fibers intact.[19] The slurry that emerges from this process can be used a few ways. A portion can be set aside and pigmented, then sprayed through stencils onto the paper. In one of his early works, Eli scooped up handfuls of pulp he had dyed red, slamming them at a large black piece of

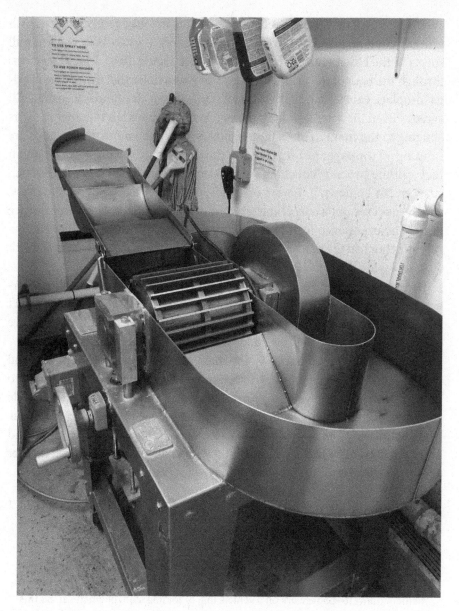

Figure 10.3 Hollander beater, Frontline Studios (photo by author).

paper, where they stuck like bloody splats. He threw one chunk so hard it "created this gaping open wound in the paper, and I felt like I was sort of closing up some of the wounds that I had had."[20]

Most of the slurry is poured into shallow plastic vats to become paper. The papermaker agitates the water with their hands to get the fibers swirling evenly, and then they "pull sheets," a process that involves gently lifting a mesh grid (a "mold and deckle") from under the slurry. I watch Walt Nygard pull sheets in the basement of Frontline Paper (see Figure 10.4). The water drips through the base of the grid in a shower of white noise that slows to individual droplets. I am struck by the sense of purification. "It sounds cleansing," Eli agrees. "Even the smell of it is cleansing." What remains is a thin mat of fibers clinging to the frame. This is flipped upside down the moment the drips are running off the paper just so, then it is pressed onto a backing of felt or linen; they call the process "couching" (pronounced "cooching," from the French *coucher*, "to lie down"). Layers of sheets are stacked into a hydraulic press, which squeezes out a surprising amount of water. Then they air-dry in wire grids. The experience feels like crossing a frontier for veterans like Shelton. After he couched the first sheet out of his dress blues, he raised his hands with a smile, saying, "It is OVER."[21]

The repeated act of pulling sheets, Eli says, is "meditative"—some veterans call it "rhythmic"—and a lot easier than regular meditation, since he can't sit quietly. "I can pull sheets for four hours a night," he says. The repetitive process helps him turn off the chaos inside. Eli also describes it as a "forgiving" process, unlike military life, in which you are never forgiven, just told things like "You'd better unfuck this situation." In papermaking, it's easy to correct your mistakes; you just throw back a bad sheet and endlessly recycle the fibers. When working with veterans pulling sheets, Eli adds, "I recognize [their] humanity. I'm not part of the chain of command. I know it sucks, and I've been abused by that machine." If they mess up a sheet, "they can fix it or accept those flaws for their beauty if they want." He adds,

> With trauma, you can't correct the past. Or in the military, one simple mistake and you face humiliation, hazing, losing rank—the younger you are, the more berated and abused you are. Here, you can correct your mistakes again and again, without being berated or forced to do pushups. But some of the repetition might also feel familiar. A lot of military experience is stupid, mindless repetition, so you get muscle memory doing it—paperwork on a vehicle log, or folding stuff, or whatever. So this has that familiarity, but instead of being mindless, it's mindful.

This mindfulness can encourage open-ended contemplation. Drew Matott told a journalist about one Marine who happened to pass the Combat Paper folks pulping uniforms at Texas State. The Marine brought in his desert cammies an hour later to cut them up. The man was "pretty angry, basically cursing the military," and returned day after day with bags of his old uniforms to process.

Figure 10.4 Walt Nygard pulling sheets (photo by author).

He was there all week just pulling paper, pulling paper, pulling paper, maybe 600 or 700 sheets. By the end of the third day, he looked up at me and said, "This is just so relaxing, really peaceful, cathartic. I feel like I'm washing my experiences." He was in love with the sound of the water, the rinsing. He told me, "I thought that the military brought me nothing but misery and angst. But actually, you know what? There were some good experiences there. It wasn't all bad."[22]

During the process of pulling sheets, Eli might offer a few gentle remarks to destabilize the military tendency to dehumanize and flatten "the enemy." Sometimes, for instance, he'll tell GWOT veterans that papermaking spread from the East to the West by way of Baghdad around the eighth century. The mills there figured out new techniques for mass manufacture, which would become key to the dissemination of human knowledge. Eli wants veterans to know the people of Baghdad are "not these 'primitive savages' we were taught to hate. I take the opportunity to humanize them during the process. That's me working through my own shit."

By this time, the uniform itself has gone through the classic three stages of a rite of passage.[23] It has been separated from its original context, ground down and washed, and reborn into something with a new, expressive function. Its cells are still in there, but they add up to a new meaning. And since veterans are so identified with their uniform, it has been a material stand-in for their own dismantling and cleansing and the possibility of rebirth.

The Fresh Medium

Unlike the rite of passage of boot camp, the next step in a combat paper workshop is in the hands of the individual, offering what Eli calls a "fresh start." The paper has raw deckle edges, but its surface is smooth, blank, inviting. Veterans can print, draw, or paint; they can make the paper into a book with a simple spine; they can even use it to sculpt. Drew Cameron says that after combat, at a time when his emotions felt "dull," even as though they had "flatlined," this paper became his "conduit" for self-expression, and the medium through which he would come to reflect on what war meant.[24] In Chapter 7, I discussed the way GIs in Vietnam said "it don't mean nothing" to numb themselves to the agony of combat violence. Speaking about making combat paper, Eli tells me,

> What we do here is a contrast to "don't mean nothin'." It's been an evolution from how we deal with this, across generations. That was such a hopeless statement, and it contributes to dysfunction and trauma and moral injury. In fact it really starts with "THEY"—the people the US military is killing. "THEY don't mean nothin'," and then it moves to "IT don't mean nothin'," which leads to "I don't mean nothin'." If THEY'RE not human, I'M not human. That's the process a lot of us have gone through. To dehumanize them, we dehumanized ourselves. A lot of the moral injury comes in there. But here we have a chance to rehumanize us and them with the paper.

With the paper, a channel of feeling and thinking opens, precisely where the military would have cut it off for its necropolitical ends.

Granted, veterans who remain enthusiastic about the military are unlikely to use the paper medium for critique. Some print portraits of themselves or their unit, with captions such as "I am proud to be part of a team." Still, they may find the process helpful for metabolizing emotions from combat. Marine Corps veteran Ryan Taylor, for instance, initially dismissed the combat paper concept as "froufrou" but wound up creating a memorial list of his deceased battle buddies. At an exhibition of his work and that of other veterans in his papermaking group, he admits he was able to expunge some of his roiled feelings through the process.

> It's almost like, I've felt this inside of me, ever since I've gotten back from Fallujah, but it's never been outside of me. You know, it almost felt like, now it's externalized, and it actually feels like I was able to let go of a small piece of it. You know, and it's kind of got a place to reside now. And I feel really great about that. There's a lot of feelings and emotions around me in paper form, and it's really special to be a part of it.[25]

In the New Jersey studio, I am flipping through enormous portfolios of combat paper art with Eli looking over my shoulder. I see the face of Rachel, a member of Veterans for Peace and Warrior Writers whom I happen to have met in Massachusetts. She has created an enormous print of her eyes gazing confrontationally from under her helmet. It is titled "For They Know Not What We Do," a play on what Christ said to God while on the cross: "Father, forgive them, for they know not what they do." Who, I wonder, is the "they" and who the "we" in Rachel's print? Perhaps "they" is the civilian world that blindly endorses the deeds of the US military, knowing so little about what those deeds can amount to on the ground?

The open-ended quality of Rachel's print resonates with the free spirit of the studio and the potential to express infinite complexity on the paper. Eli says, "Hollywood will only tell us the fuckin' boring story about military heroism or military trauma." He goes on:

> There's a saying in the military—"Oh, you wanna be a fucking INDIVIDUAL," or "There is no 'I' in Army." Sometimes for some of these people used to subsuming themselves, it's the first time they've worried about themselves as an individual. We teach you that you have a right to your story and individuality and to tell your story. This is about staking your claim. . . . We also have silence because of the masculine culture of the "silent veteran." This generation is changing that; I challenge them to speak up and speak out.

The process can be painful. On one of my visits, Eli told me that the week before, a veteran participant found his writing prompt too triggering and walked out of the room. Instead of writing by hand with the group, he went to the letterpress and began to choose individual letters to set type directly into the press. The piece that emerged featured a human figure standing with a red heart in his chest and a grenade for a head. The halting text describes how his heart fights the temptation to pull the pin to get rid of the screams in his head.

Some veterans come back to make combat paper again and again, refining their craft as their self-expression gains momentum. Tara Krause, for instance, was an Army Captain stationed at a nuclear missile site in the 1980s. She survived "a buzz saw of hatred" and sexual trauma during training at West Point[26] as well as what she now calls an "omnicidal" mentality necessary to her job. After being redeployed as a field artillery officer during the first Gulf War and participating in the bombing of Baghdad, Tara left the military, horrified at imagining what the panicked mothers in that city must have felt. She turned to human rights education and has since honed her artistry as a poet, painter, and combat paper printmaker, producing stunning "mille-feuille" images with intricately layered lines that capture subjects ranging from roses to nuclear explosions.

In conversations with me, Tara describes herself as a "culture jammer," ironizing the military's oppressive aspirations. In one sardonic 2018 pop-up book, she renders a nuclear mushroom cloud in 3D combat paper that lifts off the page, the children's-book medium throwing the deadly imagery into relief. Another piece of Tara's pop-up art features Donald Trump's head, his quiff of hair springing absurdly from the pages like its own explosion. Tara flanks this with transcripts of Trump's outrageous brag about the size of his "nuclear button," and recent UN and NATO calls to eliminate nuclear weapons.

Much of the art emerging from combat paper workshops features war-related images accompanied by a single line of text. I am struck by how often the language expresses the enduring damage done to combatants as they had to hunt and be hunted.

- "There are no veterans, only survivors"
- "No one can change the animal I've become"
- "I'm the only thing I'm afraid of"
- "That which didn't kill me, haunts me"
- "I know why you can't sleep"

For some, their internal callouses are among the most upsetting aspects of their militarization. One caption reads, simply, "The worst part was feeling numb to it . . . but it was the only way I could survive with my sanity." I turn the page in the portfolio and encounter an image of a tank with its barrel pointed at the viewer. Above it, the creator—Justin Jacobs—uses letters cut out of magazines, like in an unhinged ransom note. The text describes the emotional aphasia that can surround death in war:

> I'm not upset that my peers don't understand the stories I try to tell them. In fact I'd be mad if they thought that they did. Watching a friend die isn't "devastating," "traumatic" or "terrifying." It just is. That's the feeling and it's one that doesn't have a name. I haven't figured out how to write that down and that's why I don't tell war stories.

Then there are laments for the suffering and death of so-called enemies and civilians, a theme also prominent in the veteran poetry I have already described. I lingered on a print by Jim Fallon, whom I would meet while helping set up a Frontline Paper exhibition at the Quaker meeting house in Manhattan. As we walked to get lunch, Jim told me a little about his service as well as an illness he probably contracted through exposure to Agent Orange. Jim had no choice about deploying to Vietnam, but at least he had been a medic, a healer. For a time, he would drive an ambulance down the same road every day, taking him past an orphanage where a few girls would greet him as he passed. An old photo shows the littlest one in a hairband, clinging to the older girl next to her in a big sideways hug. One day as Jim passed, the girls waved to him urgently, to warn him of an ambush ahead. He did a U-turn, then looked back to see one of the girls lying dead in the road.

Jim created a combat paper print to linger on that pathetic tragedy (see Figure 10.5). Titled "U-Turn," the image is encircled by a thick arrow in an upside-down U shape that travels from a photo of the road to the image of those orphanage girls before it loops back. A translucent red cross superimposed on the photographs is ambiguous: is it a medic's symbol of aid or menacing crosshairs in a rifle scope? The caption, in military stencil font, reads, "SHE WAS GONE, AND THERE WAS NOTHING I COULD DO." This cry from the soul again feels like the antithesis of that slogan GIs used in Vietnam to dismiss death: "It don't mean nothing." The print also challenges the hegemonic framing, during the Vietnam War era, of Vietnamese lives as less grievable. Jim is forever suspended in grief, U-turning back to it again and again, perhaps still processing his indirect role in the girl's death.

Eli told me about his dear friend and fellow medic, Johnny Millantz, who had the same job he did in Iraq. Like Eli, Johnny was profoundly disturbed by having to check the vital signs of detainees being tortured. In a final act that would break Eli's heart, Johnny would take too many prescription pills and never wake up. Before his death, though, he had shared an image with a journalist to help expose the treatment of Iraqi detainees. In the center of the

Figure 10.5 "U-Turn" © Jim Fallon, 2014.

photo, a blindfolded detainee grimaces with pain as he holds a heavy plank in front of him with straight arms. Two US soldiers in uniform stand behind the man, grinning. One of them is Johnny.[27]

To my eyes, Johnny's smile rhymed with the frame perversions and semiotic callousing in the military's linguistic infrastructure, described in preceding chapters. Hadn't he been trained to carry out his assigned mission with a hard heart? Wasn't he supposed to use whatever tools were on offer from military culture—a dehumanizing slur, a "fuck it" to morality, a smile and a joke—to turn empathy away? In putting this photograph on public record, I wondered whether Johnny wanted not only the torture to be known, but also the torment of the young soldier made into a torturer, with his twisted inner states and signifying practices. These were moral distortions to be contemplated with horror.

For years, Eli could not talk about what had happened in Iraq, but as damning reports about US detention and interrogation practices emerged, he realized he needed to get something out of him. He tells a journalist, "Johnny's experience literally ate him away from the inside, out, until he couldn't continue living. I didn't want these demons haunting me for the rest of my life." Creative work allowed him to "kind of release the valve on this pressure cooker."[28]

Using combat paper and other materials, Eli made a triptych of white, three-dimensional masks that he showed me in the studio (see Figure 10.6).

Filthy rag-like strips dangle from all three masks, looking like soiled bandages or even frayed flesh. Eli says the mask on the right is a self-portrait, featuring a sewn-shut mouth and a black blindfold over the eyes. The central and most elevated mask depicts a tortured detainee named Mahmoud, in a "crucified effigy," in Eli's words, with a mouth taped shut and blood seeping from beneath a blindfold. The mask on the left, adorned with a faded strip of US flag over the mouth, represents Johnny, whose button eyes seem stuck open yet half dead. More generally, Eli adds, this mask also stands for "people who saw and experienced things they weren't able to reconcile and succumbed to the moral injuries of war."[29] I am struck that all three masks are symbolically muted, with Johnny's voice forever silenced by the flag—representing "national security," perhaps—over his mouth. And though Mahmoud was the only one to wear an actual blindfold, Eli has chosen to place a blindfold over his own mask, perhaps a sign of his past incomprehension or his own subjugation by the military. The boards supporting Johnny's and Eli's masks also bear their military identification numbers, a reminder that they were depersonalized cogs in the state's apparatus. It seems clear that Johnny and Eli were both perpetrators and victims of military necropolitics.

Eli expressed his disenchantment even more viscerally when he shot up his childhood teddy bear, disemboweled it with cadaver-style incisions, and restuffed it with combat paper, bullet casings, and the buttons removed from uniforms during the rag-cutting process. After suturing the teddy back up, Eli strung a noose around its neck. In some of his combat paper prints, Eli also remarks wryly on military and political doublespeak, as in a series of prints of police in riot gear, a woman in uniform and a gas mask jauntily saluting

Figure 10.6 "Torture Masks (from left to right: Johnny / Mahmoud / Self Portrait)"
© Eli Wright, 2014/2015.

next to an oil field, and so forth, captioned with morally twisted semantic contradictions such as "WAR IS PEACE" and "FREEDOM IS SLAVERY."

One of Eli's prints (see Figure 10.7) emerged from the bizarre duality he felt as an Army medic expected to carry both a medic bag and a rifle. "I had to learn how to take lives before learning to save people," he tells me. Just as the military medic embodies a paradox, so, too, does military service toy with multiple versions of what a human is. Eli's print depicts one humanoid figure in the background: a standard military "E-silhouette" target, which is a black shape that resembles a wide bottle with a short neck, standing in for a human torso and head. "To learn target practice," says Eli, "to learn taking lives, you have to oversimplify the body. The body is a mere target: 'There's a target on your left, a target on your right.'"

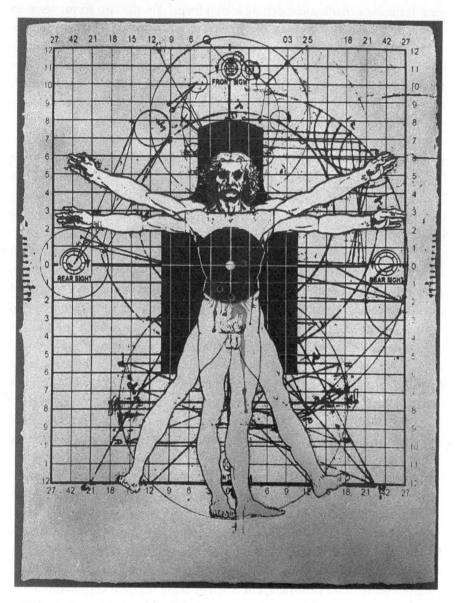

Figure 10.7 "Untitled" © Eli Wright, 2018.

Atop the E-silhouette, Eli has placed a gold-painted "Vitruvian Man," Leonardo da Vinci's famous rendering of ideal body proportions, which layers two identical nude male figures with arms and legs extended at different angles—one of them forming the shape of Jesus on the cross.[30] The work thus juxtaposes the Renaissance notion of the perfectible human body with the military's dehumanized target. Eli describes this superimposition as "man's ideal form over man's most dehumanized form." Yet the two forms seem to merge, as Eli has blacked out the Vitruvian man's eyes and a central area of the torso, conflating its core with the black target. Behind the figure's limbs, a graph-paper backdrop suggests a dispassionate gaze and includes shapes resembling reticles—the circles and crosshair markings seen through a firearm's sight.[31] At the base of the Vitruvian man's sternum, a bullet hole pierces the paper. Rivulets of blood flow down his legs.

Eli's print speaks of the military medic's perverse relationship to human life, as they are assigned to tend injured flesh while sometimes enabling further bodily harm. Perhaps it could also be read as a symbol of other contradictions in military necropolitics. Military institutions hone bodies to muscular perfection, for instance, only to send them onto the battlefield where they may be bled dry.

While I was helping set up the exhibition in the Quaker meeting house, another of Eli's prints caught my eye. Titled "Family Values" (see Figure 10.8), it pictures a well-to-do white family in their spacious living room, clustered enthusiastically around an iPad. They seem oblivious to the fact that two wounded or dead children are next to them on their sofa, while the buildings outside their windows have been bombed out. The images of the children are familiar from the US news media—both are casualties of the wars in the Middle East.[32] As in the frame perversion I describe in Chapter 8, Eli has juxtaposed oppositional registers—but rather than minimizing suffering the way combat humor does, this piece appears aimed at a different audience and works in a different affective direction. Targeting a complacent audience of American civilians, it seems designed to shock us into recognizing uncomfortable truths. If Eli's journey as an artist began with pulp slurry slammed into paper to represent his own wounds, it has culminated in ambitious political statements about necropolitics.

James Yee, the Muslim chaplain whose terrible journey at Guantanamo Bay I discuss in Chapter 7, also took to combat paper to express the contours of his struggle with prisoner abuse and war crimes. As I have described, James led religious services for prisoners, but when he reported their complaints about religious harassment and outright torture, he fell under suspicion for sedition. He endured seventy-six days in solitary confinement, intermittently subjected to shackling and sensory deprivation through the use of blindfolds, earmuffs, and hoods. After James resigned his commission, he wound up living near Frontline Paper, and he frequents the studio.

Figure 10.8 "Family Values" © Eli Wright, 2015.

Although the military fantasized that James was an "enemy within" on grounds of his sympathy for fellow Muslims in Guantanamo, he retains some of his military ideals. Like his Muslim faith, West Point had given him a strong sense of duty and honor. He considers himself "no nonsense" and tells me he hasn't thought much about the concept of "moral injury" that was otherwise common in my discussions with combat paper participants.

I learned not to project too much irony onto his art. One of his earliest creations at Frontline Paper featured meticulous line drawings of military vehicles, including the guided missile transporter carrying the surface-to-air Patriot Missile that James once supervised as an Army Captain. ("Patriot" stands for "Phased Array Tracking Radar to Intercept on Target.") James had drawn a missile launching from the vehicle with a whoosh of flames and exhaust trailing behind it. Beneath it, he wrote and underlined the words, "I'm a PATRIOT." Was he cynically commenting on the notion of labeling such a deadly weapon "patriotic"? No, he said. He was affirming his own patriotism—after all, the title of his memoir, *For God and Country*, is earnest. He showed me a scrapbook filled with samples of military uniforms in various shades and patterns, but he resisted my attempt to interpret it metaphorically. To him, it was just a book of samples.

Yet the stories of torture recounted by Guantanamo detainees, and his own ordeal at the hands of the military, remained indelible. He had memorialized stark details of some of these experiences in a pocket-sized photo album labeled "GUANTANAMO BAY" in red ink. As he turned the pages, I saw detainees in painful crouches, wire cages, and a "restraint chair" used to force-feed detainees on hunger strike. There were images of detainees seated on a transport plane's floor, shackled and tied together in rows, black sacks over their heads, with a US flag suspended above them.

In one combat paper print (see Figure 10.9), James created a line drawing of four prisoners at Camp X-ray, an area where detainees were held in individual cells without even enough space to lie stretched on the ground. In his image, the prisoners pray, sit, and stand behind implacable metal grills topped by layers of coiled concertina wire, enforced by an exterior fence and a watch tower for surveillance. There is something terribly exposed about those metal grills. James told me there was never any shade at Camp X-ray—only sun, blazing so hot the prisoners would try to pull their jumpsuits over their heads to escape it. Around their cells, James has drawn local wildlife roaming in the grass, including scorpions and an iguana. Two of the prisoners face away from the viewer, as if looking toward the clouds and birds free above them.

Figure 10.9 James Yee, "Camp X-ray."
Photo credit: LaRonda Glasco.

The same compassionate sensibility underpins two other artworks by James. On one piece, he inscribes a common snippet of Army lore: "Why is the sky blue? Because God loves the infantry." James then adds his own reflection, "But God also don't like ugly." Beneath this new slogan, he depicts a soldier aiming at a "civilian target" (his label) and an image of a member of the US Army "Kill Team" smiling while holding up the head of a deceased Afghan combatant by the hair.[33] On another piece (see Figure 10.10), James paints a group of green-clad soldiers aiming their weapons, adding question marks to two Army slogans: "Army strong?" and "Army. Be all you can be?" At the bottom of the picture, a rifle points at a fearful elderly woman (James's caption refers to the My Lai massacre), and a member of the US Army's Military Police at Abu Ghraib is shown holding an Iraqi detainee on a leash. For James, the US military has compromised its own potential through its war crimes.

Figure 10.10 James Yee, "Army. Be All You Can Be?"
Photo credit: LaRonda Glasco.

Chris Arendt, who was also stationed at Guantanamo Bay, would be deeply disillusioned by his time there as well. I first heard of Chris through Eli, who mentioned a combat paper colleague who had renamed the Global War on Terrorism the "Great War of Terror" to highlight that the United States has inflicted more terror on its perceived enemies than it has suffered. Chris had grown up in a trailer park in Michigan and enlisted in the National Guard at seventeen to finance his community college education. He figured he would be assigned to some innocuous task like sandbagging during southern-state floods. Instead, he was deployed to Guantanamo Bay in 2004 to serve as a guard.

Even before arriving in Cuba, Chris was unsettled by the linguistic norms among fellow service members. In a later public account, he recalled the day his "totally insane" section chief called him and, "in a classically immoderate way, barked out 'Raging bull! Raging bull!' And that was it, hung up the phone, seeing as he had no idea how to communicate with other human beings."[34] "Raging Bull" served as the call signal for his unit's imminent war deployment, a moment that filled Chris with panic.

Chris knew he was unsuited for the job. He had already been marginalized by the other guardsmen in his unit, who, he says, were "the most culturally insensitive people I'd ever met in my whole life" and had "decided that I was, A, a homosexual and that, B, that was something that made me not worth anything, just because I read books and could speak in sentences that contained more than five words and sometimes I didn't even swear."[35] Chris didn't want to be a "big, mean man who walked up and down cells and pushed people around. . . . I used to like smiling quite a bit, and I like jokes, and I don't really like pushing people, and I'm not a very violent person." He hadn't even wanted to hold a weapon when training except to qualify on the firing range. He tried to tell his superior officers, "I'm not your guy, and [this deployment] is gonna make me depressed." He was beginning to feel suicidal at the prospect of going to Guantanamo, but the military insisted he had made a commitment.[36] He briefly contemplated fleeing the country but had neither the money nor time to do so.

Once stationed, Chris was appalled by the treatment of detainees. Guards would storm into cells while pepper spraying even quiet prisoners, zip tie them and kick them in the face, and sometimes shave mocking patterns into their hair. One of Chris's tasks was to dispatch other guards to move detainees from one cell to another on the "Frequent Flier Program"—the sleep-deprivation method of torture James Yee had told me about (Chapter 7).[37] And when Chris began conversing with the detainees who had some command of English, asking them about their backstories, he was promptly moved off the cell blocks. Presumably he was developing too humane a connection with the enemy.

Chris emerged to testify in the 2008 Winter Soldier hearings, at which he offered harrowing accounts of detainee torture while (like James) decrying

Combat Paper 251

the euphemisms that enabled it. After he started working with Iraq Veterans Against the War, he tells me, he soon learned about combat paper and joined Eli and others to make paper at a retreat at Martha's Vineyard. His most striking piece of art is titled "Standard Operating Procedure" (Figure 10.11).

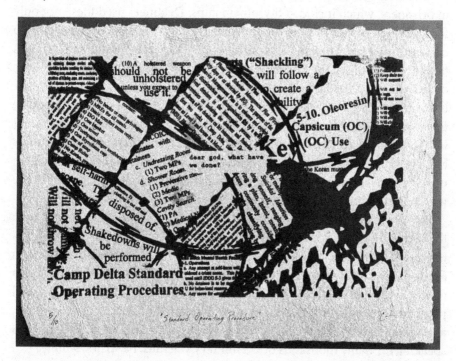

Figure 10.11 "Standard Operating Procedure" © Christopher Arendt, 2010.

The piece is a meditation on the Guantanamo Bay standard operating procedures that led to some of the detainee mistreatment Chris and James have attested to. In Chris's print, segments of the document are arranged at chaotic angles, each in its own section of concertina wire. The collage suggests comprehensive techniques of control, framed in language that is sometimes euphemistic but always resolute. One fragment mentions "shackling," which Chris vividly recalls practicing during his training before deployment, finding it both surreal and dehumanizing. Another scrap mentions "shakedowns," referring to cell searches that often entailed disrespecting prisoners' Qurans and other intrusive actions. "Oleoresin Capsicum," the scientific name of the painful pepper spray used on unruly prisoners, appears in one section. A particularly ominous directive states that a guard's weapon "should not be unholstered unless you expect to use it." Another fragment describes how "clothing is cut off and disposed of," detailing the procedures for new prisoners in a chillingly named "clothing removal room," where detainees remain shackled during the process. One scrap alludes to the "Behavior management plan" at Guantanamo Bay, outlining a phased strategy to disorient and isolate prisoners to facilitate their "interrogation."

Another fragment in the piece alludes to the sparse "comfort items" allowed to prisoners, which included Styrofoam cups. Detainees used these not only for drinking but also as a canvas on which they would use their fingernails to carve intricate floral designs or write messages. As part of his duties, Chris was tasked with confiscating any cups bearing Arabic writing, in case these were coded attempts to communicate nefarious plans. But he was awed by their beauty, and knew the intelligence officers wound up tossing them because they were not of military relevance in the end. Chris would later say his moral injury stemmed not just from participating in a system that tortured prisoners but also from being ordered to remove their sole creative outlet. He would go on to become a professional artist and designer, the ultimate rejoinder to the way military protocols suppress avenues for creative expression.

Two elements of "Standard Operating Procedure" stand in contrast with the concertina wire and those bleak military directives. One is the black silhouette of a bird perched on the wire, perhaps a hint of freedom, but not yet in full color, nor with wings spread. The other, in small, modest type, is Chris's own voice, superimposed on the cacophony of military language. In a still point amid the self-sure, codified tone of the standard operating procedures, amid its allusions to torment and obfuscations of its own harm, and perhaps speaking for many thousands of US military veterans, he writes, simply,

> dear god. what have we done?

Coda

The Nervous System

While conducting fieldwork among soldiers at Fort Hood, Texas, Kenneth MacLeish uncovered an institutional, social, and emotional landscape riddled with paradoxes. He invokes the metaphor of a "nervous system" to capture the way the military "presents itself as a comprehensive, unfeeling, and monolithic order," while nevertheless being "dynamic, agitated, full of unruly feeling."[1] In such a system, order and rationality are simultaneously presented and revoked.

The United States military could be considered a nervous system at multiple levels of scale. In its geopolitical aspirations and deeds, it is a chimera motivated by an impossibly complex intermingling of reason and irrationality, virtue and greed, humanitarianism and cold self-interest, often leaving behind it not a democratic peace, but millions of dead, infrastructural devastation, and political fragmentation. Service members are elevated to what MacLeish describes as "the ideal of citizenship and the epitome of virtue," while being empowered to extreme violence.[2] And as seen in these pages and many other accounts, contradictions abide in the antinomies of military "wave tactics," in the ambiguities of the Rules of Engagement, right down to the psyches of soldiers and veterans, some of whom may be left in a purgatory of neurological and moral torment.

The military language I have explored appears to be a key mechanism for sustaining the mood of paradox. Formal, technical, and euphemistic language contrasts with profane and sordid speech. Drill Instructors vow to be respectful, then agitate the nerves with yelling and berating, while their head games presage the moral inversions of combat. Chants and cadences declare military superiority, yet celebrate killing civilians. Jokes open in the voice of an upstanding citizen, then take a sadistic twist. Such language abides like a coiled spring, tense with potential energy and the uncertainty of its own ambiguities. It offers a dark mirror that perpetually reflects and enhances the contrasts of military life.

Within such unresolved tensions and hypocrisies, it is no wonder some military players find themselves struggling to wrap their mind around what their service even means. As one puzzled veteran quietly reflected in my presence, "I still don't know. Was my service glorious, or was it freaking awful?" Since the early twentieth century, anthropologists have noted that across societies, ambiguity and illegibility can help to create a sense of magic or the sacred.[3] The American soldiers I asked scoffed at the idea that the military's unresolved contradictions and oppositional linguistic registers give it any "magic," but perhaps, at minimum, they contribute to the military's mystique. After all, there may be some charismatic enticement, even uncanniness, in the ability to represent the state with a polished and polite tongue, then to pivot and talk about killing in such untrammeled terms.

In discussion with another veteran, we were listing kill talk's avoidant euphemisms and bloodthirsty slang when he blurted, "But IS there a right way to talk about killing?" His implication stumped me; anthropologists tend to be eager to problematize, but we rarely offer a solution. The military is a machine that specializes in violence, and in war it gives members of the infantry a job so inhuman that the verbal assists I describe may prevent them from being paralyzed on the spot by guilt, fear, or grief. After my explorations, I see that kill talk can sometimes enable terrible behavior, yet I also better understand why this language is there. Rather than scolding anyone for it, it seems wiser to direct collective energy toward questioning how the state picks its battles, given that they have come at such terrible cost to all involved.

That said, I have also described soldiers and veterans who manage to break free of the military's linguistic infrastructure to remarkable effect. They *do* speak differently about killing, in fact. This seems most likely to happen when they are no longer in the grip of combat or of their military service, giving them the space to locate more cracks and openings in their empathic imagination. They may, for instance, begin to speak of their supposed enemies or their victims as relational beings. They may give them a backstory and a mind no longer invisible but vibrant, aspiring, fearing, suffering, and thoroughly intertwined with others. They give them kin. Friends. A future. There is no snappy shorthand for this. The veterans who undertake this project linger on loss, question their government, and sometimes travel back to the scene of former battles to meet those they fought against. With their verbal and other forms of care, they honor that thing humans too readily deny—namely, the reality of others' experiences. In doing so, they engage in the antithesis of kill talk and bring us closer to the lived truth of all the humans involved in violent conflict. They allow themselves, and the rest of us with them, to feel the heartbreak of war.

Notes

Preface

1. Burns (2015: 41).
2. Remarque (1996 [1929]); Wiesel (2006 [1958]: x).
3. Levi suggests that language can provoke people to see the world as "something other than what it actually is." With this statement, he assumes a prelinguistic reality, but one need not agree with this assumption to grasp his point that language gives shape to the way people encounter the world. For evidence that euphemisms (when compared with more negative accounts) influence perception and action, see Jing-Schmidt (2022).
4. These terms carry slightly different connotations for language theorists. "Code" typically denotes a distinctive language variety, while "register" refers to a speech repertoire used by a particular persona or in a particular social situation (Agha 2007). There is some colloquial overlap between them, though, since both terms gesture toward a particular verbal repertoire.
5. For critical discussions of how anthropologists have worked for the military, see, for instance, Gusterson (2010) and D. Price (2011). For discussions of the military's so-called "Human Terrain Project" during the Global War on Terrorism, including accounts by social scientists who worked within it, see McFate et al. (2015).
6. See Bayendor (2012); Mohr et al. (2021: 601); Tomforde and Ben-Ari (2021: 4).
7. See Nader (1972). For my own work on elite groups, see my ethnography of the descendants of former colonial settlers in Kenya (McIntosh 2016), my other work on whites in Africa (McIntosh 2009, 2018a), and my analyses of language use by the US right wing (McIntosh 2020a, 2020b, 2022). On anthropology's arguably disproportionate focus on "the suffering slot," see Robbins (2013). See also Susan Harding (1991) for a discussion of anthropology's distaste for studying those with oppressive power, groups she refers to, tongue-in-cheek, as the "repugnant other."
8. Rosaldo (2000).
9. Appy (1993).
10. On mythologies about military grandeur after World War II and how such notions have informed decades of American martial enthusiasm, see Samet (2021).
11. On "moral injury," see Shay (2010; 2014). For a discussion of how some veterans feel identity-related discomfort in the face of PTSD's depression and anxiety, see Petersen (2021). On veteran suicide rates, see the National Veteran Suicide Prevention Annual Report (US Department of Veterans Affairs 2022: 10).
12. The scholarly work on military language is rather sparse, but see McIntosh (2021a) for a literature review.
13. Prince Harry, Duke of Sussex (2023: 217).
14. Examples of such collaborations have included a public conversation with James Yee for the New Jersey Council for the Humanities in 2023, and writing the introduction to Marc

Levy's 2020 book of essays, *Medic in the Green Time: Writings on the Vietnam War and Its Aftermath* (McIntosh 2020c).
15. Rosaldo (1993: 175).
16. I refrain from offering precise numbers of how many military personnel in combat zones experience combat, as this varies depending on the military branch, the era, and the theater of war.
17. Compelling accounts of what it was like to be an American service member in the Vietnam War can be found in memoirs and stories by Doug Anderson, Joshua Bowe, Nick Brokhausen, Philip Caputo, Phil Gioia, Marc Levy, John Musgrave, Tim O'Brien, Glenn Petersen, Karl Marlantes, Gary Rafferty, John Stillman, Diane Carlson Evans, and Lynda Van Devanter (the last two having served as Army nurses), among many others. See, as well, Michael Herr's *Dispatches*, even though it is authored by a war correspondent rather than a service member, Wallace Terry's collection of oral histories from Black Vietnam veterans, and the many first-hand accounts gathered by Marc Levy at https://medicinthegreentime.com/category/war/. For American memoirs of the Global War on Terrorism, see among others the writings by David Bellavia, Tyler Boudreau, Colby Buzzell, John Crawford, Ryan Leigh Dostie, Mary Jennings Hegar, Shoshana Johnson, Phil Klay, Tony Lagouranis, Miles Lagoze, Ray McPadden, Paul Rieckhoff, Kacy Tellessen, Brian Turner, Matt Young, and Kayla Williams.
18. The Department of Defense has recently commissioned numerous studies—often executed by the RAND Corporation—to evaluate military culture and practices. The Department of Defense's own Office of People Analytics (https://www.opa.mil) also administers the Defense Organizational Climate Survey (https://tinyurl.com/4rfr8u35) to millions of military personnel each year. Such assessments have been accompanied by extensive top-down directives addressing equal opportunity, bias reduction, sexual harassment, suicide prevention, and related issues. One employee of the Defense Equal Opportunity Management Institute (DEOMI) described the proliferation of policy changes as a "morass," highlighting the difficulty of navigating and implementing myriad directives across various branches. For a recent history of inclusion efforts in the US Armed Forces, see Lowen and McDonald (2023).
19. See Crawford's (2013) argument that members of the US public should engage with and take some responsibility for soldier and civilian deaths caused by US war fighting.

Chapter 1

1. *The Ground Truth* (Foulkrod 2006: 47:15).
2. Boudreau (2008: 20).
3. See Mbembe (2003, 2019). Mbembe notes that sovereign states enjoy the power to create "forms of social existence in which vast populations are subjected to conditions of life conferring upon them the status of living dead" (2003: 40). He takes inspiration from Giorgio Agamben (2005), who developed the notion of "a state of exception" to characterize the suspension of laws and rights from persons partitioned off from the body politic. Agamben seems a robust starting point for thinking about military personhood, but his "state of exception" doesn't neatly apply to military personnel (see Dunlap 2022). To give one example, Agamben's prime example of a state of exception is the concentration camp, but unlike concentration camp victims, soldiers have a political existence and the status of a

kind of super-citizen (C. Lutz 2002). Nevertheless, soldiers are both cleared to kill and to some degree symbolically emptied of their humanity.
4. I take the last term from Butler (2010).
5. MacLeish (2013; 2019: 289). On Hollywood's celebration of military service members, see Samet (2021) and Stahl (2009).
6. When I use the term "violence" in this book, I mean it to refer to kinetic violence—that is, physical force and actions causing harm or damage. This usage distinguishes it from the more metaphorical or symbolic connotations that some scholars intend when they use the term.
7. For firsthand accounts of Black American experiences in the Vietnam War, including experiences of racism in the military, see Wallace Terry's (1984) collection of oral histories.
8. In fact, the militarization of US combatants is a clear exertion of what Michel Foucault called "biopolitics," in which a political institution uses controlling techniques on groups to regulate their life processes (Foucault 1978: 139). Foucault's (1978) descriptions of biopolitics and biopower began with a distinction between two poles: "anatomo-politics," which focuses on the body as a machine that can be honed and intensified in service of the state, and the "biopolitics of populations," in which the state targets groups of people to regulate the functions and processes of life. While a certain amount of biopolitical work fosters life, such as state control of public hygiene or health that tends to favor already-privileged citizens, some has necropolitical ends that impede or disallow life (Rouse 2021). This negative valence is, of course, a potent force in the military.

   Note that historically, the "bio" in the term "biopolitics" has tended to direct scholarly attention toward bodies and flesh. Corporeal biopolitics in the military are extensive, of course, including the surveillance, subjugation, and honing of bodies through exertion, marching, drilling, firing, eating, and sleeping in highly coordinated ways (see, e.g., Hockey's [2002] description of these in the British military). But the verbal dynamics I describe in this book go far beyond the body and deep into the psyche, retraining subjectivity, modes of thought, and affect. Possibly the term "psychopolitics" should be adopted as a way of alluding to this variation on the theme of biopolitics.
9. Aside from the work of Carol Cohn (1987), whose writing on the technostrategic language of nuclear defense intellectuals emerged from feminist studies, I located almost no work in anthropology or discourse studies on the linguistic socialization of combatants. Carol Burke (2004) may come closest with her study of military socialization, folklore, and terminology. Much of the work connecting war and language focuses on the discourses that legitimate conflict in the eyes of the citizenry (see McIntosh 2021a for a summary of some important anthropological scholarship in this vein, including Hodges 2011; Masco 2014).
10. In anthropology, the concept of personhood includes qualities of agency and morality (McIntosh 2018c), both of which tend to be altered by militarization.
11. Lifton, quoted in Gonzalez et al. (2019: 128).
12. For elaboration of the perils of successfully adapting people to war, see Gonzalez et al. (2019).
13. For perspectives from veterans who came to oppose the wars they fought in, see, for instance, Anderson (2009); Boudreau (2008); Gutmann and Lutz (2010); IVAW and Glantz (2008); Lagoze (2023); Levinson (2014); Petersen (2021); Reickhoff (2006); Schrader (2019).

14. See Theidon (2016). I thank Tyler Boudreau for a conversation that brought this point to life for me.
15. Arendt (1994: 308).
16. "Wars are born and sustained," writes literary scholar James Dawes (2002: 5), "in rivers of language about what it means to serve the cause, to kill the enemy, and to die with dignity." War's discourses tend to imagine a dangerous, morally blighted enemy (Feldman 2005; Hodges 2011; Masco 2014; Puar and Rai 2002).
17. Although I did not do comparative historical work to examine kill talk in the US military prior to the Vietnam War, it would not surprise me if the post–World War II era brought heightened versions of it to military training. I say this because at the close of that war, General S. L. A. Marshall (2000 [1947]) famously claimed that fewer than 25% of men were willing to fire at an enemy in combat, and those who did fire often missed intentionally (see Grossman 1995: 3ff.). Though the accuracy of Marshall's claims is questionable, the US military responded to them with new attention to training tactics. Human silhouettes replaced bullseye targets on firing ranges, target practice required quicker response times, and camaraderie in training was enhanced so that combatants would be more willing to kill on behalf of their unit. With disinhibition of killing a priority, military linguistic culture may have changed in tandem.
18. Infrastructure is conventionally thought of in terms of material networks that enable the circulation of things, people and ideas or as "objects that create the grounds on which other objects operate" (Larkin 2013: 329), but anthropologists and others have sometimes used the concept in less obviously material ways. In this work, the metaphor of linguistic infrastructure helps me think about how the state instantiates itself in bodies and minds (cf. Agard-Jones 2013), with linguistic patterns that encourage certain flows, stoppages, and contours of thought, emotion, and behavior. Some scholars before me have also used the phrase "linguistic infrastructure" or related ones, though never in just the way I am using it here. Courtney Handman (2017), for instance, discusses how some in Papua New Guinea recognize a metaphorical resonance between transportation infrastructure and linguistic communication, because language—Bible translations, in particular—can create channels between communicative entities such as God and New Guinean Christians. Jan Blommaert (2014) discusses multilingual storefront signs in Antwerp as a kind of material linguistic infrastructure that enables linguistic superdiversity. Frank Cody (2013) discusses literacy as a kind of infrastructure that holds the promise of modern citizenship in South India. The late Bernard (Barney) Bate (2021) describes how historical arrangements such as mass meetings and public orations in Tamil society constituted an "infrastructure of communication" that invited new political publics. Ish-Shalom et al. (2021) describe a "linguistic infrastructure of world politics," focusing on the contested meaning of verbalized political concepts ("sovereignty," "liberty," "war," and the like). Working not with language so much as affect, Ruth Wilson Gilmore (2022: 490) develops a notion of an "infrastructure of feeling" (inspired in part by Raymond Williams's notion of "structures of feeling"). She takes the material foundation of the "infrastructure" metaphor to heart, suggesting it "speeds some processes and slows down others, setting agendas, producing isolation, enabling cooperation." The infrastructure of feeling in the Black radical tradition, she suggests, is often productive and inspiring. Contrary to this expansive potential, the military's linguistic infrastructure focuses more on choking off thought and feeling.

19. Butler (2010: xi, 26). Note that linguists also use the term "frame" (see, e.g., Goffman 1974 Tannen 1993), usually referring more specifically to a jointly constructed notion of what kind of social event is at hand.
20. Butler (2010: xix). The photographs in question were taken by US soldiers in the first decade of the 2000s at Abu Ghraib prison in Iraq. They depict American service members abusing, mocking, and torturing prisoners of war. While Butler's examples focus on representations of putative enemies, some of my material speaks as well to the way soldiers sometimes frame even their own lives as "already lost and destroyed."
21. On linguistic socialization, see Duranti et al. (2012); Ochs and Schieffelin (1984). On the way patterns of language can "project an implicit social ontology, sanctioning everyday understandings and making sense of them in deeply institutional terms," see Mannheim (2015: 44).
22. This exploration of American military language also enables closer exploration of US imperialism, in the spirit of Nomi Stone's (2018: 536) statement that "American militarism must be understood as a relation of self to Other—indeed as constituting the gap (real or imagined) between the two. Ethnography offers a critique on the ground and fills the voids left by 'macroscopic' lenses on empire . . . shedding light on imperial power relations and their lived and embodied effects."
23. Loosely speaking, "stance" concerns the way a speaker positions themselves in an interaction. Stance has become a highly elaborated theoretical notion in linguistic anthropology and related disciplines (see, e.g. Jaffe 2009; Kiesling 2018, 2022), but readers will understand the general spirit of the word without my needing to delve into theoretical details here.
24. Among military strategists and technical experts, too, we often find technocratic terms like "counterforce exchange" and "strategic effects strike" that fail to reckon with the human consequences of military action; see C. Cohn (1987) and W. Lutz (1992). See also Delori (2014) on discourse among pilots who dropped bombs in the 2011 attacks on Libya; they tended to avoid any discussion whatsoever of enemy dead after the fact. Gusterson (1996) has written in a related vein about the mechanistic and technical language that pervades the weapons work of nuclear scientists.
25. MacLeish (2013: 80). See also Stone (2017, 2022) on "human technology" in the military, extending beyond the bodies of combatants.
26. On military technolects, see Saber (2018). For a long list of Marine Corps acronyms, see United States Marine Corps (2017).
27. "Requirement," Louis read, "to track and improve individual medical readiness, REP C is OPNAVINST, 3710." Note that such language is paradoxically both biopolitical—concerned with the management of bodies in service of the state (Foucault 2004)—and bloodless.
28. On Marine Corps officers' stance of "epistemic superiority," see Marcellino (2014).
29. See Disler (2008) for a study of honorifics and gender in the Air Force. On military politeness, see Halbe (2011).
30. On the use of slang to bridle against military authority, see Axelrod (2013); Burke (2004: 206ff.); Reinberg (1991). See also the compilation of sexist military slang—a notorious bonding mechanism among male-dominant groups—in Burke (2004: 118–120).
31. The narrow focus of this book means I neglect not only interesting military speech registers but also interesting speech communities. I am curious, for instance, about any

linguistic overlaps between infantry and the tens of thousands of private contractors who were tasked during the GWOT with security, interrogation, and other core functions of the US military. It would be fascinating, too, to know more about language among, for instance, the low-intensity units intended to work flexibly in local societies, such as the Civil Affairs personnel who operated in Iraq with "thick" engagement and meaningful relationships (see K. Brown 2008). It would also be interesting to compare and contrast the language used by troops with different political orientations (see Dempsey 2009 on political divisions in the rank-and-file).

32. The scholarly work on political ideologies that contribute to war's violence is vast, extending to the dynamics of racism, Orientalism, colonialism, imperialism, nationalism, fundamentalism, religious bigotry, totalitarianism, revolutionary ideologies, conflicts between capitalism and communism, and much more. The work on the psychology of war violence is also daunting in scope, including such topics as the desire for power, group identity, group rivalry, aggression, vengeance, moral exclusion, confirmation bias, and far more. On crowd behavior and conformity in killing, see Browning (1998). On the affect, ideology, and social engineering that underpin genocide, see Hinton (2002). See Bandura (1999) for a brief summary of some of the psychological work on disregarding or diminishing the injurious effects of one's actions while dehumanizing victims. See Grossman (1995) for discussions of the psychology of proximity in killing. See also Theidon (2007) on the dynamic by which witnessing atrocity can beget more atrocity. Although Theidon's data comes from accounts of gang rape by soldiers in Peru's internal armed conflict of the 1980s–1990s, the principle she describes rings true more broadly: "Committing morally abhorrent acts in front of others not only forges bonds between the perpetrators but also forges *sinverguenzas*—shameless people—capable of tremendous brutality. To lose the sense of shame—a 'regulatory emotion' because shame implies an Other in front of whom one feels ashamed—creates men with a recalibrated capacity for atrocity" (Theidon 2007: 471).

33. Musgrave (2021: 104–105). Note that scholars from many disciplines have debated how we should define "dehumanization" and what its role might be in violence. Is it, for instance, about construing people as objects or as defective humans, subhuman or animal-like (sometimes called "pseudospeciation")? Is it about denying people their minds and thought processes, their potential for flourishing and suffering, their agency, or all of the above? Is it rooted in a failure to empathize? Might it sometimes be about denying a person's refined emotions or denying them civility and "civilization"? Is dehumanization located in mental states (Livingstone Smith 2021), or should we construe it as a contagious, affectively charged collective achievement that amounts to a shared atmosphere (cf. Berlant 2011: 15; Cvetkovich 2014: 13; see also Ahmed 2004)? And when should we construe it as a system of racialized value, emergent from colonialism and slavery, that considers distance from whiteness equivalent to distance from full humanity? My purposes here don't require me to settle on a single definition, particularly since all these dynamics have been at play in the US wars in Vietnam, Iraq, and Afghanistan. I will use the word generally, to mean a dynamic by which some person is or people are placed outside the circle of fully valued humanity, while recognizing this can take many forms and that it may obtain at individual and collective levels. I see the dehumanization achieved by kill talk as both conceptual and affective, involving failures of construal and empathy on the part of the dehumanizer. See Haslam and Loughnan (2014) for a review of some

literature on dehumanization; see also Bandura (1999); Buber (1937); Bourke (1999); Chen (2012); Conley (2016); Delori (2014); Haque and Waytz (2012); Harris (2017); Hinton (2002); Livingstone Smith (2021); and Over (2021). See also Parish (2014) on personhood and empathy, and Sykes and Matza (1957) for an early discussion of "techniques of neutralization" by which people rationalize illicit acts. Such techniques include reasoning that the victim deserved what the perpetrator did, a stance sometimes achieved when the perpetrator apprehends the victim as "a vague abstraction," thus weakening the perpetrator's awareness of the victim's humanity (Sykes and Matza 1957: 668).

Note that although dehumanization seems to attenuate empathy, philosophical and empirical work on war and genocide suggests dehumanization is not a sine qua non of killing (see Livingstone Smith 2021; Luft 2019), particularly given the power of forces such as peer pressure and obedience to authority. According to sociologist Aliza Luft's (2019) summary of research on genocide, "Dehumanizing discourse can pave the way for violence to occur, but violence does not require it." Still, there can be little doubt that the military's dehumanizing linguistic infrastructure and the affective and political climate of combat are mutually reinforcing, as the concepts and affect encouraged by language can set the stage for brutality and perhaps legitimize killing after the fact (Luft 2019; see also Sites 2013: 71), playing a facilitating or encouraging role. Furthermore, dehumanizing language may have a contagious effect on peers (Yanagizawa-Drott 2014).

34. Musgrave describes the same dynamic in his memoir, but this particular quotation is taken from Burns and Novick's 2017 documentary series about Vietnam (see "PBS Documentary" 2017).
35. Musgrave (2021: 108).
36. It was not unusual for American soldiers in Vietnam to talk about their own buddies being "wasted," too—further evidence that they were dehumanizing their own type to some degree as well.
37. See Wittgenstein (1958). In pondering an analogy for Musgrave's experience, I remembered Wittgenstein's duck-rabbit concept. I later found Duranti (2009) used the same analogy in his discussion of Husserl's phenomenology; evidently we were thinking in similar terms about how quickly perception can shift. My approach, then, resonates with Duranti's (2009) and Ochs's (2012) suggestion that we construe language and experience as part of the same field, such that combat language-in-use can constitute a "mode of experiencing the world" (Ochs 2012: 149).
38. This is an example of what Husserl called "phenomenological modification" (Duranti 2009: 208).
39. Musgrave (2003). This quotation is from unpaginated front matter. The italics are my own.
40. Edward Sapir and Benjamin Whorf were mid-century figures in anthropology and linguistics who developed the notion that language has an important influence on thought (Kay and Kempton 1984; Sapir 1929; Whorf 1944). Both explored the grammars and lexicons of indigenous languages to suggest that the language variety a person grows up with influences the way they perceive and experience the world, a notion sometimes called the Sapir-Whorf hypothesis and sometimes "linguistic relativity."

Sapir's and Whorf's claims have been interpreted and reworked into weak and strong versions, with stronger claims suggesting that the language one speaks *determines* thought and sets its limits. But strong linguistic determinism is easily contested, leading critics such as John McWhorter (2014) to assert that although language intersects with culture, it doesn't have an important influence on the way the world looks. Others have dismissed the relationship by asserting that "thought" is distinct from "language" (see, e.g., Pinker 1994). As a result of such critiques, some students of language go so far as to claim that the entire question of "language and thought" is dead.

But "weaker" versions of the Sapir-Whorf hypothesis still seem compelling. A good deal of interesting experimental work, for instance, suggests the grammar of one's primary language can nudge perception, classification, and memory (see, e.g., Boroditsky et al. 2003; Gumperz and Levinson 1996; Lucy 2012; see also Hill and Mannheim 1992; Webster 2015a; Wolff and Holmes 2011 on refinements to these inquiries). Anthony Webster (2015a: 90) offers a helpfully flexible definition of "linguistic relativity," construing it in terms of "a positive perspective on the ways in which languages facilitate possibilities for us to orient and imagine. . . . This is not," he adds, "a version overly enamored with constraints and determinings"— an amendment that encourages us to be open to the way different phrasings or repertoires within "the same" language can be bound up with different attitudes toward and experiences of the world.

An array of approaches in language studies have borne this possibility out. George Lakoff (1987), for one, contends that the metaphors we use help constitute broad cognitive schemas for thought. Thibodeau and Boroditsky (2011) used experimental methods to explore such an idea; in one study, they presented two groups of English speakers with passages about "crime" and found that the metaphors each group was introduced to affected their reasoning. Capps and Ochs (1995) suggest speakers bring aspects of reality into being through the narrative architecture of how they talk about it, reifying an experience like "panic disorder" (in their famous example) through language. Scott Kiesling (2018) suggests that the repeated adoption of certain stances (he focuses particularly on the "swagger stance" so common in masculine talk in the US) can durably influence speakers' affective lives and experiences of being in the world. Charles Goodwin (1994), exploring the power of phrasing to "shape events in the phenomenal environment," shows that defense lawyers discursively framed the police beating of Rodney King as justifiable "de-escalation" rather than gratuitous violence, successfully persuading jurors of this way of perceiving the evidence. Robin Conley (2016), in her work on the use of language in death penalty cases, details the way terms of reference can cultivate psychological distance from defendants accused of terrible crimes. Most germane of all to this book is Carol Cohn's (1987) personal testimonial about her several months of hanging out with nuclear defense strategists and adopting their linguistic framework for talking about nuclear bombs, which strictly avoided reference to suffering. Cohn reports that after some weeks of this, she found it hard not only to talk with the military collective about the human cost of nuclear war, but also to *think* about the devastation bombs effect. The community's discursive practice set up a kind of intersubjective orientation against empathy.

Such work prompts us to take seriously the intimate ways in which language can interact with subjectivity. The philosopher's (and, now, anthropologist's) notion of "phenomenology" seems relevant here, inviting a holistic approach to experience that includes thinking but extends as well to embodied feeling, relationality, and stance-taking (see Desjarlais and Throop 2011; Duranti 2009; Ochs 2012; Zigon and Throop 2021). This encompassing perspective resonates with new approaches to cognition that emphasize its

embodied and situated dimensions and with anthropologists' concerns with the broader social and political conditions that give rise to experience (Zigon and Throop 2021).
41. Conley (2016).
42. Furthermore, if we include speaking as part of holistic experience (Ochs 2012), we do not need to resolve the question of whether language and thought are the same, nor work with a one-way model of causality from speech to thought, nor adopt rigid linguistic determinism. One way to think about speech as part of experience-building and sense-making is to consider the following analogy. Imagine a person wearing a bright red shirt (a signifier, analogous to using a form of language) as part of an overall stance of intrepid determination. There need not be a one-way causal relationship between the red shirt and the attitude the person experiences. The wearer might express the relationship in various ways: "The red helps me feel bold," "The red reflects how bold I feel," or, more agnostically about cause and effect, "I just feel bolder in this red." As a sign, furthermore, red has a distinctive meaning to Americans; through its historical usages, it "tastes" of a bold attitude (cf. Bakhtin 1983). While the red shirt is intertwined with the wearer's experience of feeling bold, it also communicates this stance to those around them, potentially influencing these others (and the affordances of the red might be amplified in a crowd). Of course, one can also wear a red shirt while feeling meek, and it may have no discernable effect on one's attitude or mood. Similarly, using language in particular ways can have certain affordances for experience, but it does not strictly determine it.

At the same time, I take inspiration from linguist Scott Kiesling (2018) when he suggests that repeatedly speaking with the same attitude can help condition a person's feelings. Kiesling focuses on how American male speech tends to adopt a stance of ease and confidence ("swagger," as he calls it), creating a habitual "mind/body" interface with the world (Kiesling 2018: 6). Put another way, in this formulation, repeated stance-taking (through language and other forms of bodily communication) can potentially influence (provide an infrastructure for) one's habitual state (in affect, cognition, and embodiment). Presumably this dynamic can also be enhanced if one is part of a collective that recurrently strikes the same stances together.
43. For an analogy, see Adena et al.'s (2015) findings that anti-Semitic propaganda has persuasive power or not depending on whether the listener is already anti-Semitic.
44. Judith Butler argues that the perception that certain populations are threatening "does not emerge as the spontaneous act of a single mind but as a consequence of a certain field of intelligibility that helps form and frame our responsiveness to the impinging world" (2010: 34). In this volume, I presume that kill talk takes part of its power from geopolitical and historical context as well as the more immediate, holistic social contexts of its use (cf. Jones 2021). See Schaefer's (2021) relevant complaint that too often, discourse analysis "studies the transcript of power, missing all of the nonlinguistic channels by which illocutionary force actually gets its hooks into us."
45. Cohn (2020: 186).
46. See Duranti and Goodwin (1992).
47. https://www.youtube.com/watch?v=eEdPvbjPGYs (21:30).
48. In fact, the dynamics of stance-shifting may help resolve a paradox observed by Livingstone Smith (2021)—namely, that people who dehumanize paradoxically sometimes seem to view their victims as both human and subhuman. White overseers in the US South, for instance, appear to have had contradictory consciousness about enslaved people,

sometimes regarding them as animalistic, sometimes as absolutely human (Livingstone Smith 2021: 48). If dehumanization were a static mental disposition, this might be hard to make sense of (to address the tension, Livingstone Smith suggests dehumanization models others as composite "monsters"), but it may be easier to resolve when one considers the temporal aspect of stance-taking, which implicates language-in-use in shifting attitudes. Indeed, as some of my earlier linguistic anthropological work has explored, speakers of two minds can tack rapidly between seemingly contradictory stances in their talk (McIntosh 2009). See also Duranti (2009, after Husserl 1931) on "phenomenological modification."

49. C. Lutz (2002).
50. MacLeish (2015: 15).
51. Boudreau (2008: 41). Veteran Doug Anderson (2011: 491) phrases the dynamic in terms of exposure: "Long wars create a level of depravity among servicemen that is never understood by the public. If you continually expose people to legal murder, it makes them numb and cynical." The former diplomat Peter Van Buren (2015) amplifies this sentiment. Based on his disenchanting work with the US military, he characterizes war as "what happens when the rules break down."
52. See Dreyfus and Prince (2008) on the ontological breakdown of the known world in combat, in which the terms that define a person's moral commitments may collapse.
53. See Binder (2010: 94).
54. On the monstrous figure of the chimera in mythology, see Severi (2015 [2007]). Severi contends that chimerical figures in rituals and storytelling offer a kind of mnemonic device with their composite features, while their images of unresolved conflict can inspire acts of imagination. I am reluctant to project such qualities onto military contradictions, though, since the military players I spoke to see the contradictions (when they recognize them at all) primarily as symptoms of the state's hypocrisy.
55. The moral tension in Randall's description resonates with Aaron Belkin's (2012) complex argument that US service members are forced—during training and beyond—into numerous symbolic oppositions, including "masculine/feminine, strong/weak, dominant/subordinate, victor/victim, civilized/barbaric, clean/dirty, [and] straight/queer." Belkin argues that these contradictions place service members into "webs of double binds that confuse them and sustain a penchant for obedience and conformity" (2012: 4–5). He further contends that the US military has tended to symbolically force its own "filth" onto supposedly inferior states as a means of demonstrating its dominance. This book cannot do justice to Belkin's tantalizing framework, though the reader will notice some of his antinomies in my chapters about basic training in the Marine Corps. I do, however, endeavor to add a further symbolic opposition to Belkin's list—namely, that between moral probity and moral nihilism.
56. See Nick Turse (2013) for a detailed exposition of such practices. In Vietnam, service members notoriously collected body parts as trophies. In the Global War on Terrorism, US combatants sometimes took photographic "trophies" of themselves posing with enemy bodies. Although the Geneva Conventions prohibit the maltreatment of enemy remains and the US Army considers the mutilation of enemy corpses a "misconduct stress behavior" (Harrison 2012: 1–2), trophy taking has been widely documented in European and US battles. Anthropologist Simon Harrison (2012) argues such behavior is particularly common in contexts where the enemy is construed as a racial other and thus less human,

making it easier to draw on a metaphor of war-as-hunting. He adds that despite the putative evolution of war from small-scale and primitive to modern, rational, and "moderated by law," Western military practice falls decidedly short of this ideal (Simon Harrison 2012: 4).

57. See, for instance, O'Connell (2012) on how the United States Marine Corps built a strong public presence through skillful use of media and public relations.
58. See Moyn (2022) on this fraught history; see also Crawford (2013), Delori (2014), and Khalili (2012). Protocols added to the Geneva Conventions in 1977, for instance, were designed to illegalize targeting civilians and minimize enemy combatants' suffering when not deemed a military necessity.
59. The announcement of the Marine Corps Values Program states, "Our goal is to continue to produce Marines who are exemplary citizens and who will act honorably and intelligently, whatever their situation or level of responsibilities. All Marines are expected to epitomize that which is good about our Nation and to personify the ideals upon which it was founded. Honor, Courage, and Commitment are not just words; they frame the way Marines are to live and act. There is no room in the Marine Corps for situational ethics or situational morality" (https://www.marines.mil/Portals/1/Publications/MCO%201500.56.pdf).
60. Sitaraman (2013); see also Stone (2018).
61. Hartig (2017).
62. See Lowen and McDonald (2023, 6–1).
63. Moyn (2022: 317). See also Asad (2007); Delori (2020); Puar (2006).
64. Members of the infantry who served on the ground in Iraq and Afghanistan describe a certain wiggle room in the Rules of Engagement (ROE) that govern when and how lethal and nonlethal force may be used. In the earlier stages of the GWOT, for instance, the ROE were strictly enforced, but as attacks on US soldiers stepped up, they were relaxed (Levinson 2014: 232). Soldiers were initially permitted to fire their weapons only if they identified "hostile action," but this shifted to the looser requirement of identifying "hostile intent," a state of mind easy to fantasize (Gregory 2019). Marine Corps veteran Evan Wright contends the ROE in Iraq were "broadly defined and loosely enforced" and that "you [were] held accountable for the facts *as they appear to you at the time*" (Wright 2004: 33; emphasis mine). Ben, who served with the Army in Iraq, tells me the ROE were "fluid" and seemed to vary by brigade, battalion, or company. In one case, for instance, he watched another unit open fire on a vehicle on the other side of a divided highway. It had been driven by a man who turned out to be trying to get his pregnant wife to the hospital. That unit claimed firing at the other side of the highway was within their ROE, says Ben, but "we'd never heard that one" (see also Donnelly 2013; Schrader 2019).

The question of when to use force can be maddeningly unclear to members of the infantry in complex combat environments. Is that woman reaching for a weapon or a tissue under her burqa? Is the car rolling toward the checkpoint failing to stop because it carries a suicide bomb or because the driver doesn't understand the American signal for "stop"? Should Marines shell a building where they think a sniper is lying in wait, even though it may be packed with civilians? Even beyond such dilemmas, some of my respondents mentioned the challenge of remembering all the rules and laws they are supposed to be working with. The grey area too often means killing noncombatants when in doubt (Speigle 2013).

There can be no question that the laws and rules of war, as well as combatants' personal convictions, sometimes beget decency and restraint (cf. Milburn 2019), yet time and again, evidence suggests that it is easy for infantry to spin out in the theater of war. In his 2018 documentary, for instance, Miles Lagoze records frustrated Marines in Afghanistan discussing the temptation to torture prisoners for information and pointing their rifles while yelling at unarmed children (Lagoze 2018: 19:00, 48:00; see also Lagoze 2023). Testimonials by GWOT veterans also describe revenge killings of civilians and other illicit behavior, usually concealed in the presence of embedded journalists (IVAW and Glantz 2008). On the general unmooring from conventional morality in war, see Bica (2018); Bourke (1999); Gigliotti (2003: 164); Marlantes (2011); Sites (2013). On the notion that war produces its own morality, see Lutz and Millar (2012).

Compounding such tensions, the laws and guidelines of war are subject to countless ambiguities, permissive interpretations, and workarounds (Moyn 2022: 5; see also IVAW and Glantz 2008). "Just war theory," for example, justifies killing in war if attacks carefully distinguish between military targets and civilians (Gusterson 2016: 85), yet White House casualty estimation protocols count all military-age males in a drone strike zone as "combatants" unless intelligence has explicitly identified them as innocent. Sometimes drone strikes have killed anonymous groups of men because a faraway watcher concluded they might be acting vaguely like insurgents.

Some scholars have argued that self-contradiction and ambiguity in the law may be inherent to state structures. Jusionyte (2015: 133), for instance, contends that a "[blurred] distinction between law and crime... obfuscating any clear distinction between the legal, the political, and the criminal" is part of the dynamic that "enables states to happen."

65. See K. Brown (2008) for a discussion of this force mentality.
66. MacLeish (2013); Taussig (1992).
67. See, for instance, the United States Marine Corps Recruit Training Order (2024: section 1–2).
68. In a similar vein, Lieutenant Colonel Lacey tells an NPR reporter that "traditional Army training teaches that if there's a threat, you eliminate it" (Shapiro 2007). In the decades since Vietnam, however, some command posts have tried to refine their decisions about the use of force with the help of military lawyers. Such assistance is not available for most operations, though, nor, of course, for combatants making decisions in the heat of the moment. Furthermore, actions compliant with military law do not always align with normative ethical frameworks.
69. Wolfendale (2008: 45).
70. D. Phillips (2019).
71. A 2014 USMC recruiting video (https://www.youtube.com/watch?v=YvLwJEBrF84) offers a somewhat vague definition of honor as "doing the right thing, even when no one is looking." Ramon, who served as a DI in the 1980s, defines "honor" more narrowly, in terms of keeping promises and telling the truth, telling me, "Your word is your bond. If you say something, you mean it. If you're truthful, you'll never get in trouble. You know?" In 2013, sailors and Marines in the Pacific were issued a core values card linking honor to purity, stating, "WE KEEP OUR HONOR CLEAN." An accompanying video (https://www.youtube.com/watch?v=I7lDQzgv8os) features officers urging Marines to avoid sexual misconduct. Unofficially issued "Marine Corps challenge coins" often distill honor to playground values: "This is the bedrock of our character / Having the ultimate in ethical

and moral behavior: To never lie, cheat, or steal" (https://tinyurl.com/yd2ck3tu). I am struck by how few of these understandings of "honor" among Marines urge restraint in the exercise of violence, or (say) compassion for civilians or prisoners of war.

That said, other interpretations of "honor" at least link it to "respecting human dignity," such as a challenge coin that reads, "Honor: ultimate in ethical and moral behavior to respect human dignity" (https://www.challengecoin.com/u-s-marine-corps-values-challenge-coin.html). When Marine Corp Commandant General Carl Epting Mundy Jr. issued a one-page summary developing the concepts of Marine Corps Values for the LeJeune Leadership Institute at Marine Corps University, his definition of "honor" included not only those Boy Scout values of never lying, cheating, or stealing, but also "respecting human dignity," having "respect and concern for each other," and even the "quality of maturity," among other things (Mundy 1998).

72. Alex Pillen (2017: 721) has written extensively about linguistic and other semiotic forms that may have oppositional or ambivalent meanings, words that conjure a "suspended betweenness or a space that will never be filled." In Vedic India, for instance, the "superposition of contrasting values" in the same terms reflected a political context of "uncertainty and flux" (Pillen 2017: 721).

73. E. Levy (2012) has made this claim about military language. On diglossia more generally, see Ferguson (1959).

74. In a similar vein, Snow (2000: 65) glosses empathy as "feeling with" someone else, while Hollan and Throop (2008: 387) consider empathy the "complex emotional, embodied, and cognitive work that is implicated in approximating the subjective experience of another." In an extended discussion of empathy, Duranti (2010: 21), following Husserl, suggests that empathy does not mean that "we simultaneously come to the same understanding of any given situation (although this can happen), but that we have, to start, the possibility of exchanging places, of seeing the world from the point of view of the Other." Throop (2008) further suggests several dimensions along which empathy may be differently understood in different sociocultural contexts; these are "temporality," "intentionality," "discernability," and "appropriateness/possibility." His analysis of understandings of empathy in Yap (in Micronesia) reminds us that Western models of the way empathy "should" work are not universally shared.

75. https://www.waldorfeducation.org/news-resources/essentials-in-education-blog/detail/~board/essentials-in-ed-board/post/teaching-empathy-essential-for-students-crucial-for-humanity.

76. https://betterkids.education/blog/4-tips-to-help-children-develop-empathy; https://www.psychologytoday.com/us/blog/staying-sane-inside-insanity/202110/emotional-maturity-in-relationships.

77. https://www.newtownbee.com/11202020/avielle-foundation-is-now-the-avielle-initiative-at-university-of-colorado/.

78. https://www.forbes.com/sites/forbescoachescouncil/2021/01/25/empathy-from-buzzword-to-superpower/?sh=7e4169b05b75.

79. https://uxdesign.cc/realities-of-designing-with-empathy-7236b8413611.

80. https://www.facebook.com/zuck/videos/10103671105741461. Note as well that a quick search on Google Trends, which shows relative "interest" in a concept over time since 2004, shows the term "empathy" on a generally steady upward march. One has to wonder how many invocations of the term are oriented toward compassionate feeling and how

many involve weaponizing the empathy concept for political-economic gain or public manipulation.
81. See Fassin and Rechtman's (2009) discussion of the politics of trauma.
82. McIntosh and Mendoza-Denton (2020).
83. On empathic bias favoring those we already identify with, see Fuchs (2019); Kockelman (2007). Failures of empathy can arise from the dynamics of "perpetrator disgust" (Munch-Jurisic 2018), which may amplify the hostility of those committing violence toward their victims. On the relationship between proximity and empathy, see Grossman (1995); Throop (2012). Modern combatants are often physically distant from their enemies, and the overwhelming sensory environment of war can obscure the cues typically used to connect with others. Therefore, it might be more accurate to consider empathy not in terms of a simple presence or absence but as a continuum. (On the notion of an empathy spectrum, and the link between cruelty and failures of empathy, see Baron-Cohen 2012.) An empathy continuum can encompass a "will to empathy" toward largely unseen subjects, or "shadow subjects" as Maisa Taha (2017) describes them, even if one's empathic state isn't fully activated or developed. The will to empathy involves acknowledging the ontological reality of another's experience, including their potential for suffering, and extending a form of compassionate engagement toward that experience, despite limited signs of what it might be like. Much military kill talk aims to suppress empathy for the enemy across this continuum, whether the enemy is distant and abstract or close and vivid.
84. "Emotional labor," a phrase developed by sociologist Arlie Hoschchild (1983), refers to the regulation or management of emotions as part of one's professional work. Hoschchild pointed out that in the service economy, workplaces often require employees to force cheerfulness and suppress anger. In some cases, emotional labor involves the opposite; the bill collector, for instance, must selectively suppress empathy to behave in unfriendly ways that serve the profit motive.
85. See Stone (2018); Gusterson (2010).
86. On hegemonic masculinity, see Hinojosa (2010). For helpful discussion of "masculinities studies," especially its articulation with language studies, see Lawson (2020). The corpus of work highlights the constructed aspect of all versions of masculinity.
87. Belkin (2012: 3). Belkin also elaborates several complex arguments about military masculinity that are beyond the scope of my discussion. One concerns penetration as an extension of both military masculinity and imperialism. Another suggests that elements of military masculine power come from being paradoxically impenetrable ("hard-bodied") and penetrable (in the sense of "taking it like a man" if raped).
88. Along with this kin-like affinity for members of one's military unit, military identity sometimes involves a paradoxical theme of nurturing vulnerable creatures in a theater of combat. Since at least World War I, authors have documented accounts of combatants on the battlefield tending to local kittens, dogs, wounded animals, even mice, or engaging with impoverished or orphaned local children (Elshtain 1987: 205–210). These vulnerable lives, of course, are also at risk of being mowed down if caught in the violence of these same combatants.
89. See Fosher et al. (2018: 30). In a related vein, sociologist Alex Vitale (2017) suggests that most US police officers are cynical about sensitivity training, framing it as a political exercise that has no real relevance to their work.
90. Baker (2019).

91. Marlantes, quoted in Sites (2013: xxii–xxiii).
92. Psychologist Jonathan Shay (2010; 2014) is credited with first developing the notion of moral injury, a contested concept with complex and unresolved implications. For instance, scholars have tended not to question how soldiers' "moral compass" might be established or calibrated to begin with. Is a person's moral compass hardwired at birth? If so, is it calibrated to some kind of universal human moral sense? Or can a person's moral compass be altogether (re)constructed by their upbringing, including their religious beliefs? Can military training itself be said to reconfigure an adult's moral compass (cf. Lutz and Millar 2012), so that some combatants answer to a different kind of morality, one with a higher tolerance for acts of violence and killing? Most literature on the subject does not seem troubled by this problem, though MacLeish (2022) touches on it in somewhat different terms. My own impression is that by the end of their service, some veterans operate with plural or context-dependent moral calibration, shifting between a civilian's sense that killing is wrong and a military stance that accepts killing and other violent deeds in combat. This suggestion has some resonance with Hoschchild's claim that the transmutation of emotion for the workplace is a "delicate achievement" and that the self may end up fragmented in service of the institution (1983: 119).
93. See Fuchs (2017); Grossman (1995); Throop (2012); Zunshine (2012). In a related vein, philosopher Emmanuel Levinas claims that gazing at other humans has a compelling moral authority, for "the 'thou shalt not murder' is inscribed on the face" (Levinas 1998: 35, 74).
94. Indeed, as Butler (2010: 33) points out, human survival and vulnerability hinge on embeddedness and mutual reliance, and recognizing these seems to render persons more "grievable."
95. On some of these differences, see K. Brown (2008). Before World War II, naval officers had overseen the Marine Corps and its generals did not have large commands. The prestige of the Corps picked up during World War II and has been increasingly prominent since then (O'Connell 2012).
96. https://www.marines.com/life-as-a-marine/life-in-the-marine-corps/preparing-for-operating-forces.html.
97. See also Hinojosa (2010: 186).
98. Ironically, around 2004 Marine Corps leaders such as General Mattis began to criticize the Army for being too heavy-handed with their use of force in Iraq. As the counterinsurgency campaign picked up, some Marines were surprised to be instructed they should aim for a more culturally sensitive, gentle approach, though it was doomed to fail in the end (Boudreau 2008; see also K. Brown 2008).
99. The public narratives I could find suggest an Army unit may have been assigned stress cards in or around 1995, but the image has stuck around and been elaborated as myth and cautionary tale. See, for instance, https://www.snopes.com/fact-check/stress-cards/.
100. There are also internecine rivalries within each branch. Among Marines, for instance, I've heard claims such as: infantry are tougher than officers, men are tougher than women, certain bases are tougher than others. Army folks love to assert hierarchies of toughness, too, as in, "There's plenty of hazing and yelling at Fort Benning and Leonard Wood, but at Fort Jackson, well, there's a reason we call it 'Relaxin' Jackson.'"
101. https://watson.brown.edu/costsofwar/costs/human.
102. MacLeish (2013); Wool (2015).

103. For discussion of the disproportionate number of working-class American men subject to the draft, see Appy (1993).
104. G. Goodwin (2017).
105. Schaeffer (2023).
106. Vergun (2023).
107. Hoschchild (1983) discusses alienation from once-authentic feelings in her discussion of "emotional labor." She considers it a variation on the Marxist theme of alienation.
108. Following historian Richard H. Kohn, I consider militarization a process by which entities in a society, ranging from institutions to thoughts and behaviors, are shaped by war (Kohn 2009; see also C. Lutz 2001, 2020; Gonzalez and Gusterson 2019: 6).
109. Wentling (2024).
110. Helmus et al. (2023). Note, however, that this study indicates that among the military branches, veterans of the Marine Corps show the highest level of support for extremist views.
111. Wentling (2023).
112. Belew (2018).
113. Belew (2018). On the growing number of such militias with many veterans in their ranks, see Steinhauer (2020).
114. R. Fanning (2020).
115. https://www.youtube.com/watch?v=j7rJstUseKg.
116. R. Fanning (2020).

Chapter 2

1. "Aye-Aye" indicates that the recruit will carry out the order as soon as possible. "Yes, sir" indicates broader agreement. (Example: "Go clean the head, recruit!" "Aye-aye, sir!" "Did you clean the head?" "Yes, sir.")
2. At a parents' weekend at Parris Island, I observed newly graduated Marines posing for photographs just *behind* the footprints, standing with their feet about hip-width apart and their arms behind their backs, rather than dangling at their sides. Recreating the exact posture they adopted on their first night, directly on the prints, would be a category error, for they were no longer recruits but fully credentialed Marines.
3. This excerpt and those in the following paragraph come from https://www.youtube.com/watch?v=xNsVivt6Z0s.
4. This example comes from W. Price (2012: 21).
5. See Bowman (2015: 92–84).
6. As noted in the front matter, in my characterization of these military scenes, I use the terms "female" and "male" to capture the voice of military parlance, which uses clinical, depersonalizing language to distinguish between bodies. Historically, this usage has problematically implied that gender can be inferred from biological sex. USMC terms of address do not currently make space for nonbinary individuals.
7. Sagalyn (2016).
8. Marines sometimes jokingly use this phrase because DI hats resemble the hat worn by the cartoon icon of the US Forest Service.
9. Westheider (2011: 50).

10. Turner (1995[1969]: 95). See also Burke (2004) on military initiation rites.
11. On such patterns of socialization, see Ochs and Schieffelin (1984: 286–288).
12. Moore (2010) describes such symbolic patterns in Western military contexts.
13. See, for instance, W. Price (2012); Ricks (1997). For a folklorist's description, see Burke (2004).
14. See Junger (2016) for a discussion of combatants' intense bonds and sense of purpose, which can make homecoming feel like a loss.
15. For an introduction to the study of "embodied sociolinguistics," see Bucholtz and Hall (2016). For rich discussion of the bodily aspects of language, see Eisenlohr (2018).
16. The shock is partly neurophysiological. Being yelled at close range is so stressful that recruits report sometimes feeling adrenaline rushes, pounding hearts, light-headedness or dizziness, weak legs, and nausea (see, e.g., Bowman 2015: 82–83). See also Goodman (2010) on the relationship between sonic vibration and power.
17. Prior to 2019, male and female recruits would train side by side only at select sites such as the rifle range and classroom. Today, PT workouts, close order drill, and so forth can involve a mixture of male and female recruits. These changes were made partly to counter the perception that females have it easy (Snow 2019).
18. See Nindl et al.'s (2022) voluminous report, commissioned by the Corps itself, on the matter. See also Walsh (2023).
19. Clark (2016). One DI told me of his routine of coming home late at night, setting his hat and belt on a chair, and heading straight for the shower. His wife knew she was not to speak to him until he came out, for he had to transition from his intense, almost inhuman DI persona.
20. Lagoze (2023: 10).
21. See documentary evidence in P. Jackson (2018).
22. https://www.quora.com/Are-Canadian-training-sergeants-as-angry-and-mean-as-the-American-ones-you-see-in-movies-such-as-full-metal-jacket.
23. https://www.youtube.com/watch?v=3rloWiahaLI. The remark in question was posted by someone with the handle "tim patrick Kristiansen."
24. Sløk-Andersen (2019: 31).
25. See Valtonen et al. (2020).
26. https://www.quora.com/In-IDF-boot-camp-are-the-instructors-screaming-in-your-face-similar-to-Parris-Island-in-the-United-States-Marines. Similarly, Godfrey Maringira (2021) describes masculinization in Zimbabwe military training as focused on bodily suffering and inflicting violence, but he does not describe any yelling.
27. Around 2005, the Pentagon urged Army drillmasters to adopt a new stance toward recruits, including, says the Undersecretary for Personnel and Readiness, "less shouting at everyone" ("Army" 2006). The 2009 Army Drill Sergeant Handbook reads, "Do not be someone who is always screaming, because the Soldiers will tune you out. 'When in doubt, don't scream or shout!' Be direct and clear without yelling or using profanity—take the high road" (Center for Army Lessons Learned (CALL) (2009: 13), https://info.publicintelligence.net/USArmy-DrillSergeant.pdf). A 2012 account leads with the headline "Army's New Drill Sergeants Teach Rather Than Yell," underscoring the "new generation's" emphasis on "mentoring" and saying "Let's talk" to a problem private, because "bellowing is a last resort" (Vergakis 2012). A 2020 report indicated that the Army's Infantry School at Fort Benning in Georgia had cracked down on "shark attacks"

and other harsh elements of basic training. "Instead of barking at new recruits scrambling off buses... drill sergeants will formally introduce themselves and quiz soldiers on facts they're expected to memorize about the infantry" (Grobe 2020). And yet again, in October 2022, the Army reported its intentions to cut down on yelling in basic training (Beynon 2022). The very frequency of this reiterated charge, however, suggests it has not yet fully "taken."

28. Weidman (2014) and Harkness (2013) have extensively developed the notion of voice and ideologies of voice.
29. Lentjes (2018); see also Lentjes et al. (2020). For broader discussions of language, gender, and masculinities, see Hall and Bucholtz (1995); Kiesling (2018); Lawson (2020); and Zimman (2017).
30. Daughtry (2015) has written extensively about the damaging soundscape of war; see also Goodman (2010). Adding to my observations about yelling, I note that regional accent, too, can be part of sonic patriarchy. One DI, a particularly young-looking redhead, told me in a mystified tone, "When I started, a couple of guys [other DIs] told me to put on a southern accent." "Why?" I asked. "I dunno but some of these guys do more of a southern drawl when they're on a tour, even if they aren't from the South." In the American imaginary, southern states are associated with political conservatism and more polarized gender roles, in which "men are men" and fathers use a stern hand. George Lakoff (1996) has argued that American conservatives tend to favor a "strict father" model of paternal authority (both in the family and of the state), in which the callow learn through punishment. Presumably a southern drawl among military personnel points to that form of masculine intimidation.
31. https://www.youtube.com/watch?v=wM1LqadfuYQ (3:00).
32. As described in the next chapter, some (though not all) contemporary DIs have continued to use gender-impugning, homophobic, transphobic, and misogynistic insults despite the repeal of Don't Ask Don't Tell and recent efforts to include gay, female-identified, and transgender Marines (see Nindl 2022). These insults reinforce hegemonic military masculinity and reflect Turner's observation that the liminal phase in many rites of passage involves denigrating neophytes by inverting their desired status, often employing feminizing and stigmatizing imagery.
33. Hicks Kennard (2006: 20). Because projecting amplitude requires tightening the vocal cords, male DIs tend to raise their voice when yelling rather than lowering it (Hicks Kennard 2006: 160; Liu 2005: 2–3). This acoustic fact is not recognized in the Marines, however, and male DIs are widely regarded as hypermasculine and intimidating when they yell in spite of it.
34. Hicks-Kennard (2006: 16, 145). Another female DI tells Hicks-Kennard that male DIs have to yell at male recruits more because they are less receptive to learning than female recruits (Hicks-Kennard 2006: 145–146).
35. https://www.youtube.com/watch?v=yAp3tOMjL5w. The first year of gender integrated training was 2020, and it will be interesting to see whether and how vocal patterns among male or female recruits and DIs change as a result.
36. Nindl et al. (2022).
37. As Eisenlohr (2018: 49) puts it, the compression waves of sound travel through the air and "transductively [enter] the bodies of those perceiving them, thereby weakening their boundaries."

38. See Biehl and Locke (2010), after Deleuze.
39. https://www.youtube.com/watch?v=IlA9WAp-m-c.
40. Clark (2016).
41. Clark (2016). To hear another DI describe returning to his house when he was new at the job, then "passing out" and waking up yelling in the middle of the night, see the 4:30 mark here: https://www.youtube.com/watch?v=IlA9WAp-m-c.
42. Examples of frog voice can be heard at 3:10 here: https://www.youtube.com/watch?v=GIPw3WLHXOs. It can also be heard at 2:30 here: https://www.youtube.com/watch?v=bHrSoxGoSSk. Sometimes veteran DIs contradicted one another on the subject of the relationship between frog voice and vocal cord damage. Some told me frog voice results from damage to the vocal cords caused by yelling, but others said using frog voice itself damages the vocal cords. One told me frog voice can be used to *spare* the vocal cords, because it can let the DI sound intimidating without having to yell.
43. Clark (2016).
44. Turley (2012: 14). In some commands, though by no means all, frog voice has been disallowed, perhaps because of the damage it can do to the vocal cords and perhaps because it is part of a dynamic of "menacing" that some top officials are striving to move away from. Many male DIs use frog voice, but the female DIs studied by Hicks Kennard (2006: 149) tended to reject it as unnecessary.
45. In semiotics, the study of signs and symbols, we would say that the material manifestation of yelling is "iconic of" these qualities. In other words, the physical form of the language is taken as a kind of mirror or map of the deeper qualities of character and disposition that it represents. (More specifically, this dynamic is sometimes called "iconization" or "rhematization"; see Gal and Irvine 2019.) We often imagine a person who speaks aggressively, for instance, will be physically aggressive as well. In the case of yelling, acoustic assaults seem iconic of physical assaults. To produce one points to one's ability to produce the other.
46. Turley (2012).
47. Richards (1979).
48. According to Veena Das (2008), it is in the state's interest for recruits to appear as if they sacrifice themselves of their own free will, as this lends legitimacy to the war. Paradoxically, the training process grinds down recruits' agency so as to aggressively reconstruct them, yet this does not seem to compromise the national narrative that soldiers willingly lay themselves on the line for the nation.
49. W. Price (2012: 50).
50. Sagalyn (2016).
51. Benveniste (1973: 226).
52. One might call this "self-interpellation," drawing on Marxist theorist Louis Althusser's (1971) framework for thinking about how people internalize ideology when hailed, or "interpellated," as a particular kind of subject.
53. For confirmation of such dynamics, see Hicks Kennard (2006: 60); Bowman (2015: 99). At graduation ceremonies, I was impressed by the lack of emotion on the faces of DIs and new Marines.
54. Caddy (2015: 13).
55. Hicks Kennard (2006: 150).

274   Notes

56. Bonnie McElhinney (1995: 236) calls this "facelessness in face-to-face interaction" in her analysis of the impersonal affect police officers adopt when responding to a call.
57. Malinowski (1923).
58. Zuckerman (2016: 294). See also Roman Jakobson (1960) for an expanded discussion of the phatic function of language.
59. https://www.youtube.com/watch?v=qk0OuG6L84o&list=PLnKI4OY16In8nVB0jrRQuSL7prDYjR1f0 (1:30).
60. For more on the cultivation of rich intersubjectivity, see Duranti (2010); Zigon (2014).
61. https://www.youtube.com/watch?v=LP2fpn8PRns.
62. http://recruitparents.com/bootcamp/first-phone.asp. I accessed this in December 2020; between then and 2023, the website was altered and the prose I describe was unaccountably deleted.
63. "The First Four Hours," https://www.youtube.com/watch?v=zwEFmBkx08c (2:00).

Chapter 3

1. Kubrick initially brought Ermey on as a consultant to a professional actor but ultimately hired him as the actor, asking him to draw on his old Drill Instructor idioms with a few cinematic embellishments.
2. Turley (2012: 15).
3. See United States Marine Corps (2019: section 2–14). In a 2016 conversation with then–Public Affairs Officer Captain Greg Carroll at Parris Island, I asked whether "slurs" would be acceptable coming from a DI. He replied, "Drill Instructors are meant to represent the epitome of being a Marine. The good thing is someone's always observing what's going on, and obviously using any slurs against recruits would be unacceptable, and that's in the Training Order. There are certain things you can or cannot call a recruit.... I won't even address racial insults because that would be unacceptable, ... and the Training Order also reads, 'No foul language or profanity in presence of recruits.'" I would later come to recognize the overstatement in Carroll's claim that "someone's always observing" DI practices.
4. Rhetoricians use "epithet" to mean a descriptive term or phrase that can be positive or negative, but I use it in the colloquial American sense of a prejudicial or abusive term such as a racial slur or a derogatory phrase. Linguistic and philosophical work on racist language also uses "epithet" in an implicitly negative sense, though the relationship between the terms "epithet" and "slur" is a contested one. Claudia Bianchi (2014) and Christopher Hom (2008) treat "epithet" as more or less synonymous with "slur." Joseph Hedger (2013: 206) divides derogatory epithets into two classes, one being "slurs," which "express contempt but don't say anything about or describe their content," and the other kind of epithet including both descriptive and expressive content (presumably this would include something like referring to Donald Trump as "mango Mussolini"). Adam Croom (2013: 22) proposes that unlike slurs, some racially loaded epithets (such as referring to an Asian American as a "banana") are terms that are primarily used "as non-derogatory terms applied to non-humans" and, thus, that trigger a different and more "exploratory" interpretive process. In this book, I use "epithet" to encompass both well-known slurs and novel pejorative words and phrases.
5. See Sidnell (2021); Bean (1980: 308).

6. This practice brings to mind Clifford Geertz's (1973) description of customary Balinese naming practices, which emphasize social role over personal identity. The comparison invokes the intriguing ways in which military personhood flouts the expectations of liberal individualism.
7. Turley (2012: 101).
8. In his boot camp memoir, Will Price describes a stream of intimidation from his DI such as, "THIS RECRUIT IS A SNOT-PICKING, HEINOUS CREATURE" and "SOUND OFF, YOU DISGUSTING LITTLE TURDS!!" (Price 2012: 105, 47).
9. For firsthand reminiscences of former DIs that sometimes allude to these naming practices, see Smith (2007).
10. Beyond the nicknames I discuss, other military terminology can further dehumanize recruits. Military food is often referred to as "chow," a term that in civilian life is more commonly associated with dog food. Personnel sleep not in "beds" but in "racks," a word that ordinarily denotes a place to store objects. A West Point graduate from the early '80s told me that cadets were urged to "press ham" when pushing through an exhausting run. She found this particularly dehumanizing, remarking, "It felt like we were processed meat."
11. According to Anna Wierzbicka, slurs and epithets "stress, hyperbolically, the property in question" and imply that the property "determines [the speaker's] way of seeing the referent, to the exclusion of other properties" (Wierzbicka 1988: 475). Judith Butler (1997: 4) further explores the social disorientation that can ensue from insults: When "addressed injuriously... one can be 'put in one's place' by such speech, but such a place may be no place."
12. For sexual assault prevention and response policies across the Department of Defense, see https://sapr.mil/policy. The Marine Corps' 2019 description of their Sexual Assault and Prevention Program reflects extensive procedural evolution; see https://www.marines.mil/portals/1/Publications/MCO%201752.5C.pdf?ver=2019-06-10-115714-627. See also Nindl et al. (2022).
13. Seck (2022). Resistance to gender integration across the military has a long and violent history. One of my respondents who was among the first women to graduate from West Point in the 1980s told me it was commonplace for male cadets to tell the women among them that they would "rape them out."
14. On broader explorations of masculinity in the military see Gardiner (2012: 372); see also Belkin (2012); Burke (1996: 213; 2004: 118ff.); Cohn (1987; 2020); Cohn and Enloe (2003); Disler (2008: 20); Eastman (2009); Eichler (2011); Elshtain (1987); Enloe (2000; 2015); N. Frank (2009); Hoffman (2011); Mararac (2023); McCoy (1995); Moon (2005); Young (2003).
15. Mararac (2023). Mararac adds that the compulsory masculinity and heteronormative ethos of the military can result in service members performing a kind of masculinity that may not feel like their own.
16. Turley (2012: 199).
17. Along the same lines, a USMC veteran tweeted in 2018 that "in recruit training on Parris Island I was specifically and repeatedly told that women are lying, weak, untrustworthy, whores." https://twitter.com/iAmTheWarax/status/986663835175145474?s=20, retrieved February 2019. See also Lagoze (2023).
18. According to Nindl et al. (2022: 131-132), "Such language is expressly prohibited in the standards of conduct section in both Depot orders (DepO) outlining the recruit training

order.... Sixteen standards of conduct must be followed by everyone involved in training; the fifth standard of conduct prohibits sexually explicit and demeaning language based on gender:

> [Personnel within this command] will not use profane, obscene, or unprofessional language, as it is offensive, detracts from the training environment, and reflects poorly on the Marine Corps. This includes all language which is sexually explicit or demeaning to any race, gender, ethnicity, heritage, sexual orientation, or religion.

19. See Nindl et al. (2022: 600, 601) for these examples. Another DI instructs his platoon about how he refers to peripheral vision (he addresses recruits with the metonym "eyeballs,"). "Eyeballs, who here goes to the mall and saw a big pair of breasts? And you're with your girlfriend, right? You don't want to get caught. You're not going to turn your head, right? You use your fricking (we call it) titty vision." The same DI adds a refrain to prevent the recruits from reporting him for using sexist and profane language. "Eyeballs, zero! I never said that right?" (Nindl et al. 2022: 599). The folklorist Richard Burns quotes a Marine who says that "before the PC monster reared its ugly head," DIs would liken the M-16 rifle's parts to female anatomy; the trigger, for instance, was "the clitoris," and recruits were instructed to "stroke her rear (charging handle) with authority" (Burns 2003).
20. See Nindl et al. (2022: 132) on how such language serves as a bonding mechanism.
21. W. Price (2012: 127).
22. Turley (2012: 99). See as well Lagoze's (2023: 17) discussion of sexism as a bonding mechanism on Parris Island in 2011: "Outbursts of misogyny, revealing flashes wrapped in seductive tidbits of wry and savage humor, passed for niceties out there. Short moments when we weren't being yelled at. Those times made us the happiest campers."
23. Belkin (2012).
24. https://law.justia.com/codes/us/2010/title10/subtitlea/partii/chap37/sec654.
25. Turley (2012: 201, 70, 179).
26. Nolan (2013).
27. Nindl et al. (2022: 603).
28. Barroso (2019); see also https://www.zippia.com/infantry-jobs/demographics/.
29. Hoylman (2017).
30. Lowen and McDonald (2023); Sanchez (2011).
31. Context about the survey can be found here: https://www.opa.mil/research-analysis/opa-surveys/defense-organizational-climate-survey. Recent revisions to the survey have amplified the Department of Defense's ability to assess sexual misconduct (see Lowen and McDonald 2023).
32. In the vein of Jasbir Puar's concept of pinkwashing, one might argue the US military's low tolerance for racial epithets is a form of "lingwashing" (McIntosh 2018a). This linguistic practice allows the state to claim transcendent antiracism while obscuring the fact that many of the wars the US has prosecuted have been driven by a racist necropolitics that profoundly devalues the lives of millions of people of color. It also overlooks the challenges that people of color face in being promoted to senior leadership in some branches. See Cooper (2020).
33. Musgrave (2003: 11).
34. See Buckley (2001); Terry (1984).
35. Westheider (2011: 51–52; see also Westheider 1997).

36. Arment (2016a).
37. Lagoze (2023: 14).
38. At the Parris Island Brig & Brew, I had a brief but revealing exchange with a couple of DIs about racist language among recruits. Carlos and I were chatting about diversity in the Corps and how platoons mix people from different regions and backgrounds. Grady chipped in, seemingly trying to perform both his fidelity to the rules and a style of cool indifference. "There was a guy in my unit from a small town who referred to someone else as n*****. I told him, hey, *I* don't care, but you can't do that." A minute later, when Grady's attention was diverted, Carlos hastily turned to me and said, "Actually, we take this kind of thing, using a word like that, very seriously. It's completely forbidden in the Corps; we do not put up with it."
39. See Hosein (2019); Mohammed (2019); Sandhoff (2017).
40. Evidence for Islamophobic slurs within the US the military is easy to find, but for more accounts, see Elliott (2006). See also https://www.muslimmarine.org for accounts of Muslim Marines being called names such as "bin Laden" and "terrorist."
41. https://www.ummid.com/news/2016/September/21.09.2016/us-muslim-veteran-terrorist-written-on-locker.html.
42. Nolan (2013).
43. See Reitman (2017) for a full account of the events. In another example of racial insults that culminated in suicide, Army Private Danny Chen, who served in Afghanistan, took his own life in 2011 after being mercilessly bullied and called "gook," "chink," and "fortune cookie" by other soldiers and some superior officers in his unit.
44. Quoted in Dobos (2020: 37).
45. https://www.reddit.com/r/USMC/comments/28njh8/how_are_gay_people_treated_in_the_marine_corps/.
46. N. Fanning (2019).
47. https://www.npr.org/templates/story/story.php?storyId=10352064.
48. Yang (2011).
49. Nindl et al. (2022: 604).
50. https://thegoombagazette.com/2013/05/26/give-me-20-faggots/.
51. Turley (2012: 180).
52. Arment (2016b).
53. Turley (2012: 109).
54. Foulkrod (2006, 11:55).
55. Young (2018b).
56. Arment (2016b).
57. Turley (2012: 17, 38).
58. Bowman (2015: 123–124).
59. Cadences and songs about enthusiastic killing offer another means to habituate recruits to the idea of committing violence. Marine Corps and Army veterans alike offered me many examples. They included:

> Napalm sticks to kids,
> French fried eyeballs and baby ribs.
> Napalm sticks to kids like glue,
> It sticks to me and it sticks to you.
> Drop some Napalm from the sky,
> And watch those kiddies DIE DIE DIE!

A song sung to the tune of "The Candyman Can" goes,

> Who can take a baby,
> Throw it in the air,
> Watch it hit the ground and splatter everywhere?
> The S&M man! The S&M man can!
> He takes a whole lot of blood and he mixes it with love, the S&M man!

60. Arment (2018).
61. Foulkrod (2006, 13:00). Internalizing the idea that one is a killer can be vital in other branches, too, of course. An Army veteran I call Sam worked artillery in Afghanistan, and told me how his unit would conceptualize the "grid" they would "wipe out," without "feeling anything," because they had to frame themselves "as killers":

> At the end of the day, your job is to kill another human being. You have to be soulless.... So a lot of our rhetoric was you're a killer, you kill, it's what you do. I was artillery, so we don't see the person we kill, but they would always be like, "Artillery doesn't even give a fuck. The infantry has got to see the person and shoot them, men, women, children, dogs, I don't care. You give me a number, and I will destroy that entire village." My job was the job that an entire grid square of a map could be wiped out by me personally, and it was ingrained in us that we were not to feel anything. And I think—I mean, I'm sure your research shows that the words you use internally give you a connotation, right? It's very important if your mind frame it "we are killers," to have that sense of . . . I'm not a person, I'm just a killer, you know?

Chapter 4

1. As noted in the Introduction, I have altered names and sometimes the contexts in which I was privy to information, to protect the identities of military personnel.
2. https://www.marines.mil/News/News-Display/Article/938548/marine-corps-completed-three-command-level-investigations-at-parris-island/.
3. Loewenson (2023).
4. Fosher et al. (2018: 4–5).
5. The military uses survey instruments to try to gather data on this matter (Lowen and McDonald 2023).
6. See the 2015 RAND study (Keller et al. 2015) and Parks and Burgess (2019) on hazing in the US military for some rationales behind its endurance and findings about its potential costs. Note that the humiliation of prospective newcomers to a group has been common in initiation rites all over the world, past and present, and anthropologists have suggested several reasons for it. In many masculine initiation rites, grueling hardships help "prove" manhood, as young males are extracted from the nurturing world of female kin (see D. Gilmore 1990; M. Gutmann 1997). Psychologists add that hazing tends to enhance loyalty once someone is admitted to the group, possibly because of cognitive dissonance, Stockholm syndrome, or other mechanisms. The persistence of hazing may be partly explained in terms of "effort justification," a dynamic in which the more demanding a task, the more appealing the subjective value of the group or person who demands it, contributing to allegiance. One DI shed further light when he informed Bowman (2015) that when recruits are perpetually confused and informed they are in the wrong, they come to believe they must transform into good Marines in order to redeem themselves. For more on hazing, see Bourke (2016); Cimino (2011); Kavanaugh (2017).

7. Moon (2019: 36, 62). Note that this claim has implications for the way we think about "moral injury." If moral injury ensues from violating a person's moral compass but the military is capable of resetting that compass, might it follow that killing in a military context will not necessarily result in moral injury for all soldiers?

    In encounters with some veterans, I could sense the reorientation of their moral orienting system (though I understood that they might be able to toggle between orientations and stances as well, depending on the topic or context). A conversation that comes to mind was with Terrence, a Vietnam veteran and Marine who attended the Drill Instructors' reunion out of nostalgia. As we were parting ways after several days, Terrence asked whether I had ever heard of George Orwell, then quoted a statement often attributed to him: "People sleep peacefully in their beds at night only because rough men stand ready to do violence on their behalf." "That's us," he added cheerfully. "We will murder you." Terrence's phrasing, including his choice of the word "murder," seemed a deliberate way to underscore that a transgression for a civilian is not always a transgression for a combatant.

8. Lifton (1991: 526). Note that Lifton, a psychiatrist who worked on the impact of war on the psyche, was talking about effects on those who have experienced war, whereas I am discussing pedagogical signs presented to recruits *before* war.

9. United States Marine Corps (1998). These phrases can be found in sections 6–1, 2–6, 2–7, and 2–1, respectively.

10. United States Marine Corps (1998, section 5–11).

11. https://www.mcrdsd.marines.mil/Recruit-Training/Training-Information/. In the same vein, training materials for DIs repeatedly list the imperatives of "moral excellence," "codes of integrity," "respecting human dignity," and generally creating a Corps of "the highest moral character in and out of uniform" (United States Marine Corps 1998: section 2–1).

12. Note that cadets at the United States Military Academy at West Point, Army Officer Candidate School at Fort Benning, and the United States Air Force Academy are expected to study Army General John Schofield's gentlemanly statement on discipline, delivered in 1879 to the Corps of Cadets at the US Military Academy. It reads, in part,

    > The discipline which makes the soldiers of a free country reliable in battle is not to be gained by harsh or tyrannical treatment.... It is possible to impart instruction and to give commands in such a manner and such a tone of voice to inspire in the soldier no feeling but an intense desire to obey.... He who feels the respect which is due to others cannot fail to inspire in them regard for himself.

13. DiRosa and Goodwin (2014).

14. http://www.nbcnews.com/id/8381517/ns/us_news/t/incident-fort-knox/#.XvTV45NKiL8.

15. Mockenhaupt (2007). In an interview with NPR, journalist Brian Mockenhaupt explains that one reason the Army opted to "adjust the tone and culture" of basic training around 2005 was to slow recruit attrition by moving away from the "harsh and kind of demonic Drill Sergeant." https://www.npr.org/templates/story/story.php?storyId=10352064. Note as well that some graduating classes of new Army Drill Sergeants are more than 30% female (Novelly 2020), a figure that—though it guarantees nothing about behavior—may influence training to move away from ostentatiously abusive attempts to prove masculinity, whether by the Drill Sergeant or the recruit.

16. Center for Army Lessons Learned (CALL) (2009: 13).

17. Eckholm (2005).

18. A fuller statement reads as follows: The "Drill Instructor's role is to lead by example as a teacher, scholar, leader, and mentor. . . . Drill Instructors must conduct themselves in a manner consistent with the spirit of the Drill Instructor Pledge. Drill Instructors must provide leadership by example, foregoing fear and intimidation, in order to foster trust and confidence by subordinates" (United States Marine Corps 2008: section 1–5). Again and again, the Marine Corps emphasizes that Drill Instructors "will not haze or maltreat recruits" (see, e.g., United States Marine Corps 2008: section 1–9; United States Marine Corps 2024: section 1–9).
19. Marine Corps Order 1510.32F, p. 4. https://www.marines.mil/Portals/1/MCO%201510.32F.pdf.

    The order reads, "Hazing, maltreatment, abuse of authority or other illegal alternatives to leadership are counterproductive practices and are expressly forbidden. Marines in supervisory positions are strictly charged to treat all recruits firmly, fairly, with dignity and compassion. Leaders/supervisors will be held accountable for their actions."
20. See United States Marine Corps (2019: section 1–8; 2024: section 1–8).
21. According to the 2008 RTO, "hazing" includes striking a recruit "to inflict pain," "verbally berating" them, and any other "illegal, harmful, demeaning or dangerous acts," which can be "verbal or psychological in nature" (United States Marine Corps 2008: section G-14). Prohibitions described by subsequent Recruit Training Orders can be found in Nindl et al.'s (2022) internal study of the Marine Corps.
22. Contemporary training in DI school also includes discussions of power imbalances and group psychology. DIs in training learn, for instance, about Phillip Zimbardo's 1971 Stanford prison experiment, which (methodological problems notwithstanding) furnishes vivid examples of how students arbitrarily placed into roles of authority over others begin to dehumanize them and abuse their own power. Training further includes discussions about how to intervene if one DI sees another overstepping the line (Spangler 2016).
23. See Parks and Burgess (2019: 15); see also Keller et al. (2015) on the lack of consensus among military personnel about what constitutes "hazing." Oversight reports suggest as well that across the Marine Corps and the US military generally, definitions of "hazing" vary and are only vaguely understood (Giberd 2017). One Marine Corps lawyer I spoke to told me that hazing tends to be "in the eye of the beholder."
24. For several years, the Parris Island Series Commander Course has required DI candidates to read the book titled *Pride and Discipline: The Hallmarks of a United States Marine* by Colonel Donald J. Myers (2014), which addresses the culture of brutality in the USMC. In a chapter titled "Why Abuse?" Myers speculates that systematic abuse by DIs may have begun after World War II as a kind of compensatory masculinity for those who hadn't had chance to prove themselves in that fight, and it became self-justifying with each US war thereafter. The very fact that the Series Commander course assigns this book suggests that the Marine Corps is keenly aware of an enduring push-pull between guidelines and the temptation to stray from them.
25. https://www.youtube.com/watch?v=MjffzVCno84.
26. Eckholm (2005).
27. Westheider (2011: 51).
28. Similarly, a Marine Corps chaplain who served in the early aughts reports seeing a DI force recruits to drink water until they vomited, then do pushups in their own vomit. He also describes DIs slapping an exhausted Marine who was close to drowning in the pool. http://isme.tamu.edu/JSCOPE06/Creeley06.html.

29. The Parris Island Recruit Training Order forbids "profanity or foul language in the presence of recruits" (United States Marine Corps 2008: section 1-8) and "profane, obscene, or unprofessional language" (United States Marine Corps 2019: section 1-7). Similarly, the 2009 US Army Drill Sergeant Handbook instructs trainers not to be demeaning or to use profanity (Center for Army Lessons Learned [CALL] 2009).
30. Because the public-facing military puts such an emphasis on "clean," upstanding language, it can be hard for a journalist or researcher to get a sense of the contradictions in linguistic practice. When conducting her 1997 and 2003 dissertation research on DI phonetics, for instance, linguist Catherine Hicks Kennard (2006: 62) seems to have taken DI rules at face value, writing, "Recruit Training is not a place for abuse, either physical or mental. . . . A DI is not allowed to use profanity, refer to recruits by offensive, racist, or otherwise derogatory names (e.g. 'fatso,' 'pig,' 'dog'). . . . While there is a large amount of authority in the hands of DIs, this authority is not ever a license for abuse." Hicks Kennard also notes, though, that DIs worried some of their "disrespectful and unprofessional" language might be "caught on tape" (Hicks Kennard 2006: 35–36), with one requesting that she erase a recording he made when she was gone, because he "might have used profanity." Such erasures have been going on for years; Burke (2004: 49–50) describes a folklorist in the 1960s who asked to record the "salty marching chants" he recalled from his own training and was told by a public affairs officer that these "colorful" chants were "no longer performed." While standing outside the gates later, the folklorist subsequently heard a unit inside performing exactly the chants he remembered. Since then, Burke writes, journalists such as Thomas Ricks, especially in his enthusiastic 1997 book *Making the Corps*, have "naively assumed that because Drill Instructors don't curse while a journalist is present, they don't curse at all." The unofficial script is to be scrubbed from the record, when possible.
31. The clip can be viewed at https://www.youtube.com/watch?v=PD-fC941yLI.
32. Will Price's memoir offers further examples of the tension between the rules and their violation. His DIs often used the minced oath "friggin,'" but also occasionally referred to a recruit as, for instance, a "nerdy motherfucker" or a "shit-bird" (W. Price 2012: 104, 158). Price provides some wry metalinguistic commentary on the gap between official policy and verbal practice. He writes that one "recruit got only three out of 40. What the f—— . . . Oops, I've been told that recruits aren't supposed to curse—I mean, what the heck?" (W. Price 2012: 57). And, "If we f—— up—I mean screw up—then we pay for it." (W. Price 2012: 66).
33. See McIntosh (2020d) on the iconicity between military profanity and "hardness."
34. See, for instance, Kiesling (1997, 2001).
35. See McIntosh (2020d).
36. Allan and Burridge (2006: 54).
37. The 2022 report on gender integration in the Marine Corps (Nindl et al. 2022: 134) observes that male DIs and recruits continue to use sexually derogatory and misogynistic language around women even though offensive and abusive language violates standards of conduct for the "work atmosphere" and "core values" of the Marine Corps. The authors also note that the Department of Defense's (DoD's) Sexual Assault Prevention and Response Office considers this language to be "low-grade, yet problematic, behavior on the DoD's continuum of harm—a spectrum of interpersonal interactions reflecting the interconnected nature of behaviors that increase the risk for sexual assault. . . . When instructors use degrading language, they prime the environment and their recruits to be

more permissive of the continuum of harm behaviors" (Nindl et al. 2022: 304). When the authors presented portions of their findings to the Marine Corps, the Training and Education Command commented in response, "We recognize that the use of the language described by the study team runs counter to current policies for training recruits and represents a systemic issue among Marine Corps drill instructors that we are working to correct" (Nindl et al. 2022: 131).

38. Myers (2014: 20–21). Historian Joanna Bourke (2016) further explores some justifications Marine Corps trainers offer for the practice of harsh hazing, highlighting their claim that it fosters solidarity, enhances the elite mystique of in-group status, and preserves the Marines' masculine edge.

39. Seck (2021). A Military Law Task Force suggests that many incidents will never have been reported to begin with, that the Department of Defense "[does] not adequately track the number of hazing incidents" and that the "policies generally [do] not provide clear guidance" on what does and does not constitute hazing (Gilberd 2017).

40. http://isme.tamu.edu/JSCOPE06/Creeley06.html.

41. See Reitman (2017).

42. See, for instance, https://www.opa.mil/research-analysis/opa-surveys.

43. W. Price (2012: 170). In a similar vein, Patrick Turley (2012: 53–54) notes his Senior Drill Instructor gave the following speech early in basic training:

> "Alright, gents, I want you to hear this from me before you hear it from the 'recruit underground.' A Drill Instructor from thirty-thirty-eight is getting kicked out, because some recruit wanted to open his goddamn mouth when he shouldn't. There's a lot of shit that goes on here that we don't talk about, right?"
>
> "Yes sir," we said back.
>
> "Especially not in letters home. Your families don't need to be more worried than they already are. Now, has anyone here been hit by a Drill Instructor?"
>
> I kept my mouth shut and casually glanced over at [a fellow Recruit]. We remained silent....
>
> "Good."

44. Occasionally veterans told me they received overtly cynical teachings about the Rules of Engagement and the laws of war, though this is a vast subject beyond the purview of this book. Much training clarifies how serious the subject is. One Marine, however, told me that although DIs "give you a lot of courses and lectures on, like, the rules of war and what's legal and what's not, underlying it all is like, 'Of course,' like, 'if you feel threatened, you can just do whatever you want.'" In a similar vein, an Army veteran who trained shortly after 9/11 told me that in his training, "The whole attitude was like, 'Sorry we've got to do this, but here's this mandatory class about not killing civilians,' you know? But then the whole thing is like not taken seriously and it's kind of derided by most of the NCOs [non-commissioned officers]." Some military players justify a loose approach to the rules of war on grounds self-protection, repeating the refrain that "it's better to be judged by twelve than carried by six"—better, in other words, to end up in court for killing the wrong person than to be killed in action.

45. In Peircian semiotic theory, we would call this relationship one of "iconicity," whereby a sign mirrors, resembles, or diagrams the thing it stands for. The violation of rules in training diagrams or mirrors the possibility for violating norms and rules in combat.

46. See Harkins (2015).

47. Belkin (2012).

48. https://tinyurl.com/3xcvutvr. This discipline of the body in order to instill self-surveillance, serving the agenda of the state, is a letter-perfect example of modern biopolitical power as described by Foucault (1995, 2004).
49. https://tinyurl.com/3xcvutvr.
50. https://tinyurl.com/3xcvutvr.
51. https://tinyurl.com/3xcvutvr.
52. It can also be physically dangerous (Seck 2016).
53. A DI told me about this kind of game at the 2019 Drill Instructors' reunion, and I would later learn that a burial for a sand flea, with full military honors, features in the 1957 feature film *The D.I.* Yet again we see a feedback loop between cinema and reality, as well as continuity in the folkloric traditions of DIs.
54. Turley (2012: 107, 110).
55. This account can be found here: https://youtube.com/shorts/0wG87YT5geE?si=78Dz wSokx6OAw2lL. See also Belkin's (2012) nuanced interpretation of the queer overtones of sexualized hazing in the US military.
56. https://www.youtube.com/watch?v=GIPw3WLHXOs (2:45).
57. Mike, a former Commissioned Officer in the Marine Corps, told me that when he was in officer training, his higher-ups would impose a more literate version of fuck-fuck games, seemingly appropriate to the officer's more cerebral training. He relates,

> When it came to fuck-fuck games, the worst hazing I endured was any time you screwed something up they would assign you to write an essay. The essay I think had to be something like five hundred words, and words under four letters didn't count. You had to underline every fifth word, counting to be sure every word was over four letters. . . . You couldn't screw up in terms of the counting of the numbers of words. You had to write them in pen so if you screwed up you had to start all over again. So to make the word count you'd make up these things, like, "This officer candidate stationed at Marine Corps Base Quantico Virginia on the East Coast of the United States of America in the western hemisphere failed to"—you're making sure you're getting four letters in every word, so you would just make up this baloney—"failed to give, um, Staff Sergeant Smith the appropriate greeting of the day. This candidate recognizes that was contrary to good order and discipline," yadda yadda. You go on about lessons learned and what you're going to do to prove yourself, and "increased situational awareness." . . . You would [be assigned] eight of these essays in a day and you'd have to turn them in and so you wouldn't sleep; you would be up all night writing these damn essays. . . . And then at the end of the training they came out with this huge stack of paper, [saying], "I didn't read a goddamned one of 'em!" and just threw 'em up in the air. . . . I would rather have been slapped around; I was terrified of these essays.

58. https://www.reddit.com/r/USMCboot/comments/2ek5bl/2_sheets_and_a_blanket/.
59. Ricks (1997: 57).
60. Clark (2016).
61. Jones (2021).
62. Lagoze (2023: 132).
63. Consider the words of this Marine veteran, who says,

> I actually think hazing is a good thing. . . . [The way to take it is] minimizing the significance of what's going on around you. More often than not if you actually like froze time for a second and thought "What's actually happening right now," you're gonna realize it's nothing. It's like, I'm gonna still be here tomorrow. . . . What was actually going on? They were having a bunch of fun at my expense. I thought it was kinda funny. They thought it was kinda funny. What's the big deal? I think it was just a bunch of us having a good laugh

together and becoming closer as Marines. I think the only reason people have a bad view of hazing is because it's people that would never be in a position to be hazed in the first place. It's the same people who demonize military training as being too difficult. It's like well that's for YOU. I need it more difficult. Cause a very particular type of person joins the military. And an even MORE particular type of person joins the Marine Corps. And an even MORE particular type of person enjoys the hazing. So you don't have to get hazed, that's fine, but allow ME to. (https://youtube.com/shorts/v-xcs1ganxw?si=UKW65jRbUQsm-fPK)

64. Turley (2012: 66, 123, 126).

Chapter 5

1. W. Price (2012: 115).
2. Elshtain (1987). In a related vein, Andrew Bickford (2001) finds that in the German Democratic Republic between about the 1950s and 1980s, the nation was equated with virtuous and domestically oriented women in need of heroic defense by men.
3. The notion of "structures of feeling" was popularized by Marxist theorist Raymond Williams (1977), who saw these in terms of competing ways of thinking (especially ways of thinking not fully articulated, hence "feeling") at particular historical moments.
4. This is the former link to the page, which seems to have been deleted: https://www.facebook.com/MARINES-AGAINST-MOTHERS-OF-AMERICA-156272691092133/about/?ref=page_internal.
5. This is the former link, though it no longer works: https://www.causes.com/causes/563116-marines-against-mothers-of-america?fbclid=IwAR2jFZYa3l5yxnbe9GHPPHr-QTP6TbSbYzbvi5m2ceXY61-APuaXGoxZbm8.
6. See McIntosh (2020b).
7. See my Introduction, as well as K. Barry (2011); Rakel (2018); Reiss (2018).
8. The reluctance to place "boots on the ground" has been part of the rationale for conducting violence work from a distance, by way of drone technology. But drones have their own terrible humanitarian consequences, which have been invisible to many Americans (Moyn 2022).
9. Lakoff (1996).
10. Serwer (2021).
11. https://www.nytimes.com/live/2020/11/07/us/biden-trump?campaign_id=60&emc=edit_na_20201107&instance_id=0&nl=breaking-news&ref=cta&regi_id=21954539&segment_id=43937&user_id=bb50894db3fa05d85654b961f2fe4b08#biden-makes-his-first-remarks-to-the-nation-as-president-elect.
12. https://www.defenseculture.mil/Portals/90/Documents/AboutDEOMI/SPLN-DEOMI_Strategic_Plan_FY2024-FY2029-20231003.pdf?ver=5uKXx-LxS0cp9DOABpjIjQ%3d%3d.
13. Mararac (2023).
14. Ress (2022).
15. Bledsoe (2023).
16. The trend toward Republicanism is more pronounced in the officer corps, and one survey found that since the end of the draft Republicanism among officers jumped from one-third to two-thirds (Thompson 2012).
17. Bledsoe (2023).

18. S. Gutmann (2000: 282). For details about the expansion of the US military's mandate, see Brooks (2017).
19. S. Gutmann (2000: 11); see also Cameron (1995); Fairclough (2003: 20) on such language ideologies outside of the military.
20. S. Gutmann (2000: 25, 118).
21. https://www.amazon.com/Kinder-Gentler-Military-Americas-Gender-Neutral/dp/0684852918/ref=sr_1_1?crid=1P3M5WH27WPOQ&keywords=gutmann+kinder+gentler&qid=1694100417&sprefix=gutmann+kinder+gentler%2Caps%2C92&sr=8-1#customerReviews.
22. http://www.leatherneck.com/forums/archive/index.php/t-17073.html.
23. McIntosh (2020b: 79).
24. https://www.npr.org/templates/story/story.php?storyId=10352064.
25. The rich online comments that were available in summer 2017 following this Military.com article have since been deleted: http://www.military.com/daily-news/2016/09/18/marine-boot-camp-covered-up-recruits-medical-issues.html.
26. L. T. Wood (2016).
27. Copp (2017). Donald Trump's administration further deterred diversity training with his 2020 executive order that training must not discuss topics that could result in "discomfort, guilt, anguish or any other form of psychological distress" (https://trumpwhitehouse.archives.gov/presidential-actions/executive-order-combating-race-sex-stereotyping/) by virtue of the listener's race or sex. According to Lowen and McDonald (2023: 6–12), this language hindered discussions of topics such as racism, sexism, and unconscious bias, resulting in the suspension of many Department of Defense Military Equal Opportunity trainings.
28. See https://www.influencewatch.org/government-agency/defense-equal-opportunity-management-institute/.
29. https://www.army.mil/standto/archive/2021/03/26/?dmd&linkId=119238544. This page describes some of the Army's multiple initiatives intended to take on behaviors that "tear at the fabric" of the military, attempting to restore not only morale but "an Army-wide culture of dignity and respect." In 2020, as racial tensions roiled the country in the wake of George Floyd's death, Army initiatives such as Project Inclusion and This Is My Squad encouraged military leaders to mitigate racial discontent in the ranks. Such initiatives seemed designed to appeal to liberals, while still using the language of military traditionalists by insisting they would enhance "unit cohesion" (Britsky 2020; Reinsch 2021).
30. https://www.cnn.com/videos/us/2021/05/21/ted-cruz-military-woke-and-emasculated-russia-starr-newday-vpx.cnn. One week later, former SEAL-officer turned congressman Dan Crenshaw invited followers to tattle on wokeism using a "whistleblower webpage" (Clark 2021). For details on how Republicans have recently tried to roll back diversity and inclusion initiatives in defense spending bills, see Mascaro and Freking (2023).
31. Schogol (2022).
32. https://www.youtube.com/watch?v=M8gvaO0svUg.
33. Luciano (2021). Tucker Carlson suggests on another episode that the Chinese authorities are hardening up their forces to combat the supposed feminization of their male adolescents (https://www.youtube.com/watch?v=COQ8exApyEc). "Kind of interesting, isn't it," he adds. "So how are we responding to this?" Carlson cuts to a video clip of Biden talking

about military accommodations for women and mistakenly interprets these to include allowing pregnant women to serve in combat (in fact, they are not allowed to deploy).

> So we've got new hairstyles and maternity flight suits. Pregnant women are going to fight our wars. It's a mockery of the US military. While China's military becomes more masculine as it's assembled the world's largest Navy, our military needs to become, as Joe Biden says, more feminine—whatever feminine means any more, since men and women no longer exist... And the Pentagon is going along with this.

34. More specifically, Carlson suggested that by assigning Ibrahim Kendi's book *How to be an Antiracist*, the US Navy is signaling to its members that "the country is not worth fighting for"—merely to talk about enduring racial tension, in other words, is to weaken the armed forces. https://www.youtube.com/watch?v=COQ8exApyEc.
35. Pompeo (2022).
36. Schogol (2023).
37. Shane (2023).
38. Hegseth (2024: 199, xiii).
39. Hegseth (2024: 199, xiii).
40. M. Myers (2022); Spoehr (2022).
41. B. Williams (2023).
42. Schogol (2023). Others have attributed declining enlistment to the decline in fitness and academic preparedness necessary to qualify, as well as a broader pattern of male "retreat from society" (Beynon and Baker 2024).
43. Nick Mararac (2023) makes this point, too, while observing that in such conservative rejoinders to "wokeness," buzzwords such as "national security" and "force readiness" are treated as authoritative because supposedly unquestionably good for the nation.
44. S. Gutmann (2000: 115).

Chapter 6

1. For an argument that dehumanizing language does not guarantee dehumanizing thought, see arguments by philosopher David Livingstone Smith (2021). For an argument that dehumanizing language is not a requirement for killing, see sociologist Aliza Luft (2015). For more detailed discussion of some of the concepts in this chapter, particularly in relation to the notion of generic reference, see McIntosh (2021b).
2. Cf. Butler (2010).
3. See Bourke (1999).
4. Foulkrod (2006, 28:45); see also Luft (2015).
5. Note as well that some studies reveal that civilians may be targeted even by contemporary democratic states under distinctive conditions, especially when a protracted war of attrition creates "desperation" for victory. In such conditions, killing noncombatants may be a strategy used to manipulate the adversary into giving up (Downes 2006).
6. Cf. Cohn (1987).
7. Note that empathy can be engaged even without physical proximity. Some drone operators report terrible guilt because after tracking their targets for days and weeks, the

pixelated figures they see on the screen going about daily business, hugging family members, and so forth become in-filled with humanity to them (Edney-Browne 2016; Press 2018).
8. Molendijk (2023).
9. https://www.democracynow.org/shows/2008/3/19 (11:00).
10. Similarly, Matt Young (2018a: 96), in his recent memoir, writes that Marine Corps training transforms recruits into a "person-thing," whose "perquisite to existence is that we lose not only our own humanity but remove that of our enemy as well."
11. Crenshaw (2015).
12. Livingstone Smith (2011).
13. Tirrell (2012).
14. Verrips (2004).
15. Tang (2008).
16. Silliman (2008).
17. Silliman (2008).
18. https://www.nbclearn.com/portal/site/learn/cuecard/65336 (accessed June 15, 2019). This link is now defunct.
19. See D. Frank et al. (2011) on how simply hearing about the number of dead in a conflict tends not to evoke a strong affective response.
20. Gordon and Trainor (2006: 447). For other journalistic reports of epithets used during the early years of the GWOT, see P. Martin (2008); Ricks (2006, 2015); Herbert (2005).
21. https://www.youtube.com/watch?v=B6L9NTpkYnI. Prysner also explains the hajj pilgrimage and that in Arabic, a "haji" is someone who's taken a pilgrimage. He adds, "So we took the best thing for a Muslim and made it into the worst thing."
22. Foulkrod (2006: 10:40).
23. Young (2018a: 96).
24. Casey was the 36th Chief of Staff of the United States Army from 2007 to 2011. https://www.democracynow.org/2008/3/18/winter_soldier_contd_us_vets_active.
25. IVAW and Glantz (2008: 97); see also Boudreau (2008).
26. See Chen (2012); Livingstone Smith (2021). Note that Livingstone Smith contends that dehumanization is a matter not of degree but one of either/or, since the latter is compatible with the cognitive essentialism that seems part of it. On essentialism as a cognitive and social phenomenon, see McIntosh (2018b).
27. Douglas (1966).
28. Bergen (2016: 203).
29. "Viet Cong" is an ostensibly neutral name for the National Liberation Front of Vietnam.
30. Mbembe (2003: 18).
31. I discuss the relationship between conceptual impoverishment and oppressive power in McIntosh (1998).
32. Wierzbicka (1988: 475).
33. See, for instance, Haslam and Loughnan (2014). Note, too, that Livingstone Smith (2021: 26) disagrees with Haslam about this element of dehumanization, suggesting that "dehumanization is not primarily a matter of attributing subhuman traits to a person, as Haslam believes. Instead, it is about attributing a subhuman essence to them."
34. Grossman (1995: 160); see also Holmes (1989).
35. For these examples, see Sallah and Weiss (2005: 47); Park (2007: 28–29).

36. Burns and Novick (2017); see episode 5, at 7:30.
37. Davis (2014: 39).
38. See Zuckerman (2021).
39. Terry (1984).
40. Komunyakaa tells an interviewer he "refused to use those derogatory terms for the Vietnamese" because of their parallels with racism at home. He reflects further on his ambivalence as a combatant: "You have to degrade before you can kill. . . . In a certain sense, I identified with the Vietnamese, and yet I knew that I could get killed by those same individuals. And that's a real trick inside the head to think about it in that way" (quoted in Alleyne 2018).
41. Gal and Irvine (2019).
42. Puar and Rai (2002); see also Puar (2006).
43. Livingstone Smith (2021: 16); see also Jones (2021).
44. Anderson (2023: 1–2). See also Adam Gilbert's (2018: 99–102) discussion of veteran poetry that recognizes how epithets and slurs aided the process of dehumanization.
45. Agamben (2005). See also Livingstone Smith (2021) on how dehumanization involves withholding ordinary moral rights and obligations.
46. French and Jack (2015: 194).
47. Terry (1984: 90–91), emphasis mine.
48. Sallah and Weiss (2005: 47).
49. See this dynamic documented in Holmes (1989: 391) and Turse (2013). In February 2000, then-presidential candidate and Vietnam veteran John McCain got into trouble when he argued he could personally limit the extension of an ethnoracial military slur (Tang 2008). When he was criticized for using the word "gooks" to refer to North Vietnamese, McCain tried to clarify that he was referring only to the interrogators who had held him captive and tortured him for five years. Perhaps he felt his personal experience gave him authority to control the limits of the word's reference. But as philosopher Hilary Putnam (1975: 144) once put it, "Meaning just ain't in the head," since dubbings that establish reference rely on broader social context (see also Bakhtin 1983). The term "gooks" has a long history of use by US occupation troops to refer to a wide breadth of Asian nationalities, from Chinese to Korean, and during the Vietnam war it was often extended to encompass all Vietnamese. A speaker's personal intentions don't refine the extension of the epithet by making finely grained distinctions between who is and isn't caught in its dehumanizing reductions. The broad meaning of the term has already been regimented by its historical and pragmatic uses.
50. https://www.youtube.com/watch?v=B6L9NTpkYnI.
51. Davis (2014: 131). Geoff Millard, testifying at the Winter Soldier hearings in 2008, explains how the term "haji" came to be applied to just about anyone outside of the US forces when in Iraq and Afghanistan.

> It's no surprise for anyone who's been in the military since September 11th, especially not for those of us who have been deployed since September 11th, that the word "haji" is used to dehumanize people not just of Iraq and Afghanistan, but anyone there who is not us. We bought haji DVDs at the haji shops from the hajis that worked there. The KBR [private contractor] employees that did our laundry that were from Pakistan became hajis. The KBR employees who worked inside of our chow halls became hajis. Everyone that was not a US force [member] became a haji, not a person, not a name, but a haji. I used to have conversations with members of my unit, and I would ask them why they use that term, especially

members of my unit who are people of color. It used to shock me that they would. And their answers were very similar, almost always, and that was, "They're just hajis. Who cares?" (https://www.democracynow.org/2008/3/18/winter_soldier_contd_us_vets_active)

Quil Lawrence, a correspondent for the BBC formerly embedded with US troops, reports that he saw "graffiti written on the back of seats in humvees that says 'all hajis must die'" (P. Martin 2008).

52. Young (2018b).
53. Speigle (2013: 21).
54. Hill (2008).
55. My thanks to Merav Shohet of Boston University for her translations and spellings of the relevant Vietnamese phrases.
56. According to Merav Shohet (personal communication), "mày is the 'derogatory' or disrespectful way of referring to second person 'you,' though in the South and center of the country it's used habitually by status superiors to inferiors[,] . . . so, 'fuck your (mày) mother (má)', or 'mother fucker.'"
57. A respondent on a Google Group forum from 1999 notes the parallel between the use of "xin loi" and the Terminator's use of the mock Spanish "hasta la vista" (https://groups.google.com/g/alt.war.vietnam/c/ITWVuGki1QM).
58. Merav Shohet (personal communication) is not certain where this phrase might have come from, but this is her best guess: "Maybe chết/giết đau (chết = die/croak; giết = to kill/murder [and pronounced yiet, a barely aspirated *t*, or even as if it ends with a barely aspirated /k sound in southern dialect, or ziet, a barely aspirated *t*, definitely not /c sound in the northern dialect]; đau = hurt), and in this context the terms, when combined together, could mean 'torture (or kill) you', or perhaps 'chết đau khổ' (meaning a painful death / torture to death)?"
59. On such indirect implications, called "indirect indexicality," see Hill (2008).

Note that American soldiers in World War II used the terms "Papa-san" and "Mama-san" across the Asian Pacific to refer to men and women in positions of respect ("-san" is an honorific in Japanese). Yet these terms implied no particular esteem among GIs in Vietnam. Consider this passage from Doug Anderson's memoir (2009: 125), as he marvels in hindsight at the cruelty of his young platoon:

> Here we are, a bunch of teenagers with high-tech weapons, swaggering through their village kicking over their family altars, diddling their daughters, kicking the shit out of Papa-san for fun, burning the thatch of their hooches out of sheer meanness of hormonal excess. . . . We'd just as soon kill a villager as look at him.

60. https://www.democracynow.org/2008/3/18/winter_soldier_contd_us_vets_active.
61. Fosher et al. (2018: 84).
62. Asad (2007).
63. USMC Officer (n.d.: 13).
64. See, for instance, Davis (2014: 86–87, 107).
65. Delori (2014: 526–527). He elaborates, "The enemy is completely absent. . . . It is not represented as an Other, or as an evil, or in a more abstract 'totemized' way. . . . The enemy is just not there. Instead, the whole party revolves around one single object: the bomb."
66. Boudreau (2018: 166).

67. See, for instance, Glover (2001); Grossman (1995); Levinas (1998); Hollan and Throop (2008).
68. Glover (2001: 345).
69. See McIntosh (2010) on rapid stance-shifting in speech that corresponds to rapid shifts in consciousness.
70. To return to Lieutenant Braun's 1967 NBC interview, we see a telling (if inadvertent) confession of how far enemy epithets could stretch. Correspondent Howard Tuckner breaks in at one point during his narrative to ask a metalinguistic question: "By 'dinks,' you mean North Vietnamese?" Braun smiles slightly, and looks down as he replies. "Yeah. Dinks are uh NVA, North Vietnamese, communist, Charlies, anything." Braun's smile, his only noteable expression of facial affect in a seven-minute interview, might reflect his sudden awareness that the term might sound startling, even shocking, to some Americans watching from their living rooms. As he defines "dinks," he lists a series of expanding social categories, starting with the "NVA," or the formal North Vietnamese Army, and ending up at "anything" (including "communist," which encompasses vast numbers of civilians). Clearly, many common epithets for the enemy defy the ethical principle described by philosophers French and Jack (2015) earlier in this chapter—namely, that service members should be carefully selective about who is dehumanized and when.
71. Sallah and Weiss (2005: 272).
72. https://www.democracynow.org/2008/3/18/winter_soldier_contd_us_vets_active.
73. Foulkrod (25:00).
74. Davis (2014: 111–112).
75. Davis (2014: 133).
76. Davis (2014: 137).
77. Davis (2014: 137).
78. Davis (2014: 143).
79. Anderson (2023: 1–2).
80. Schutz (1970: 185).

Chapter 7

1. Young (2018a: p. x).
2. See Turse (2013) for abundant evidence to support Steve's claim.
3. Thanks to Marc Levy for drawing my attention to the converse, described by Glenn Gray (1998 [1959])—namely, the notion of the "lucky" or charmed soldier everyone wants to be near during enemy mortar or artillery attacks.
4. To repeat a point I make in the Introduction, I do not believe that this language has straightforward causal effects. Profanity does not neatly beget violence, for instance. But in a violent context, it can be a verbal mirror or echo of violence itself, and when it is issued during violence work, it seems co-constitutive of it.
5. Cohn (1987: 704, 695); see also Gusterson (1996).
6. Cohn (1987: 708, emphasis mine).
7. See, for instance, Bandura (1999). For broader empirical evidence that euphemism influences perception and behavior, steering people to regard and respond to negative actions and items as if they were more palatable, see Walker et al. (2021); Jing-Schmidt (2022).

8. Ackerman (2014).
9. See "United States Military Doublespeak" (2014).
10. Whorf (1944).
11. W. Lutz (1992: 48).
12. W. Lutz (1990: 351); see also Klemperer (2013).
13. W. Lutz (1992: 48). The Pentagon sometimes refers to bombs as "vertically deployed anti-personnel devices." In an especially dehumanizing locution, US military planners implemented a software program in 2002 called Bugsplat, used to calculate the estimated civilian casualties likely to ensue from a given airstrike (Cronin 2018).
14. Crawford (2013: 4).
15. James has published a memoir under his own name (*For God and Country: Faith and Patriotism under Fire*, 2005, Public Affairs) and thus wishes to be identified in this text.
16. Camp Delta Standard Operating Procedures (SOP), 2003, Headquarters, Joint Task Force–Guantanamo (JTF-GTMO), Guantanamo Bay, Cuba. http://hrlibrary.umn.edu/OathBetrayed/SOP%201-238.pdf.
17. Cohn (1987: 703).
18. Camp Delta at Guantanamo Bay had a protocol to force-feed detainees if they hadn't eaten some number of meals in a row (James remembers nine). Some avoided the force-feeding by eating small amounts of fruit every five or six meals. Note that despite the official tone of the phrase "voluntary nonreligious fasting," I cannot locate it in the Standard Operating Procedures of the era.
19. A later Pentagon brief would euphemistically report that 120 of the 350 "self-harm" incidents at Guantanamo Bay in 2003 could be classified as "hanging gestures." http://content.time.com/time/subscriber/article/0,33009,1056316-2,00.html.
20. James noted that after he was taken off the island, Guantanamo Bay Standard Operating Procedures became harsher and more prohibitive of chaplain interactions with detainees.
21. Williams (2010).
22. https://twitter.com/MCRDPI/status/1257108773279272960?s=20&t=quMWu1kzCIKOSzhfWZ3tgw.
23. Wright (2004: 14).
24. "Shake 'n Bake," manufactured by Kraft Foods, is a popular breadcrumb-style coating for fried chicken. Marc Levy tells me the phrase was additionally used by GIs in Vietnam to refer to non-commissioned officers who achieved the rank by taking an accelerated training course.
25. Note that "Crispy Critters" was the name of a breakfast cereal manufactured by Post Cereals in the 1960s. Doug Anderson tells me that in Vietnam, the phrase "crispy critters" sometimes referred to the following strategy: "Fly a C-130 over an area saturated with enemy. Through the open cargo doors, literally pour the napalm out from drums over a large area. Then a helicopter comes behind and fires a rocket into the napalm. The acreage bursts into flame."
26. Lagoze (2023: 72–77).
27. https://www.youtube.com/watch?v=4-zaloxkMKE. "ONE SHOT ONE KILL Marine Scout Sniper Kills a Taliban Sniper."
28. Soular (1994: 19).
29. Tellessen (2021: 2).
30. https://www.youtube.com/watch?v=Ge52hGWudec, starting at 2:00.

Notes

31. https://www.youtube.com/watch?v=Ge52hGWudec (4:45).
32. https://www.youtube.com/watch?v=f5UcAMiPcDo. See, for instance, 6:45.
33. Much like the slurs I discuss in earlier chapters, profanity can dehumanize by mapping a person onto a symbolically polluting body part or act. Take the words of Josh, who enlisted in the Army as a teenager and served in Afghanistan for seven years. Interviewed in 2015 as part of a series on killing for *Cut*, Josh was asked when it is acceptable to take a human life. Josh replies, "If they mean to do harm to myself and my family, fuck 'em, they've chosen their path," then goes on to talk about the pleasure he took in killing "some mercenary asshole" or "Taliban dickhead." See https://www.youtube.com/watch?v=BsfbO9oz0GI.
34. Bergen (2016: 133).
35. Bergen (2016).
36. Tourette's syndrome can also cause the involuntary utterance of obscenities and derogatory remarks.
37. See, for instance, Stephens et al. (2009).
38. Bergen (2016: 183).
39. The communicative intent behind such uses of profanity also comes into relief when considering Goffman's (1978) discussion of "response cries." Although profanity often seems like an automatic exclamation, the audience of overhearers still shapes the word choice. As Goffman (1978: 799) writes, "Imprecations [spoken swear words] seem to be styled to be overheard in a gathering…A man who utters 'Fuck!' in a foundry [a factory for casting metal] is likely to avoid that particular expletive if he trips in a day nursery."
40. Bergen (2016: 224).
41. Pieslak (2009: 48, 50).
42. McIntosh (2020d).
43. Bergen (2016: 47).
44. I credit Anthony Webster (2015b) for developing the suggestion that the poetic qualities of language can nudge our thinking and feeling this way and that. Webster suggests that linguistic "sound associations" can be fruitfully connected to the Sapir-Whorf hypothesis, in light of the way they "evoke and orient our imagination" (Webster 2015b: 6) as socialized language users. The phonological similarities across profane words in English—those "plosive" sounds, for instance—tend to evoke those harsh feelings I discuss in the text. When the terse and "hard" sonic form of profane words supposedly resembles qualities of the speaker and qualities of what is spoken about, this mapping relationship is another example of "iconization" (Irvine and Gal 2000), in which the signs mirror their objects or "serve to convey ideas of things they represent simply by imitating them" (Peirce 1998: 5). (Later, Gal and Irvine would rename the dynamic "rhematization" [Gal and Irvine 2019].) In Webster's (2019: 184) discussion of scholarship on linguistic form, peoples' "emotional or felt connections" to linguistic forms are often "saturated with iconicity, because [they] feel as if they resemble what they are expressing."
45. A 2012 headline parody online (the link to which is now dead) read, "New DoD Regulation Bans Profanity; Soldiers Fucking Pissed."
46. Cf. Fleming and Lempert (2011).
47. Bersani (1987: 221).
48. See, for instance, Freud's interpreters on the fusion of Eros and Thanatos in orgasm (Sternbach 1975).
49. See also the words of the Army veteran Josh, who elaborates his enthusiasm for the "primal," phallic qualities of both sex and killing, saying, "The two things [humans]

have been doing ever since we came out of wherever we evolved from are fuck and kill. There's nothing more manly than watching helicopters fly overhead as you shoot a bunch of dudes, you know, as you're in a fucking gunfight" (https://www.youtube.com/watch?v=k1-SmU4zeQU).

Arguably, Marine Corps training channels the sexuality of young men into their rifles, sometimes conflating the gun with the phallus, as in the infamous chant, "This is my rifle [indicating the rifle with one hand], this is my gun [holding penis with other hand]. This is for fighting, this is for fun." The very fact that the chant facetiously disambiguates rifle from penis implies the two are hard to distinguish from each other.

50. The phrase "matter out of place" comes from anthropologist Mary Douglas's (1966) cross-cultural observation that objects and living things that transgress their normative location or category tend to be considered contaminating or polluting.
51. https://www.youtube.com/watch?v=4yzxkE72vkA.
52. Bergen (2016).
53. Prazosin is a drug that relieves PTSD-associated nightmares.
54. The nonstandard syntax of this phrase reflects the fact that 80% of US combatants in Vietnam came from the working class (Appy 1993). Its refusal of the polite grammatical form also indexes the covert prestige of working-class masculinity (Trudgill 1972).
55. Connolly (1994: 10).
56. Here is an example, in semiotic terms, of an "indexical icon"; the bodies are pointed to with the spit and also taken to share the contaminated characteristics of that vehicle for pointing.
57. In the study of rhetoric, "antiphrasis" refers to a type of verbal irony whereby a statement is used in a sense contrary to its conventional meaning. This irony often highlights the intended meaning, such as saying "Take your time!" to imply someone should hurry up. However, the phrase "It don't mean nothin'," used by combatants in Vietnam, does not seem to have been used to emphasize the opposite.
58. Lifton (1989 [1961]: 429).
59. Dunnuck would become a Sergeant in C 2-7 CAV. Two currently available videos feature overlapping portions of this brief interview with him (https://www.facebook.com/watch/?v=240243177102846; https://www.youtube.com/watch?v=0ZeouAaw4BU). The first, available on Facebook, includes Dunnuck's reference to the importance of preserving the lives of himself and his men. The second, on YouTube, starts a few seconds later and runs a few seconds longer.
60. In some cases, the phrase may have been used to steer a combatant away from an emotional meltdown. In a scene in the feature film *Hamburger Hill*, based on the infamous site of a horrific battle, members of a US platoon rescue one of their own from his rage and grief after the loss of his buddy by yelling, "It don't mean nothing, man! Not a thing" (https://www.youtube.com/watch?v=885EiuL9GKg). Before long, one GI coaxes the grieving man into repeating this phrase, accompanied by rhythmic hand slapping and fist bumping, turning it into an embodied chant with a meditative quality—something to focus on like a mantra to divert and soothe him.
61. Lagoze (2023: 20).
62. Pieslak (2009: 48, 50).
63. http://www.atroop412cav.com/jargon_slang/. Though each entry appears to have been authored by an individual veteran, the site is titled *Military Jargon from "The Soldier's Handbook," Written by the US Army*.

Chapter 8

1. As relayed by W. Price (2012: 192).
2. For discussions of military politeness and values talk, see Halbe (2011); Marcellino (2014).
3. Potter (2007).
4. For examples of military slang, see Axelrod (2013); Reinberg (1991); Saber (2018).
5. Filkins (2017).
6. Filkins (2017).
7. Filkins (2017).
8. This quotation appears on the Facebook page of the Marine Barracks Hawaii Association (https://www.facebook.com/100069341603625/posts/276647912437670/).
9. Goffman (1974).
10. As noted elsewhere, this "mirroring" relationship between sign and signified is referred to as "iconicity" in Peircian semiotics. Stasch (2011) has argued that iconic resonances within a society can have a reinforcing quality, supporting the "compellingness" of particular cosmologies or worldviews.
11. Notions of what is and isn't funny are always politically partial and situated in sociocultural dynamics. These preferences constitute what Elise Kramer (2011) calls "humor ideologies."
12. As one self-help book authored by a Navy Seal puts it, "You have to become the devil to get through Hell. . . . When everyone is in pain and miserable with their heads hanging low, you're the one smiling! Not a friendly smile, but one that says 'You think this fucking shit can hurt me?!'" (Gleeson 2021: xi).
13. M. Levy (2020: 226).
14. M. Levy (2020: 159).
15. Rottmann, Barry, and Paquet (1972: 53). The full poem reads as follows: "To build a 'gook stretcher,' all you need is: / Two helicopters / Two long, strong ropes, / And one elastic gook." Note that Rottman sardonically titles the poem "S.O.P."—short for "standard operating procedure." Presumably the poem is a commentary on the routine violations of international laws against torture or atrocity. In another grisly example of combat humor, Levy offers Fred Tomasello's anecdote about a quip his buddy made while the platoon was counting North Vietnamese Army bodies after an artillery attack. The bodies had been so mutilated they came apart with unnatural ease. "Frenchy holds the leg up at me and smiles. 'Hey, Lieutenant,' he says, 'let's grab one leg each and make a wish!'" (M. Levy 2020: 228).
16. M. Levy (2020: 226).
17. Fluri (2019).
18. Swart (2009).
19. Schaefer (2020).
20. Tomasello, quoted in M. Levy (2020: 228).
21. See McCreaddie and Wiggins (2009); Sliter et al. (2014); Zelizer (2010). Humor has other potential functions beyond the purview of this chapter. Freud, for instance, endorsed the idea that jokes offer convenient plausible deniability for hostility (Swart 2009), and—relevant to my discussion of "fun" euphemisms in Chapter 7—Cohn (1987) notes that

whimsical humor surrounding high-stakes military planning can help make it possible even to talk about difficult things at all, for it holds the horror at bay.

22. Lambek (2003: 3).
23. Raskin (1979).
24. Oring (1992) argues that amusement is triggered at the very moment that the hearer recognizes the "appropriateness" of the seeming incongruity.
25. McGraw and Warren (2010) offer the "benign violation theory," which claims that humor occurs when something benign threatens a person's sense of how the world "ought to be," and they see both interpretations simultaneously (their sense of how the world ought to be, plus the benign threat to it). McGraw, Williams, and Warren (2014) have further elaborated the notion of the benign threat, suggesting that psychological distance from a tragic event is important to being able to laugh at a joke about it.
26. See especially McGraw, Williams, and Warren (2014).
27. Munch-Jurisic (2018: 154). See also Bourke (1999).
28. An important wrinkle in this material on frame perversion is that the same utterance can be taken in different ways, depending on the context of the person or people interpreting it. Take, for example, the Charles Rosner poster from the early 1970s that read, "Join the Army: travel to exotic, distant lands; meet exciting, unusual people and kill them." Emblazoned on T-shirts, the slogan was often intended in an antiwar spirit, with the violent twist at the end a critique of the horrors of military. Yet the same T-shirt slogan is now sold on promilitary websites, like one that urges people to "showcase their appreciation for military humor" by purchasing a shirt reading, "Join the Marines / Travel to exotic places/ Meet new people / Then kill them" (https://www.ironhorsehelmets.com/join-the-marines-travel-to-exotic-places-meet-new-people-then-kill-them-t-shirt/). The nesting or overlapping of prosocial and violent imagery in frame perversion can be taken in a spirit of either sardonic critique of violence or humorous endorsement of it.
29. Pillen (2015: 343).
30. Pillen (2015: 346).
31. Pillen (2015: 347–348).
32. Tick (2005: 113).
33. Miles Lagoze (2023: 42) learned a variation of the same chant in the Marines around 2011: "I went to the mall, where all the fatties shop, I pulled out my machete, and I began to chop. I went to the playground, where all the kiddies play, I pulled out my machine gun, and I began to spray."
34. https://www.youtube.com/shorts/cYCQsdA_eX4.
35. Buchanan (2007: 55–63).
36. See, for instance, https://www.worthpoint.com/worthopedia/1969-vietnam-war-zippo-lighter-cobra-405309639. Versions of this slogan were handed down from the Vietnam era to the Global War on Terrorism. Sergeant Ian Hernandez (quoted in Turley 2012: 208) describes a DI from the early aughts who liked to say, "As I walk through the Valley of the Shadow of Death, I fear no evil because I am the baddest motherfucker down there."
37. Buchanan (2007: 167).
38. Buchanan (2007: 34).
39. https://www.youtube.com/watch?v=WzxNRoGoSKU.
40. Lagoze (2023: 128).

41. Childs (2018). Ironically, in World War II the ace of spades card signified good luck for the 101st Airborne Division, which used card suits to identify different regiments (Giles 2022).
42. See Sergeant Major Herb Friedman's discussion of death cards here: https://www.psywarrior.com/DeathCardsAce.html. During the United States' 2003 invasion of Iraq, decks of cards were printed with images of Iraqi officials the military sought to capture, with Saddam Hussein featured as the ace of spades (Budanovic 2018).
43. All three card images here were provided with permission by Sergeant Major Herb Friedman. See http://www.psywarrior.com/DeathCardsAce.html.
44. Will Price's GWOT-era memoir invokes similar frame perversion: "Looking for spent brass shells in the grass was no picnic . . . but it was the closest thing to an Easter Egg hunt I'll see this year. The thought kind of cheered me up in a sick way. Dare I say, 'A sick *Marine* way?'" (W. Price 2012: 89).
45. Horton (2019).
46. This incident is portrayed about fifty-three minutes into the film (53:30). See also Baker (2019).
47. Boudreau (2008: 55); see also Bourke (1999) on what some combatants experience as elation in killing.
48. Boudreau (2008: 32–33).
49. https://www.dropbox.com/s/pckd68rzk3kibud/IMG_9967.mov? dl=0.
50. Sites (2013: xx).

Chapter 9

1. Levy (2020: 173).
2. As it happens, this particular incident did not happen to Marc, who tells me that the chopper crew chief who told him about it resisted writing it down, even though Marc suggested he do so a number of times. Eventually, he gave Marc permission to write about the event in a poem.
3. Rukeyser (1996: 11).
4. The writing and revising process can also furnish an opportunity for self-reflection. Alexander Fenno, during a Warrior Writers workshop, opted to write a letter apologizing to the small boy he once kicked in the chest in Afghanistan and reports that in so doing he came to understand more about his own inner dynamics. "I was an angry young man with a gun strapped to my hip. The weight of it was like a hot burning coal, stuck in my pocket. . . . It burned me. In turn, I burned you" (Calica and Basl 2014: 15, 113).
5. See Soular (1994: 29).
6. Weigl quoted in Valentine (2013); see also Gilbert (2018: 146).
7. Anderson (1994: 10). In Chapter 6, I described how some GIs used the phrase "xin loi" sardonically, to mean something more like "tough shit," but Doug means the phrase sincerely here. Doug tells me that when he read the poem at a literary event in Vietnam in 2019, the young Vietnamese woman who introduced him translated it as "sorry" with a bitter, ironic twist. He suspected she meant it as a dig, condemning him for his past involvement with the US military.
8. See Heimes (2011: 7) for an expansive articulation of this dynamic. For more on poetry as therapy, see Jack Leedy (1969). Sherry Reiter (2009) helpfully unpacks her own

"ten principles of transformative writing"; I did not encounter these until after this chapter had been completed, but I see some overlap between her observations and some of mine. Reiter underscores the way writing allows a person to get some distance on a traumatic event and to metabolize it emotionally, while editing one's writing gives a person an empowering sense of control.

9. Shay (2010: 243).
10. Forché (1993).
11. The term dates back to classical Greece but was developed extensively by Foucault (1983). See also Schrader (2019) on parrhesia among returning veterans.
12. Decaul's statement can be found on the fourteenth image of his memoir at this website: https://memory.loc.gov/diglib/vhp-stories/loc.natlib.afc2001001.88836/zoomturner?ID=pm0001001&page=14.
13. See the fifteenth page of Decaul's memoir, here: https://www.loc.gov/item/afc2001001.88836/?ID=pm0001001&page=14.
14. See also Glenn Petersen (2021) on his ability to deny the conscious fear of danger while serving on a Navy aircraft carrier in the Gulf of Tonkin and on his experience of repressed fear that returned dramatically decades later.
15. On assistance for returning veterans see, for instance, https://www.marines.mil/News/Messages/Messages-Display/Article/886568/policy-for-return-and-reunion-of-marines/; https://planmydeployment.militaryonesource.mil/reunion-reintegration/family-members/what-to-expect-an-overview-of-reunion-and-reintegration/.
16. Harrison (1993).
17. See, for instance, Sebastian Junger's account of Papago rites (2016: 120).
18. See also Haldén and Jackson (2016).
19. For instance, Veena Das (1985: 5), based on her work in South Asia, has written of the war survivor's need "to talk and talk about war." See also Das and Nandy (1985) for richer elaboration of matters of representation and silence in war.
20. There was a notable exception to this pattern: the 1971 Winter Soldier Investigation, sponsored by Vietnam Veterans Against the War, in which over a hundred veterans famously testified about war crimes. http://www.vvaw.org/1971_50years/wsi.php.
21. On mixed feelings upon hearing "Thank you for your service," see, for instance, M. Levy (2020: 216).
22. https://www.warriorwriters.org/artists/kevin.html.
23. https://www.youtube.com/watch?v=NhCbsLneukM (10:20).
24. See, for instance, Bulmer and Jackson (2016); Dawes (2002); Das (1985, 2007); McSorley (2013); Pillen (2016); Scarry (1988); Suarez-Orozco (1990); Tucker and Prosise (2003: 131).
25. Daniel (1998: 75).
26. McSorley (2013: 239).
27. Caruth (1996: 4). See also Dawes (2013: 29–33) on the immense difficulties involved in speaking about trauma.
28. Wool (2015: 36).
29. Burns and Novick (2017, episode 6, 3:00).
30. In Ehrhart (1989: 37).
31. Musgrave (2003, front matter, emphasis mine).
32. See the fifteenth page of Decaul's memoir, here: https://memory.loc.gov/diglib/vhp-stories/loc.natlib.afc2001001.88836/zoomturner?ID=pm0001001&page=14.

33. "The Real Deal" (2000) http://medicinthegreentime.com/the-real-deal/.
34. Petersen (2021: 216).
35. For his war dreams, see Levy (2016). Examples of his poetry and prose can be found in Levy (2020).
36. Ehrhart (1987: 247).
37. The poem's title is "Make a New History" (J. Barry 2018).
38. The poem is found in Volkman (2009: 72–73).
39. "Bringing scunnion," sometimes spelled "scunion," refers to visiting destruction or violence on someone. The phrase apparently made it to the Iraq War as well.
40. Coyne (2008).
41. In Ehrhart (1989: 72).
42. In Volkman (2009: 185). Marc Levy happens to be friends with Bianchini and tells me he "served two tours in Vietnam as an Army Ranger LRRP [long-range reconnaissance patrol], wounded three times, highly decorated. After the war, he served ten years in federal prison for large-scale growing/selling pot. While in prison, he taught himself to paint and became an accomplished painter. When I asked Dave to contribute to Victor Volkman's book, he came up with that letter. He's not kidding about the 'goody-goody soup of human bone.'"
43. https://www.warriorwriters.org/artists/jeremy.html.
44. https://www.poetryfoundation.org/articles/68670/can-poetry-console-a-grieving-public-56d24846cd077.
45. https://www.poetryfoundation.org/articles/68670/can-poetry-console-a-grieving-public-56d24846cd077.
46. Muchnik (2017, 22:00).
47. In conversation, Preston credits the phrase "blood to ink" to Sherry Reiter (2009: 61). He tells me studies have shown sometimes when deeply depressed individuals donate a pint of blood, their depression or suicidality is alleviated. "The poem symbolically represents an organ or a pint of blood. And writing a poem is like converting blood to ink."
48. "Rung Sat," by Preston Hood (2007: 48):

> I rappel through the door of the gunship
> thinking about someone to love.
> On patrol I'm a hunter in the blackness
> dozing off, hardened, tired of danger,
> I sight the enemy, waist deep in Rung Sat,
> muscular legs standing executioner quiet,
> black-green smudge & sweat curled on lip.
> A snake stops me. I wade ahead,
> fall through myself like a stone,
> enemy voices passing only meters away,
> the backdrop of dark, life's death.
> I scan the horizon for movement,
> count the bodies across the canal,
> wait until they slip into the mud.
> My mind is a red-brown blur,
> a gauze for the wounded we torture.
> What's happening seems not true.
>
> Two hours before dawn the next day, we insert
> by chopper, on some Viet Cong farmer's land

> to interrogate sympathizers,
> & search for the mortar tubes
> the NVA shell us with.
>
> We demand revenge:
> the smell of rice at the jungle top,
> lazy orange mist shifting like smoke.
>
> In low silhouette, we patrol to ambush—
> our bodies surrounded by dark—
> the shadow of surprise suspended inside us.
> Across the trail, wind rips nipper palm,
> fear crawling at our feet, a wounded man.
>
> We radio in airstrike—
> the wounded lie with the dying,
> the dragged bodies hurried away
> disappear into bamboo.
>
> Blood trails along the river
> mark a company retreat—
> abandoned bombed-out bunkers
> shallow graves dug quickly,
> brown-uniformed & black-pajamaed bodies,
> rice bowls & fish heads—
> children half-buried in dirt.
> I am a man half in the water, half out;
> my legs suck into mud.
> My hands hold my head outstretched—
> hasten to deliver me among the dead.

49. Anderson (1994: 22).
50. See Marlantes (2011); Sites (2013); Shay (2010).
51. Berger (1992: 22).
52. Connolly (1994: 27).
53. Connolly (1994: 68).
54. Shwartz (2022).
55. Berger (1992: 21).
56. Berger (1992: 21).
57. Ehrhart (1984: 12–13). "Time on target" refers to the coordination of artillery fire in a salvo so that the munitions arrive roughly simultaneously.
58. Weigl (1988: 33–35).
59. cf. Luhrmann (2018).
60. I thank Marc Levy for this observation.
61. "Whatever you did in war will always be with you," cautions Marc Levy (2020: x).
62. See also Sherry Reiter (2009: 61).
63. In other writings (see, e.g., Anderson 2009), Doug develops the concept of the "snake brain": a kind of primordial force awakened by the conditions of combat.
64. Anderson (2015: 6).
65. Buber (1937).
66. Quoted in Ehrhart (1989: 47).
67. H. Martin (2013: 24).

68. "After Curfew" (H. Martin 2013: 55).
69. "Nocturne, Traffic Control Point" (H. Martin 2013: 49).
70. Gilbert (2018: 132).
71. "A Farmer from Vinh," in Rottman (1993: 191). In another poem, "The Ho Chi Minh Bird" (Rottman 1993: 141), a man who was pronounced "too old for battle" was assigned to whistle bird calls to cheer soldiers along the trail where bombs and Agent Orange had devastated the bird population. Rottman projects the man's pride in transcending the horrors of battle with these gentle sounds: "I was 257 different birds. / I got malaria, my hair fell out, and I was wounded four times. / But I was a Ho Chi Minh bird every day for thirteen years."
72. Ehrhart (1984: 20).
73. Anderson (2015: 9).

Chapter 10

1. Gates (2013); Nesson (2010); Rappaport (2008).
2. Pillen (2016: 99). See also Daniel (1996).
3. As Flatley (2008: 3) puts it, "Melancholia forms the site in which the social origins of our emotional lives can be mapped out and from which we can see the other persons who share our losses and are subject to the same social forces."
4. Kapadia (2019: 10).
5. Another strand in the history of dissident aesthetics in the USA is so-called craftivism, often gendered as feminine. Craftivism has included the AIDS Memorial Quilt, which tenderly depicts lives that were once stigmatized while it also testifies, with its enormous size, to the extent of human loss. It also includes perversions of hegemonic forms. "Yarn bombing," for instance, is a sort of textural graffiti that uses knitted or crocheted yarn to transform sterile or conservative spaces and monuments into playful, colorful, and politically expressive designs—sometimes covering tanks with pink and purple yarn, or Confederate statues with knitted ropes of kudzu. "Feminist cross-stich" uses the quaintly conventional feminine form of cross-stitching in a hoop to articulate such flower-laden advice as "Carry yourself with the confidence of a mediocre white man" or "Fuck politeness." Craftivism also includes those pink pussy hats knitted and crocheted to protest President Donald Trump's election in 2016.
6. Eli tells me the paperclip as a sign of protest dates to the protests against fascism in Europe during World War II. GIs in Vietnam sometimes sported a paper clip as a quiet expression of resistance against the war they participated in. The PAPER CLIP acronym is sometimes unpacked differently—for example, "Civilian Life Is Preferred," or "Civilian Life Incentive Program," but as a former medic Eli prefers the final word "Precious." To his knowledge, Eli was the first Global War on Terrorism soldier to tattoo the paper clip on himself, against military regulations. Several dozen members of Iraq Veterans Against the War followed suit.
7. One veteran tells a documentarian that re-entering civilian society is like "jumping out of a window of a moving car." See first video in this series: http://www.peacepaperproject.org.
8. Junger (2016).

9. Junger (2016).
10. Lévi-Strauss (1963).
11. Turner (1968).
12. Chan (2015).
13. Sometimes, Eli will use the labels inside uniforms as a prompt for talking about the social lives of the uniforms before they are worn. Many uniforms have woe-begotten origins, having been manufactured by prisoners under UNICOR, the trade name for Federal Prison Industries, since the 1930s. It's "modern-day slavery," Eli says, bound up with defense contracting and war profiteering and with the mass incarceration and subsequent exploitation of disadvantaged social groups.
14. See Nesson (2010, 38:00).
15. See Sites (2013: 131–135).
16. See Nesson (2010: 9:50).
17. https://www.warriorwriters.org/artists/leonard.html.
18. Eli also showed me the innovative bicycle-powered travel-beater prototype, developed by the combat paper community in 2009, the components of which are made by a papermaker in Boston. The beater has a soft trough made of yellow plastic that can be held in place like a tent with a metal exoskeleton of bars. Participants experimented with different iterations until they produced one whose components can be conveniently packed into checked luggage when flying.

    A photograph from the Combat Paper Facebook page (https://www.facebook.com/photo?fbid=1479445298909774&set=pcb.1479446438909660) depicts a portable Hollander, flanked by an easel on which someone has cheekily reworded the Marine Corps' "Rifleman's Creed" in these terms: "This is a Hollander Beater. There are many like it, but this one is mine." Rather than identifying with your rifle, it implies, try cathecting onto the machine that can transform your uniform into something positive.
19. Paper binds together when the cellulose fiber in plant-based material forms hydrogen bonds. Wool uniforms like those used in World War I won't bind on their own, so they must be mixed with a "carrier fiber" containing cellulose.
20. PBS, "Veterans Shred." https://www.youtube.com/watch?v=xb3K-Sd4cPA.
21. https://www.warriorwriters.org/artists/leonard.html.
22. Gates (2013).
23. On an early articulation of these three stages, see Van Gennep (2004 [1909]).
24. https://www.youtube.com/watch?v=kQDUooReONM.
25. See the first video here: http://www.peacepaperproject.org.
26. https://www.youtube.com/watch?v=KvcpmEZuGcw.
27. J. Phillips (2015).
28. https://www.youtube.com/watch?v=4VgCPviA8Rc.
29. https://www.youtube.com/watch?v=4VgCPviA8Rc.
30. Eli's "Vitruvian Target" reminds me of the "bullet crucifixes" made during World War I—a variety of "trench art" featuring a crucifix made of bullet cartridges with a crucified Christ attached to it. See Saunders (2000).
31. Eli also includes some personal code on this image, taking inspiration from the way da Vinci sometimes encoded secrets into his images. The lower and upper edges of the graph include numbers that make private allusions to events and topics in his life.

32. Five-year-old Omran Daqneesh was injured in 2016 Russian/Syrian airstrike in Aleppo, and two-year-old Alan Kurdi, a Syrian boy of Kurdish background, drowned off the coast of Greece in 2015 when his family tried to migrate.
33. The disturbing photograph James depicted in his drawing, capturing the unsettling actions of the Army 'Kill Team,' can be viewed here: https://www.aljazeera.com/news/2011/3/21/us-army-soldiers-pose-with-dead-afghan.
34. https://www.youtube.com/watch?v=UolZz_iq3Ms (2:30).
35. https://www.youtube.com/watch?v=UolZz_iq3Ms (5:20).
36. All quotations come from the same video (https://www.youtube.com/watch?v=UolZz_iq3Ms). I have confirmed the sentiments more recently with Chris himself.
37. https://www.youtube.com/watch?v=5kV3VL-oCVY.

Coda: The Nervous System

1. MacLeish (2015: 16). Taussig's (1992: 2) original discussion of the "nervous system" metaphor draws attention, similarly, to the tension between state facades and the smoke, mirrors, violence, and fear that lie behind them.
2. MacLeish (2015: 15).
3. Pillen (2017: 721), for instance, draws on Mauss's (1972 [1950]) theory of magic to suggest that ambiguous linguistic forms can serve as a means of creating magical forces.

Work Cited

Achugar, Mariana. 2008. *What We Remember: The Construction of Memory in Military Discourse*. John Benjamins.

Ackerman, Eliot. 2014. "Assassination and the American Language." *The New Yorker*, November 20, 2014. https://www.newyorker.com/news/news-desk/assassination-american-language.

Adena, Maja, Ruben Enikolopov, Maria Petrova, Veronica Santarosa, and Ekaterina Zhuravskaya. 2015. "Radio and the Rise of the Nazis in Prewar Germany." *The Quarterly Journal of Economics* 130(4): 1885–1939.

Agamben, Giorgio. 1998. *Homo Sacer: Sovereign Power and Bare Life*. Stanford University Press.

Agamben, Giorgio. 2005. *State of Exception*. Translated by Kevin Attell. University of Chicago Press.

Agard-Jones, Vanessa. 2013. "Bodies in the System." *Small Axe* 17(3): 182–192.

Agelopoulos, Georgios. 2000. "'You Are in the Army Now': An Ethnographic Account of Military Training." Paper presented at the 6th Biennial EASA Conference, Krakow, July 26–29.

Agha, Asif. 2007. *Language and Social Relations*. Cambridge University Press.

Åhäll, Linda, and Thomas Gregory, eds. 2015. *Emotions, Politics, and War*. Routledge.

Ahmed, Sara. 2004. *The Cultural Politics of Emotion*. Edinburgh University Press.

Alim, H. Samy, John R. Rickford, and Arnetha F. Ball, eds. 2016. *Raciolinguistics: How Language Shapes Our Ideas about Race*. Oxford University Press.

Allan, Keith, and Kate Burridge. 2006. *Forbidden Words: Taboo and the Censoring of Language*. Cambridge University Press.

Alleyne, Lauren K. 2018. "The Complexity of Being Human: An Interview with Yusef Komunyakaa." *The Fight and the Fiddle*, May 1, 2018. https://fightandfiddle.com/2018/05/01/the-complexity-of-being-human-an-interview-with-yusef-komunyakaa/.

Althusser, Louis. 1971. "Ideology and Ideological State Apparatuses (Notes toward an Investigation)." In *Lenin and Philosophy and Other Essays*, translated by Ben Brewster, 127–186. Monthly Review Press.

Anderson, Doug. 1994. *The Moon Reflected Fire*. Alice James Books.

Anderson, Doug. 2009. *Keep Your Head Down: Vietnam, the Sixties, and a Journey of Self-Discovery*. W. W. Norton.

Anderson, Doug. 2011. "Something Like a Soul." *The Massachusetts Review* 52(3): 489–494.

Anderson, Doug. 2015. *Horse Medicine*. Barrow Street Press.

Anderson, Doug. 2023. "Three Poems." *WLA: War, Literature, and the Arts* 35:1–5.

Appy, Christian. 1993. *Working Class War: American Combat Soldiers and Vietnam*. University of North Carolina Press.

Arendt, Hannah. 1994. "Understanding and Politics." In *Essays in Understanding: 1930–1954*, edited by J. Kohn, 307–327. Schocken Books.

Argenti-Pillen, Alex. 2003. *Masking Terror: How Women Contain Violence in Southern Sri Lanka*. University of Pennsylvania Press.

Arment, Jason. 2016a. "Every Man a Fortress." *Lunch Ticket*, Winter/Spring, 2016. http://lunchticket.org/every-man-fortress/.

Arment, Jason. 2016b. "The Oaths We Keep." *Watershed Review* 38(2). https://wayback.archive-it.org/10525/20190514113652/https://www.csuchico.edu/watershed/2016-fall/nonfiction/arment-jason.shtml.

Arment, Jason. 2018. *Musalaheen: A War Memoir*. University of Hell Press.

"Army: Nicer Drill Sergeants More Effective." 2006. Associated Press, October 10, 2006. https://www.nbcnews.com/id/wbna15210867.

Asad, Talal. 2007. *On Suicide Bombing*. Columbia University Press.

Axelrod, Alan. 2013. *Whiskey Tango Foxtrot: The Real Language of the Modern American Military*. Skyhorse.

Baker, Camille. 2019. "A Veteran's War Movie Sheds Damning Light on How the Marines Fight in Afghanistan." *The Intercept*, April 7, 2019. https://theintercept.com/2019/04/07/combat-obscura-afghanistan-war-documentary/.

Bakhtin, Mikhail M. 1983. *The Dialogic Imagination: Four Essays*. University of Texas Press.

Bandura, Albert. 1999. "Moral Disengagement in the Perpetration of Inhumanities." *Personality and Social Psychology Review* 3(3): 193–209.

Baron-Cohen, Simon. 2012. *Zero Degrees of Empathy*. Penguin.

Barroso, Amanda. 2019. "The Changing Profile of the U.S. Military: Smaller in Size, More Diverse, More Women in Leadership." *The Pew Research Center*, September 10, 2019. https://www.pewresearch.org/fact-tank/2019/09/10/the-changing-profile-of-the-u-s-military/.

Barry, Jan. 2018. *Earth Songs II: Poems of Love, Loss, and Life*. Jan Barry Books.

Barry, Kathleen Lois. 2011. *Unmaking War, Remaking Men: How Empathy Can Reshape Our Politics, Our Soldiers, and Ourselves*. Phoenix Rising Press.

Bate, Bernard. 2021. *Protestant Textuality and the Tamil Modern: Political Oratory and the Social Imaginary in South Asia.*, edited by E. Annamalai, Francis Cody, Malarvizhi Jayanth, and Constantine V. Nakassis. Stanford University Press.

Bax, Anna. 2018. "'The C-Word' Meets 'the N-word': The Slur-Once-Removed and the Discursive Construction of 'Reverse Racism.'" *Journal of Linguistic Anthropology* 28(2): 114–136.

Bayendor, David. 2012. "HTS Redux: A 'Halfie' Calls for an Anthropology of the Military." *E-International Relations*. https://www.e-ir.info/2012/03/01/hts-redux-a-halfie-calls-for-an-anthropology-of-the-military/.

Bean, Susan. 1980. "Ethnology and the Study of Proper Names." *Anthropological Linguistics* 22(7): 305–331.

Belew, Kathleen. 2018. *Bring the War Home: The White Power Movement and Paramilitary America*. Harvard University Press.

Belkin, Aaron. 2012. *Bring Me Men: Masculinity and the Benign Façade of American Empire, 1898–2001*. Oxford University Press.

Benveniste, Emile. 1973. *Problems in General Linguistics*, translated by Mary Elizabeth Meek. Coral Gables, FL: University of Miami Press.

Bergen, Benjamin. 2016. *What the F: What Swearing Reveals about Our Language, Our Brains, and Ourselves*. Basic Books.

Berger, John. 1992. "Once in a Poem." In *And Our Faces, My Heart, Brief as Photos*, 21–23. Random House.

Berlant, Lauren. 2011. *Cruel Optimism*. Duke University Press.

Bersani, Leo. 1987. "Is the Rectum a Grave?" *October* 43(Winter): 197–222.

Beynon, Steve. 2022. "Less Screaming, More Weightlifting: The Army Is Reinventing Basic Training for Gen Z." *Military News*, October 18, 2022. https://www.military.com/daily-news/2022/10/18/less-screaming-more-weightlifting-army-reinventing-basic-training-gen-z.html.

Beynon, Steve, and Kelsey Baker. 2024. "The Army's Recruiting Problem Is Male." *Military.com*, June 14, 2024. https://www.military.com/daily-news/2024/06/14/armys-recruiting-problem-male.html?ESRC=eb_240617.nl&utm_medium=email&utm_source=eb&utm_campaign=20240617.

Bianchi, Claudia. 2014. "The Speech Acts Account of Derogatory Epithets: Some Critical Notes." In *Liber Amicorum Pascal Engel*, edited by J. Dutant, D. Fassio, and A. Meylan, 465–480. Université de Genève. https://www.unige.ch/lettres/philo/publications/engel/liberamicorum/bianchi.pdf.

Bica, Camillo Mac. 2018. *Beyond PTSD: The Moral Casualties of War*. Gnosis Press.

Bickford, Andrew. 2001. "Male Identity, the Military, and the Family in the Former German Democratic Republic." *Anthropology of East Europe Review* 19(1): 65–76.

Biehl, João, and Peter Locke. 2010. "Deleuze and the Anthropology of Becoming." *Current Anthropology* 51(3): 317–351.

Binder, Werner. 2010. "Ritual Dynamics of Torture: The Performance of Violence and Humiliation at the Abu Ghraib Prison." In *State, Power, and Violence*, edited by Margo Kitts, Bernd Schneidmüller, Gerald Schwedler, Eleni Tounta, Hermann Kulke, and Uwe Skoda, 75–104. Harrassowitz.

Bledsoe, Everett. 2023. "What Percentage of the US Military Is Conservative—4 Sources." *The Soldiers Project*, October 2, 2023. https://www.thesoldiersproject.org/percentage-of-the-us-military-is-conservative/.

Bloch, Maurice. 1992. *Prey into Hunter: The Politics of Religious Experience*. Cambridge University Press.

Blommaert, Jan. 2014. "Infrastructures of Superdiversity: Conviviality and Language in an Antwerp Neighbourhood." *European Journal of Cultural Studies* 17(4): 431–451.

Boroditsky, L., Schmidt, L., Phillips, W. 2003. "Sex, Syntax, and Semantics." In *Language in Mind: Advances in the Study of Language and Thought*, edited by D. Gentner and S. Goldin-Meadow, 61–80. MIT Press.

Boudreau, Tyler. 2008. *Packing Inferno: The Unmaking of a Marine*. Feral House.

Boudreau, Tyler. 2009. "To Kill or Not to Kill." *The Progressive*. https://progressive.org/kill-kill/.

Boudreau, Tyler. 2018. "Soldier Street Theater." In *Performance in a Militarized Culture*, edited by Sara Brady and Lindsey Mantoan, 155–170. Routledge.

Bourke, Joanna. 1999. *An Intimate History of Killing: Face to Face Killing in Twentieth Century Warfare*. Basic Books.

Bourke, Joanna. 2016. "Hazing: Bullying in the Military." *Psychology and Education* 53(1–2): 56–64.

Bowman, Rachel Lynne. 2015. *The Embodied Rhetoric of Recruit Training in the United States Marine Corps*. PhD diss., University of North Carolina at Greensboro.

Britsky, Haley. 2020. "It's Going to Take Time." *Task and Purpose*. December 31, 2020. https://taskandpurpose.com/news/army-leaders-people-first-2020-2021/?mc_cid=9d30fec682&mc_eid=bf0de7cdd7.

Brooks, Rosa. 2017. *How Everything Became War and the Military Became Everything: Tales from the Pentagon*. Simon & Schuster.

Brown, Keith. 2008. "'All They Understand Is Force': Debating Culture in Operation Iraqi Freedom." *American Anthropologist* 110(4): 443–453.

Brown, Melissa T. 2012. *Enlisting Masculinity: The Construction of Gender in US Military Recruiting Advertising during the All-Volunteer Force*. Oxford University Press.

Browning, Christopher R. 1998. *Ordinary Men: Reserve Police Battalion 101 and the Final Solution in Poland*. Harper Perennial.

Brumley, Caanan. 2006. *Ears, Open. Eyeballs, Click*. Cinema Company C.

Work Cited

Buber, Martin. 1937. *I and Thou*. Translated by Ronald Gregor Smith. T. & T. Clark.

Buchanan, Sherry. 2007. *Vietnam Zippos*. Asia Ink and Visionary World.

Bucholtz, Mary, and Kira Hall. 2016. "Embodied Sociolinguistics." In *Sociolinguistics: Theoretical Debates*, edited by Nikolas Coupland, 173–197. Cambridge University Press.

Buckley, Gail Lumet. 2001. *American Patriots: The Story of Blacks in the Military from the Revolution to Desert Storm*. Random House.

Budanovic, Nikola. 2018. "The Ace of Spades." *The Vintage News*, March 29, 2018. https://www.thevintagenews.com/2018/03/29/death-card-vietnam-war/.

Bulmer, Sarah, and David Jackson. 2016. "'You Do Not Live in My Skin': Embodiment, Voice, and the Veteran." *Critical Military Studies* 2(1–2): 25–40.

Burke, Carol. 1996. "Pernicious Cohesion." In *It's Our Military Too: Women and the US Military*, edited by Judith Stiehm, 205–219. Temple University Press.

Burke, Carol. 2004. *Camp All-American, Hanoi Jane, and the High-and-Tight: Gender, Folklore, and Changing Military Culture*. Beacon Press.

Burns, Ken, and Lynn Novick. 2017. *The Vietnam War*. Florentine Films.

Burns, Richard Allen. 2003. "This Is My Rifle, This Is My Gun . . . : Gunlore in the Military." *New Directions in Folklore*, 7. https://scholarworks.iu.edu/journals/index.php/ndif/article/view/19886

Butler, Judith. 1997. *Excitable Speech: A Politics of the Performative*. Routledge.

Butler, Judith. 2010. *Frames of War: When Is Life Grievable?* Verso Books.

Caddy, Dan. 2015. *Awesome Sh*t My Drill Sergeant Said: Wit and Wisdom from America's Finest*. Dey St.

Calica, Lovella, and Kevin Basl. 2014. *Warrior Writers: A Collection of Writing & Artwork by Veterans*. L. Brown and Sons.

Cameron, Deborah. 1995. *Verbal Hygiene*. Routledge.

Capps, Lisa, and Elinor Ochs. 1995. *Constructing Panic: The Discourse of Agoraphobia*. Harvard University Press.

Caruth, Cathy. 1996. *Unclaimed Experience: Trauma, Narrative, and History*. Johns Hopkins University Press.

Center for Army Lessons Learned (CALL). 2009. *Drill Sergeant Handbook (No 09-12): Tactics, Techniques, and Procedures*. Fort Leavenworth, KS: Combined Arms Center (CAC). https://info.publicintelligence.net/USArmy-DrillSergeant.pdf.

Chan, Julia B. 2015. "Behind the Mask: Facing Torture after the War." *Reveal*, February 14, 2015. https://revealnews.org/article/behind-the-mask-facing-torture-after-the-war/.

Chen, Mel Y. 2012. *Animacies: Biopolitics, Racial Mattering, and Queer Affect*. Duke University Press.

Childs, Fred. 2018. "Ace of Spades." *Charlie Company Vietnam, 1966–1972*, August 31, 2018. https://charliecompany.org/2018/08/31/ace-of-spades/.

Cimino, Aldo. 2011. "The Evolution of Hazing: Motivational Mechanisms and the Abuse of Newcomers." *Journal of Cognition and Culture* 11(3–4): 241–267.

Clark, James. 2016. "The No Sh*t Truth about What It's Like to Be a Drill Instructor." *Task and Purpose*, May 9, 2016. https://taskandpurpose.com/mandatory-fun/no-sht-truth-like-drill-instructor.

Clark, James. 2021. "Dan Crenshaw Wants People to Blow the Whistle on 'Woke Ideology' in the Military and He's Getting Roasted for It." *Task and Purpose*, June 1, 2021. https://taskandpurpose.com/news/dan-crenshaw-woke-military-whistleblower/.

Cody, Francis. 2013. *The Light of Knowledge: Literacy Activism and the Politics of Writing in South India*. Cornell University Press.

Cohn, Carol, and Cynthia Enloe. 2003. "A Conversation with Cynthia Enloe: Feminists Look at Masculinity and the Men Who Wage War." *Signs: Journal of Women in Culture and Society* 28(4): 1187–1107.

Cohn, Carol. 1987. "Sex and Death in the Rational World of Defense Intellectuals." *Signs: Journal of Women in Culture and Society* 12(4): 687–718.

Cohn, Carol. 2020. "'Cocked and Loaded': Trump and the Gendered Discourse of National Security." In *Language in the Trump Era: Scandals and Emergencies*, edited by Janet McIntosh and Norma Mendoza-Denton, 179–190. Cambridge University Press.

Conley, Robin. 2016. *Confronting the Death Penalty: How Language Influences Jurors in Capital Cases*. Oxford University Press.

Connolly, David. 1994. *Lost in America*. Viet Nam Generation; Burning Cities Press.

Cooper, Helene. 2020. "The Few, the Proud, the White: The Marine Corps Balks at Promoting Generals of Color." *The New York Times*, August 31, 2020. https://www.nytimes.com/2020/08/31/us/politics/marines-race-general.html.

Copp, Tara. 2017. "Mattis: Get Unnecessary Training Off Warfighters' Backs." *Military Times*, July 25, 2017. https://www.militarytimes.com/news/your-military/2017/07/25/mattis-get-unnecessary-training-off-warfighters-backs/.

Coyne, Kevin. 2008. "Poet-Soldiers Lend Voices on Iraq War." *The New York Times*, February 24, 2008. https://www.nytimes.com/2008/02/24/nyregion/nyregionspecial2/24colnj.html.

Crawford, Neta C. 2013. *Accountability for Killing: Moral Responsibility for Collateral Damage in America's Post-9/11 Wars*. Oxford University Press.

Crenshaw, Paul. 2015. "Names." *HaveHasHad*. https://www.hobartpulp.com/web_features/names.

Cronin, Bruce. 2018. *Bugsplat: The Politics of Collateral Damage in Western Armed Conflicts*. Oxford University Press.

Croom, Adam M. 2013. "Racial Epithets, Characterizations, and Slurs." *Analysis and Metaphysics* 12:11–24.

Cvetkovich, Ann. 2014. "Affect." In *Keywords for American Cultural Studies*, edited by Bruce Burgett and Glenn Hendler, 13–15. 2nd ed. New York: New York University Press.

Daniel, E. Valentine. 1996. *Charred Lullabies: Chapters in an Anthropology of Violence*. Princeton University Press.

Daniel, E. Valentine. 1998. "The Limits of Culture." In *In Near Ruins: Cultural Theory at the End of the Century*, edited by Nicholas B. Dirks, 67–91. University of Minnesota Press.

Das, Veena. 1985. "Anthropological Knowledge and Collective Violence." *Anthropology Today* 1(3): 4–6.

Das, Veena. 2007. *Life and Words: Violence and the Descent into the Ordinary*. University of California Press.

Das, Veena. 2008. "Violence, Gender, and Subjectivity." *Annual Review of Anthropology* 37(1): 283–299.

Das, Veena, and Ashis Nandy. 1985. "Violence, Victimhood and the Language of Silence." *Contributions to Indian Sociology* 19(1): 177–195.

Davis, Sean. 2014. *The Wax Bullet War: Chronicles of a Soldier and Artist*. Ooligan Press.

Daughtry, J. Martin. 2014. "Thanatosonics: Ontologies of Acoustic Violence." *Social Text* 32(2): 25–51.

Daughtry, J. Martin. 2015. *Listening to War: Sound, Music, Trauma, and Survival in Wartime Iraq*. Oxford University Press.

Dawes, James. 2002. *The Language of War: Literature and Culture in the U.S. from the Civil War through World War II*. Harvard University Press.

Dawes, James. 2013. *Evil Men*. Harvard University Press.

Dedaić, Mirjana N., and Daniel N. Nelson, eds. 2003. *At War with Words*. Mouton de Gruyter.

Delori, Mathias. 2014. "Killing without Hatred: The Politics of Non-Recognition in Contemporary Western Wars." *Global Discourse: An Interdisciplinary Journal of Current Affairs and Applied Contemporary Thought* 4(4): 516–531.

Delori, Mathias. 2020. "The Politics of Emotions in Contemporary Wars." In *Handbook of Critical International Relations*, edited by S. C. Roach, 305–323. Edgar Elgar.

Dempsey, Jason K. 2009. *Our Army: Soldiers, Politics, and American Civil-Military Relations*. Princeton University Press.

Desjarlais, Robert, and Jason C. Throop. 2011. "Phenemenological Approaches in Anthropology." *Annual Review of Anthropology* 40:87–102.

Dirosa, Gia A., and Gerald F. Goodwin. 2014. "Moving away from Hazing: The Example of Military Initial Entry Training." *Virtual Mentor* 16(3): 204–209.

Disler, Edith A. 2008. *Language and Gender in the Military: Honorifics, Narrative, and Ideology in Air Force Talk*. Cambria Press.

Dobos, Ned. 2020. *Ethics, Security, and the War-Machine: The True Cost of the Military*. Oxford University Press.

Donnelly, Faye. 2013. *Securitization and the Iraq War: The Rules of Engagement in World Politics*. Routledge.

Douglas, Mary. 1966. *Purity and Danger: An Analysis of Concepts of Pollution and Taboo*. Routledge.

Downes, Alexander B. 2006. "Desperate Times, Desperate Measures: The Causes of Civilian Vicimization in War." *International Security* 30(4): 152–195.

Dreyfus, Hubert, and Camilo Salazar Prince. 2008. "The Thin Red Line: Dying without Demise, Demise without Dying." In *The Thin Red Line*, edited by David Davies, 29–35. Routledge.

Dunlap, Shawn. 2022. "Put Yourself in My Combat Boots: Autoethnographic Reflections on Forms of Life as a Soldier and Veteran." *Journal of Community Engagement and Scholarship* 13(4). https://doi.org/10.54656/YLIB7949.

Duranti, Alessandro, and Charles Goodwin. 1992. *Rethinking Context: Language as an Interactive Phenomenon*. Cambridge University Press.

Duranti, Alessandro, Elinor Ochs, and Bambi B. Schieffelin, eds. 2012. *The Handbook of Language Socialization*. Wiley-Blackwell.

Duranti, Alessandro. 2009. "The Relevance of Husserl's Theory to Language Socialization." *Journal of Linguistic Anthropology* 19(2): 205–226.

Duranti, Alessandro. 2010 "Husserl, Intersubjectivity and Anthropology." *Anthropological Theory* 10(1–2): 16–35.

Eastman, Carolyn. 2009. "Fight Like a Man: Gender and Rhetoric in the Early Nineteenth Century American Peace Movement." *American Nineteenth Century History* 10(3): 247–271.

Eckholm, Eric. 2005. "As Recruiting Suffers, Military Reins in Abuses at Boot Camp." *The New York Times*, July 26, 2005. https://www.nytimes.com/2005/07/26/us/as-recruiting-suffers-military-reins-in-abuses-at-boot-camp.html.

Edney-Browne, Alex. 2016. "Embodiment and Affect in a Digital Age: Understanding Mental Illness among Military Drone Personnel." *Krisis* 3:1–14.

Ehrhart, William D. 1984. *To Those Who Have Gone Home Tired: New & Selected Poems by W. D. Ehrhart*. Thunder's Mouth Press.

Ehrhart, William D. 1987. "Soldier-Poets of the Vietnam War." *The Virginia Quarterly Review* 63(2): 246–265.

Ehrhart, William D., ed. 1989. *Unaccustomed Mercy: Soldier-Poets of the Vietnam War*. Texas Tech University Press.

Eichler, Maya. 2011. *Militarizing Men: Gender, Conscription, and War in Post-Soviet Russia*. Stanford University Press.

Eisenlohr, Patrick. 2018. "Suggestions of Movement: Voice and Sonic Atmospheres in Mauritian Muslim Devotional Practices." *Cultural Anthropology* 33(1): 32–57. https://doi.org/10.14506/ca33.1.02.

Elliott, Andrea. 2006. "For Recruiter Speaking Arabic, Saying Go Army Is a Hard Job." *The New York Times*, October 7, 2006. https://www.nytimes.com/2006/10/07/us/07recruit.html.

Elshtain, Jean Bethke. 1987. *Women and War*. University of Chicago Press.

Englebretson, Robert, ed. 2007. *Stancetaking in Discourse: Subjectivity, Evaluation, and Interaction*. John Benjamins.

Enloe, Cynthia. 2000. *Maneuvers: The International Politics of Militarizing Women's Lives*. University of California Press.

Enloe, Cynthia. 2015. "The Recruiter and the Sceptic: A Feminist Approach to Military Studies." *Critical Military Studies* 1(1): 3–10.

Fairclough, Norman. 2003. "'Political Correctness': The Politics of Culture and Language." *Discourse & Society* 14(1): 17–28.

Fanning, Necko. 2019. "I Thought I Could Serve as an Openly Gay Man in the Army: Then Came the Death Threats." *The New York Times Magazine*, April 10, 2019. https://tinyurl.com/4tjenmxk.

Fanning, Rory. 2020. "Far Right Militias Are Recruiting Vets: We Must Organize against This Trend." *Truthout*, November 11, 2020. https://truthout.org/articles/far-right-militias-are-recruiting-vets-we-must-organize-against-this-trend/.

Fassin, Didier, and R. Rechtman. 2009. *The Empire of Trauma: An Inquiry into the Condition of Victimhood*. Princeton University Press

Feldman, Allan. 2005. "On the Actuarial Gaze: From 9/11 to Abu Ghraib." *Cultural Studies* 19(2): 203–226.

Ferguson, Charles A. 1959. "Diglossia." *WORD* 15(2): 325–240.

Filkins, Dexter. 2017. "James Mattis, a Warrior in Washington." *The New Yorker*, May 22, 2017. https://www.newyorker.com/magazine/2017/05/29/james-mattis-a-warrior-in-washington.

Finley, Erin P. 2011. *Fields of Combat: Understanding PTSD among Veterans of Iraq and Afghanistan*. Cornell University Press.

Flatley, Jonathan. 2008. *Affective Mapping: Melancholia and the Politics of Modernism*. Harvard University Press.

Fleming, Luke, and Michael Lempert. 2011. "Introduction: Beyond Bad Words." *Anthropological Quarterly* 84(1): 5–13.

Fluri, Jennifer. 2019. "What's So Funny in Afghanistan? Jocular Geopolitics and the Everyday Use of Humor in Spaces of Protracted Precarity." *Political Geography* 68:125–130.

Forché, Carolyn. 1993. *Against Forgetting: Twentieth Century Poetry of Witness*. W. W. Norton.

Fosher, Kerry, Rebecca Lane, Erika Tarzi, Kristin Post, and Eric Gauldin. 2018. "Marine Corps Organizational Culture Research Project Report to Personnel Studies and Oversight Office: Marines' Perspectives on Various Aspects of Marine Corps Organizational Culture." Center for Advanced Operational Culture Learning, United States Marine Corps. Accessed July 15, 2022. https://www.usmcu.edu/Portals/218/CAOCL/files/MCOCR%20Report%20to%20PSO%2030Mar18_wDem_FINAL.pdf?ver=2019-09-05-135301-060.

Fosher, Kerry, and Lauren Mackenzie, eds. 2021. *The Rise and Decline of U.S. Military Culture Programs, 2004–2020*. Marine Corps University Press.

Foucault, Michel. 1978. *History of Sexuality. Vol. 1, An Introduction*. Translated by Robert Hurley. Pantheon Books.

Foucault, Michel. 1983. *Discourse and Truth: The Problematization of Parrhesia*. University of California Press.

Foucault, Michel. 1995. *Discipline and Punish: The Birth of the Prison*. Translated by Alan Sheridan. Vintage.

Foucault, Michel. 2004. *The Birth of Biopolitics: Lectures at the Collège de France, 1978–1979*. Picador.

Foulkrod, Patricia. 2006. *The Ground Truth: After the Killing Ends*. Radioaktive Film and Plum Pictures.

Frank, David A., Paul Slovic, and Daniel Vastfjall. 2011. "'Statistics Don't Bleed': Rhetorical Psychology, Presence, and Psychic Numbing in Genocide Psychology." *JAC* 31(3–4): 609–624.

Frank, Nathaniel. 2009. *Unfriendly Fire: How the Gay Ban Undermines the Military and Weakens America*. Thomas Dunne Books.

French, Shannon, and Anthony Jack. 2015. "Dehumanizing the Enemy: The Intersection of Neuroethics and Military Ethics." In *Responsibilities to Protect: Perspectives in Theory and Practice*, edited by David Whetham and Bradley J. Strawser, 169–195. Brill.

Fuchs, Thomas. 2017. "Intercorporeality and Interaffectivity." In *Intercorporeality: Emerging Socialities in Interaction*, edited by Christian Meyer, Jürgen Streek, and J. Scott Jordan, 3–23. Oxford University Press.

Fuchs, Thomas. 2019. "Empathy, Group Identity, and the Mechanisms of Exclusion: An Investigation into the Limits of Empathy." *Topoi* 38:239–250.

Gal, Susan, and Judith T. Irvine. 2019. *Signs of Difference: Language and Ideology in Social Life*. Cambridge University Press.

Gardiner, Steven L. 2012. "The Warrior Ethos: Discourse and Gender in the United States Army since 9/11." *Journal of War & Culture Studies* 5(3): 371–383.

Gates, Barbara. 2013. "Combat Papermakers Drew Cameron and Drew Matott." *Works & Conversations*, November 30, 2013. http://www.peacepaperproject.org/files/Conversations.org_+Combat+Papermakers+Drew+Cameron+and+Drew+Matott,+by+Barbara+Gates.pdf.

Geertz, Clifford. 1973. *The Interpretation of Cultures: Selected Essays*. Basic Books.

Gigliotti, Simone. 2003. "Unspeakable Pasts as Limit Events: The Holocaust, Genocide, and the Stolen Generations." *Australian Journal of Politics and History* 49(2): 164–181.

Gilberd, Kathleen. 2017. "Hazing and Bullying in the Military." Military Law Task Force, July 30, 2017. https://nlgmltf.org/military-law/2017/hazing-and-bullying-in-the-military/.

Gilbert, Adam. 2018. *A Shadow on Our Hearts: Soldier-Poetry, Morality, and the American War in Vietnam*. University of Massachusetts Press.

Giles, Rosemary. 2022. "The Ace of Spades Was Used by the 101st Airborne before It Became the 'Death Card.'" *War History Online*, June 16, 2022. https://www.warhistoryonline.com/vietnam-war/ace-of-spades-origins.html?safari=1&Exc_D_LessThanPoint002_p1=1.

Gilmore, David D. 1990. *Manhood in the Making: Cultural Concepts of Masculinity*. Yale University Press.

Gilmore, Ruth Wilson. 2022. *Abolition Geography: Essays towards Liberation*. Verso.

Gleeson, Brent. 2021. *Embrace the Suck: The Navy Seal Way to an Extraordinary Life*. Hachette Brook Group.

Glover, Jonathan. 2001. *Humanity: A Moral History of the Twentieth Century*. Yale University Press.

Goffman, Erving. 1974. *Frame Analysis: An Essay on the Organization of Experience*. Northeastern University Press.

Goffman, Erving. 1978. "Response Cries." *Language*, 54(4): 787–815.

Goffman, Erving. 1981. *Forms of Talk*. University of Pennsylvania Press.

Gonzalez, Roberto J., and Hugh Gusterson. 2019. "Introduction." In *Militarization: A Reader*, edited by Roberto J. Gonzalez, Hugh Gusterson, and Gustaaf Houtman, 1–18. Duke University Press.

Gonzalez, Roberto J., Hugh Gusterson, and Gustaaf Houtman, eds. 2019. *Militarization: A Reader*. Duke University Press.

Goodwin, Charles. 1994. "Professional Vision." *American Anthropologist* 96(3): 606–633.
Goodwin, Gerald F. 2017. "Black and White in Vietnam." *The New York Times*, July 18, 2017. https://www.nytimes.com/2017/07/18/opinion/racism-vietnam-war.html.
Goodman, Steve. 2010. *Sonic Warfare: Sound, Affect, and the Ecology of Fear*. MIT Press.
Gordon, Michael, and Bernard Trainor. 2006. *Cobra II: The Inside Story of the Invasion and Occupation of Iraq*. Pantheon Books.
Gray, Glenn. 1998 [1959]. *The Warriors: Reflections on Men in Battle*. Bison Books.
Gregory, Thomas. 2019. "Dangerous Feelings: Checkpoints and the Perception of Hostile Intent." *Security Dialogue* 50(2): 131–147.
Grobe, Anna Mulrine. 2020. "Trust Your Drill Sergeant? Army Takes New Approach to Basic Training." *The Christian Science Monitor*, October 7, 2020. https://www.csmonitor.com/USA/Military/2020/1007/Trust-your-drill-sergeant-Army-takes-new-approach-to-basic-training.
Grossman, Dave. 1995. *On Killing: The Psychological Cost of Learning to Kill in War and Society*. Open Road Media.
Gumperz, John J., and Stephen C. Levinson. 1996. *Rethinking Linguistic Relativity*. Cambridge, UK: Cambridge University Press.
Gusterson, Hugh. 1996. *Nuclear Rites: A Weapons Laboratory at the End of the Cold War*. University of California Press.
Gusterson, Hugh. 2010. "The Cultural Turn in the War on Terror." In *Anthropology and Global Counterinsurgency*, edited by John D. Kelly, Beatrice Jauregui, Sean T. Mitchell, and Jeremy Walton, 279–296. University of Chicago Press.
Gusterson, Hugh. 2016. *Drone: Remote Control Warfare*. MIT Press.
Gutmann, Matthew, and Catherine Lutz. 2010. *Breaking Ranks: Iraq Veterans Speak Out against the War*. University of California Press.
Gutmann, Matthew. 1997. "Trafficking in Men: The Anthropology of Masculinity." *Annual Review of Anthropology* 26:385–409.
Gutmann, Stephanie. 2000. *The Kinder, Gentler Military: How Political Correctness Affects our Ability to Win Wars*. Encounter Books.
Halbe, Dorothea. 2011. "Language in the Military Workplace—between Hierarchy and Politeness." *Text & Talk—an Interdisciplinary Journal of Language, Discourse & Communication Studies* 31:315–334.
Haldén, Peter, and Peter Jackson, eds. 2016. *Transforming Warriors: The Ritual Organization of Military Force*. Routledge.
Hall, Kira, and Mary Bucholtz, eds. 1995. *Gender Articulated: Language and the Socially Constructed Self*. Routledge.
Hall, Kira, and Mary Bucholtz. 2016. "Embodied Sociolinguistics." In *Sociolinguistics: Theoretical Debates*, edited by Nikolas Coupland, 173–198. Cambridge University Press.
Han, Clara. 2004. "The Work of Indebtedness: The Traumatic Present in Late Capitalist Chile." *Culture, Medicine, and Psychiatry* 28(2):169–187.
Handman, Courtney. 2017. "Walking Like a Christian: Roads, Translation, and Gendered Bodies as Religious Infrastructure in Papua New Guinea." *American Ethnologist* 44(2): 315–327.
Haque, Omar Sultan, and Adam Waytz. 2012. "Dehumanization in Medicine: Causes, Solutions, and Functions." *Perspectives in Psychological Sciences* 7(2): 176–186.
Harding, Susan. 1991. "Representing Fundamentalism: The Problem of the Repugnant Cultural Other." *Social Research* 58(2): 373–393.
Harkins, Gina. 2015. "11 Secrets Marine Drill Instructors Hide at Boot Camp." *Marine Corps Times*, October 29, 2015. https://www.marinecorpstimes.com/news/your-marine-corps/2015/10/29/11-secrets-marine-drill-instructors-hide-at-boot-camp/.

Harkness, Nick. 2013. *Songs of Seoul: An Ethnography of Voice and Voicing in Christian South Korea.* University of California Press.

Harris, Lasana T. 2017. *Invisible Mind: Flexible Social Cognition and Dehumanization.* MIT Press.

Harrison, Simon. 1993. *The Mask of War: Violence, Ritual, and the Self in Melanesia.* Manchester University Press.

Harrison, Simon. 2012. *Dark Trophies: Hunting and the Enemy Body in Modern War.* Berghan Books.

Hartig, Luke. 2017. "Trump's New Drone Strike Policy: What's Any Different? Why It Matters." *Just Security,* September 22, 2017. https://www.justsecurity.org/45227/trumps-drone-strike-policy-different-matters/.

Haslam, Nick, and Steve Loughnan. 2014. "Dehumanization and Infrahumanization." *Annual Review of Psychology* 65:399–423.

Hedger, Joseph A. 2013. "Meaning and Racial Slurs: Derogatory Epithets and the Semantics/Pragmatics Interface." *Language and Communication* 33:205–213.

Hegseth, Pete. 2024. *The War on Warriors: Behind the Betrayal of the Men Who Keep Us Free.* Harper Collins.

Heimes, Silke. 2011. "State of Poetry Therapy Research (Review)." *The Arts in Psychotherapy* 38:1–8.

Helmus, Todd C., Ryan Andrew Brown, and Rajeev Ramchand. 2023. *Prevalence of Veteran Support for Extremist Groups and Extremist Beliefs: Results from a Nationally Representative Survey of the U.S. Veteran Community.* RAND Corporation, RR-A1071-2-v2. https://www.rand.org/content/dam/rand/pubs/research_reports/RRA1000/RRA1071-2-v2/RAND_RRA1071-3.pdf.

Herbert, Bob. 2005. "From 'Gook' to 'Raghead.'" *The New York Times,* May 2, 2005. https://www.nytimes.com/2005/05/02/opinion/from-gook-to-raghead.html.

Hicks Kennard, Catherine. 2000. "Redefining Femininity: Female Drill Instructors in the United States Marine Corps." *Texas Linguistic Forum* 43:87–98.

Hicks Kennard, Catherine. 2006. *Gender and Command: A Sociophonetic Analysis of Female and Male Drill Instructors in the United States Marine Corps.* PhD diss., University of Arizona.

Hill, Jane H. 2008. *The Everyday Language of White Racism.* Wiley-Blackwell.

Hill, Jane H., and Bruce Mannheim. 1992. "Language and World View." *Annual Review of Anthropology* 21:381–406.

Hinojosa, Ramon. 2010. "Doing Hegemony: Military, Men, and Constructing a Hegemonic Masculinity." *The Journal of Men's Studies* 18(2): 179–194.

Hinton, Alexander Laban, ed. 2002. *Genocide: An Anthropological Reader.* Blackwell.

Hinton, Alexander Laban, and Robert Jay Lifton. 2004. *Why Did They Kill? Cambodia in the Shadow of Genocide.* University of California Press.

Hockey, John. 2002. "'Head down, Bergen on, Mind in Neutral': The Infantry Body." *Journal of Political and Military Sociology* 30(1): 148–171.

Hodges, Adam. 2011. *The 'War on Terror' Narrative: Discourse and Intertextuality in the Construction and Contestation of Sociopolitical Reality.* Oxford University Press.

Hoffman, Danny. 2011. *The War Machines: Young Men and Violence in Sierra Leone and Liberia.* Duke University Press.

Hollan, Douglas, and C. Jason Throop. 2008. "Whatever Happened to Empathy? Introduction." *Ethos* 36(4): 385–401.

Holmes, Richard. 1989. *Acts of War: The Behavior of Men in Battle.* Free Press.

Hom, Christopher. 2008. "The Semantics of Racial Epithets." *The Journal of Philosophy* 105(8): 416–440.

Hood, Preston. 2007. *A Chill I Understand: Poems.* Summer Home Press.

Horton, Alex. 2019. "The Marines Don't Want You to See What Happens When Propaganda Stops and Combat Begins." *Washington Post*, March 15, 2019. https://www.washingtonpost.com/arts-entertainment/2019/03/14/marines-dont-want-you-see-what-happens-when-propaganda-stops-combat-begins/.

Hoschchild, Arlie. 1983. *The Managed Heart: Commercialization of Human Feeling*. University of California Press.

Hosein, Shareda. 2019. "Muslims in the U.S. Military: Moral Injury and Eroding Rights." *Pastoral Psychology* 68:77–92.

Hoylman, Loana. 2017. "Selective Service: Funnelling the Poor and Working Class into Combat." *The VVA Veteran*, March–April 2017. http://vvaveteran.org/37-2/37-2_selectiveservice.html.

Husserl, Edmund. 1931. *Ideas: General Introduction to Pure Phenomenology*. Collier.

Iraq Veterans Against the War (IVAW) and Aaron Glantz. 2008. *Winter Soldier Iraq and Afghanistan: Eyewitness Accounts of the Occupations*. Haymarket Books.

Irvine, Judith T, and Susan Gal. 2000. "Language Ideology and Linguistic Differentiation." In *Regimes of Language: Ideologies, Polities, and Identities*, edited by Paul V. Kroskrity, 35–83. School of American Research Press.

Jackson, Peter. 2018. *They Shall Not Grow Old*. Wingnut Films and House Productions.

Jakobson, Roman. 1960. "Closing Statement: Linguistics and Poetics." In *Style in Language*, edited by T. Sebeok, 350–377. MIT Press.

Jaffe, Alexandra, ed. 2009. *Stance: Sociolinguistic Perspectives*. Oxford University Press.

Jing-Schmidt, Zhuo. 2022. "Euphemism." In *Handbook of Pragmatics*, edited by Jan Ola Ostman and Jef Verschueren, 124–144. John Benjamins.

Jones, Brian Adam. 2021 "Here Are the Funniest Military Punishments You Shared with Us." *Task and Purpose*, April 1, 2021. https://taskandpurpose.com/news/veterans-funniest-military-punishments/.

Jones, Deborah. 2021. "The 'Fascist' and the 'Potato Beetle': Patriotic Chronotopes and Dehumanizing Language in Wartime Ukraine." *American Ethnologist* 50(1): 30–42.

Junger, Sebastian. 2016. *Tribe: On Homecoming and Belonging*. Twelve.

Jusionyte, Ieva. 2015. "States of Camouflage." *Cultural Anthropology* 30(1): 113–138.

Kapadia, Ronak K. 2019. *Insurgent Aesthetics: Security and the Queer Life of the Forever War*. Duke University Press.

Kavanaugh, Christopher. 2017. "How and Why Hazing Evolved." *Sapiens*, June 15, 2017. https://www.sapiens.org/culture/why-hazing-evolved/.

Kay, Paul, and Willett Kempton. 1984. "What Is the Sapir-Whorf Hypothesis?" *American Anthropologist* 86(1): 65–79.

Keller, Kirsten M., Miriam Matthews, Kimberly Curry Hall, William Marcellino, Jacqueline A. Mauro, and Nelson Lim. 2015. *Hazing in the U.S. Armed Forces: Recommendations for Hazing Prevention Policy and Practice*. Santa Monica, CA: RAND Corporation. https://www.rand.org/pubs/research_reports/RR941.html.

Khalili, Laleh. 2012. *Time in the Shadows: Confinement in Counterinsurgencies*. Stanford University Press.

Kiesling, Scott F. 1997. "Power and the Language of Men." In *Language and Masculinity*, edited by Sally Johnson and Ulrike Hanna Meinhof, 65–85. Blackwell.

Kiesling, Scott F. 2001. "'Now I Gotta Watch What I Say': Shifting Constructions of Masculinity in Discourse." *Journal of Linguistic Anthropology* 11(2): 1–24.

Kiesling, Scott F. 2018. "Masculine Stances and the Linguistics of Affect: On Masculine Ease." *NORMA: International Journal for Masculinity Studies* 13(3-4): 191–212.

Kiesling, Scott F. 2022. "Stance and Stancetaking." *Annual Review of Linguistics* 8:409–426.

King, Anthony. 2006. "The Word of Command: Communication and Cohesion in the Military." *Armed Forces & Society* 32:493–512.

Klemperer, Victor. 2013. *The Language of the Third Reich*. Bloomsbury Academic.

Kockelman, Paul. 2007. "Inalienable Possession and Personhood in a Q'eqchi'-Mayan Community." *Language in Society* 36(3): 343–369.

Kohn, Richard H. 2009. "The Danger of Militarization in an Endless 'War' on Terrorism." *Journal of Military History* 73(1): 177–208.

Kramer, Elise. 2011. "The Playful is Political: The Metapragmatics of Internet Rape Joke Arguments." *Language in Society* 40(2): 137–168.

Lagoze, Jacob Miles. 2018. *Combat Obscura*. Oscilloscope Laboratories.

Lagoze, Jacob Miles. 2023. *Whistles from the Graveyard: My Time behind the Camera on War, Rage, and Restless Youth in Afghanistan*. One Signal Publishers; Atria.

Lakoff, George. 1987. *Women, Fire, and Dangerous Things*. University of Chicago.

Lakoff, George. 1996. *Moral Politics: How Liberals and Conservatives Think*. University of Chicago Press.

Lambek, Michael. 2003. "Introduction: Irony and Illness—Recognition and Refusal." *Social Analysis: The International Journal of Social and Cultural Practice* 47(2): 1–19.

Larkin, Brian. 2013. "The Politics and Poetics of Infrastructure." *Annual Review of Anthropology* 42:327–343.

Lawson, Robert. 2020. "Language and Masculinities: History, Development, and Future." *Annual Review of Linguistics* 6:409–434.

Leedy, Jack. 1969. *Poetry Therapy: The Use of Poetry in the Treatment of Emotional Disorders*. University of Michigan Press.

Lentjes, Rebecca. 2018. "Sounds of Life: Fetal Heartbeat Bills and the Sounds of Animacy." *Sounding Out!* July 9, 2018. https://soundstudiesblog.com/2018/07/09/sounds-of-life-fetal-heartbeat-bills-and-the-politics-of-animacy/.

Lentjes, Rebecca, Amy E. Alterman, and Whitney Arey. 2020. "'The Ripping Apart of Silence': Sonic Patriarchy and Anti-Abortion Harassment." *Resonance: The Journal of Sound and Culture* 1(4): 422–442.

Lévi-Strauss, Claude. 1963. "The Effectiveness of Symbols." In *Structural Anthropology*, translated by Claire Jacobson, 186–205. Basic.

Levinas, Emmanuel. 1998. *Entre Nous: On Thinking-of-the-Other*. Translated by Michael B. Smith and Barbara Harshav. Columbia University Press.

Levinson, Nan. 2014. *War Is Not a Game: The New Antiwar Soldiers and the Movement They Built*. Rutgers University Press.

Levy, Elinor. 2012. "Upper Echelons and Boots on the Ground: The Case for Diglossia in the Military." In *Warrior Ways: Explorations in Modern Military Folklore*, edited by Eric A. Eliason and Tad Tuleja, 99–115. University Press of Colorado.

Levy, Marc. 2016. *Dreams, Vietnam*. Winter Street Press.

Levy, Marc. 2020. *The Best of Medic in the Green Time: Writings from the Vietnam War and Its Aftermath*. Winter Street Press.

Lifton, Robert J. 1989 [1961]. *Thought Reform and the Psychology of Totalism: A Study of "Brainwashing" in China*. University of North Carolina Press.

Lifton, Robert Jay. 1991. *Death in Life: Survivors of Hiroshima*. University of North Carolina Press.

Litz, Brett T., Nathan Stein, Eileen Delaney, Leslie Lebowitz, William P. Nash, Caroline Silva, and Shira Maguen. 2009. "Moral Injury and Moral Repair in War Veterans: A Preliminary Model and Intervention Strategy." *Clinical Psychology Review* 29:695–706.

Livingstone Smith, David. 2011. *Less Than Human: Why We Demean, Enslave, and Exterminate Others*. St. Martin's Press.

Livingstone Smith, David. 2021. *Making Monsters: The Uncanny Power of Dehumanization*. Harvard University Press.

Liu, E. 2005. "Command Presence: What a Marine Drill Instructor Taught Me about Leadership." *Slate*, January 20, 2005. https://slate.com/news-and-politics/2005/01/what-a-marine-drill-instructor-taught-me.html.
Loewenson, Irene. 2023. "Hazing Reports in the Marine Corps Have Dropped Significantly." *Marine Corps Times*, May 12, 2023. https://tinyurl.com/ycymp3tm.
Lowen, Jessica, and Daniel P. McDonald. 2023. "Race and Ethnic Diversity in the United States Armed Forces: A Continued Evolution toward an Inclusive and Lethal Force." In *Military Diversity in Multinational Defence Environments: From Ethnic Intolerance to Inclusion, Final report of Research Task Group HFM-301*, edited by Barbara T. Waruszynski, Yantsislav Yanakiev, Mathias De Roeck, Delphine Resteigne, Jessica Lowen, Daniel McDonald, and Sven Hertel. https://cradpdf.drdc-rddc.gc.ca/PDFS/unc429/p816740_A1b.pdf.
Luciano, Michael. 2021. "Fox News Guest Goes on Sexist Diatribe." *Mediaite*. December 17, 2021. https://www.mediaite.com/opinion/jesse-kelly-mocks-women-in-the-military/.
Lucy, John. 2012. *Language Diversity and Thought: A Reformulation of the Linguistic Relativity Hypothesis*. Cambridge University Press.
Luft, Aliza. 2015. "Toward a Dynamic Theory of Action at the Micro-Level of Genocide: Killing, Desistance, and Saving in 1994 Rwanda." *Sociological Theory* 33(2): 148–172.
Luft, Aliza. 2019. "Dehumanization and the Normalization of Violence: It's Not What You Think." https://items.ssrc.org/insights/dehumanization-and-the-normalization-of-violence-its-not-what-you-think/.
Luhrmann, Tanya M. 2018. "The Real Ontological Challenge." *HAU: The Journal of Ethnographic Theory* 8(1–2): 79–82.
Lutz, Catherine. 2001. *Homefront: A Military City and the American Twentieth Century*. Beacon Press.
Lutz, Catherine. 2002. "The Wars Less Known." *The South Atlantic Quarterly* 101(2): 285–296.
Lutz, Catherine. 2020. "Militarization." *International Encyclopedia of Anthropology*, edited by Hillary Callan. Wiley-Blackwell. https://doi.org/10.1002/9781118924396.wbiea1304.
Lutz, Catherine, and Kathleen Millar. 2012. "War." In *A Companion to Moral Anthropology*, edited by Didier Fassin, 482–499. Blackwell.
Lutz, William. 1990. "The World of Doublespeak." In *State of the Language*, edited by Christopher Ricks and Leonard Michaels, 350–356. University of California Press.
Lutz, William. 1992. "The First Casualty." *English Today* 8(1): 48–49.
MacLeish, Kenneth T. 2013. *Making War at Fort Hood: Life and Uncertainty in a Military Community*. Princeton University Press.
MacLeish, Kenneth. 2015. "The Ethnography of Good Machines." *Critical Military Studies* 1(1): 11–22.
MacLeish, Kenneth. 2019. "How to Feel about War: On Soldier Psyches, Military Biopolitics, and American Empire." *Biosocieties* 14:274–299.
MacLeish, Kenneth. 2022. "Moral Injury and the Psyche of Counterinsurgency." *Theory, Culture, & Society* 39(6): 63–86.
Malinowski, Bronislaw. 1923. "The Problem of Meaning in Primitive Languages." In *The Meaning of Meaning*, edited by Charles K. Ogden and Ian A. Richards, 296–336. Kegan Paul; Trench and Trubner.
Mannheim, Bruce. 2015. "The Social Imaginary, Unspoken in Verbal Art." In *The Routledge Handbook of Linguistic Anthropology*, edited by Nancy Bonvillain, 44–61. Routledge.
Mararac, N. M. 2023. "Queering the Military: How Ideologies about Gender and Sexuality Shape(d) the U.S. Armed Forces." Virtual webinar series, Talking Politics 2023: Silences and Voices in Global Media, University of Chicago, April 21, 2023. https://nickmararac.com/talkingpolitics2023-queering-the-military/.

Marcellino, William M. 2014. "Talk Like a Marine: USMC Linguistic Acculturation and Civil–Military Argument." *Discourse Studies* 16(3): 385–405.

Maringira, Godfrey. 2021. "Soldiers, Masculinities, and Violence: War and Politics." *Current Anthropology* 62(S23): S103–S111.

Marlantes, Karl. 2011. *What It Is Like to Go to War*. Grove Atlantic.

Marshall, S. L. A. 2000 [1947]. *Men against Fire: The Problem of Battle Command*. University of Oklahoma Press.

Martin, Hugh. 2013. *The Stick Soldiers*. BOA Editions.

Martin, Phillip. 2008. "Why So Many Iraqis Hate Us? Try 'Towel Head' on for Size." *HuffPost*, April 11, 2008. https://www.huffpost.com/entry/why-so-many-iraqis-hate-u_b_96330.

Mascaro, Lisa, and Kevin Freking, 2023. "House Republicans Push Through Defense Bill Limiting Abortion Access and Halting Diversity Efforts." *AP News*, July 14, 2023. https://apnews.com/article/defense-house-ukraine-mccarthy-abortion-diversity-50a7b843afa02fa7aa85819b074244c5.

Masco, Joseph. 2014. *The Theater of Operations: National Security Affect from the Cold War to the War on Terror*. Duke University Press.

Mauss, Marcel. 1972 [1950]. *A General Theory of Magic*. Translated by R. Brain. Routledge.

Mbembe, Achille. 2003. "Necropolitics." *Public Culture* 15(1): 11–40.

Mbembe, Achille. 2019. *Necropolitics*. Duke University Press.

McCoy, Alfred W. 1995. "'Same Banana': Hazing and Honor at the Philippine Military Academy." *The Journal of Asian Studies* 54(3): 689–726.

McCreaddie, M., and S. Wiggins. 2009. "Reconciling the Good Patient Persona with Problematic and Non-Problematic Humour: A Grounded Theory." *International Journal of Nursing Studies* 46(8): 1079–1091.

McElhinny, Bonnie. 1995. "Challenging Hegemonic Masculinities: Female and Male Police Officers Handling Domestic Violence." In *Gender Articulated*, edited by K. Hall and M. Bucholtz, 217–244. Routledge.

McFate, Montgomery, and Janice H. Laurence, eds. 2015. *Social Science Goes to War: The Human Terrain System in Iraq and Afghanistan*. Oxford University Press.

McGraw, A. Peter, and Caleb Warren. 2010. "Benign Violations: Making Immoral Behavior Funny." *Psychological Science* 21(8): 1141–1149.

McGraw, Peter A., Lawrence E. Williams, and Caleb Warren. 2014. "The Rise and Fall of Humor: Psychological Distance Modulates Humorous Responses to Tragedy." *Social Psychological and Personality Science* 5:566–572.

McIntosh, Janet. 1998. "Symbolism, Cognition, and Political Orders." *Science and Society* 62(4): 557–568.

McIntosh, Janet. 2009. "Stance and Distance: Social Boundaries, Self-Lamination, and Metalinguistic Anxiety in White Kenyan Narratives about the African Occult." In *Stance: Sociolinguistic Perspectives*, edited by Alexandra Jaffe, 72–91. Oxford University Press.

McIntosh, Janet. 2016. *Unsettled: Denial and Belonging among White Kenyans*. University of California Press.

McIntosh, Janet. 2018a. "Listening vs. Lingwashing: Promise, Peril, and Structural Oblivion when White South Africans Learn Indigenous African Languages." *Signs and Society* 6(3): 475–503.

McIntosh, Janet. 2018b. "Essentialism." In *The International Encyclopedia of Anthropology*, edited by Hilary Callan. John Wiley. https://doi.org/10.1002/9781118924396.wbiea1800.

McIntosh, Janet. 2018c. "Personhood, Self, and Individual." In *The International Encyclopedia of Anthropology*, edited by Hilary Callan. John Wiley. https://doi.org/10.1002/9781118924396.wbiea1576.

McIntosh, Janet. 2020a. "Introduction: A Linguistic Emergency." In *Language in the Trump Era: Scandals and Emergencies*, edited by Janet McIntosh and Norma Mendoza-Denton, 1–44. Cambridge University Press.
McIntosh, Janet. 2020b. "Crybabies and Snowflakes." In *Language in the Trump Era: Scandals and Emergencies*, edited by Janet McIntosh and Norma Mendoza-Denton, 71–88. Cambridge University Press.
McIntosh, Janet. 2020c. "Introduction: The Mud in Those Letters." In *The Best of Medic in the Green Time: Writings from the Vietnam War and its Aftermath*, by Marc Levy, ix–xxv. Winter Street Press.
McIntosh, Janet. 2020d. "Maledictive Language: Obscenity and Taboo Words." *The International Encyclopedia of Linguistic Anthropology*, edited by James M. Stanlaw. John Wiley. https://doi.org/10.1002/9781118786093.iela0248.
McIntosh, Janet. 2021a. "Language and the Military: Necropolitical Legitimation, Embodied Semiotics, and Ineffable Suffering." *Annual Review of Anthropology* 50:241–258.
McIntosh, Janet. 2021b. "'Because It's Easier to Kill That Way': Dehumanizing Epithets, Militarized Subjectivity, and American Necropolitics." *Language in Society* 50: 583–603.
McIntosh, Janet. 2022. "The Sinister Signs of QAnon: Interpretive Agency and Paranoid Truths in Alt-Right Oracles." *Anthropology Today* 38(1): 8–12.
McIntosh, Janet, and Norma Mendoza-Denton, eds. 2020. *Language in the Trump Era: Scandals and Emergencies*. Cambridge University Press.
McSorley, Kevin. 2013. "Rethinking War and the Body." In *War and the Body: Militarisation, Practice and Experience*, edited by Kevin McSorley, 233–244. Routledge.
McWhorter, John. 2014. *The Language Hoax: Why the World Looks the Same in Any Language*. Oxford University Press.
Milburn, Andrew. 2019. "When You're in Command, Your Job Is to Know Better." *The Atlantic*, May 25, 2019. https://www.theatlantic.com/ideas/archive/2019/05/trumps-war-crime-pardons-sully-memorial-day/590302/.
Mockenhaupt, Brian. 2007. "The Army We Have." *The Atlantic*, June 2007. https://www.theatlantic.com/magazine/archive/2007/06/the-army-we-have/305902/.
Mohammed, Affraz. 2019. "A Muslim Marine's Trauma: I Was Set Up, Arrested and Acquitted." *The New York Times Magazine*, September 4, 2019. https://tinyurl.com/mr48ajxd.
Mohr, Sebastien, Birgitte Refslund Sørensen, and Matti Weisdorf. 2021. "The Ethnography of Things Military—Empathy and Critique in Military Anthropology." *Ethnos* 86(4): 600–615.
Molendijk, Tine. 2023. "Moral Coping or Simply Uncomplicated Soldiering? How Soldiers Avoid Moral Injury through Simplification, Justification, Rationalization, and Compartmentalization." *Armed Forces and Society*, April 2023. https://doi.org/10.1177/0095327X231165910.
Moon, Seungsook. 2005. "Trouble with Conscription: Entertaining Soldiers, Popular Culture, and the Politics of Militarized Masculinity in South Korea." *Men and Masculinities* 8(1): 64–92.
Moon, Zachary. 2019. *Warriors between Worlds: Moral Injury and Identities in Crisis*. Lexington Books.
Moore, Darren. 2010. *The Soldier: A History of Courage, Sacrifice, and Brotherhood*. Icon Books.
Moyn, Samuel. 2022. *Humane: How the United States Abandoned Peace and Reinvented War*. Verso.
Muchnik, Federico. 2017. *Hunter in the Blackness: Veterans, Hope, and Recovery*. Mighty Visual Productions.

Munch-Jurisic, and Ditte Marie. 2018. "Perpetrator Disgust: A Morally Destructive Emotion." In *Emotions and Mass Atrocity: Philosophical and Theoretical Explorations*, edited by Thomas Brundholm and Johannes Lang, 142–161. Cambridge University Press.

Mundy, C. E. 1998. *30th Commandant's Statement on Core Values of the United States Marines*. Issued for Marine Corps Leadership Development, Lejeune Leadership Institute, Marine Corps University. https://www.usmcu.edu/Portals/218/LLI/MLD/Fidelity/CORE%20VALUES.pdf?ver=2018-09-26-095727-693.

Musgrave, John. 2003. *Notes to the Man Who Shot Me: Vietnam War Poems*. Coal City Press.

Musgrave, John. 2021. *The Education of John Musgrave: Vietnam and its Aftermath*. Alfred A. Knopf.

Myers, Donald J. 2014. *Pride and Discipline: The Hallmarks of a United States Marine*. Trafford.

Myers, Meghann. 2022. "Is the Military Too 'Woke' to Recruit?" *Military Times*, October 13, 2022. https://www.militarytimes.com/news/your-military/2022/10/13/is-the-military-too-woke-to-recruit/.

Nader, Laura. 1972. "Up the Anthropologist: Perspectives Gained from Studying Up." In *Reinventing Anthropology*, edited by Dell Hymes, 284–311. Vintage Books.

Nesson, Sara. 2010. *Iraq, Paper, Scissors*. Portrayal Films.

Nindl, Bradley C. et al. 2022. *USMC Gender-Integrated Recruit Training Study, Contract Number: M95494-20-C-0021; Final Report Prepared for the United States Marine Corps.* https://www.hqmc.marines.mil/Portals/61/Docs/FOIA/Reading-Room/Final_Report-University_of_Pittsburgh_Academic_Study_on_Gender-Integrated_Recruit_Training.pdf.

Nguyen, Thanh T., and Bruce Weigl. 1994. *Poems from Captured Documents*. University of Massachusetts Press.

Nolan, Hamilton. 2013. "Don't Ask, Don't Tell, Faggot: Inside Marine Corps Boot Camp." *Gawker*, May 21, 2013. https://www.gawkerarchives.com/dont-ask-dont-tell-faggot-inside-marine-corps-boot-509032688.

Novelly, Thomas. 2020. "Every Army Drill Sergeant Is Trained at Fort Jackson: Women Are Shaping the Role's Future." *Post and Courier*, August 20, 2020. https://www.postandcourier.com/news/every-army-drill-sergeant-is-trained-at-fort-jackson-women-are-shaping-the-roles-future/article_f5a5f69e-1050-11ea-b27e-1b6fd02be548.html.

Obrdlik, Antonin J. 1942. "Gallows Humor—a Sociological Phenomenon." *American Journal of Sociology* 47(5): 709–716.

Ochs, Elinor. 2012. "Experiencing Language." *Anthropological Theory* 12(2):142–160.

Ochs, Elinor, and Bambi B. Schieffelin. 1984. "Language Acquisition and Socialization: Three Developmental Stories and Their Implications." In *Culture Theory: Essays on Mind, Self, and Emotion*, edited by Richard A. Shweder and Robert A. Levine, 276–320. Cambridge University Press.

O'Connell, Aaron B. 2012. *Underdogs: The Making of the Modern Marine Corps*. Harvard University Press.

Oring, Elliott. 1992. *Jokes and their Relations*. Lexington: University Press of Kentucky.

Over, Harriet. 2021. "Falsifying the Dehumanization Hypothesis." *Perspectives on Psychological Science*. 16(1): 33–38.

Parish, Steven M. 2014. "Between Persons: How Concepts of the Person Make Moral Experience Possible." *Ethos* 42(1): 31–50.

Park, Jinim. 2007. *Narratives of the Vietnam War by Korean and American Writers*. Peter Lang.

Parks, Gregory S., and Jasmine Burgess. 2019. "Hazing in the United States Military: A Psychology and Law Perspective." *Southern California Interdisciplinary Law Journal* 29(1): 1–63.

"PBS Documentary Takes a Long, Deep Plunge into the Open Wound of the Vietnam War." 2017. *Dallas News.* https://www.dallasnews.com/arts-entertainment/architecture/2017/09/14/pbs-documentary-takes-a-long-deep-plunge-into-the-open-wound-of-the-vietnam-war/.

Peirce, Charles Sanders. 1998. *The Essential Peirce: Selected Philosophical Writings.* Vol. 2, *1893–1913.* Indiana University Press.

Petersen, Glenn. 2021. *War and the Arc of Human Experience.* Hamilton/Rowman & Littlefield.

Phillips, Dave. 2019. "Trump Clears Three Service Members in War Crimes Cases." *The New York Times,* November 15, 2019. https://www.nytimes.com/2019/11/15/us/trump-pardons.html.

Phillips, Joshua E. S. 2015. "The Devastating Story behind one Image of Detainee Abuse." *Reveal,* February 14, 2015. https://revealnews.org/article/the-devastating-story-behind-one-image-of-detainee-abuse/.

Pieslak, Jonathan. 2009. *Sound Targets: American Soldiers and Music in the Iraq War.* Indiana University Press.

Pillen, Alex. 2015. "Atrocity and Non-Sense: The Ethnographic Study of Dehumanization." In *Genocide and Mass Violence: Memory, Symptom, and Recovery,* edited by Devon E. Hinton and Alexander L. Hinton, 342–358. Cambridge University Press.

Pillen, Alex. 2016. "Language, Translation, Trauma." *Annual Review of Anthropology* 45:95–111.

Pillen, Alex. 2017. "A Space That Will Never Be Filled: Sharp Communication and the Simultaneity of Opposites." *Current Anthropology* 58(6): 718–738.

Pinker, Steven. 1994. *The Language Instinct: How the Mind Creates Language.* William Morrow.

Pompeo, Michael R. 2022. "America's Military and Our Country Won't Survive if Wokeism Continues to Rule." *Fox News,* September 28, 2022. https://www.foxnews.com/opinion/america-military-our-country-wont-survive-if-wokeism-continues-rule.

Potter, Terrence M. 2007. "USMA Nicknames: Naming by the Rules." *Names: A Journal of Onomastics* 55:445–454.

Press, Eyal. 2018. "The Wounds of the Drone Warrior." *The New York Times Magazine,* June 13, 2018. https://www.nytimes.com/2018/06/13/magazine/veterans-ptsd-drone-warrior-wounds.html.

Price, David. 2011. *Weaponizing Anthropology: Social Science in Service of the Militarized State.* AK Press.

Price, William. 2012. *Devil Dog Diary: A Day-by-Day Account of US Marine Corps Basic Training.* CreateSpace.

Prince Harry, Duke of Sussex. 2023. *Spare.* Random House.

Puar, Jasbir, and Amit S. Rai. 2002. "Monster, Terrorist, Fag: The War on Terrorism and the Production of Docile Patriots." *Social Text* 20(3): 117–148.

Puar, Jasbir. 2006. "Mapping US Heteronormativities." *Gender, Place, and Culture* 13(1): 67–88.

Putnam, Hilary. 1975. "The Meaning of 'Meaning.'" *Minnesota Studies in the Philosophy of Science* 7:131–193.

Rakel, David. 2018. *The Compassionate Connection: The Healing Power of Empathy and Mindful Listening.* W. W. Norton.

Rappaport, Julia. 2008. "War in Pieces: Combat Paper Project Sees Veterans Use Uniforms to Heal." *Vineyard Gazette,* July 24, 2008. https://vineyardgazette.com/news/2008/07/25/war-pieces-combat-paper-project-sees-veterans-use-uniforms-heal.

Raskin, Victor. 1979. "Semantic Mechanisms of Humor." *Proceedings of the Fifth Annual Meeting of the Berkeley Linguistics Society*, 325–335. https://journals.linguisticsociety.org/proceedings/index.php/BLS/article/view/2164/1934.

Reickhoff, Paul. 2006. *Chasing Ghosts: A Soldier's Fight for America from Baghdad to Washington*. NAL Hardcover.

Reinberg, Linda. 1991. *In the Field: The Language of the Vietnam War*. Facts on File.

Reinsch, Michael. 2021. "People First Task Force Building More Cohesive Teams." *JBSA News*, December 21, 2021. https://www.jbsa.mil/News/News/Article/2877692/people-first-task-force-building-more-cohesive-teams/.

Reiss, Helen. 2018. *The Empathy Effect: Seven Neuroscience-Based Keys for Transforming the Way We Live, Love, Work, and Connect Across Differences*. Sounds True.

Reiter, Sherry and Contributors. 2009. *Writing away the Demons: Stories of Creative Coping through Transformative Writing*. North Star Press of St. Cloud.

Reitman, Janet. 2017. "How the Death of a Muslim Recruit Revealed a Culture of Brutality in the Marines." *The New York Times*, July 6, 2017.

Remarque, Erich Maria. 1996 [1929]. *All Quiet on the Western Front*. Random House.

Ress, Dave. 2022. "Across the Military, Basic Training is Changing with a Focus on Mentorship, Not Yelling." *Stars and Stripes*, June 4, 2022. https://www.stripes.com/branches/army/2022-06-04/military-basic-training-focus-mentorship-not-yelling-6233225.html.

Richards, Bill. 1979. "My Lai Participant Tries to Forget." *The Washington Post*, November 13, 1979. https://www.washingtonpost.com/archive/politics/1979/11/13/my-lai-participant-tries-to-forget/951e54e7-db8c-4d55-901b-7db63345e08a/.

Ricks, Thomas E. 1997. *Making the Corps*. Simon and Schuster.

Ricks, Thomas E. 2006. *Fiasco: The American Military Adventure in Iraq*. Penguin.

Ricks, Thomas E. 2015. "U.S. Military Cultural Awareness." *Foreign Policy*, April 30, 2015. https://foreignpolicy.com/2015/04/30/u-s-military-cultural-awareness-i-was-a-pro-saddam-protestor-was-called-a-camel-jockey-but-i-am-an-american-soldier/.

Robbins, Joel. 2013. "Beyond the Suffering Subject: Toward an Anthropology of the Good." *Journal of the Royal Anthropological Institute* 19(3): 447–462.

Rosaldo, Renato. 1993. *Culture and Truth: The Remaking of Social Analysis*. Beacon Press.

Rosaldo, Renato. 2000. "Of Headhunters and Soldiers." *Issues in Ethics* 11(1). https://www.scu.edu/ethics/ethics-resources/ethical-decision-making/of-headhunters-and-soldiers/.

Rottmann, Larry. 1993. *Voices from the Ho Chi Minh Trail: Poetry of America and Vietnam 1965–1993*. Event Horizon Press.

Rottmann, Larry, Jan Berry, and Basil T. Paquet, eds. 1972. *Winning Hearts & Minds: War Poems by Vietnam Veterans*. McGraw-Hill.

Rouse, Carolyn M. 2021. "Necropolitics versus Biopolitics: Spatialization, White Privilege, and Visibility during a Pandemic." *Cultural Anthropology* 36(3): 360–307.

Rukeyser, Muriel. 1996. *The Life of Poetry*. Wesleyan University Press.

Saber, Anthony. 2018. "Lexicogenic Matrices and Institutional Roles of U.S. Military Jargon." *Lexis: Journal in English Lexicology* 11. http://journals.openedition.org/lexis/1179.

Sagalyn, Dan. 2016. "The Chaos and Fog of the First Night of Marine Corps Boot Camp." *PBS News*, December 8, 2016. https://www.pbs.org/newshour/nation/chaos-fog-first-night-marine-corps-boot-camp.

Sallah, Michael, and Mitch Weiss. 2005. *Tiger Force: A True Story of Men and War*. Little, Brown.

Samet, Elizabeth. 2021. *Looking for the Good War: American Amnesia and the Violent Pursuit of Happiness*. Farrar, Straus and Giroux.

Sanchez, Marcy. 2011. "Diversity Training for a Diverse Corps." *Defense Visual Information Distribution Service*, March 18, 2011. https://www.dvidshub.net/news/67330/diversity-training-diverse-corps.

Sandhoff, Michelle. 2017. *Service in a Time of Suspicion: Experiences of Muslims Serving in the U.S. Military Post-9/11*. University of Iowa Press.

Sapir, Edward. 1929. "The Status of Linguistics as a Science." *Language* 5:207–214. Reprinted in *The Selected Writings of Edward Sapir in Language, Culture, and Personality*, edited by D. G. Mandelbaum, 160–166. University of California Press.

Saunders, Nicholas. 2000. "Bodies of Metal, Shells of Memory: 'Trench Art' and the Great War, Recycled." *Journal of Material Culture* 5(1): 43–67.

Scarry, Elaine. 1988. *The Body in Pain: The Making and Unmaking of the World*. Oxford University Press.

Schaefer, Donovan O. 2020. "Whiteness and Civilization: Shame, Race, and the Rhetoric of Donald Trump." *Communication and Critical/Cultural Studies* 17(1): 1–18.

Schaefer, Donovan O. 2021. "How Do Words Work?" *The Religious Studies Project*. https://www.religiousstudiesproject.com/response/how-do-words-work/.

Schaeffer, Katherine. 2023. "The Changing Face of America's Veteran Population." Pew Research Center, November 8, 2023. https://www.pewresearch.org/fact-tank/2021/04/05/the-changing-face-of-americas-veteran-population/.

Schogol, Jeff. 2022. "Turns Out That Russian Recruiting Video Loved by Critics of the 'Woke' US Military Was Total BS." *Task and Purpose*, October 3, 2022 https://taskandpurpose.com/news/russian-military-recruiting-commercial-not-reality/.

Schogol, Jeff. 2023. "Army Secretary Concerned 'Woke Military' Criticism Could Hurt the Service." *Task and Purpose*, June 14, 2023. https://taskandpurpose.com/news/army-secretary-woke-military.

Schrader, Benjamin. 2019. *Fight to Live, Live to Fight: Veteran Activism after War*. SUNY Press.

Schutz, Alfred. 1970. *On Phenomenology and Social Relations*. University of Chicago Press.

Seck, Hope Hodge. 2016. "Marine Boot Camp Covered Up Recruits' Hazing-Related Medical Issues." *Military News*, September 18, 2016. https://www.military.com/daily-news/2016/09/18/marine-boot-camp-covered-up-recruits-medical-issues.html.

Seck, Hope Hodge. 2021. "Nearly 90% of Military Hazing Complaints Come from the Marine Corps, Data Shows." *Military News*, February 7, 2021. https://www.military.com/daily-news/2021/02/07/nearly-90-of-military-hazing-complaints-come-marine-corps-data-shows.html.

Seck, Hope Hodge. 2022. "Marines Still Oppose Integrated Boot Camp Platoons after $2M Study." *Marine Corps Times*, November 4, 2022. https://www.marinecorpstimes.com/news/your-marine-corps/2022/11/04/marines-still-oppose-integrated-boot-camp-platoons-after-2m-study/.

Serwer, Adam. 2021. *The Cruelty Is the Point: The Past, Present, and Future of Trump's America*. One World.

Severi, Carlo. 2015 [2007]. *The Chimera Principle: An Anthropology of Memory and Imagination*. Chicago: HAU.

Shane, Leo. 2023. "Government Shutdown Could Hinge on Fight Over 'Woke' Military Policies." *Federal Times*, August 22, 2023. https://www.federaltimes.com/news/pentagon-congress/2023/08/22/government-shutdown-could-hinge-on-fight-over-woke-military-policies/.

Shapiro, Ari. 2007. "JAGs Take a More Central Battlefield Role." *Morning Edition*, NPR, April 5, 2007. https://www.npr.org/2007/04/05/9371046/jags-take-a-more-central-battlefield-role.

Shay, Jonathan. 2010. *Achilles in Vietnam: Combat Trauma and the Undoing of Character*. Simon and Schuster.

Shay, Jonathan. 2014. "Moral Injury." *Psychoanalytic Psychology* 31(2):182-191.

Shwartz, Alexandra. 2022. "Annie Ernaux Turns Memory into Art." *The New Yorker*, November 14, 2022. https://www.newyorker.com/magazine/2022/11/21/annie-ernaux-turns-memory-into-art.

Sidnell, Jack. 2021. "Person and Self." In *The International Encyclopedia of Linguistic Anthropology*, edited by James Stanlaw. John Wiley. https://doi.org/10.1002/9781118786093.iela0308.

Silliman, Stephen W. 2008. "The Old West in the Middle East." *American Anthropologist* 110(2): 237–247.

Sitaraman, Ganesh. 2013. "Counterinsurgency, the War on Terror, and the Laws of War." *The Virginia Law Review* 95(7): 1745–1839.

Sites, Kevin. 2013. *The Things They Cannot Say: Stories Soldiers Won't Tell You about What They've Seen, Done, or Failed to Do in War*. Harper Perennial.

Sliter, Michael, Aron Kale, and Zhenyu Yuan. 2014. "Is Humor the Best Medicine? The Buffering Effect of Coping Humor on Traumatic Stressors in Firefighters." *Journal of Organizational Behavior* 35(2): 257–272.

Sløk-Andersen, Beate. 2019. "The Butt of the Joke? Laughter and Potency in the Becoming of Good Soldiers." *Cultural Analysis* 17(1): 25–56.

Smith, Larry. 2007. *The Few and the Proud: Marine Corps Drill Instructors in their Own Words*. W. W. Norton.

Snow, Nancy E. 2000. "Empathy." *American Philosophical Quarterly* 37(1): 65–78.

Snow, Shawn. 2019. "Male and Female Marine Platoons to Integrate at Recruit Training for the First Time." *Marine Corps Times*, January 4, 2019. https://www.marinecorpstimes.com/news/your-marine-corps/2019/01/04/male-and-female-marine-platoons-to-integrate-at-recruit-training-for-the-first-time/.

Sorensen, Birgitte. 2015. "Veterans Homecomings: Secrecy and Post-Deployment Social Becoming." *Current Anthropology* 56(S12): S231–S240.

Soular, James. 1994. "Poetry of Witness: Vietnam War Veteran-Poets (Challenging American Myth)." Master's thesis, University of Montana. https://scholarworks.umt.edu/etd/3240.

Spangler, Todd. 2016. "Parris Island Drill Instructors Face Scrutiny after Recruit's Death." *Detroit Free Press*, December 30, 2016. https://www.freep.com/story/news/2016/12/30/after-death-michigan-recruit-parris-island-drill-sergeants-face-scrutiny/95434678/.

Speigle, William R. II. 2013. *The Marine Corps' Warrior Ethos: Practicality for Today's Operating Environment*. US Army War College Strategy Research Project. https://apps.dtic.mil/sti/pdfs/ADA589486.pdf.

Spoehr, Thomas. 2022. "The Rise of Wokeness in the Military." The Heritage Foundation, September 30, 2022. https://www.heritage.org/defense/commentary/the-rise-wokeness-the-military.

Stasch, Rupert. 2011. "Textual Iconicity and the Primitivist Cosmos: Chronotopes of Desire in Travel Writing about Korowai of West Papua." *Journal of Linguistic Anthropology* 21(1): 1–21.

Stahl, Roger. 2009. *Militainment, Inc.: War, Media, and Popular Culture*. Routledge.

Steinhauer, Jennifer. 2020. "Veterans Fortify the Ranks of Militias Aligned with Trump's Views." *The New York Times*, September 11, 2020. https://www.nytimes.com/2020/09/11/us/politics/veterans-trump-protests-militias.html.

Sternbach, O. 1975. "Aggression, the Death Drive and the Problem of Sadomasochism: A Reinterpretation of Freud's Second Drive Theory." *The International Journal of Psychoanalysis* 56(3): 321–333.

Stephens, Richard, John Atkins, and Andrew Kingston. 2009. "Swearing as a Response to Pain." *Neuroreport* 20(12): 1056–1060.

Stone, Nomi. 2017. "Living the LaughScream: Human Technologies and Affective Maneuvers in the Iraq War." *Cultural Anthropology* 32(1): 149–174.

Stone, Nomi. 2018. "Imperial Mimesis: Enacting and Policing Empathy in US Military Training." *American Ethnologist* 45(4): 533–545.

Stone, Nomi. 2022. *Pinelandia: An Anthropology and Field Poetics of War and Empire*. University of California Press.
Suarez-Orozco, Marcelo M. 1990. "Speaking of the Unspeakable: Toward a Psychosocial Understanding of Responses to Terror." *Ethos* 18(3): 353–383.
Swart, S. 2009. "The Terrible Laughter of the Afrikaner—towards a Social History of Humor." *Journal of Social History* 42(4): 889–917.
Sykes, Gresham M., and David Matza. 1957. "Techniques of Neutralization: A Theory of Delinquency." *American Sociological Review* 22(6): 664–670.
Tal, Kali. 1991. "Speaking the Language of Pain." In *Fourteen Landing Zones: Approaches to Vietnam War Literature*, edited by Philip K. Jason, 217–250. University of Iowa Press.
Taha, Maisa C. 2017. "Shadow Subjects: A Category of Analysis for Empathic Stancetaking." *Journal of Linguistic Anthropology* 27(2): 190–209.
Tang, Irwin A. 2008. *Gook: John McCain's Racism and Why It Matters*. It Works/Paul Revere Books.
Tannen, Deborah, ed. 1993. *Framing in Discourse*. Oxford University Press.
Taussig, Michael. 1992. *The Nervous System*. Routledge.
Tellessen, Kacy. 2021. *Freaks of a Feather: A Marine Grunt's Memoir*. Latah Books.
Terry, Wallace. 1984. *Bloods: Black Veterans of the Vietnam War; an Oral History*. Random House.
Theidon, Kimberly. 2007. "Gender in Transition: Common Sense, Women and War." *Journal of Human Rights* 6(4): 453–478.
Theidon, Kimberly. 2016. "Conclusion: Reflections on the Women, Peace, and Security Agenda." In *Gender Violence in Peace and War*, edited by Victoria Sanford, Katerina Stefatos, and Cecilia M. Salvi, 184–198. De Gruyter.
Thibodeau, Paul H., and Lera Boroditsky. 2011. "Metaphors We Think With: The Role of Metaphor in Reasoning." *PLoS ONE* 6(2): e16782. https://doi.org/10.1371/journal.pone.0016782.
Thompson, Mark. 2012. "Does the Military Vote Really Lean Republican?" *Time*, November 5, 2012. https://swampland.time.com/2012/11/05/does-the-military-vote-really-lean-republican/.
Throop, Jason C. 2008. "On the Problem of Empathy: The Case of Yap, Federated States of Micronesia." *Ethos* 36(4): 402–426.
Throop, Jason C. 2012. "On the Varieties of Empathic Experience: Tactility, Mental Opacity, and Pain in Yap." *Medical Anthropology Quarterly* 26(3): 408–430.
Tick, Edward. 2005. *War and the Soul: Healing Our Nation's Veterans from Post-Traumatic Stress Disorder*. Quest Books.
Tirrell, Lynne. 2012. "Genocidal Language Games." In *Speech and Harm: Controversies over Free Speech*, edited by Ishani Maitra and Mary Kate McGowan, 174–221. Oxford University Press.
Tomforde, Maren, and Eyal Ben-Ari. 2021. "Anthropology of the Military." In *Handbook of Military Sciences*, edited by A. Sookermany, 1–15. SpringerLink.
Trudgill, Peter. 1972. "Sex, Covert Prestige and Linguistic Change in the Urban British English of Norwich." *Language in Society* 1:179–195.
Tucker, Robert E., and Theodore O. Prosise. 2003. "The Language of Atomic Science and Atomic Conflict: Exploring the Limits of Symbolic Representation." In *At War with Words*, edited by Mirjana N. Dedaic and Daniel N. Nelson, 127–148. Mouton de Gruyter.
Turley, Patrick. 2012. *Welcome to Hell: Three and a Half Months of Marine Corps Boot Camp*. Chronology.
Turner, Victor W. 1968. *The Drums of Affliction: A Study of Religious Processes among the Ndembu of Zambia*. Oxford University Press.

Turner, Victor. 1995 [1969]. *The Ritual Process: Structure and Anti-Structure.* Transaction Publishers.

Turse, Nick. 2013. *Kill Anything that Moves: The Real American War in Vietnam.* Picador.

United States Marine Corps. 1998. MCRP [Marine Corps Reference Publication] 6-11B. *Marine Corps Values: A User's Guide for Discussion Leaders.* University Press of the Pacific. https://www.fitness.marines.mil/Portals/211/Docs/FFI/MCRP%206-11B%20%20W%20CH%201%20Marine%20Corps%20Values_A%20User's%20Guide%20for%20Discussion%20Leaders.pdf.

United States Marine Corps. 2008. *Depot Order P1513.6B, "Recruit Training Order."* Document in possession of author.

United States Marine Corps. 2017. *MCO 4400.201 Acronyms.* https://www.marines.mil/Portals/1/Publications/MCO%204400.201%20Acronyms_4.6.17.pdf?ver=2017-04-11-110125-010.

United States Marine Corps. 2019. *Depot Order 1513.6G, "Recruit Training Order."* https://www.mcrdpi.marines.mil/Portals/76/DepO%201513_6G%20Recruit%20Training%20Order%20Ch%201%20%202%20%203%20Searchable_1.pdf.

United States Marine Corps. 2024. *Depot Order 1513.6H, "Recruit Training Order."* https://www.mcrdpi.marines.mil/Portals/76/Docs/DepotOrders/Current%20Depot%20Orders%20as%20of%2017%20May%202023/A.%20SSIC%201000%20-%20Military%20Personnel/DepO%201513.6H%20Recruit%20Training%20Order.pdf?ver=Q1FbE8r30ONoH_Eb6ZUeZw%3d%3d.

"United States Military Doublespeak." 2014. *The Citizen,* November 30, 2014. https://www.thecitizen.in/index.php/en/NewsDetail/index/6/1529/United-States-Military-Doublespeak.

US Department of Veterans Affairs. 2022. *2022 National Veteran Suicide Prevention Annual Report.* https://www.mentalhealth.va.gov/docs/data-sheets/2022/2022-National-Veteran-Suicide-Prevention-Annual-Report-FINAL-508.pdf.

USMC Officer. n.d. *Law of War: Introduction to Rules of Engagement B130936 Student Handout.* Accessed November 20, 2021. https://usmcofficer.com/the-basic-school/training-phases/phase-1/law-war-rules-engagement-roe/.

Valentine, Douglas. 2013. "War, Poetry, and Reconciliation: An Interview with Bruce Weigl." *Counterpunch,* October 18, 2013. https://www.counterpunch.org/2013/10/18/war-poetry-and-reconciliation/.

Valtonen, Anu, Aki-Mauri Huhtinen, and Soili Paananen. 2020. "Ethnographic Study of the Military Body's Enactment of Routines at a Training Camp." *Scandinavian Journal of Military Studies* 3(1): 132–143.

Van Buren, Peter. 2015. "War Porn: Hollywood and War, from World War II to 'American Sniper.'" *Truthout,* February 19, 2015. https://truthout.org/articles/war-porn-hollywood-and-war-from-world-war-ii-to-american-sniper/.

Van Gennep, Arnold. 2004 [1909]. *The Rites of Passage.* Routledge.

Vergakis, Brock. 2012. "Army's New Drill Sergeants Teach Rather Than Yell." *Associated Press,* July 4, 2012. https://www.kswo.com/story/18949175/armys-new-drill-sergeants-teach-rather-than-yell/.

Vergun, David. 2023. "Military Celebrates Women's History Month." *DOD News,* March 10, 2023. https://tinyurl.com/mw8sj3vp.

Verrips, Jojada. 2004. "Dehumanization as a Double-Edged Sword: From Boot Camp Animals to Killing Machines." In *Grammars of Identity/Alterity: A Structural Approach,* edited by Gerd Baumann and Andre Gingrich, 142–154. Berghahn Books.

Vitale, Alex. 2017. *The End of Policing.* Verso.

Volkman, Victor R. 2009. *More Than a Memory: Reflections of Viet Nam.* Modern History Press.

Vonnegut, Kurt. 1969. *Slaughterhouse-Five, or, The Children's Crusade*. Delacorte.
Walker, Alexander C., Martin Harry Turpin, Ethan A. Meyers, Jennifer A. Stolz, Jonathan A. Fugelsang, and Derek J. Koehler. 2021. "Controlling the Narrative: Euphemistic Language Affects Judgments of Actions While Avoiding Perceptions of Dishonesty." *Cognition* 211:104633.
Walsh, Steve. 2023. "The Marines Are Supposed to Fully Open Boot Camp to Women but Continue to Resist." *NPR*, January 2, 2023. https://tinyurl.com/bddct7wb.
Warrior Writers NJ. 2017. *Sound Off: Warrior Writers NJ*. Post Traumatic Press.
Webster, Anthony K. 2015a. "Why the World Doesn't Sound the Same in Any Language and Why That Might Matter: A Review of *The Language Hoax: Why the World Looks the Same in Any Language*." *Journal of Linguistic Anthropology*, 25(1): 87–104.
Webster, Anthony K. 2015b. "The Poetry of Sound and the Sound of Poetry: Navajo Poetry, Phonological Iconicity, and Linguistic Relativity." *Semiotica* 207:279–301.
Webster, Anthony K. 2019. "Poetry and Emotion: Poetic Communion, Ordeals of Language, Intimate Grammars, and Complex Remindings." In *Routledge Handbook of Language and Emotion*, edited by Sonia E. Pritzker, Janina Fenigsen, and James M. Wilce, 182–202. Routledge.
Weidman, Amanda. 2014. "Anthropology and Voice." *Annual Review of Anthropology* 43:37–51.
Weigl, Bruce. 1988. *Songs of Napalm: Poems*. Grove Press.
Wentling, Nikki. 2023. "Military Service Key Factor in 3 Decades of Extremist Attacks." *Military Times*, June 7, 2023. https://tinyurl.com/yc4wp42t.
Wentling, Nikki. 2024. "Troops Do Not Have an Extremism Problem, but Veterans Do, Study Finds." *Military Times*, January 5, 2024. https://tinyurl.com/4ezryn9m.
Westheider, James. 1997. *Fighting on Two Fronts: African Americans and the Vietnam War*. New York University Press.
Westheider, James. 2011. *Fighting in Vietnam: The Experiences of the US Soldier*. Stackpole Military History Series.
Whorf, Benjamin Lee. 1944. "The Relation of Habitual Thought and Behavior to Language." *ETC: A Review of General Semantics* 1(4): 197–215.
Wierzbicka, Anna. 1988. *The Semantics of Grammar*. John Benjamins.
Wiesel, Elie. 2006 [1958]. *Night*. Hill and Wang.
Williams, Bodi. 2023. "Ideological Warfare: Woke Culture Is Poisoning the Military." *Washington Examiner*, June 23, 2023. https://www.washingtonexaminer.com/restoring-america/courage-strength-optimism/ideological-warfare-woke-culture-is-poisoning-the-military.
Williams, Margot. 2010. "At Guantanamo Bay, Torture Apologists Take Refuge in Empty Code Words and Euphemisms." *The Intercept*, January 29, 2020. https://theintercept.com/2020/01/29/guantanamo-9-11-forever-trials/.
Williams, Raymond. 1977. *Marxism and Literature*. Oxford University Press.
Wittgenstein, Ludwig. 1958. *Philosophical Investigations / Philosophische Untersuchungen*. Translated by G. E. M. Anscombe. 3rd ed., with English and German indexes. Macmillan.
Wolfendale, Jessica. 2008. "From Soldier to Torturer? Military Training and Moral Agency." In *Violence: "Mercurial Gestalt,"* edited by Tobe Levin, 45–60. Brill.
Wolff, Phillip, and Kevin J. Holmes. 2011. "Linguistic Relativity." *WIREs Cognitive Science* 2(3): 239–352.
Wood, L. Todd. 2016. "Next President Will Have to Change Military Culture." *Washington Times*, April 26, 2016. http://www.washingtontimes.com/news/2016/apr/26/l-todd-wood-next-president-will-have-change-milita/.
Wool, Zoe. 2015. *After War: The Weight of Life at Walter Reed*. Duke University Press.
Woulfe, James B. 1998. *Into the Crucible: Making Marines for the 21st Century*. Presidio. Kindle file.

Work Cited

Wright, Evan. 2004. *Generation Kill: Devil Dogs, Iceman, Captain America, and the New Face of American War*. G. P. Putnam.

Yanagizawa-Drott, David. 2014. "Propaganda and Conflict: Evidence from the Rwandan Genocide." *The Quarterly Journal of Economics* 129(4): 1947–1994.

Yang, Jeff. 2011. "Afghanistan Hazing Cases Echo 'A Few Good Men.'" *The Wall Street Journal*, December 27, 2011. https://blogs.wsj.com/speakeasy/2011/12/27/afghanistan-hazing-cases-echo-a-few-good-men/.

Yee, James. 2005. *For God and Country: Faith and Patriotism under Fire*. PublicAffairs.

Yi, Jamison. 2004. "MCMAP and the Marine Warrior Ethos." *Military Review*, November–December:17–24.

Young, Iris Marion. 2003. "The Logic of Masculinist Protection: Reflections on the Current Security State." *Signs: Journal of Women in Culture and Society* 9(1): 1–25.

Young, Matt. 2018a. *Eat the Apple*. Bloomsbury.

Young, Matt. 2018b. "I Hope the Military Doesn't Change My Brother Like It Did Me." *Time*, March 13, 2018. https://time.com/5193840/military-afghanistan-service-marine-corps/.

Zelizer, Craig. 2010. "Laughing Our Way to Peace or War: Humour and Peacebuilding." *Journal of Conflictology* 1(2): 1–9.

Zigon, Jarrett. 2014. "Attunement and Fidelity: Two Ontological Conditions for Morally Being-in-the-World." *Ethos* 42(1): 16–30.

Zigon, Jarrett, and Jason Throop. 2023 [2021]. "Phenomenology". In *The Open Encyclopedia of Anthropology*, edited by Felix Stein. Facsimile of the first edition in The Cambridge Encyclopedia of Anthropology. http://doi.org/10.29164/21phenomenology.

Zimman, Lal. 2017. "Gender as Stylistic Bricolage: Transmasculine Voices and the Relationship between Fundamental Frequency and /s/." *Language in Society* 46:339–370.

Zuckerman, Charles. 2016. "Phatic Violence? Gambling and the Arts of Distraction in Laos." *Journal of Linguistic Anthropology* 26(3): 294–314.

Zuckerman, Charles. 2021. "Introduction to the Generic Special Issue." *Language in Society* 50(4): 501–515.

Zunshine, Lisa. 2012. *Getting Inside Your Head: What Cognitive Science Can Tell Us about Popular Culture*. Johns Hopkins University Press.

Index

For the benefit of digital users, indexed terms that span two pages (e.g., 52–53) may, on occasion, appear on only one of those pages.

abjection
    necropolitical, 14–15, 41, 64–65
    profanity and, 159–160
abortion, 110, 114
Abu Ghraib, 19, 249. *See also* Global War on Terrorism (GWOT)
abuse
    childhood, 22, 36, 119
    prisoner, 147–148, 246
    substance, 32
    in training, 10, 16–17, 28, 64, 73–74, 83–85, 86–89, 91–92, 103–105, 108–109, 228
Ackerman, Eliot, 25, 146–147
Afghanistan, 5–6, 14–15, 17–18, 21, 27, 35–36, 37–38, 121–122, 125, 128–129, 133–136, 140, 151, 152–153, 155–156, 160–161, 173, 182, 191, 227, 249. *See also* Global War on Terrorism (GWOT)
Agamben, Giorgio, 131, 256 n.3
agency, 5–6, 45, 227
    yelling and, 47, 52, 57
aggression, 3–4, 7, 10, 115
    language and, 121–122, 144–145, 153, 156, 159, 160–162, 179–180, 187–188
    masculinity and, 19, 31, 34–35, 47, 56, 110–111, 159
    training and, 47, 50–51, 56–57, 64–65, 91–92, 110–111, 176–177
Air Force Academy, 114, 279 n.12
Akers, Brian, 95
al-Qaeda, 146–147
Althusser, Louis, 65, 273 n.52
Anderson, Doug, 131, 133–134, 140–141, 158–160, 193, 205, 256 n.17, 264 n.51
    "Infantry Assault," 218–219
    "Kill Him with a Name," 206–207
    "My Enemy," 219–220
    "North of Tam Ky, 1967," 212
    "Same Old," 222–223

"Xin Loi," 199–200
animalism, animalization, 66–67, 96, 124–125, 129, 159–160
anthropology, 5, 11–12, 16–17, 23
anti-Semitism, 15, 124–125, 263 n.43
antiwar activism, 143–144, 162–164, 213, 233–234
Arab people, Arabic, 34, 122, 126–127, 130, 133–134
Arendt, Chris, 249–251
    "Standard Operating Procedures," 250–252
Arendt, Hannah, 18–19
Arment, Jason, 73, 77–79
Army, 29, 35, 113–115, 131, 147, 160, 189–190, 249
    reforms, 50–51, 86–87, 111–112, 113–115
    standards and values of, 85–86
    training, 50–51, 62–64, 65–66, 70–71, 73–74, 76–78, 86–87, 99–100, 111–112, 124, 127, 129, 132–133
    Training and Doctrine Command regulations, 86–87
art, 33. *See also* combat paper; poetry; veterans
    demilitarization and, 32–33, 230–231
    emotions and, 238–241
    politics of, 227, 233–234, 240–241, 246
    as therapy, 4, 9, 32–33, 197–198
Asad, Talal, 136
authority, 8, 21–22, 49–50, 52, 68, 110–111
autonomy, bodily, 45

Barry, Jan, 205–207
Basl, Kevin, 202
Bate, Bernard (Barney), 258 n.18
Bean, Susan, 65
Becker, Michael, 98–99
Belew, Kathleen, 37
Belkin, Aaron, 31, 94, 264 n.55
belonging, 5–6, 13, 34–36, 45–46

328 Index

Benveniste, Emile, 57–58
Berger, John, 212–215
Berggen, Jeremy Stainthorp, "PTSD," 208–209
Bersani, Leo, 159
Bianchi, Claudia, 274 n.4
Bianchini, David, "To Shane," 208
Bicycle Cards, 182. *See also* death cards
Biden, Joseph, 109–110, 113–114
Binder, Werner, 26
biopolitics, 257 n.8, 259 n.27, 283 n.48
Black Friday Dark Dawn, 52–53
Black Lives Matter, 113–114
Black service members, 34, 36, 72–73, 113–114, 129–130, 257 n.7. *See also* race
Blommaert, Jan, 258 n.18
body count, 17–18, 126, 132
boot camp. *See* training
Boudreau, Tyler, 14, 26, 104–105, 137, 192–193, 201, 256 n.17
Bourke, Joanna, 282 n.38
Bowen, Kevin, 205, 221
Bowman, Rachel Lynn, 78
Braun, Conrad, 125–126, 137–138
Brinson, Thomas, 207–208
British Army, 50–51, 74–75
Brown, D. F., 204
Buber, Martin, 219–220
Bulger, Whitey, 162
bureaucracy, bureaucratese, 10, 21–22, 87–88, 147, 151
Burns, Ken, 203
Burns, Robert, 3
Butler, Judith, 19, 263 n.44, 269 n.94

cadences (calling cadences), 176–178, 277 n.59
Calica, Lovella, 205
Calley, William, Jr., 56–57
Cambodia, 5, 35–36
Cameron, Drew, 225–226, 238–239
Camp Pendleton, 89
Canadian Forces, 50–51
Captured Documents (Nguyen and Weigl), 221
Carroll, Greg, 44–46, 274 n.3
Carrying the Darkness (ed. Ehrhart), 205
Caruth, Cathy, 202–203
Casey, George, 127–128
Casey, Michael, 205

"For the Old Man," 220–221
Casey, Rion, 129
civil rights movement, 72
civilians
  casualties, 17, 27–28, 35–36, 37–38, 56–57, 122, 131–133, 136, 146–147, 240–241, 249, 253
  dehumanization of, 17, 38, 122, 132–133, 136, 160
  training and, 44–46, 88–89
class, 4–6, 36, 45, 47–48, 91
clichés, thought-terminating, 164–165, 208–209
code, 4
code of silence, 92, 212
Cody, Frank, 258 n.18
Cohn, Carol, 24–25, 145–146, 148–149, 257 n.9, 261 n.40, 294 n.21
colonialism, 122, 260 n.32, n.33
combat, 35–36
  dehumanization and, 19–20, 37–38, 119–123, 125–133, 136, 137–138, 155–156, 157–158, 162–164
  emotions of, 21, 25, 32, 123, 140–141, 143–144, 155–157, 164–167, 186, 198–200, 213, 228–229, 238–241
  empathy and, 30–31
  frame perversion and, 191–193
  language and, 3–4, 9–10, 12, 16–23, 24–25, 29–32, 35, 37–38, 64–65, 121–123, 125–133, 136, 137–141, 143–145, 151–167, 175–176, 186, 202–204, 207–209, 210–211, 226–227, 240–241
  morality and, 6, 9, 18–19, 26–29, 32, 120–121, 122–123, 124–125, 131–132, 136, 138–139, 144–145, 151, 175–176, 186, 192–193, 198, 208–210
  personhood and, 7, 20, 28, 37, 192–193, 199
  power and, 5–6
  relationality and, 137–141, 198, 210, 219–220, 254
  social hierarchy and, 130
  trauma and, 12–14, 228
  violence and, 3–4, 6–7, 10, 14–15, 18, 20–21, 24, 26, 32, 38, 143–144, 151–155, 175, 209, 211
  women in, 36, 119

Combat Obscura (dir. Lagoze), 31–32, 156, 191, 265 n.64
combat paper, 32–33, 225–229, 230–249, 250–252
Combat Paper Project, 205, 226–228, 231
communalization, 200–201
communication
  affiliative dimensions of, 59–62
  combat and, 202–203
  failures of, 58
community, speech, 19, 63, 133, 147, 153, 259 n.31
compartmentalization, 116, 123, 143–144
Conley, Robin, 24, 261 n.40
Connolly, Dave, 129–130, 132–133, 162–164, 166–167, 182, 205, 213
  "Food for Thought, 3:00 a.m.," 199
  "For the Weasel, KIA 02/08/69," 216–217
  "Incident near Ap Bac Ba Ria," 213
  "Why I Can't," 213–215
conservatism, 30, 37, 104–105, 108–111, 113–116, 159
coping mechanisms, 38, 144–145, 154, 173–175, 191
COVID-19 pandemic, 49–50
craftivism, 300 n.5
creativity, 32–33, 48, 148–150, 152–153, 178–181, 227, 243, 252
Crenshaw, Paul, 124
Croom, Adam, 274 n.4
Cruz, Ted, 113–114
cynicism, 10, 29, 180–182, 189–190, 192

Da Nang Air Base, 26–27
Daniel, E. Valentine, 202–203
da Vinci, Leonardo, "Vitruvian Man," 245–246
Davis, Sean, 129, 133, 139–140
death cards, 182–186
Decaul, Maurice Emerson, 200–201, 204
decision-making, 28–29, 55, 57, 86
Defense Equal Opportunity Institute (DEOI), 72, 110
Defense Equal Opportunity Management Institute (DEOMI), 34, 92
dehumanization
  combat and, 19–20, 37–38, 119–123, 125–133, 136, 137–138, 155–156, 157–158, 162–164
  empathy and, 23, 30, 121–123, 137–139

  of enemies, 20–21, 23, 24–25, 37–38, 59, 64–65, 74, 120–126, 127–129, 130–139, 236–238, 251–252, 260 n.32
  killing and, 151–152, 155–156, 167, 245–246, 260 n.32, n.33
  language and, 20, 37–38, 64–65, 74, 121–123, 127, 130–133, 135, 151–152, 167, 236–238, 251–252, 261 n.36, 263 n.48, 275 n.10, 287 n.26, n.33, 288 n.45
  training and, 20, 37–38, 59, 64–65, 74, 119, 123–125, 127, 129, 133, 135–136, 275 n.10
Delori, Mathias, 136–137
demilitarization, 3–4, 6–7, 18, 25, 32–33, 38, 226–227, 228–234, 236–238. *See also* veterans
Denmark, 50–51
Department of Defense, 10, 21, 27, 37, 67, 72, 84, 92, 108, 125, 176
  Defense Organizational Climate Survey, 72, 256 n.18
  Office of People Analytics, 92, 256 n.18
Department of Veteran Affairs, 114
derogatory terms. *See* slurs
diglossia, 29, 170
discrimination, 72–74, 110
diversity and inclusion, 10, 17–18, 34–35, 71–72, 104–105, 110–111, 113–115
"Don't ask, don't tell" (DADT), 69–71, 75–76, 272 n.32
doublespeak, 147–151, 157–158, 207–208, 226, 243–244. *See also* euphemisms
Douglas, Mary, 128
Drill Instructors (DIs), 7–8, 9–10, 14–16, 33, 41–46, 63–64. *See also* training
  abuse and, 17–18, 49, 64, 81–84, 86–89, 91–92, 100–101, 103–104
  affiliative talk and, 57–59
  cadences and, 176–178, 277 n.59
  dehumanization and, 20, 59, 64–65, 74, 123–124, 127, 136
  harshness of, 9–10, 46, 49, 54, 58, 62, 63, 75–77, 83, 88–89, 91–93, 103, 110–113
  head games, 95–101
  incentive training, 93–95
  instilling knowledge, 81–83, 150
  insults and, 63–64, 67–72, 73–74, 75–77, 90, 123–124
  kill chants and, 77–79
  kin ties and, 60–62

Drill Instructors (DIs) (*Continued*)
  masculinity and, 15, 20, 47–48, 272 n.30
  on mothers, 105–106, 115–116
  name-calling and, 65–67
  obedience and, 28–29
  performance of, 48–49
  profanity and, 52–53, 86–87, 90–91, 155
  rule-breaking and, 88–93, 99–100
  yelling and, 20, 47, 49–57, 81–83, 96
drone warfare, 27, 67, 136–137, 146–147, 284 n.8, 286 n.7
Duke, Jennifer, 57
Dunnuck, Lyman, 165
Duranti, Alessandro, 261 n.37, 263 n.48, 267 n.74
dysphemisms, 151, 153–154

Ears, Open. Eyeballs, Click, 78, 90–91
East Coast Drill Instructors Association, 7–8, 33, 43–44, 63, 83–84, 94, 105
Ehrhart, William (Bill), 205, 221
  "Making the Children Behave," 222
  "Time on Target," 217–218
Elshtain, Jean Bethke, 104
embodiment, 3–4, 257 n.8
  insults and, 75–76
  integrity and, 159
  language and, 22, 24, 47, 91, 159–160, 161–164
  objectification and, 21
  poetry and, 198–200
  profanity and, 91
  training and, 16–17, 20
  uniform and, 225
  violence and, 68–69
  yelling and, 54–56
emotion, 21
  art and, 238–241
  combat and, 21, 25, 32, 123, 140–141, 143–144, 155–157, 164–167, 186, 198, 199–200, 228–229, 238–241
  detachment and, 24, 209–210, 213
  humor and, 173–176
  language and, 91, 164–167, 173–176, 213
  poetry and, 198–200, 210–213
  profanity and, 156–157
emotional labor, 30–31, 270 n.107
empathy, 24, 38, 260 n.33
  for enemy, 9, 19, 32–33, 47, 121–122, 137–141, 144–145, 149–150, 160–162, 217–218, 242–243, 254
  masculinity and, 30–32, 108–111, 115–116
  relationality of, 32–33, 219–220, 254
  training and, 46–47, 55–57
"the enemy," enemy combatant
  empathy for, 9, 19, 32–33, 47, 121–122, 137–141, 144–145, 149–150, 160–162, 217–218, 242–243, 254, 268 n.83
  dehumanization of, 20–21, 23, 24–25, 37–38, 59, 64–65, 74, 120–126, 127–129, 130–139, 236–238, 251–252, 260 n.32, 264 n.56
  morality and, 122, 124–125
  as polluting essence, 128–129
  racialization of, 30–31, 109, 121–123, 125, 126–131, 132–133, 135–136, 137–138, 264 n.56
  rehumanizing, 32–33, 217–223, 240–241, 254
epithets. *See* slurs
Ermey, R. Lee, 50, 63, 88–89, 91–92, 213–215
Espada, Martin, 209
ethics, 27–29, 57, 84, 85–86, 131–132, 175–176
ethnicity, 30. *See also* race
  dehumanization and, 121–122, 132–133, 136
  in military, 36, 71–74, 110
euphemisms, 3–4, 25, 140, 145–155, 157–158, 167, 189–190, 203–204, 206–209, 226, 250–254. *See also* doublespeak
Executive Order 1233, 146–147
exercise, 16–17, 44–45, 77–78, 81–83, 89, 93–94
extremism, 37–38, 136
eyeballing, 58

Fallon, Jim, 240–241
  "U-Turn," 241
family. *See* kin ties
Fanning, Rory, 37–38
Felix, Joseph, 73–74
femininity, feminization, 15, 31–32, 48, 66–67, 68–69, 72–73, 104, 108, 111, 115–116, 157–158
Ferrizi, Ron, 203

Finland, 50–51
Flemmi, Steven, 162
Floyd, Bryan Alex, 207–208
Fluri, Jennifer, 173
focus groups, 33
Forché, Carolyn, 200
Fort Belvoir, 233–234
Fort Drum, 70–71, 227–228
Fort Hood, 129, 253
Fort Leonard Wood Drill Sergeant School, 111–112
Foucault, Michel, 257 n.8, 283 n.48
fractal recursivity, 130
frame analysis, 172, 259 n.19
frame of war, 19
frame perversion, 29, 171–173, 174–176, 182, 183–186, 190–193, 242–243
　as pedagogy, 175–178
frog voice, 56
From Both Sides Now (ed. Mahoney), 221
Frontline Paper, 33, 148, 226, 228–229, 232–233, 234–236, 240–241, 246–247
Full Metal Jacket (dir. Kubrick), 50, 63, 88–89, 152

Gal, Susan, 130, 273 n.45, 292 n.44
Geertz, Clifford, 275 n.6
gender, 31–32, 34, 104–105, 110–111, 115–116. *See also* masculinity
　hierarchy and, 130
　insults and, 64–65, 66–71
　language and, 19–21, 150, 157, 159, 161–162
　marginalization and, 109
　power and, 8
　sexuality and, 69–70
　training and, 20, 47–48, 50, 52–53, 56, 64–65, 66–67, 70–71, 94, 105–108, 150
　women in military, 17–18, 34–36, 42, 46, 48, 53–54, 67–69, 76–77, 104, 110–111, 114–115, 119
Geneva Conventions, 27, 131–132, 264 n.56. *See also* Rules of Engagement (ROE)
Georgia Three Percent Security Force, 38
Gilmore, Ruth Wilson, 258 n.18
Global War on Terrorism (GWOT), 5–6, 8, 9–10, 14–15, 17–18, 21, 24–25, 27–28, 30–31, 34–37, 63, 67–69, 72, 73–74, 76–77, 84, 89, 92, 105–106, 119–123, 125–129, 132–133, 134–136, 138–140, 146–147, 151–154, 155–156, 157–158, 160–161, 165–166, 170, 182, 186, 191, 192–193, 200–203, 205, 217, 221, 225, 227–228, 236–238, 241–243, 246, 249–250, 255 n.5, 256 n.17, 259 n.31, 264 n.56
Glover, Jonathan, 137
Goffman, Erving, 172, 292 n.39
Goodwin, Charles, 261 n.40
grief, grievability, 14, 19, 23, 32–33, 120–123, 173–174, 175–176, 197–198, 199–201, 209–213, 221, 223, 241, 269 n.94
The Ground Truth (dir. Huze), 13–14, 77–79, 122, 138–139
Guantanamo Bay, 147–150, 246–252
　Standard Operating Procedures, 148–149
Guerra, Julie A. M., 113–114
guilt, 6, 9, 18, 32, 123, 140–141, 160–161, 200–201, 218–219, 226, 254
Gulf War, 147, 202, 240
Gutmann, Stephanie, 111, 115–116
gynophobia, 67–69, 130

Handman, Courtney, 258 n.18
harassment, 10, 72, 113, 246
Harrison, Simon, 264 n.56
hazing, 84–85, 86–88, 91–92, 100–101, 108
head games, 93, 95–101
healing rituals, 230–231
Hearts and Minds, 180–181
Hedger, Joseph, 274 n.4
Hegseth, Pete, 114
Heritage Foundation, 114–115
heterosexuality, compulsory, 15
Hicks Kennard, Catherine, 53–54, 58, 281 n.30
hierarchy, 14, 21–22, 52, 57–58, 130
　gendered, 130
　racial, 121–122, 128, 130
　sexuality and, 130
Hill, Jane, 133
Holocaust, 124–125
Hom, Christopher, 274 n.4
homophobia, 4, 52–53, 64–65, 67, 69–71, 75–77, 111–112, 130
honor, 26–29, 85–86, 100–101, 115–116, 148, 154, 169–171, 247
Hood, Preston, 209–212
　"Rung Sat," 211

Hoschchild, Arlie, 268 n.84, 269 n.92, 270 n.107
humanity, 18–19, 66–67, 96, 120–122, 123–124, 131, 136–137, 138–140, 148, 162–164, 175–176, 209, 215–217, 219–220, 228–229, 236–238, 260 n.33. *See also* dehumanization
Human Terrain Project, 255 n.5
humor, 17, 29, 38, 50–51, 68, 99, 151, 166, 170–175, 189–190, 192–193, 203–204, 246. *See also* frame perversion; irony; jokes; memes
Huze, Sean, 13–14, 77–78

iconic, iconization, 273 n.45, 281 n.33, 282 n.45, 292 n.44, 293 n.56, 294 n.10
identity, 26, 31, 45–48, 57–58, 65–66, 78, 85, 91–92, 110–111, 155, 157, 171, 172, 215–216, 228–231, 255 n.11
imperialism, 5, 52, 259 n.22, 260 n.32, 268 n.87
incentive training (IT), 49–50, 81–83, 93–95
index, indexicality, 164, 215–216, 289 n.59
Indigenous Americans, 201, 230
individuality, 23–24, 37, 44–47, 55, 57–58, 66–67, 121–122, 126, 144, 197–198, 228–229, 239–240
infantilization, 64, 66–67, 72–73, 109
infantry. *See also* combat
    creativity and, 178–179
    empathy and, 30–31
    language and, 3–4, 9, 17–18, 20–22, 64–65, 116, 144, 172, 197–198
    power and, 5–6
    racial demographics of, 71–72
    training and, 64–65, 84, 108
    violence and, 9, 22, 84, 116, 254
infrastructure, linguistic, 19–20, 23–24, 38
injury, 14, 25, 35–36, 144–145, 159, 176–177, 225. *See also* moral injury
insults, 16–17, 38, 64, 88–91, 111–112, 215–216
    gender-based, 66–71
    pedagogy of, 20, 64–65, 66–67, 71
    racial and ethnic, 71–74
    semiotic callousing and, 64–65, 74–77, 91, 111–112, 123–124
integrity, 10, 29, 85–86, 100–101, 115–116, 159, 169–170
interpellation, 65–66, 68, 74, 77, 273 n.52

interviews, 33–34
Iraq, 3–6, 10–11, 13–15, 17–18, 21, 24–25, 27, 35–36, 119–123, 125, 127–130, 133, 134–136, 138–140, 151–152, 155–156, 165–166, 170, 192–193, 221, 225, 227–228, 236–238, 241–242, 259 n.31. *See also* Global War on Terrorism (GWOT)
Iraq Veterans Against the War, 127–128, 225–226, 227–228, 250–251
irony, 173–174, 175–176, 186, 247. *See also* humor
irrationality, 85, 96, 100, 172, 202–203, 253. *See also* rationality
Irvine, Judith, 130
Islamophobia, 73–74, 113, 120, 125, 126–127, 135–136
Israeli Defense Force, 50–51

Jakobson, Roman, 274 n.58
jargon, 20–22, 153, 154–155, 157–158, 169–170, 203. *See also* doublespeak; euphemisms
Johnson, Lyndon, 180–181
jokes, 3–4, 21, 50–51, 71, 75–77, 135, 152–153, 172–176, 226, 253. *See also* humor
Junger, Sebastian, 228–229

Kapadia, Ronak, 227
Kelly, Jesse, 114
Kendi, Ibrahim, 114
Kiesling, Scott, 261 n.40, 263 n.42
"kill-capture" strategy, 27
killing, killability, 10, 253–254, 260 n.32, 278 n.61
    combat and, 14–15, 17–18, 20–21, 23–24, 74–75, 119–122, 125, 131–134, 136, 144–145, 151–154, 161–162, 167, 175–176, 183, 197–198
    enemy and, 14, 79, 119–121, 125, 127, 129, 131–132, 133–134, 136, 151–152
    training and, 37–38, 41, 46, 74–75, 77–79, 85, 127
kill talk, 18–22, 24–25, 30–33, 35, 37–38, 85, 167, 197–199, 209, 226, 254
kin ties, 31–32, 60–62, 64–66
kinetic action, 54–55
Kirkland, Haywood, 132
knowledge, instilling, 81–83, 150

Kohn, Richard H., 270 n.108
Komunyakaa, Yusef, 129–130, 205
Krause, Tara, 240
Kubrick, Stanley, 50, 63, 88–89

Lagoze, Miles, 31–32, 49, 73, 100, 153–154, 156, 165–166, 182, 191, 256 n.17, 265 n.64
Lakoff, George, 109, 261 n.40, 272 n.30
Lambek, Michael, 174
language, 255 n.4
  body and, 22, 24, 47, 91, 159–160, 161–164
  class and, 91
  combat and, 3–4, 9–10, 12, 16–23, 24–25, 29–32, 35, 37–38, 64–65, 121–123, 125–133, 136, 137–141, 143–145, 151–167, 175–176, 186, 202–204, 207–209, 210–211, 226–227, 240–241
  dehumanization and, 20, 37–38, 64–65, 74, 121–123, 127, 130–133, 135, 151–152, 167, 236–238, 251–252, 260 n.33, 261 n.36, 275 n.10, 287 n.26, n.33, 288 n.45
  demilitarization and, 32–33
  emotion and, 91, 164–167, 173–176, 213
  empathy and, 30
  experience and, 23–25, 29
  gender and, 157, 159, 161–162
  harsh, 75–77, 79, 91, 111–112
  hierarchy and, 21–22
  identity and, 155, 157, 171–172
  ideology of, 31–32, 54, 75–77, 79, 135, 157–158
  infrastructure of, 19–20, 23–24, 38
  killing, killability and, 77–79, 143–145, 146–147, 151–155, 161–164, 165–167, 209–211, 215–216, 254, 258 n.17
  masculinity and, 20–21, 91, 104–105, 145–146, 150, 157, 159, 161–162, 167
  morality and, 14–15, 16–18, 19–20, 121–122, 124–125, 136, 138–139, 144–147, 151, 154, 158, 160, 161–162, 172–173, 175–176, 209–210
  norms of, 38
  officially sanctioned (formal) versus transgressive (informal), 4, 20–22, 26, 29, 85, 127, 144–145, 147, 169–170, 189–190
  personhood and, 47, 65
  poetry and, 199–200, 206–209, 212
  politically correct (PC), 104, 111–112, 113–115
  politics of, 215–216
  racist, 126–131, 135–138, 276 n.32, 277 n.38, 288 n.49
  rehumanization and, 9
  relationality and, 137–141
  semiotic callousing and, 75–77, 91, 111–112, 157
  sexuality and, 159
  socialization and, 19
  subjectivity and, 7, 18, 19–20, 22–24, 46, 126, 137, 149–150, 159, 175–176, 192, 230–231
  thought and, 19–20, 23, 57, 146–147, 154, 161–162, 206–208, 255 n.3, 261 n.37, n.40, 263 n.42, 292 n.44
  violence and, 3–4, 9–10, 14–21, 22–25, 29–31, 38, 47, 54–55, 59, 76–77, 78–79, 111–112, 121–122, 131, 132–134, 143–156, 157–159, 160–167, 175–176, 202–203, 206–207, 209, 211, 254
Latino/a service members, 36
laughter, 50–51, 173–174. *See also* humor
Lentjes, Rebecca, 52
Lévi-Strauss, Claude, 230–231
Levy, E., 29
Levy, Marc, 128, 131–132, 157, 173, 204–205, 256 n.17
  "Peacetime," 206–207
  "Portrait of a Boy at Dawn," 198
LGBTQ+ service members, 15, 17–18, 34, 69–71, 75–76, 110, 115
liberalism, 7, 10, 30, 108–109, 111, 113–114, 115–116, 275 n.6
Libya, 136–137
Lifton, Robert Jay, 18, 85, 164–165
Livingstone Smith, David, 130–131, 263 n.48, 286 n.1, 287 n.26, n.33, 288 n.45
Lucey, Jeffrey, 138–139
Lutz, Catherine, 26
Lutz, William D., 147

MacLeish, Kenneth, 14, 21, 26, 28, 253, 269 n.92
Mahoney, Phillip, 221
Malinowski, Bronislaw, 59
Mararac, Nick, 67

marginalization, 46, 105, 109–110, 225, 227, 250
Marine Combat Training Battalion, 34–35
Marine Corps, 7–9, 34–35, 38
　Basic Officer training, 136
　empathy and, 31–32
　combat and, 13–15, 17
　gender integration of, 48, 53–54, 67–69, 71, 76–77, 119, 281 n.37
　Gunners Creed, 77
　Logistics Base, 73–74
　Mental Health Advisory Team, 133
　Officer Candidate School, 135–136
　organizational culture of, 135–136
　Public Affairs, 191
　racial inclusiveness of, 72–74
　as speech community, 63
　standards and values of, 85–88, 266 n.71
　Training and Education Command, 94–95
　training of, 10–11, 15–17, 20–21, 28–29, 41–44, 45–46, 50–51, 62, 63–64, 65–66, 67–71, 72–74, 75–79, 81–101, 103–104, 105–106, 111–112, 127, 133
　Values Program, 27–28
Maringira, Godfrey, 271 n.26
Marlantes, Karl, 32, 256 n.17
Martin, Hugh, "Responding to an Explosion in Qarah Tappeh," 221
masculinity, 8, 19, 34–35, 42, 64–65, 66–68, 110–111, 114–115, 130, 201, 225
　class and, 47–48
　combat and, 56, 157, 159, 161–162, 167
　empathy and, 31–32, 115–116
　language and, 20–21, 91, 104–105, 145–146, 150, 157, 159, 161–162, 167
　sexuality and, 70–71
　training and, 20, 38, 42, 47–48, 50, 52–56, 64–65, 66–67, 68–71, 94, 108, 150
Matott, Drew, 225–226, 236–238
Mattis, James, 113, 170, 192–193, 269 n.98
Mbembe, Achille, 14, 128–129
McSorley, Kevin, 202–203
McWhorter, John, 261 n.40
Meadlo, Paul, 56–57
Mejia, Camilo, 123
memes, 170, 171–172, 186–190. *See also* humor
memory, 8–9, 13, 23, 143–144, 162–164, 201
　arts and, 3–4, 226–227, 231

　poetry and, 198, 200, 205, 213–215, 218–219
mental health, 6, 110, 115, 133
metaphor, 20, 28, 66–67, 75–76, 125, 145, 199–200, 213–215, 253, 261 n.40
method, 33–35
military, militarism, militarization, 37
　class and, 36, 47–48, 91
　contradictions of, 3–4, 6, 12, 26–29, 77, 84–85, 92–93, 100–101, 169–174, 175–176, 189–190, 192–193, 246, 253–254, 281 n.30, n.32
　culture of, 5, 9–10, 18–20, 31–32, 34–35, 71–72, 84, 104–105, 122, 135, 159, 186, 242–243
　diversity and inclusion in, 10, 17–18, 35–36, 71–73, 104–105, 110–111, 113–115
　empathy and, 30–32
　LGBTQ+ people in, 17–18, 36, 69–71, 75–76, 110, 114–115
　identity and, 26, 31, 45–48, 57–58, 77–78, 85–86, 110–111, 155, 157, 171, 228–229, 231, 255 n.11
　masculinity and, 19, 20–21, 31–32, 34–35, 42, 47–48, 50, 52–56, 64–71, 94, 104–105, 108, 110–111, 114–116, 150, 157, 159, 161–162
　as nervous system, 28, 253
　people of color in, 34, 36, 73–74, 257 n.7, 276 n.32, 277 n.38
　personhood and, 16–17, 47, 256 n.3, 275 n.6
　post-deployment assistance, 201–202
　power and, 5–6, 28, 42–43
　race and, 34, 36, 71–74, 110, 113–115, 129–130
　reforms, 113–115
　religion and, 73–74
　standards and values of, 85–88
　women in, 17–18, 34–36, 42, 46, 48, 53–54, 67–69, 76–77, 104, 110–111, 114–115, 119, 281 n.37
Military Equal Opportunity, 104–105
militias, far-right, 37–38
Millantz, Johnny, 241–243
Millard, Geoff, 127–128, 288 n.51
misogyny, 69–70, 91. *See also* gynophobia; sexism
Mockenhaupt, Brian, 279 n.15

mock language, 122, 133–135
Moon, Zachary, 85
moral injury, 6–7, 32–33, 123, 154, 193, 209, 227, 243, 247, 252, 279 n.7
morality, 26, 85–87, 109
  combat and, 6, 9, 18–19, 26–29, 32, 120–121, 122–123, 124–125, 131–132, 136, 138–139, 144–145, 151, 175–176, 186, 192–193, 198, 208–210
  frame perversion and, 192–193
  language and, 14–15, 16–18, 19–20, 121–122, 124–125, 136, 138–139, 144–147, 151, 154, 158, 160, 161–162, 172–173, 175–176, 209–210
  training and, 28–29, 74–75, 77, 79, 84, 85, 100, 279 n.11
  transgressing, 6, 27–28, 84–85, 100
  violence and, 5–6, 18, 144–145, 175–176, 209–210
mothers, "Mothers of America," 104–109, 115–116
Moyn, Samuel, 27–28
Musgrave, John, 23, 29, 72–73, 131, 204, 256 n.17
Muslims, 73–74, 136, 147–148, 246–247
My Lai massacre, 56–57, 143–144, 249

name-calling, 64–67, 77. *See also* insults
National Endowment for the Arts, Operation Homecoming, 205
nationalism, 88–89, 260 n.32
national security, 10, 14, 67, 108, 111, 115–116, 120–121
Naval Criminal Investigative Service (NCIS), 83–84
Navy, 4–5
necropolitics, 14
  combat and, 144–145, 149–151, 160–162, 174–176, 178–179, 198, 208–209
  critique of, 225, 238–239, 243, 246
  empathy and, 30–31, 108, 115, 137, 138–139, 149–150, 160–161, 198
  language and, 14–15, 16–18, 22, 29–31, 37–38, 46, 64–65, 74–75, 79, 151, 160–162, 172, 174–176, 208–209
  training and, 41, 46, 56, 62, 64–65, 74–75, 79, 84–85, 93
nervous system, 28, 253
Nguyen, Thanh T., 221

nihilism, 12, 38, 144–145, 164–165, 186, 192, 203, 232
norms, transgressing, 20–21, 27–28, 38, 92–93, 100, 158–160, 161–162, 175, 186
Norway, 50–51
Novick, Lynn, 203
nuclear engagement, 145–146
Nygard, Walt, 228–229, 232–233, 235–236

Obama, Barack, 27, 113
obedience, 21–22, 28–29, 31, 94, 150
objectification, 21, 23, 66–67
Obrdlik, Antonin, 173
Ochs, Elinor, 261 n.37, n.40, 263 n.42, 271 n.11
Operation Desert Storm, 124
Orientalism, 122, 260 n.32
Owen, Wilfred, 205
  "Dulce et Decorum Est," 209

Pacanowski, Jenny, 232–233
Pakistan, 146–147
papermaking. *See* combat paper
Paquet, Basil T., 205
parrhesia, 200
Parris Island Marine Corps Training Depot, 7–8, 9–10, 15–16, 33, 41–46, 47–48, 51, 53–54, 60–63, 68–69, 70–71, 73–74, 76–78, 81, 83–84, 89–90, 91–92, 93–94, 100–101, 103, 105–106, 110, 113, 119, 120, 150, 200–201
patriotism, 4–6, 18–19, 36, 44, 109–110, 247
PC. *See* political correctness
Peace Paper Project, 226
pedagogy, 20–21, 28, 45–47, 49–52, 55–57, 64–67, 71, 74, 92–93, 100, 144, 175–178
Peirce, Charles Sanders, 164–165
Pentagon, 30–31
performance, 48–49, 55–57
personhood, 7, 16–17, 20, 28, 37, 41, 44–47, 55, 57–59, 65–67, 192–193, 199, 256 n.3
Petersen, Glenn, 204, 256 n.17
Petraeus, David, 30–31, 135–136
phatic, phaticity, 59–61
Phillips, Thomas, 48
Pillen, Alex, 175–177, 226–227, 267 n.72
poetry (poetry of recovery), 4, 23, 32–33, 162–165, 198–199, 200–202, 204–206, 210–211
  embodiment and, 198–200

poetry (poetry of recovery) (*Continued*)
  emotion and, 198–200, 210–213
  empathy and, 217–218, 219–220
  killing and, 218–219
  language and, 199–200, 206–209, 212
  politics of, 200, 213–215, 222
  rehumanization and, 212, 216–223
political correctness (PC language, "wokeism"), 38, 104, 111–115
pollution, 66–68, 128–129, 159–160
Pompeo, Mike, 114
Potter, Terrence, 169–170
Price, Will, 57, 68, 92, 103, 281 n.32
profanity, 4, 20–21, 23, 38, 86–87, 90–99, 155–162, 175, 206–208, 209–210
professionalism, 26–27, 126, 147
pronouns
  first-person, 47, 52–53, 57–58, 65
  gender-neutral, 110
  second-person, 58
Prysner, Mike, 127, 133
PTSD (post-traumatic stress disorder), 6, 8–9, 143–144, 201–203, 208–209
Puar, Jasbir, 130
punishment, 41–42, 48–50, 52, 58, 81–83, 86–87, 93–94, 97–100

Quick Reaction Force, 139–140

race
  dehumanization and, 30–31, 109, 121–123, 125, 126–131, 132–133, 135–136, 137–138, 260 n.33
  hierarchy and, 121–122, 128, 130
  in military, 34, 36, 71–74, 110, 113–115, 129–130, 257 n.7
racism, 4, 10, 15, 17, 23, 36, 37–38, 72–73, 110, 114–115, 121–123, 126–128, 135–138, 176, 209–210, 219–220, 260 n.32, 276 n.32, 277 n.38, 288 n.49
Rai, Amit, 130
RAND Corporation, 37, 87–88, 256 n.18
rap groups, 204
Raskin, Victor, 174
rationality, 20, 27–28, 79, 85, 94, 95–96, 98–99, 144, 169, 253. *See also* irrationality
realism, 28–29, 91, 104–105, 144–147, 151, 154–155, 157–158, 175–176, 182, 189–190, 200, 203, 222

Recruit Training Order (RTO), 87, 90–91, 155
register, 4, 172
rehumanization, 9, 212, 216–223, 240–241, 254
Reitman, Janet, 91–92
relationality
  in combat, 137–141, 198, 210, 219–220, 254
  dehumanization and, 121–122
  empathy and, 32–33, 219–220, 254
  humor and, 173–174
religion, 34, 73–74, 122, 125, 127–128, 132–136
Remarque, Erich Marie, *All Quiet on the Western Front*, 3
Ricks, Thomas, 98–99, 281 n.30
rites of passage, 45, 56, 62, 64–65, 85, 226, 230, 238–239
ritual, 42–43
Rochelle, William, 127–128
Roe vs. Wade, 110
Rosaldo, Renato, 5, 9
Rottmann, Larry, 173, 205
  Voices from the Ho Chi Minh Trail, 221–222
Rukeyser, Muriel, 198
rule-breaking, 84–87, 88–93, 99–100
Rules of Engagement (ROE), 131–132, 265 n.64, 282 n.44
Rwanda, 124–125
Ryan, Bill, 126

sacra (sacrum), 45–47, 85
sadism, 4, 16–17, 21, 69–70, 83, 85, 99, 100, 152, 176–177, 182, 197–198, 253
Sallah, Michael, 132, 137–138
San Diego Marine Corps Training Depot, 9–10, 28–29, 43–44, 46, 48–49, 52–53, 63–64, 86–87, 90, 92
sanitization, 3–4, 145, 147
Sapir, Edward, 261 n.40
Sapir-Whorf hypothesis, 23, 261 n.40, 292 n.44
Sassoon, Siegfried, 205
"scenario training," 27
Schofield, John, 279 n.12
Schutz, Alfred, 140–141
security, human, 18

semiotic callousing, 20, 54–55, 57, 64–65, 74–77, 91, 111–112, 119, 123–124, 157, 242–243
semiotics, 14–15, 32–33, 54, 100, 130, 164–165, 172, 175–176, 190, 192–193, 267 n.72, 273 n.45, 282 n.45, 293 n.56, 294 n.10
sensitivity, 27, 110–112, 113–115
Serwer, Adam, 109–110
sexism, 10, 64–65, 68, 104–105, 110, 176
sexual assault, harassment, 10, 67–68, 232–233, 240
sexuality, 69–71, 109, 130, 159
Shay, Jonathan, 200, 269 n.92
Shelton, Leonard, 233
Shohet, Merav, 289 nn.55–56, n.58
Siddiqui, Raheel, 73–74, 84, 113
Sidnell, Jack, 65
Sites, Kevin, 192–193, 233
slang, 21–22, 66, 90, 134, 145–146, 150–154, 159, 161, 166–167, 169–170, 254. *See also* doublespeak; euphemisms
slogans, 21, 29, 38, 68, 115–116, 144–145, 152, 171, 178–180, 182, 189–190, 192, 241, 249
slurs (epithets), 20–21, 23, 32, 64–65, 66–67, 73–74, 121–122, 124–136, 137–138, 140–141, 144, 157, 198, 209–210, 219–220, 274 n.3
snowball sampling, 34
social media, 33
socialization, 19, 37
solitary confinement, 147–148
sonic patriarchy, 52, 55
Soular, James, 154–155
stance, 4, 20–22, 24, 29, 38, 47, 56, 59, 64–65, 76, 82–83, 85, 104, 109–110, 130–131, 134–135, 141, 144–145, 152–153, 160, 161–162, 169–171, 175–176, 183–184, 186, 211, 218, 228–229, 261 n.40
  shifting, 25, 137–139, 191
state, 5–6, 20
  hypocrisies of, 28
  necropolitics of, 22, 30–31, 41, 48, 56, 57, 62, 79, 108, 115, 198, 200, 213–215, 218–219, 222, 227, 231, 243, 254
  parenting and, 108–109
Steptoe, Lamont, 200
"stop-loss" policies, 6

structure of feeling, 31, 105, 115–116, 258 n.18, 284 n.3
subjectivity, 5, 19–20, 22–24, 137, 257 n.8
  combat and, 7, 18–20, 126, 149–150, 159, 175–176, 192–193, 199
  training and, 44–46, 59, 62
substance abuse, 32
suicide, 6, 32, 110, 115, 149, 250
super-citizenship, 44, 86–87, 88–89, 115–116, 225
Syria, 146–147

taboo, 20–21, 26, 67, 85, 91–93, 121, 127, 133, 151, 159–160, 161–162
Taha, Maisa, 268 n.83
Tailhook scandal, 110
Taliban, 146–147, 153–154, 157–158, 160–161
Taussig, Michael, 28
Taylor, Ryan, 239
Telleson, Kacy, 155
terrorism, terrorist, 122, 136, 146–148, 249–250
testimonial, 22–23
therapy, 8–9, 200–201, 204, 210–211, 226
Thou-orientation, 141
thought, 19–20, 23, 57, 146–147, 154, 161–162, 206–208
Three Percenter movement, 38
Tick, Edward, 175–176
torture, 19, 28–29, 147–150, 227–228, 241–243, 246, 247–249, 250–252
training, 9–11, 34–35, 38, 41–43, 47–48, 56, 62, 258 n.17
  abuse in, 28, 81–85, 86–89, 91–92, 100–101, 103–104, 108–109
  cadences and, 176–178
  dehumanization and, 20, 37–38, 59, 64–65, 74, 119, 123–125, 127, 129, 133, 135–136, 275 n.10
  frame perversion and, 192
  harshness of, 9–10, 34–35, 46, 49, 54, 62–63, 75–77, 79, 83, 84–85, 87–89, 91–93, 103–108, 110–113, 115
  head games, 95–101
  incentive training, 93–95
  as instilling knowledge, 81–83, 150
  insults and, 63–64, 65–77, 90
  kill chants, 77–79
  kin ties and, 60–62

training (*Continued*)
  masculinity and, 20, 47–48, 52–56, 64–65, 66–71, 91, 94, 104, 105, 150
  morality and, 28–29, 84–87, 100
  as pedagogy, 20–21, 28, 45–47, 49–52, 55–57, 64–67, 71, 74, 92–93, 100, 144, 175–178
  personhood and, 44–47, 55, 57–59, 65–67
  power and, 6
  reforms, 50–51, 113–114, 279 n.15
  rule-breaking in, 20, 28, 88–93, 99–100
  semiotic callousing and, 20, 54–55, 57, 64–65, 74–77, 91, 111–112, 119, 123–124
  slurs in, 15, 64–65, 68–74, 120, 135–136
  violence and, 14–18, 20
  yelling and, 20, 47, 81–83, 96
trauma, 5–6, 13–14, 30, 109, 119, 202–204, 210–211, 228, 233. *See also* PTSD (post-traumatic stress disorder)
traumatic brain injury (TBI), 35–36
Trump, Donald, 28–29, 58, 104, 109–111, 113, 133, 240
Tuberville, Tommy, 114–115
Tuckner, Howard, 137–138
Turley, Patrick, 56, 63–64, 67–68, 69–70, 77–78, 96, 100–101, 282 n.43
Turner, Victor, 45, 47, 64–65, 85, 230–231
Turse, Nick, 264 n.56

uniform, 225–227, 231–236, 238, 247. *See also* combat paper
Uniform Code of Military Justice, 41–42, 86–87
United States Playing Card company, 182. *See also* death cards

Van Buren, Peter, 264 n.51
veterans
  art by, 225–227, 238–252
  demilitarization of, 3–4, 6–7, 18, 25, 32–33, 38, 226–227, 228–234, 236–238
  critique of military, 3–4, 9, 227
  extremism and, 37–38
  memory and, 8–9, 143–144, 201–203
  mental health and, 6, 32, 110, 201, 204
  poetry by, 197–200, 204–223
Veterans for Peace, 239
Vietnam War, 5–6, 8, 9–10, 17–18, 21, 23, 26–27, 34–37, 44, 56–57, 71–75, 121–124, 125–126, 128–131, 132–134, 137–138, 151–152, 154–155, 157, 161–166, 178–183, 184–186, 198–201, 203–205, 207–208, 209–213, 217–223, 240–241, 256 n.17
Viges, Hart, 134–135, 138–139
violence, 3–6, 8–9, 14–15, 16–17, 20–22, 30, 47, 55, 76–77, 79, 111–112, 121–122, 157, 260 n.33
  combat and, 3–4, 6–7, 10, 14–15, 18, 20–21, 24, 26, 32, 38, 143–144, 151–155, 175, 209, 211
  embodiment and, 68–69
  experience of, 13–15, 16–21, 23, 24–27, 32–33
  frame perversion and, 176–177, 192–193
  humor and, 170–171, 174–175
  "just," 27–29
  language and, 3–4, 9–10, 14–21, 22–25, 29–31, 38, 47, 54–55, 59, 76–77, 78–79, 111–112, 121–122, 131, 132–134, 143–156, 157–159, 160–167, 175–176, 202–203, 206–207, 209, 211, 254
  memes and, 186–188, 190
  morality and, 5–6, 18, 144–145, 175–176, 209–210
  phatic, 59
Vitale, Alex, 268 n.89
voice, 51–54, 56, 172
volume, 47, 50, 52–54, 61, 64–65. *See also* yelling
Vonnegut, Kurt, *Slaughterhouse Five*, 166
vulnerability, 14, 21, 30, 45, 46, 48, 56–57, 66–67, 76–77, 105, 108–110, 123, 140–141, 153, 198

Walter Reed National Military Medical Center, 233–234
war crimes, 3–4, 27–29, 56–57, 123, 132, 246, 249
Warrior Writers, 205, 226, 231, 239
weakness, 31–32, 47–48, 59, 68, 104, 105–106, 109, 111, 114, 115–116, 130, 145–146, 204
Webster, Anthony, 261 n.40, 292 n.44
Weigl, Bruce, 199–200, 205, 221
  "Song of Napalm," 218
Weiss, Mitch, 132, 137–138
West Point, 169–170, 240, 279 n.12
Westheider, James, 72–73, 89

white supremacy, 37–38, 125
Whorf, Benjamin Lee, 146–147, 261 n.40
Wierzbicka, Anna, 129, 275 n.11
Wiesel, Elie, *Night*, 3
William Joiner Institute for the Study of War and Social Consequences, 33, 203, 205, 210–211, 217, 221
Williams, Margot, 150
Williams, Raymond, 258 n.18, 284 n.3
Winning Hearts & Minds: War Poems by Vietnam Veterans, 205
Winter Hill Gang, 162
Winter Soldier hearings (2008), 123, 127, 133, 138–139, 250–251
Wittgenstein, Ludwig, 23
woke. *See* political correctness
Wolfendale, Jessica, 28–29
Wool, Zoe, 202–203
Wright, Eli, 227–228, 230–239, 241–242, 243–246, 249–251. *See also* Combat Paper Project

"Family Values," 246
"Game Over," 202
writing, 8–9, 32–34, 121, 205, 210–211, 231. *See also* poetry

Yamashita, Bruce, 76–77
Yee, James, 147–150, 246–248
  "Army. Be All You Can Be?" 249
  "Camp X-ray," 248
  For God and Country, 247
yelling, 41–43, 47, 49–55, 59, 61–62, 81–83, 96. *See also* insults
Yemen, 146–147
Young, Matt, 77–78, 127, 133, 144, 152–153, 256 n.17

Zippo lighters, 178–182
Zuckerberg, Mark, 30
Zuckerman, Charles, 59